SHIN YOSHIDA

Yuya, Yuto, Yuri and Yugo... Finally they're all here, and the mystery surrounding this quartet kicks off! Look forward to both the mystery and the Duels!

NAOHITO MIYOSHI

What would I do if I had three additional personalities? Yuto would handle the rough layouts, Yugo would ink and Yuri would add the finishing touches! Heh heh heh... Huh? Me? I'd be sleeping like a log! :-)

MASAHIRO HIKOKUBO

Sometimes, I fantasize about a project called Yu-Gi-Go!, in which you can get cards all over town, and cafés and game centers are Duel Fields, and you can unlock rare packs by walking around a lot!! Um, sorry about that...

2

ARC-V

SHONEN JUMP MANGA EDITION

ORIGINAL CONCEPT BY
Kazuki Takahashi

PRODUCTION SUPPORT: **STUDIO DICE**

STORY BY
Shin Yoshida

ART BY
Naohito Miyoshi

DUEL COORDINATOR
Masahiro Hikokubo

TRANSLATION + ENGLISH ADAPTATION
Taylor Engel and John Werry, HC Language Solutions, Inc.
TOUCH-UP ART + LETTERING **John Hunt**
DESIGNER **Shawn Carrico**
EDITOR **Mike Montesa**

Printed in the U.S.A.

Published by VIZ Media, LLC
P.O. Box 77010
San Francisco, CA 94107

10 9 8 7 6 5 4 3 2 1
First printing, September 2017

www.viz.com   www.shonenjump.com

2

Turbo Duel!!

ORIGINAL CONCEPT BY **Kazuki Takahashi**

PRODUCTION SUPPORT: **STUDIO DICE**

STORY BY **Shin Yoshida**

ART BY **Naohito Miyoshi**

DUEL COORDINATOR **Masahiro Hikokubo**

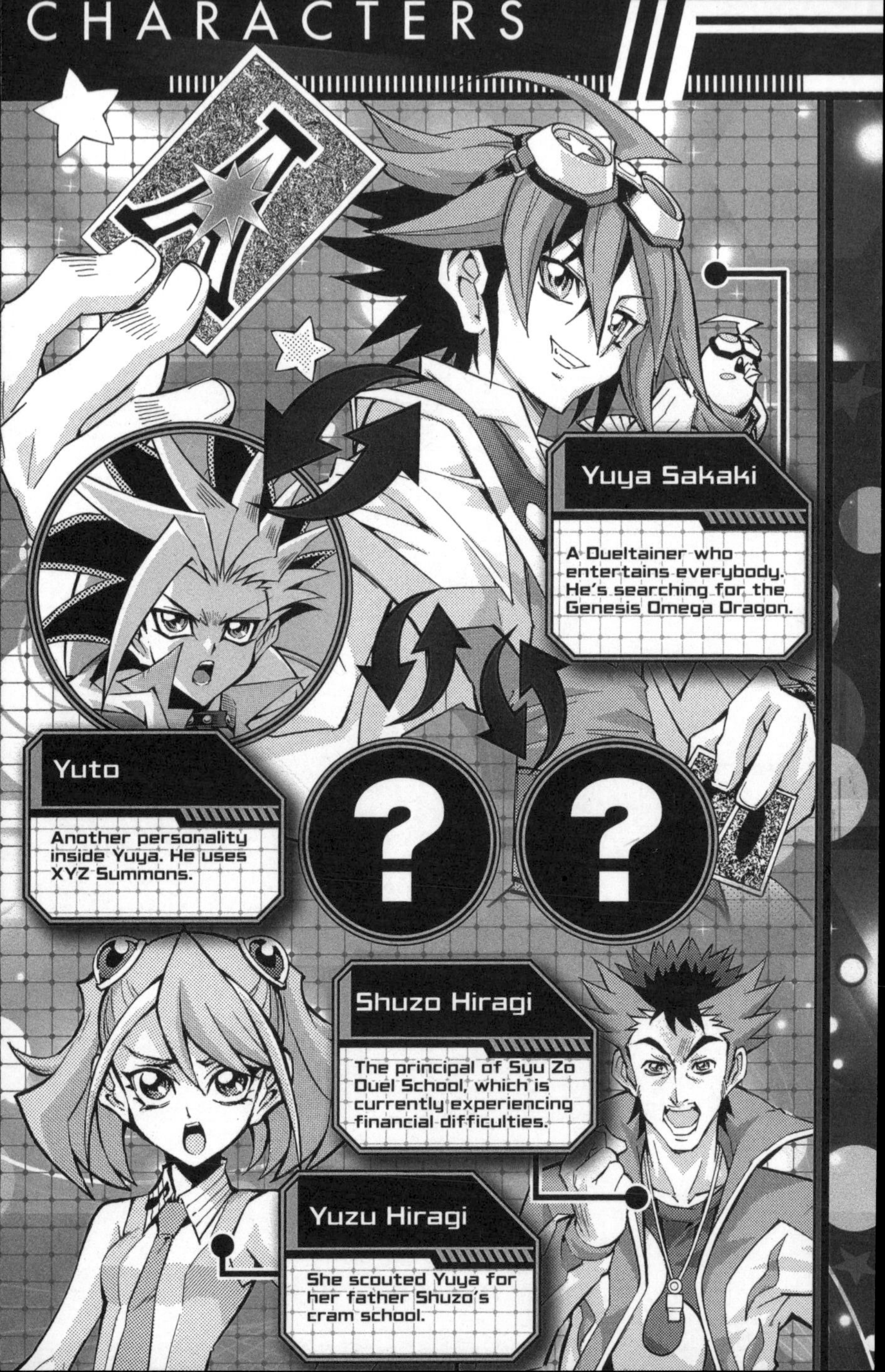
CHARACTERS
Yuya Sakaki
A Dueltainer who entertains everybody. He's searching for the Genesis Omega Dragon.
Yuto
Another personality inside Yuya. He uses XYZ Summons.
?
?
Shuzo Hiragi
The principal of Syu Zo Duel School, which is currently experiencing financial difficulties.
Yuzu Hiragi
She scouted Yuya for her father Shuzo's cram school.

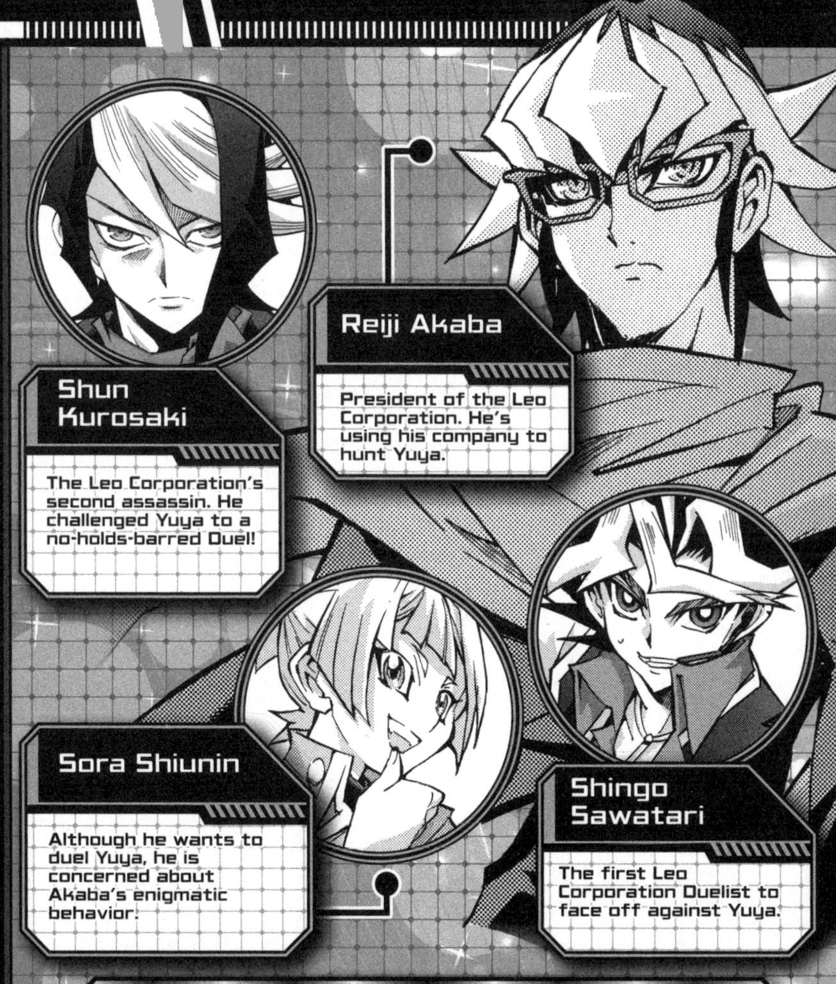

Reiji Akaba

President of the Leo Corporation. He's using his company to hunt Yuya.

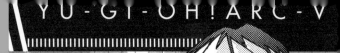

Shun Kurosaki

The Leo Corporation's second assassin. He challenged Yuya to a no-holds-barred Duel!

Shingo Sawatari

The first Leo Corporation Duelist to face off against Yuya.

Sora Shiunin

Although he wants to duel Yuya, he is concerned about Akaba's enigmatic behavior.

STORY

Solid Vision with mass has plunged the world into the era of Action Duels. The Duelists of the Leo Corporation are in hot pursuit of Yuya Sakaki, a Dueltainer who can hack that technology. The Leo Corporation's first assassin, Sawatari, squares off against him only to discover that the person he has been chasing is someone else–a guy who introduces himself as Yuto! However, during the Duel, Yuto transforms into Yuya, who wins and escapes. Yuzu Hiragi, who happens to be present at the Duel, becomes Yuya's manager and joins him in pursuit of the Genesis Omega Dragon [G.O.D.]. Then the second assassin, Kurosaki, takes Yuzu's father, Shuzo, hostage and Yuya ends up dueling him. After winning, Yuya tells Yuzu and her father that he has four personalities!!

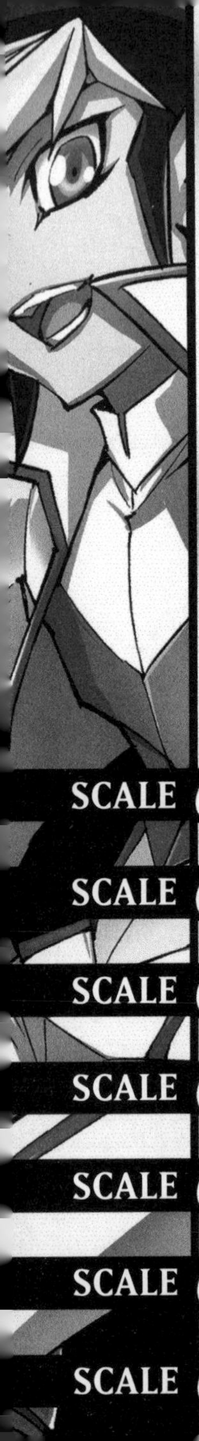

YU-GI-OH! ARC-V

2 Turbo Duel!!

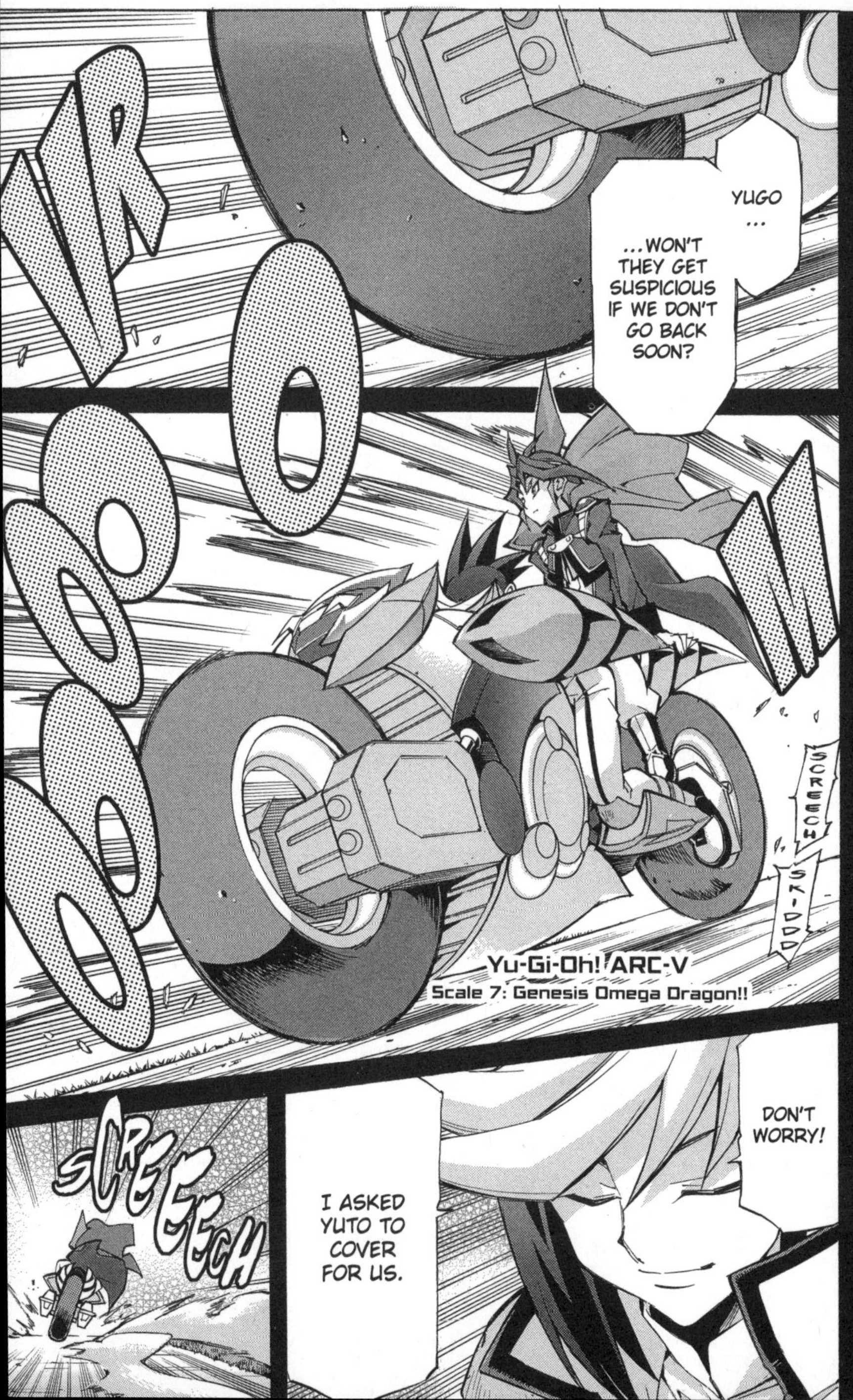
YUGO...
...WON'T THEY GET SUSPICIOUS IF WE DON'T GO BACK SOON?
SCREECH
SKIDDD
Yu-Gi-Oh! ARC-V
Scale 7: Genesis Omega Dragon!!
DON'T WORRY!
I ASKED YUTO TO COVER FOR US.
SCREEECH

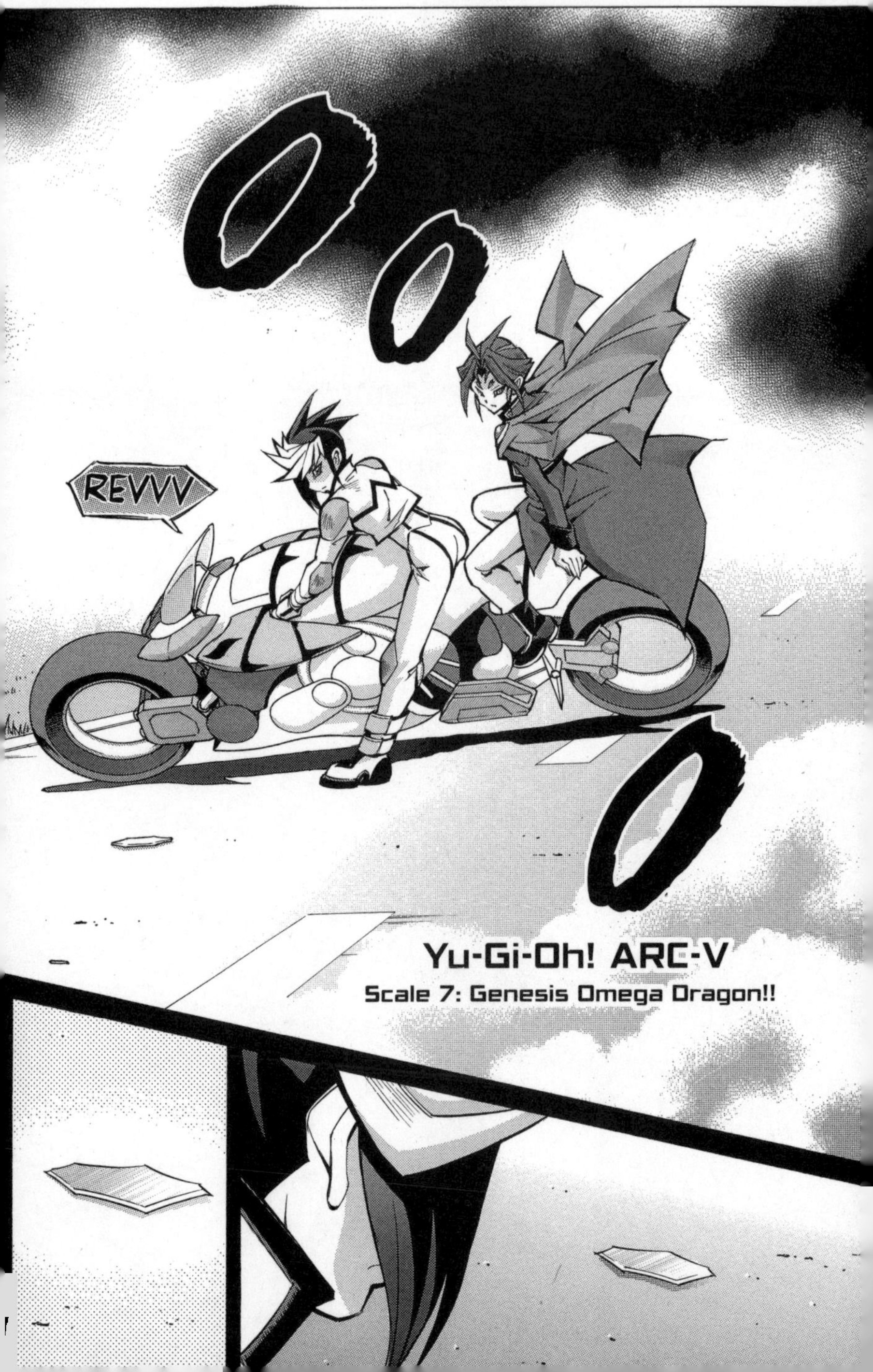
VRRRRRRR
REVVV
VRRRRRRR
Yu-Gi-Oh! ARC-V
Scale 7: Genesis Omega Dragon!!

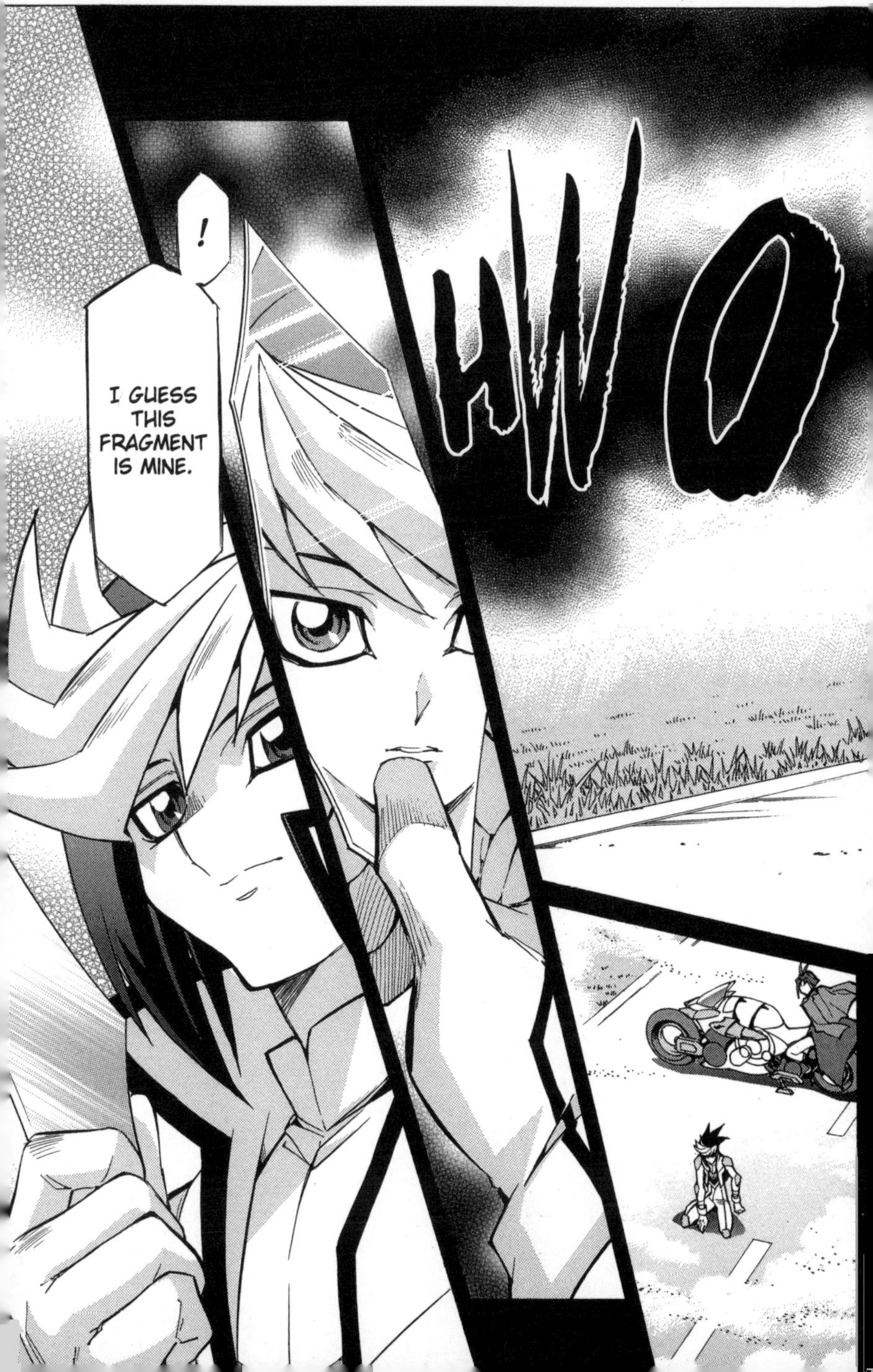
!
I GUESS THIS FRAGMENT IS MINE.
HWO

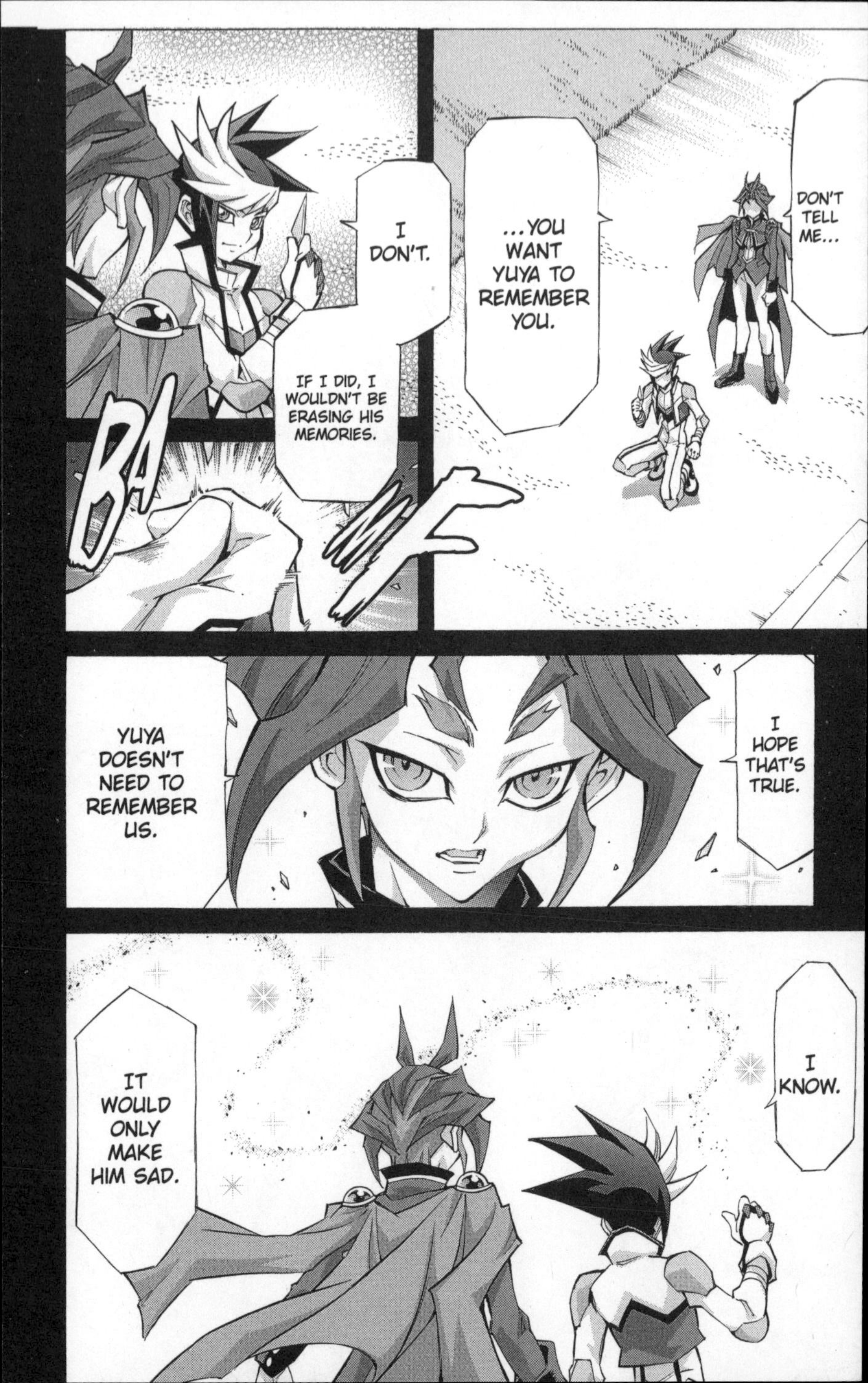
DON'T TELL ME...
...YOU WANT YUYA TO REMEMBER YOU.
I DON'T.
IF I DID, I WOULDN'T BE ERASING HIS MEMORIES.
BAM
I HOPE THAT'S TRUE.
YUYA DOESN'T NEED TO REMEMBER US.
I KNOW.
IT WOULD ONLY MAKE HIM SAD.

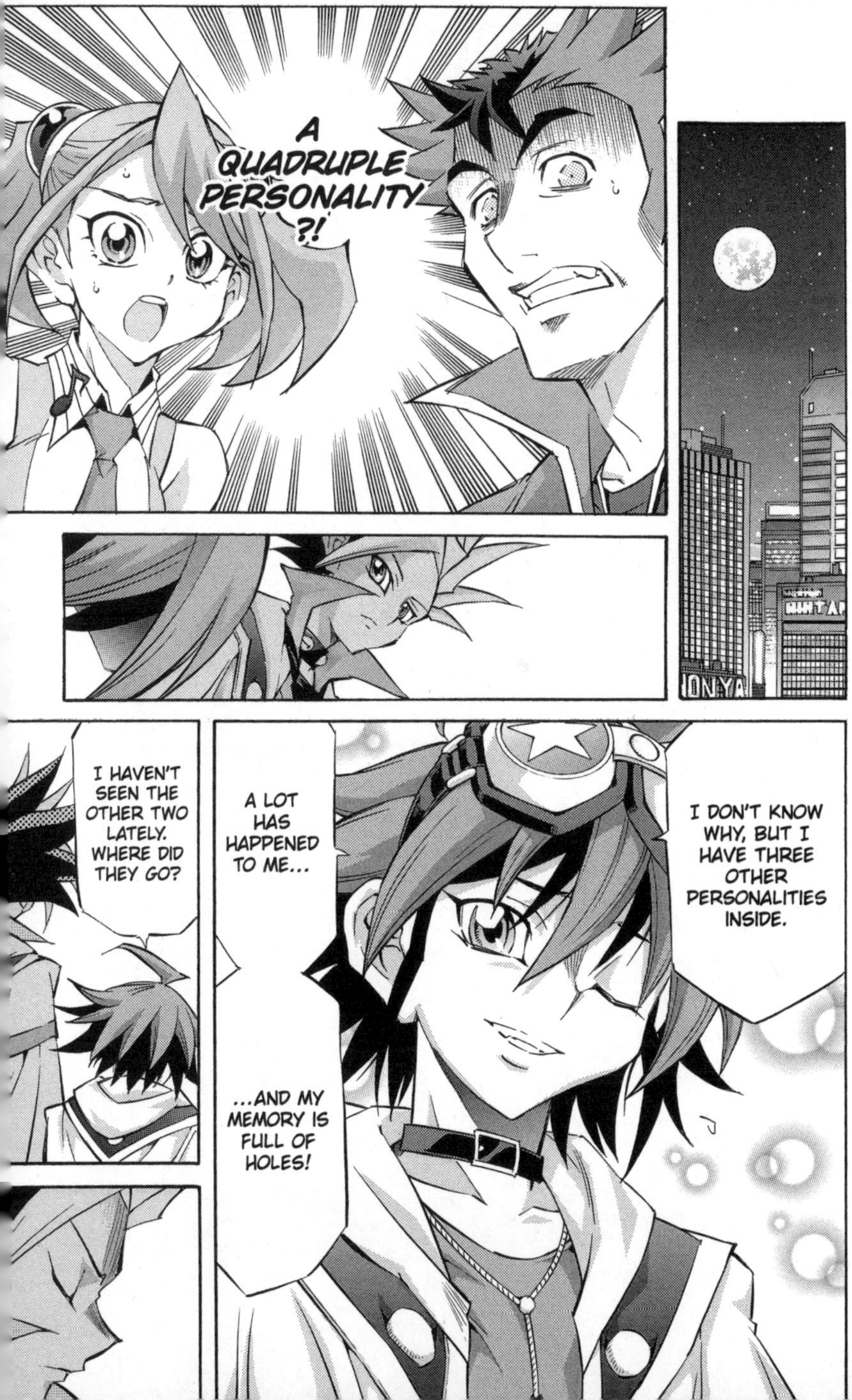
A QUADRUPLE PERSONALITY ?!
I DON'T KNOW WHY, BUT I HAVE THREE OTHER PERSONALITIES INSIDE.
A LOT HAS HAPPENED TO ME...
...AND MY MEMORY IS FULL OF HOLES!
I HAVEN'T SEEN THE OTHER TWO LATELY. WHERE DID THEY GO?

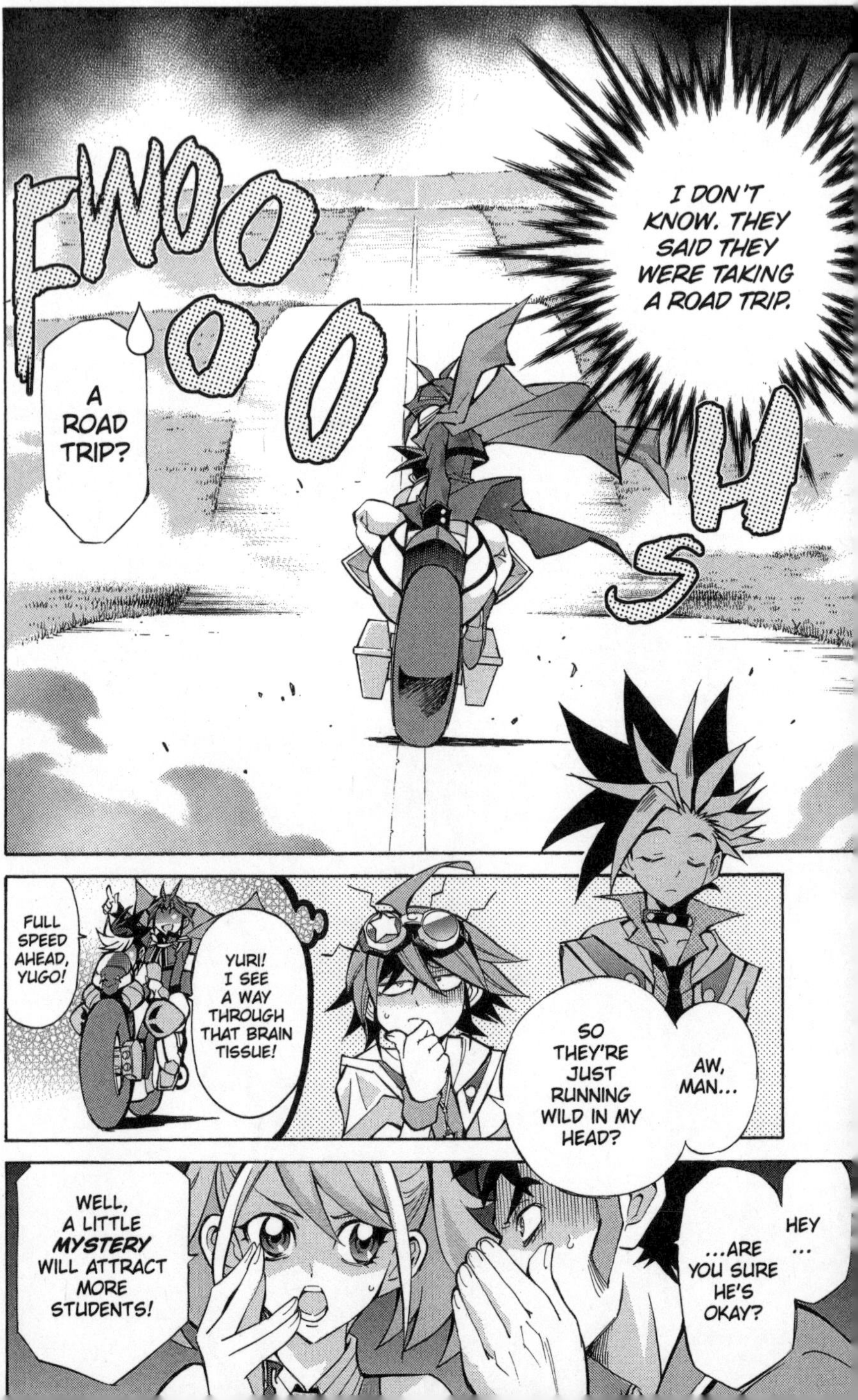
I DON'T KNOW. THEY SAID THEY WERE TAKING A ROAD TRIP.
FWOOOOOSH
A ROAD TRIP?
AW, MAN...
SO THEY'RE JUST RUNNING WILD IN MY HEAD?
YURI! I SEE A WAY THROUGH THAT BRAIN TISSUE!
FULL SPEED AHEAD, YUGO!
HEY ...
...ARE YOU SURE HE'S OKAY?
WELL, A LITTLE ***MYSTERY*** WILL ATTRACT MORE STUDENTS!

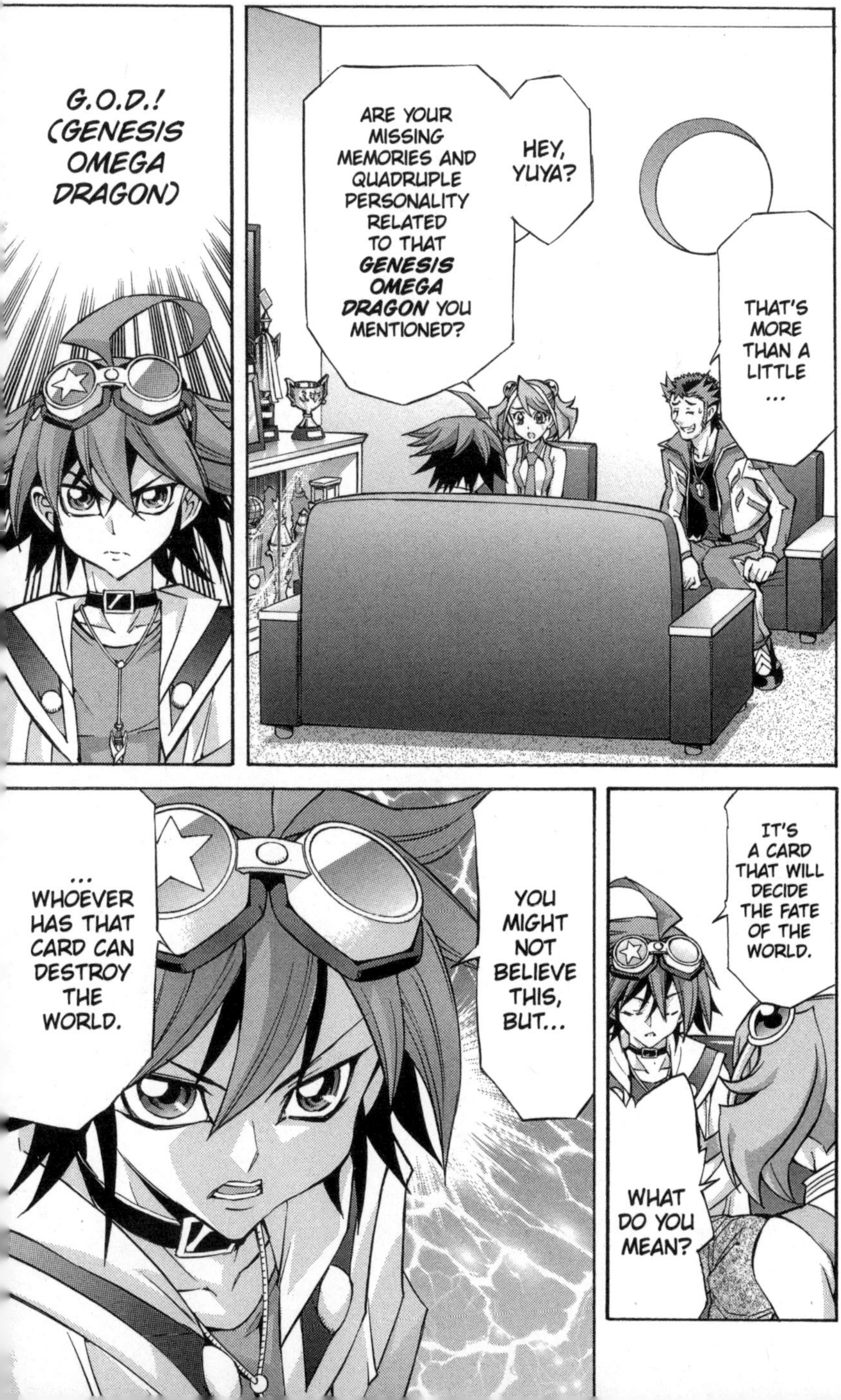
HEY, YUYA?
ARE YOUR MISSING MEMORIES AND QUADRUPLE PERSONALITY RELATED TO THAT **GENESIS OMEGA DRAGON** YOU MENTIONED?
THAT'S MORE THAN A LITTLE ...
G.O.D.! (GENESIS OMEGA DRAGON)
IT'S A CARD THAT WILL DECIDE THE FATE OF THE WORLD.
WHAT DO YOU MEAN?
YOU MIGHT NOT BELIEVE THIS, BUT...
... WHOEVER HAS THAT CARD CAN DESTROY THE WORLD.

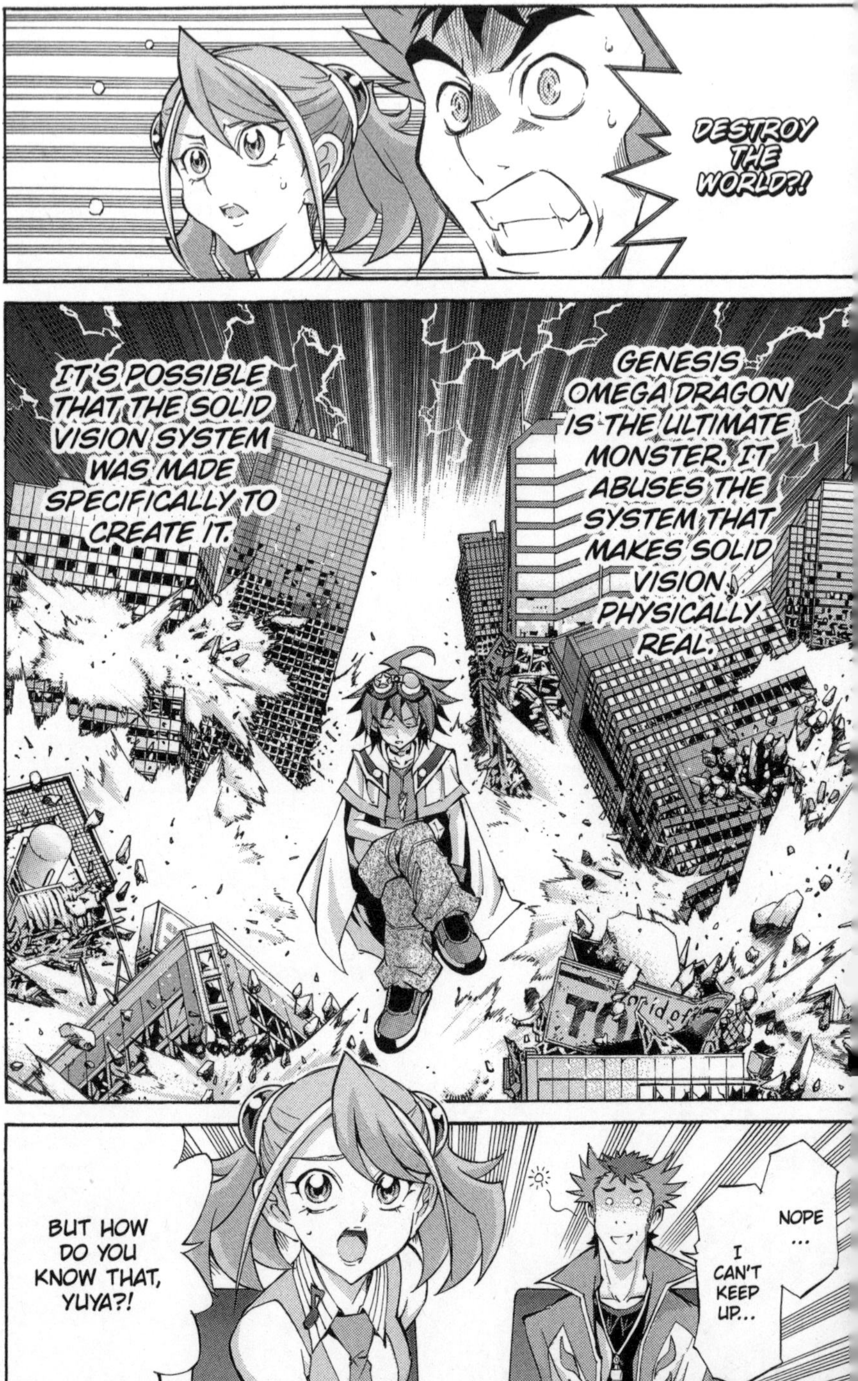
DESTROY THE WORLD?!
GENESIS OMEGA DRAGON IS THE ULTIMATE MONSTER. IT ABUSES THE SYSTEM THAT MAKES SOLID VISION PHYSICALLY REAL.
IT'S POSSIBLE THAT THE SOLID VISION SYSTEM WAS MADE SPECIFICALLY TO CREATE IT.
NOPE...
I CAN'T KEEP UP...
BUT HOW DO YOU KNOW THAT, YUYA?!

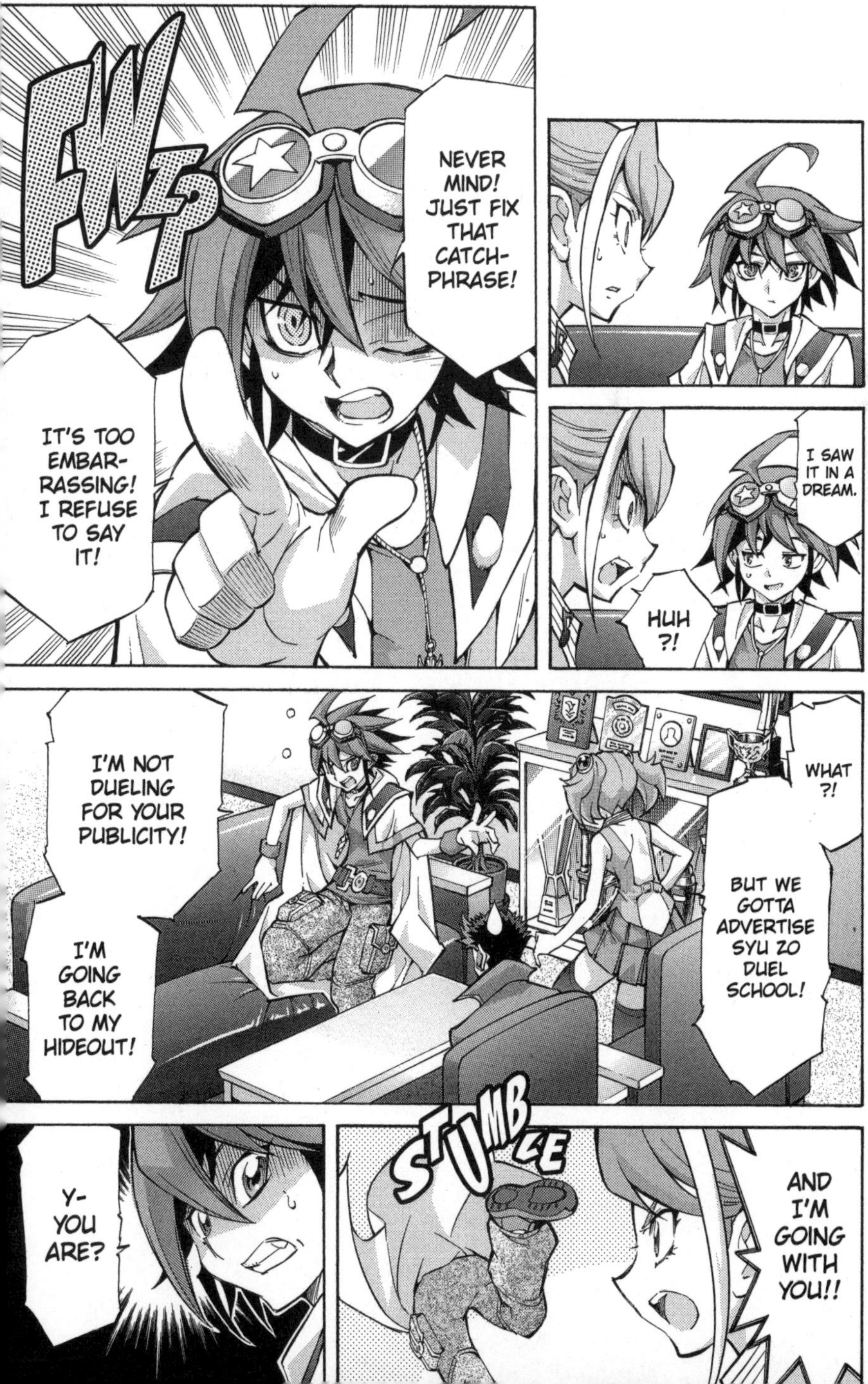
I SAW IT IN A DREAM.
HUH ?!
NEVER MIND! JUST FIX THAT CATCH-PHRASE!
FWIP
IT'S TOO EMBAR-RASSING! I REFUSE TO SAY IT!
WHAT ?!
BUT WE GOTTA ADVERTISE SYU ZO DUEL SCHOOL!
I'M NOT DUELING FOR YOUR PUBLICITY!
I'M GOING BACK TO MY HIDEOUT!
STUMBLE
AND I'M GOING WITH YOU!!
Y-YOU ARE?

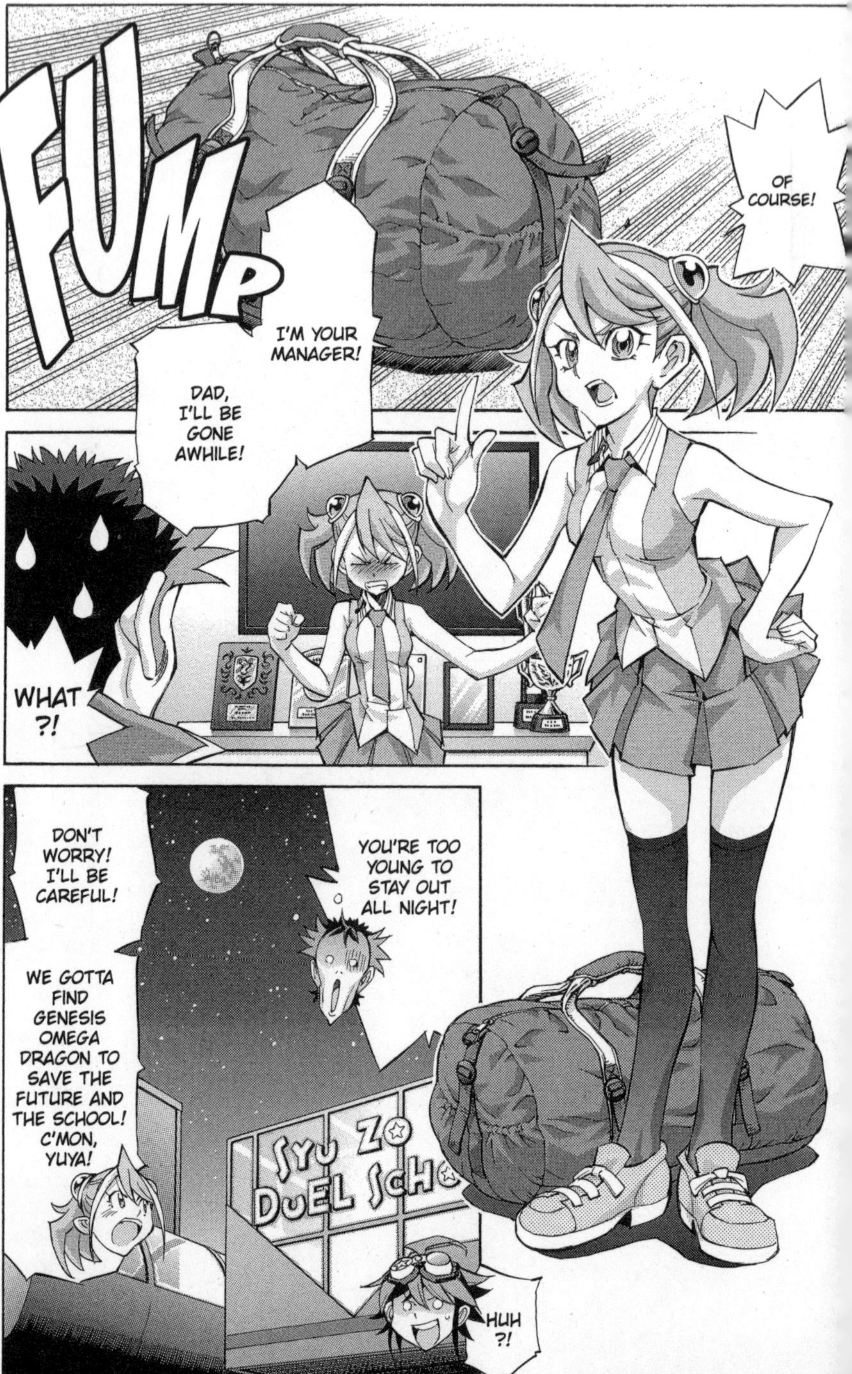
FUMP
OF COURSE!
I'M YOUR MANAGER!
DAD, I'LL BE GONE AWHILE!
WHAT ?!
YOU'RE TOO YOUNG TO STAY OUT ALL NIGHT!
DON'T WORRY! I'LL BE CAREFUL!
WE GOTTA FIND GENESIS OMEGA DRAGON TO SAVE THE FUTURE AND THE SCHOOL! C'MON, YUYA!
SYU ZO DUEL SCHO
HUH ?!

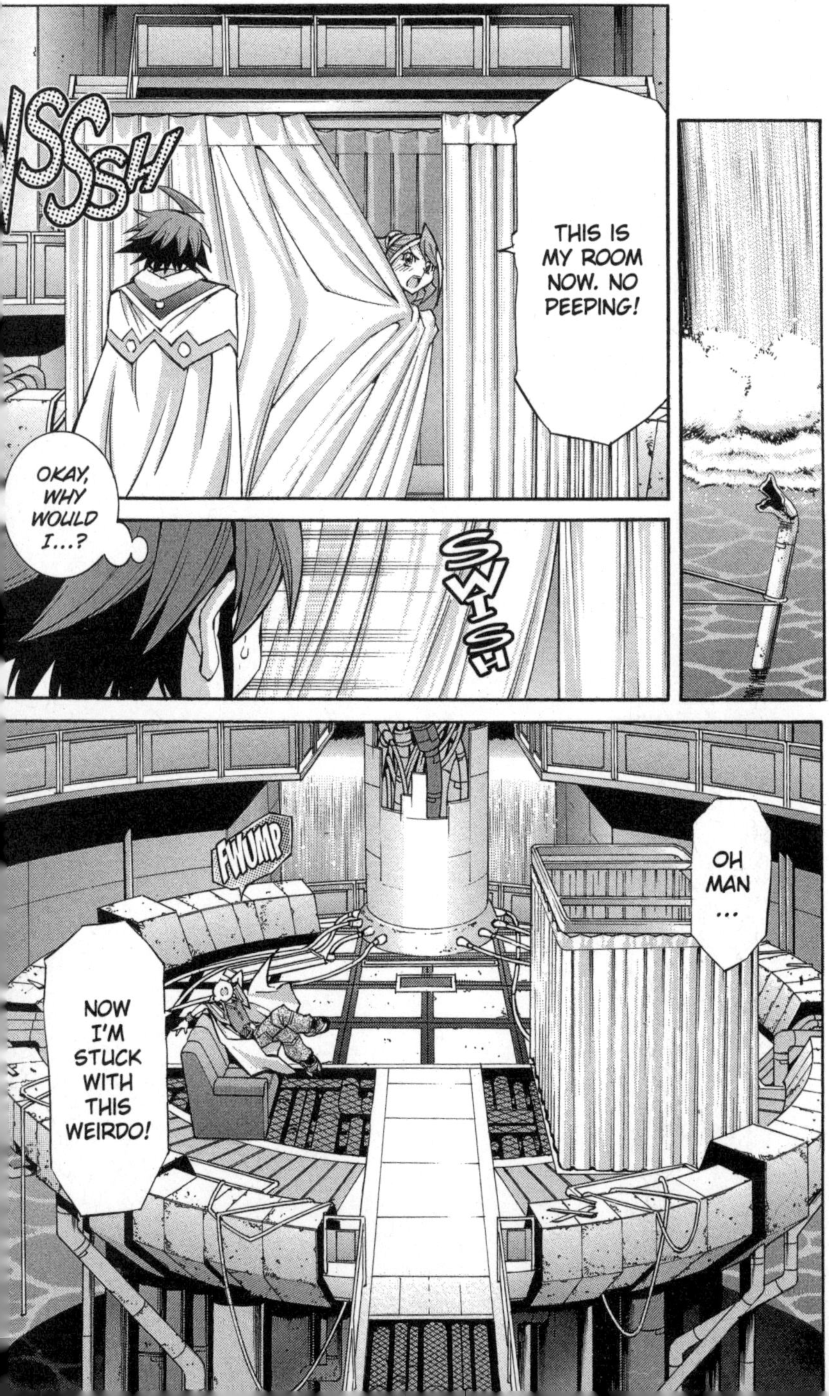
THIS IS MY ROOM NOW. NO PEEPING!
ISSSH
SWISH
OKAY, WHY WOULD I...?
OH MAN ...
FWUMP
NOW I'M STUCK WITH THIS WEIRDO!

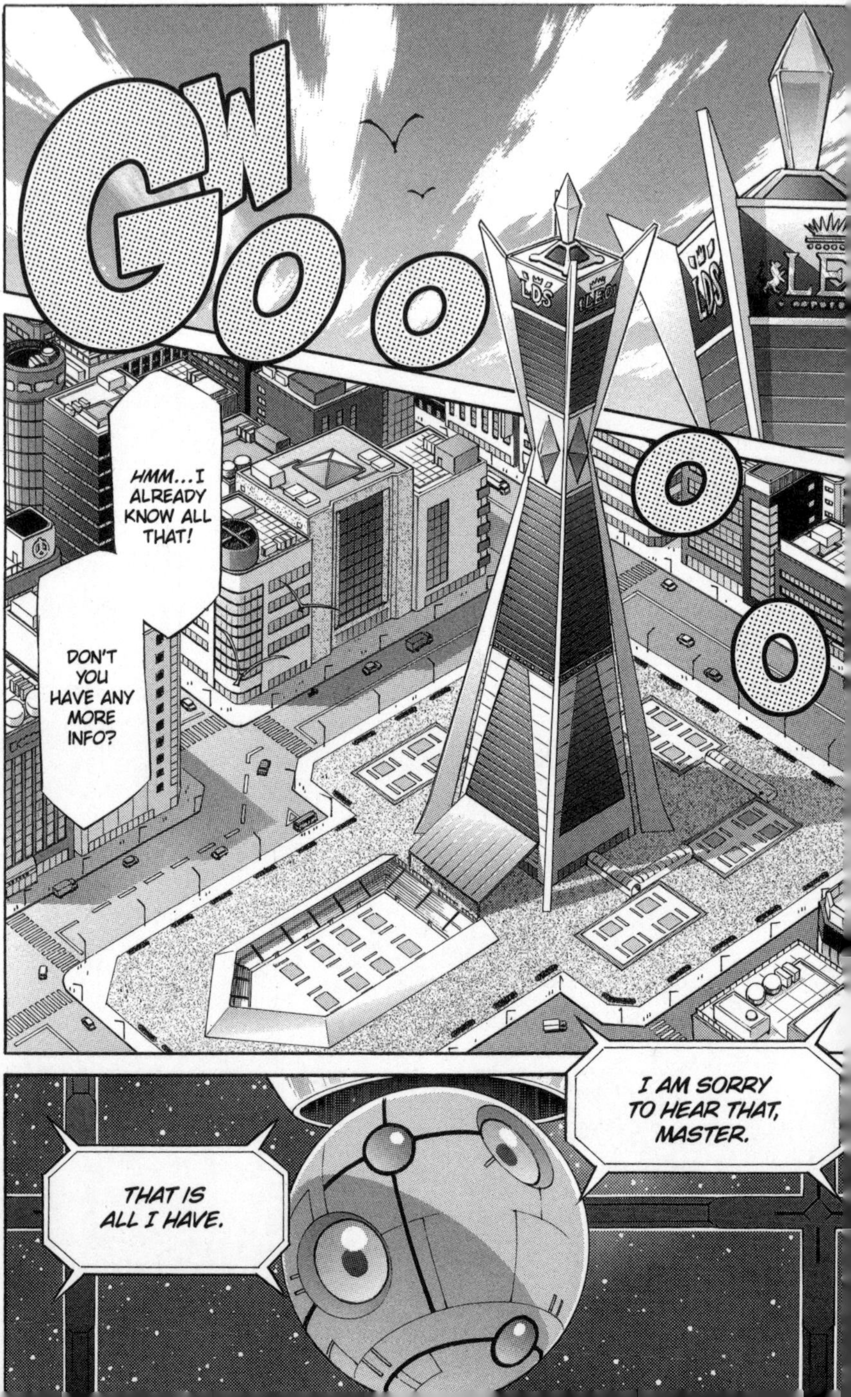
GWOOOOO
HMM...I ALREADY KNOW ALL THAT!
DON'T YOU HAVE ANY MORE INFO?
I AM SORRY TO HEAR THAT, MASTER.
THAT IS ALL I HAVE.

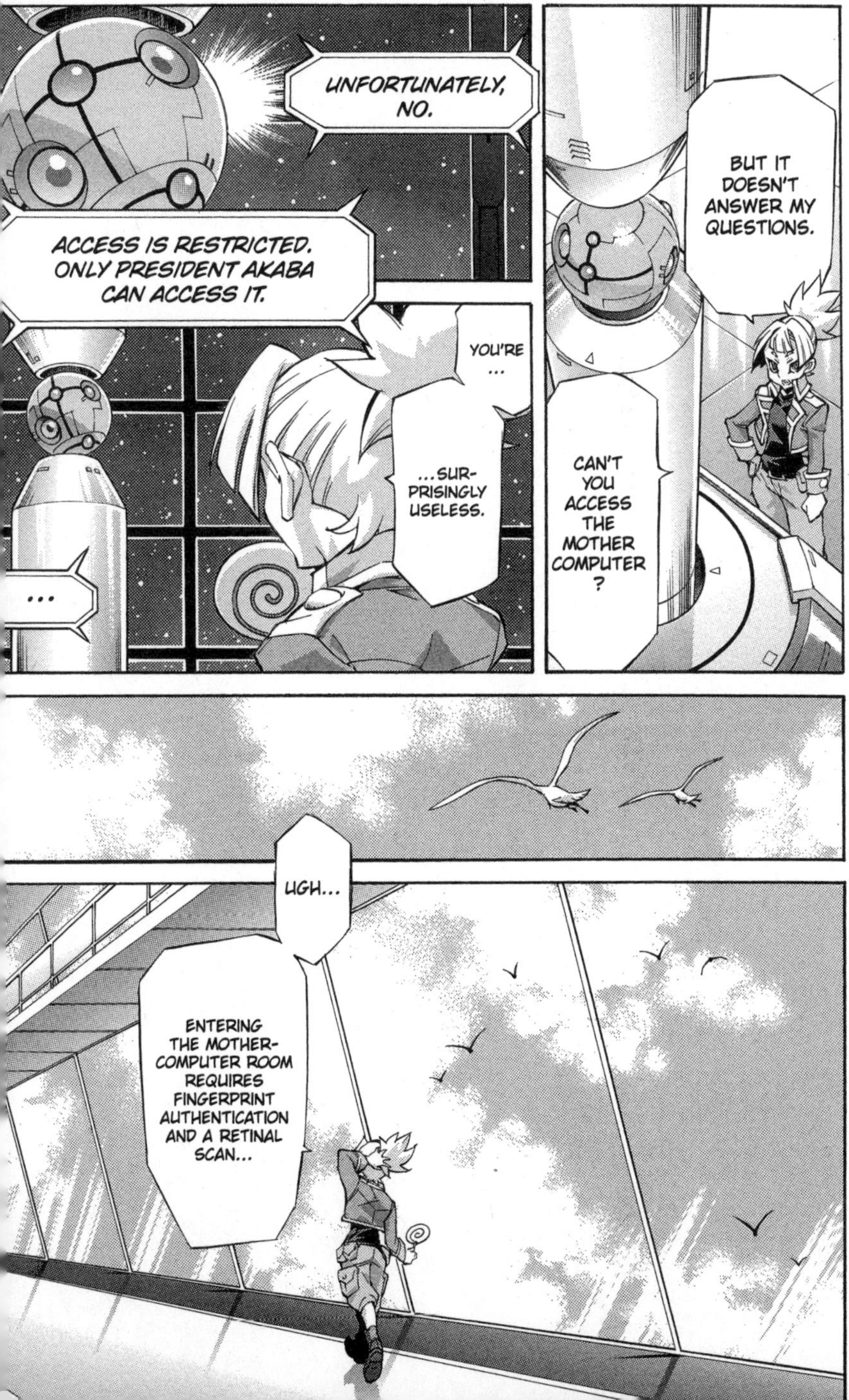

BUT IT DOESN'T ANSWER MY QUESTIONS.
CAN'T YOU ACCESS THE MOTHER COMPUTER?
UNFORTUNATELY, NO.
ACCESS IS RESTRICTED. ONLY PRESIDENT AKABA CAN ACCESS IT.
YOU'RE...
...SUR-PRISINGLY USELESS.
...
UGH...
ENTERING THE MOTHER-COMPUTER ROOM REQUIRES FINGERPRINT AUTHENTICATION AND A RETINAL SCAN...

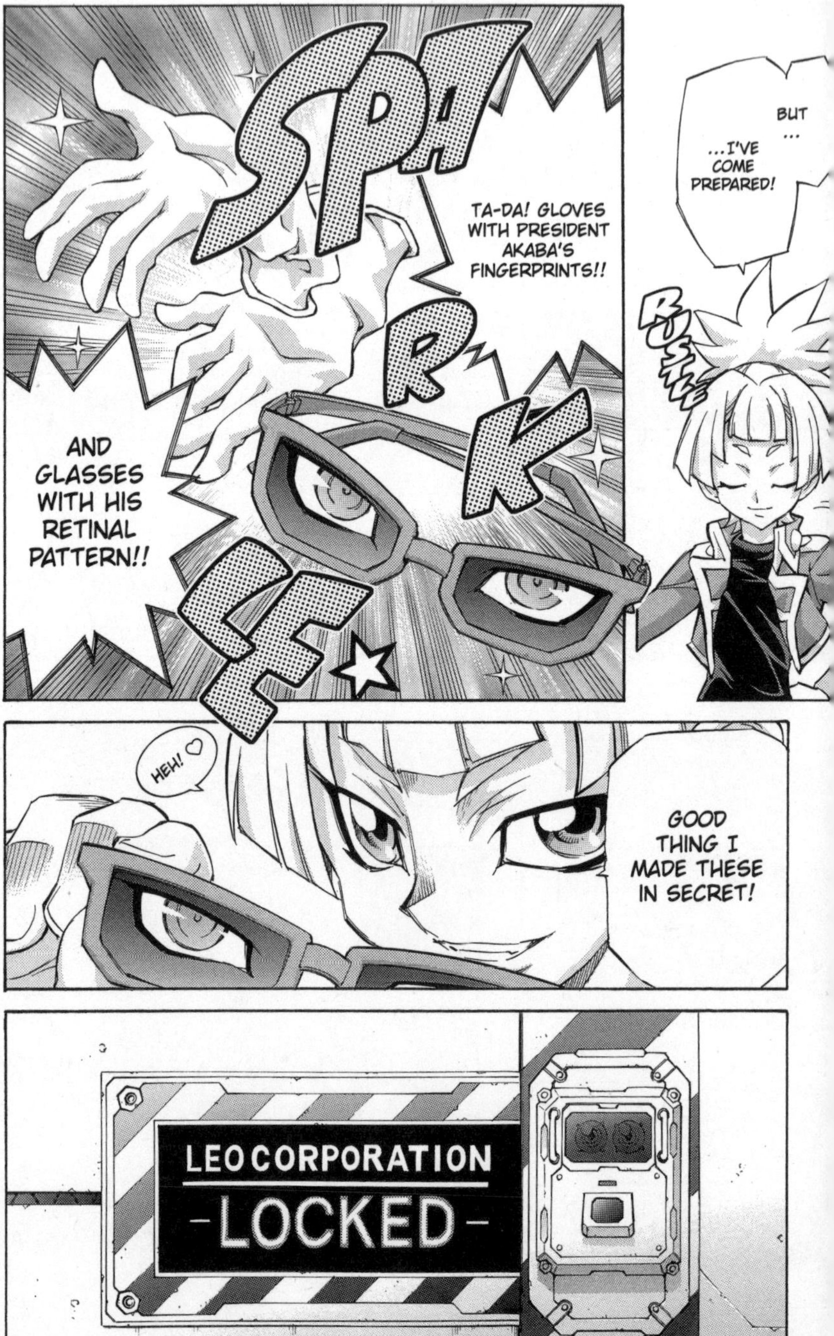
BUT ...
...I'VE COME PREPARED!
RUSTLE
SPARKK
TA-DA! GLOVES WITH PRESIDENT AKABA'S FINGERPRINTS!!
AND GLASSES WITH HIS RETINAL PATTERN!!
GOOD THING I MADE THESE IN SECRET!
HEH! ♡
LEO CORPORATION
-LOCKED-

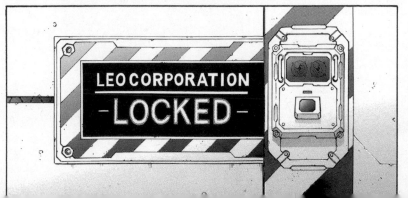

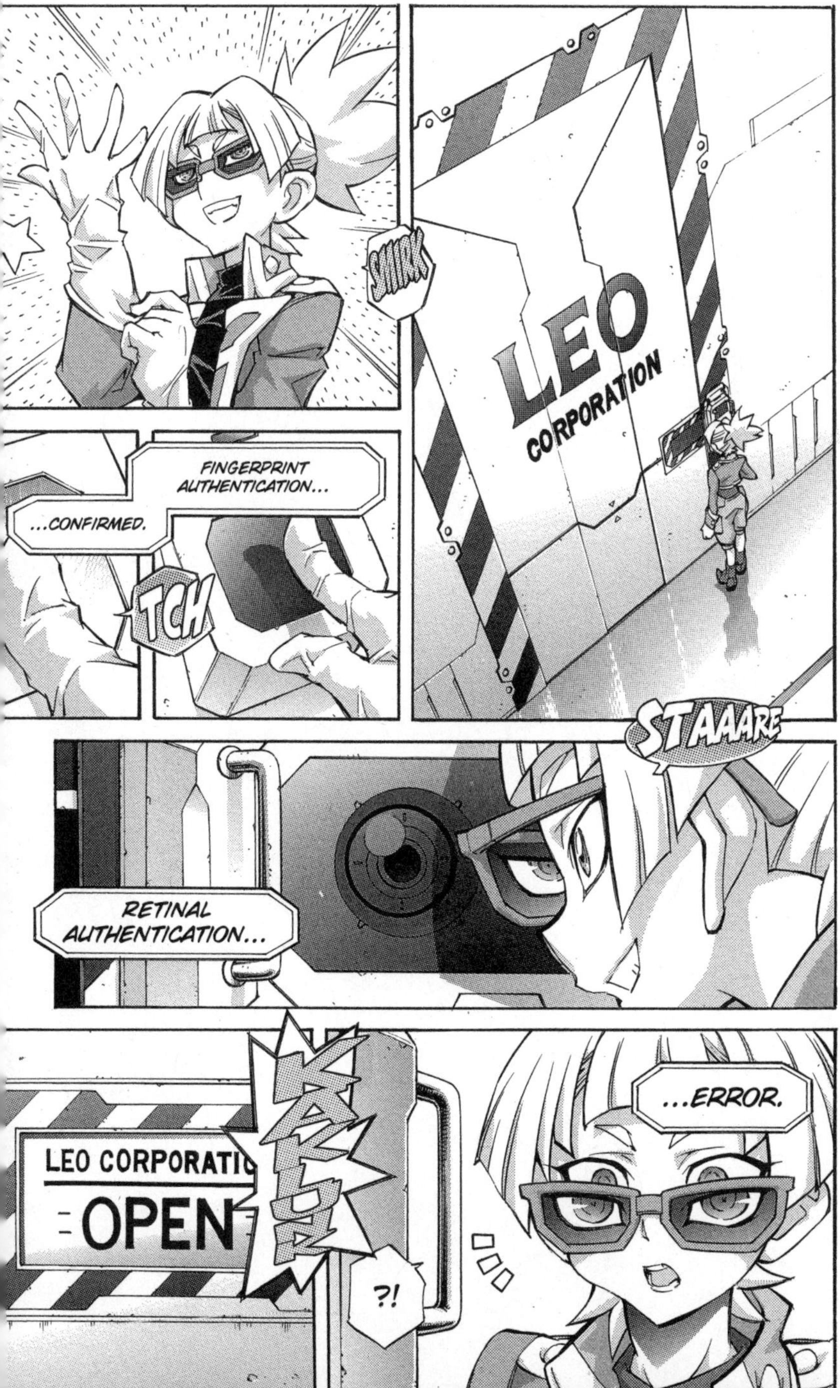
LEO
CORPORATION
SHIKK
FINGERPRINT AUTHENTICATION...
TCH
...CONFIRMED.
STAAARE
RETINAL AUTHENTICATION...
...ERROR.
?!
LEO CORPORATI
OPEN

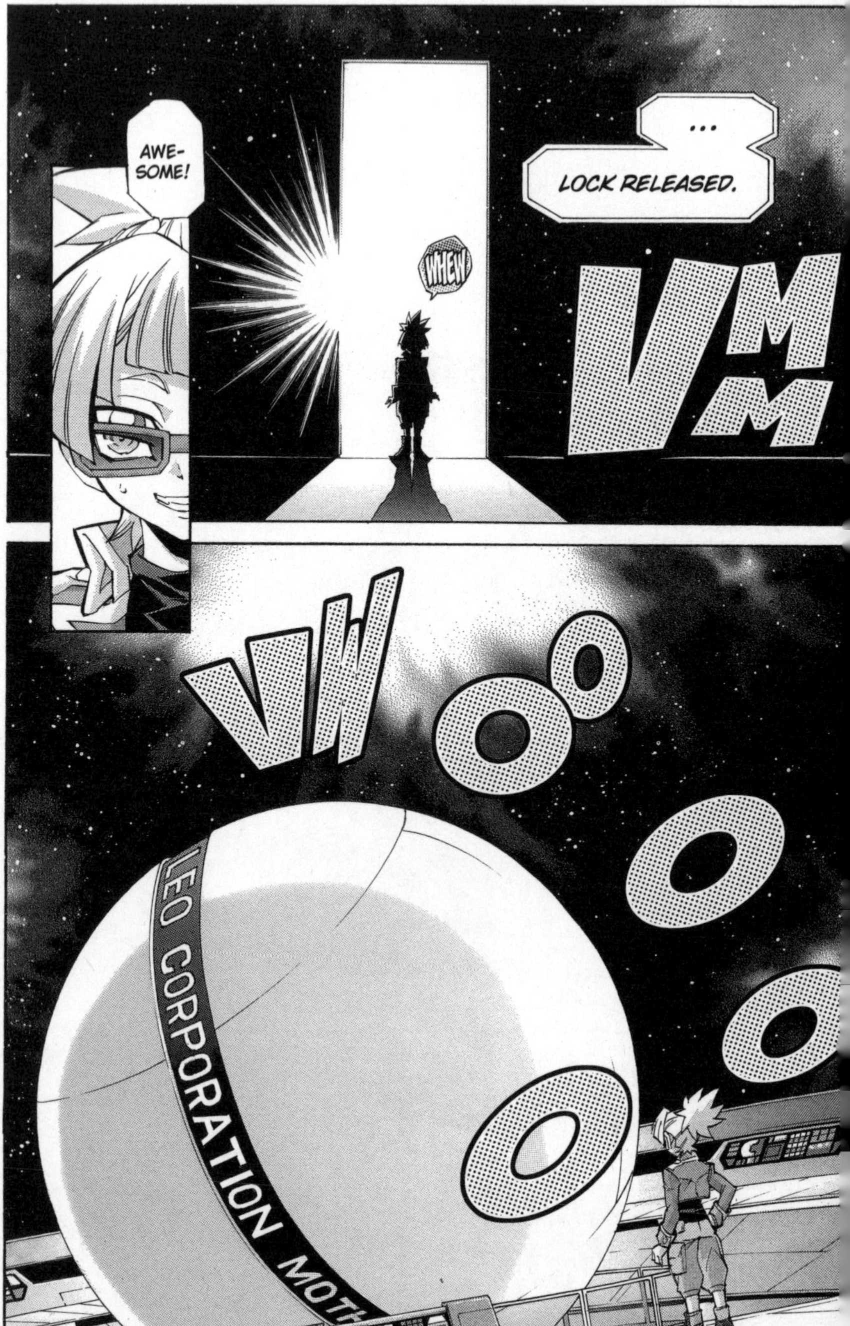
...
LOCK RELEASED.
WHEW
VMM
AWE-SOME!
VWOOOOOO
LEO CORPORATION

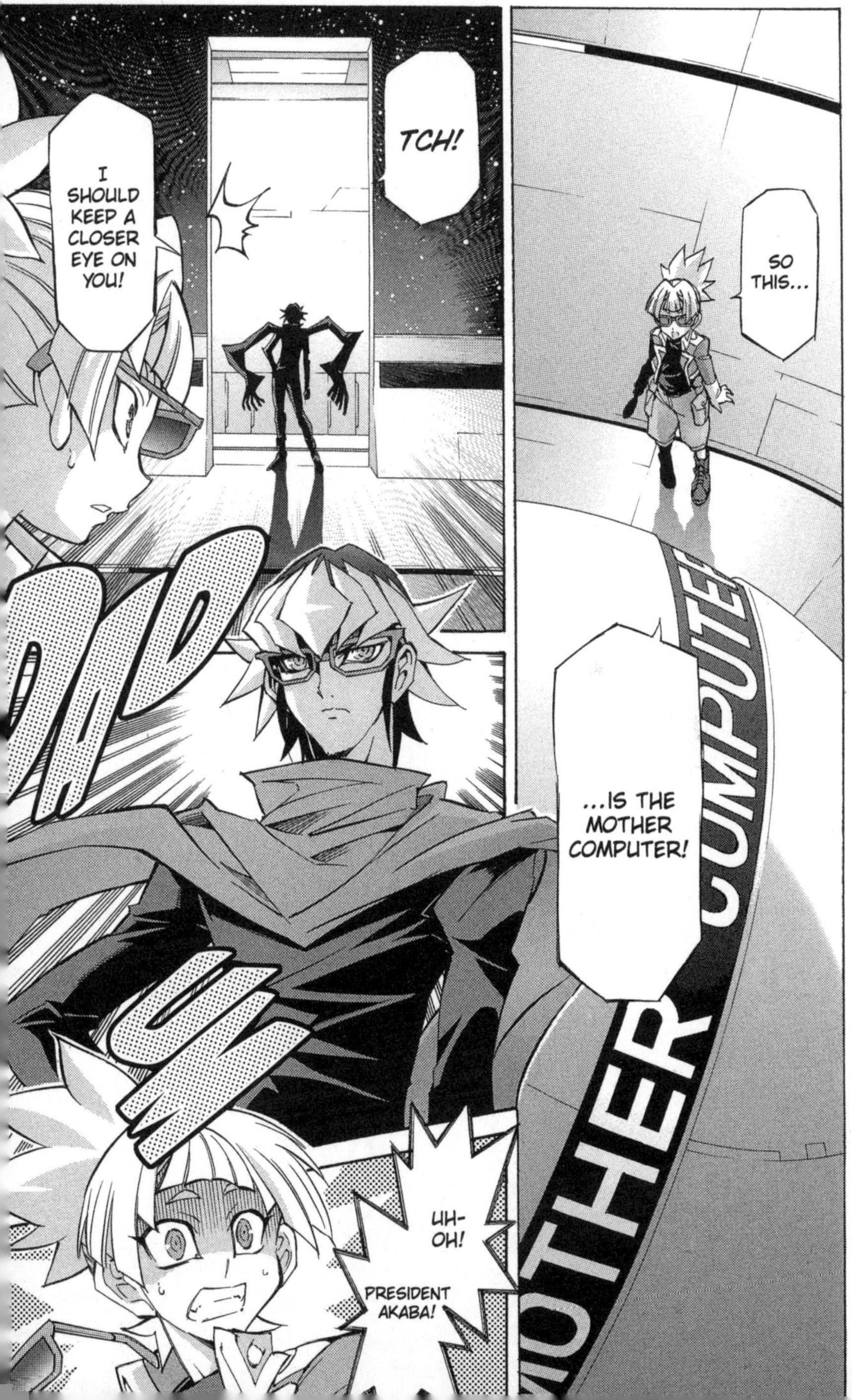
SO THIS...
...IS THE MOTHER COMPUTER!
MOTHER COMPUTER
TCH!
I SHOULD KEEP A CLOSER EYE ON YOU!
UH-OH!
PRESIDENT AKABA!

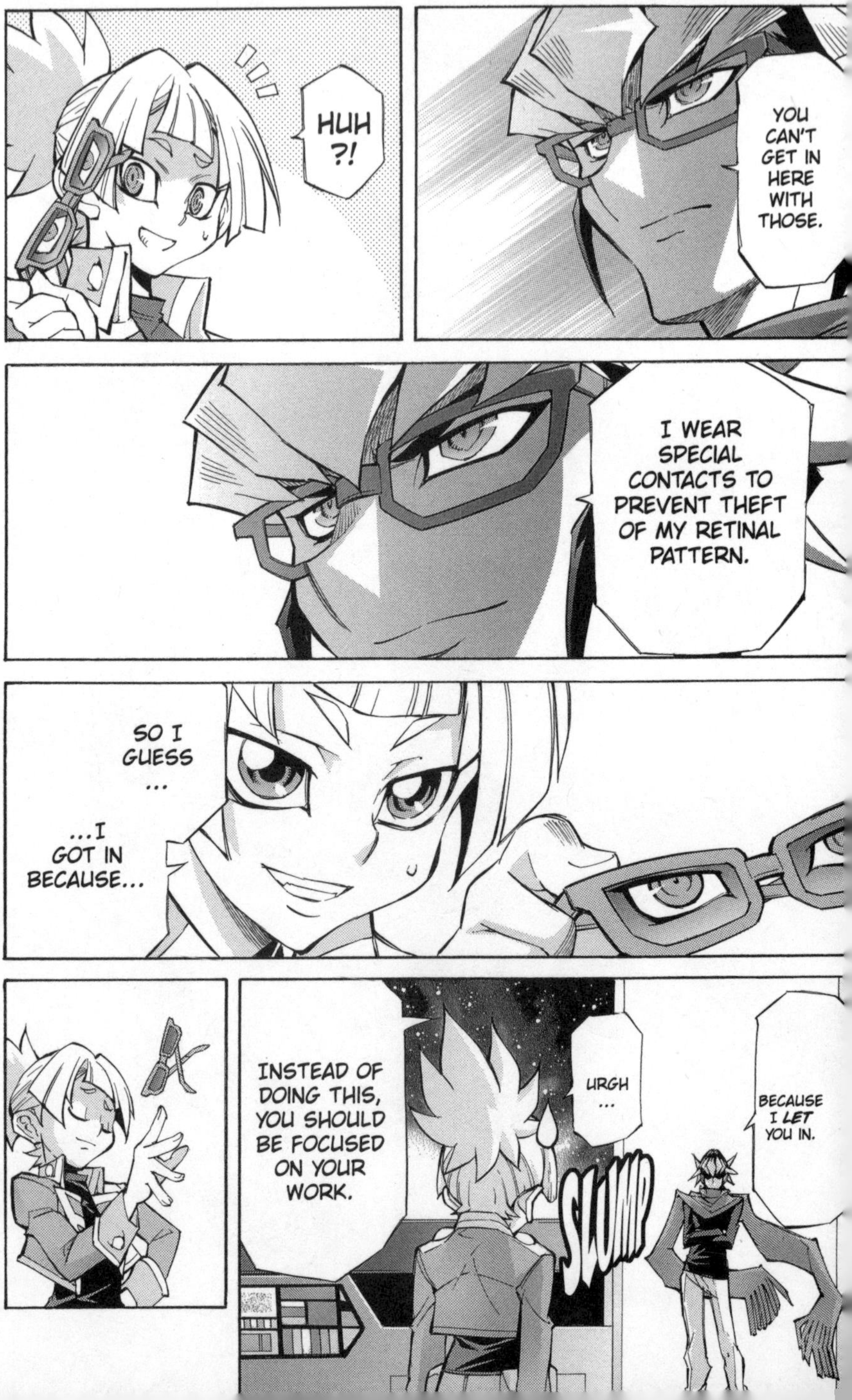
YOU CAN'T GET IN HERE WITH THOSE.
HUH ?!
I WEAR SPECIAL CONTACTS TO PREVENT THEFT OF MY RETINAL PATTERN.
SO I GUESS ...
...I GOT IN BECAUSE...
BECAUSE I *LET* YOU IN.
URGH ...
INSTEAD OF DOING THIS, YOU SHOULD BE FOCUSED ON YOUR WORK.
SLUMP

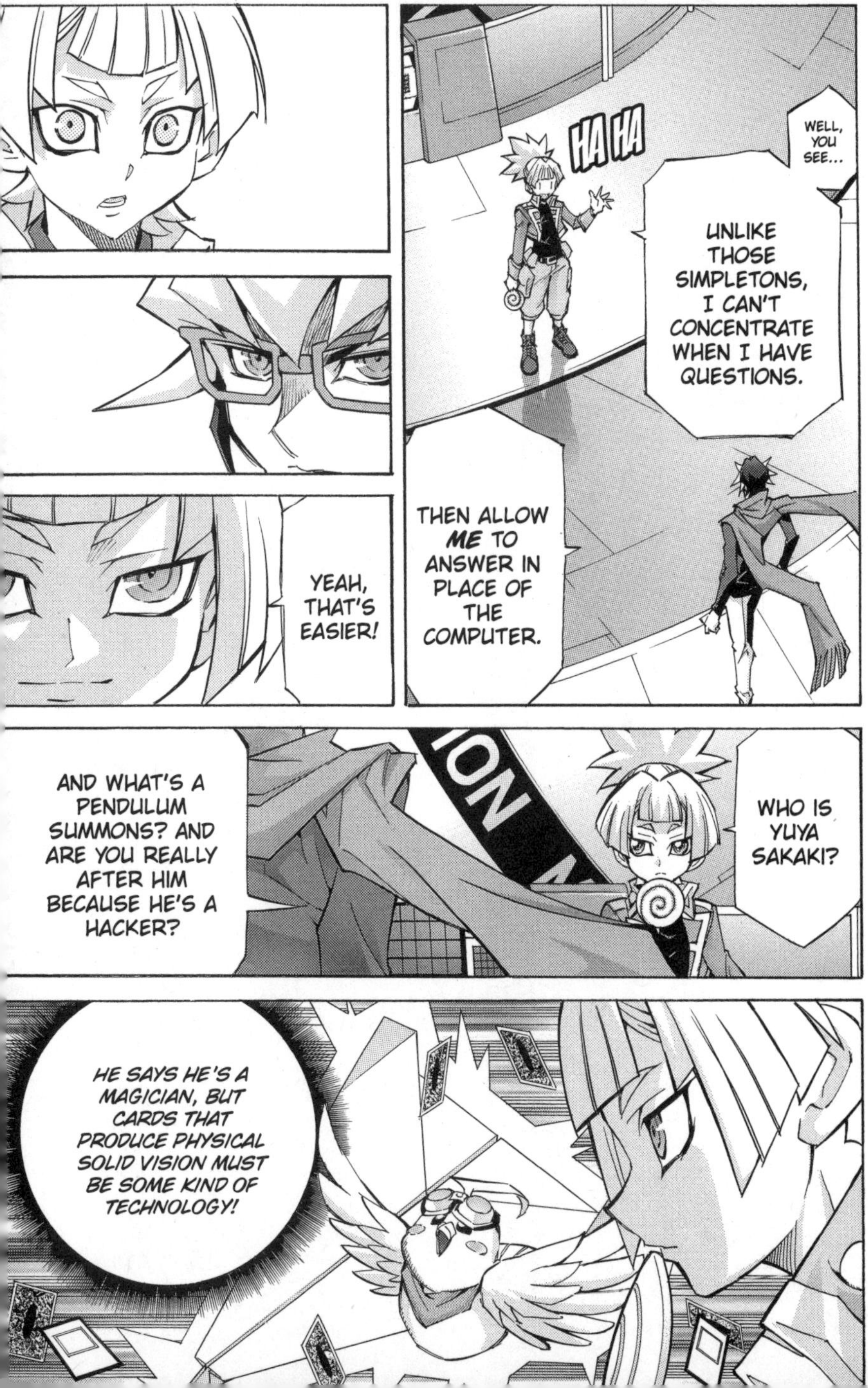
WELL, YOU SEE...
HA HA
UNLIKE THOSE SIMPLETONS, I CAN'T CONCENTRATE WHEN I HAVE QUESTIONS.
THEN ALLOW *ME* TO ANSWER IN PLACE OF THE COMPUTER.
YEAH, THAT'S EASIER!
WHO IS YUYA SAKAKI?
AND WHAT'S A PENDULUM SUMMONS? AND ARE YOU REALLY AFTER HIM BECAUSE HE'S A HACKER?
HE SAYS HE'S A MAGICIAN, BUT CARDS THAT PRODUCE PHYSICAL SOLID VISION MUST BE SOME KIND OF TECHNOLOGY!

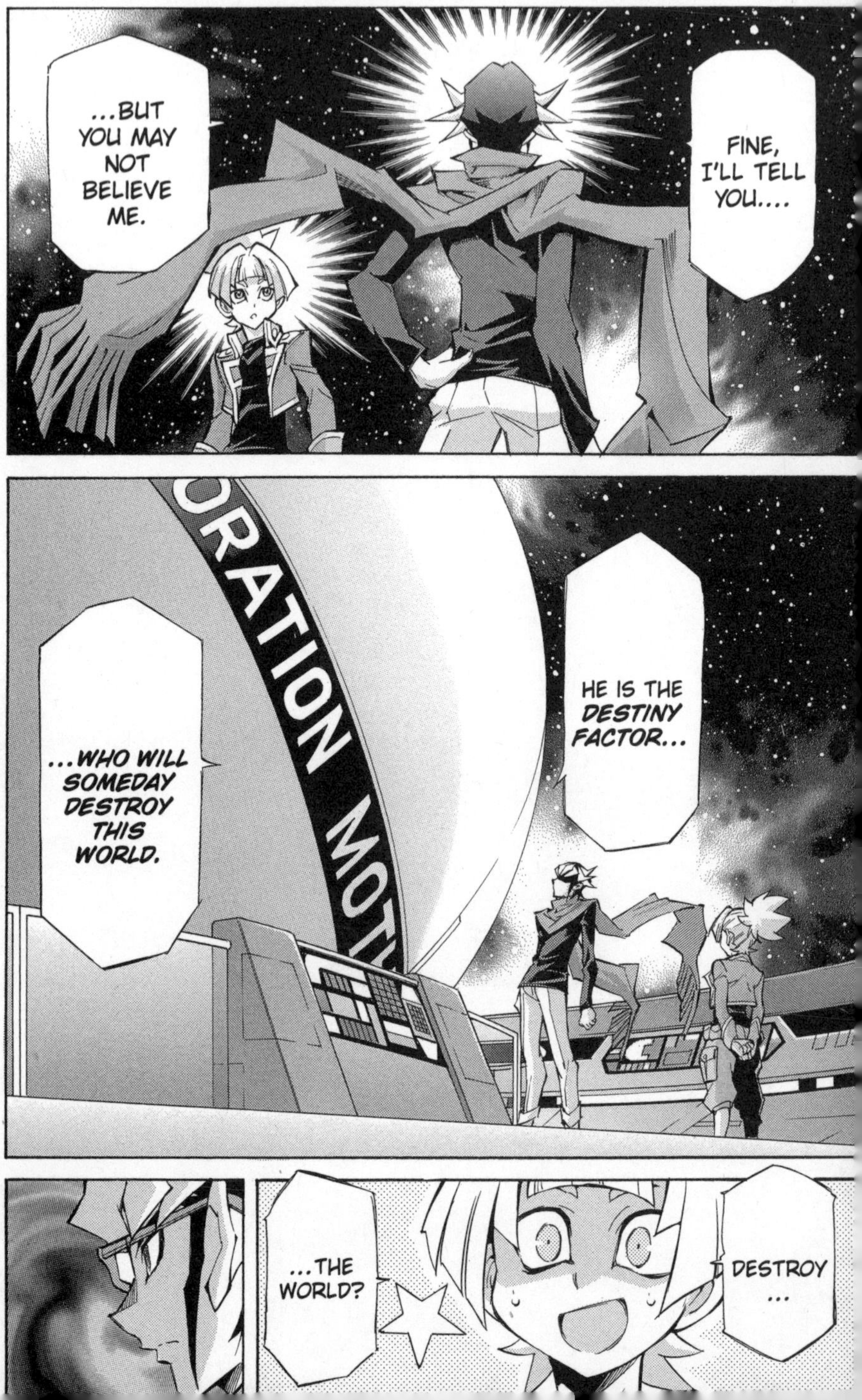
FINE, I'LL TELL YOU....
...BUT YOU MAY NOT BELIEVE ME.
HE IS THE *DESTINY FACTOR*...
...WHO WILL SOMEDAY DESTROY THIS WORLD.
DESTROY ...
...THE WORLD?

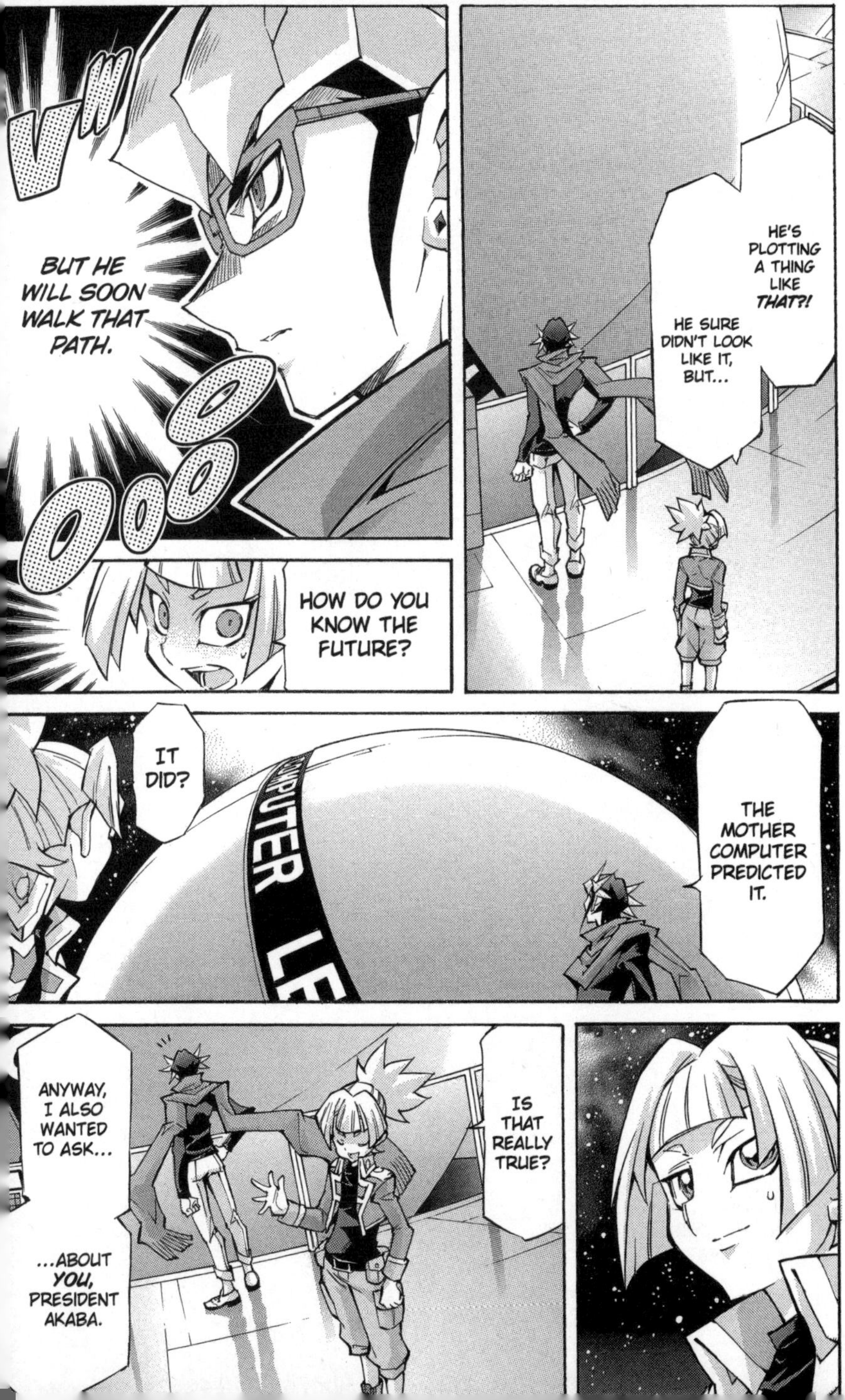
HE'S PLOTTING A THING LIKE *THAT?!*
HE SURE DIDN'T LOOK LIKE IT, BUT...
VMM
BUT HE WILL SOON WALK THAT PATH.
OOOO
HOW DO YOU KNOW THE FUTURE?
THE MOTHER COMPUTER PREDICTED IT.
IT DID?
IS THAT REALLY TRUE?
ANYWAY, I ALSO WANTED TO ASK...
...ABOUT *YOU,* PRESIDENT AKABA.

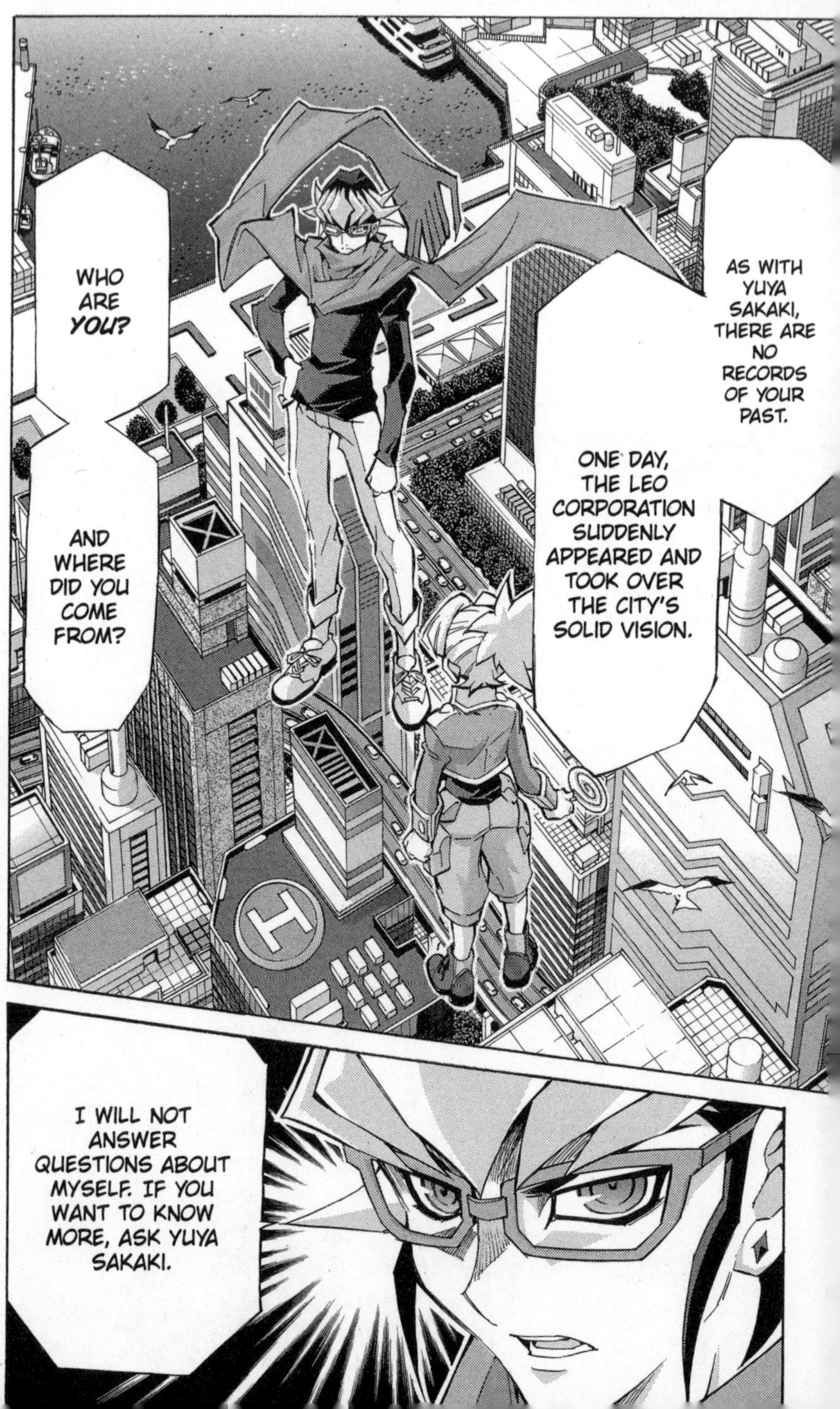
AS WITH YUYA SAKAKI, THERE ARE NO RECORDS OF YOUR PAST.
ONE DAY, THE LEO CORPORATION SUDDENLY APPEARED AND TOOK OVER THE CITY'S SOLID VISION.
WHO ARE *YOU?*
AND WHERE DID YOU COME FROM?
I WILL NOT ANSWER QUESTIONS ABOUT MYSELF. IF YOU WANT TO KNOW MORE, ASK YUYA SAKAKI.

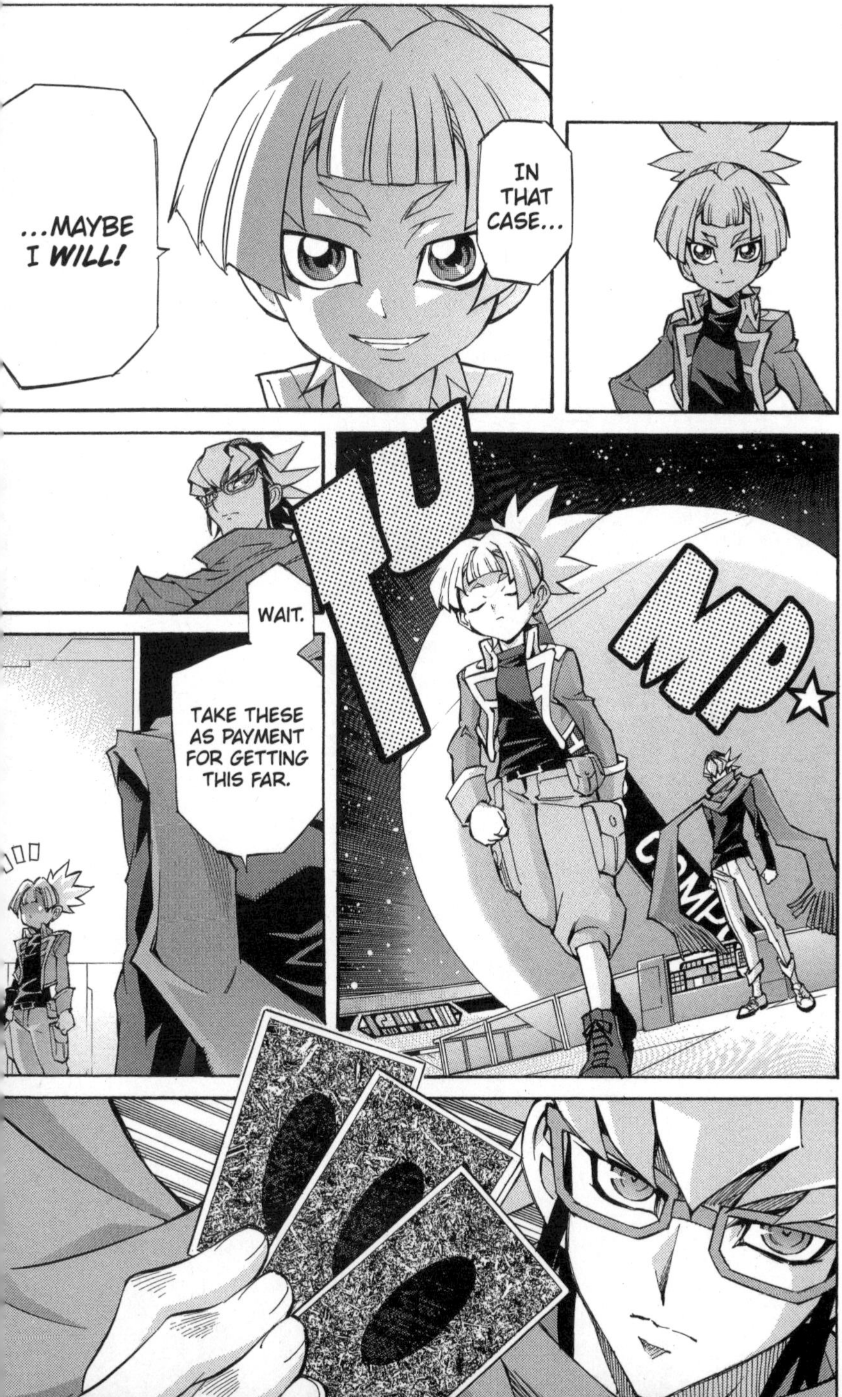
IN THAT CASE...
...MAYBE I WILL!
YUMP☆
WAIT.
TAKE THESE AS PAYMENT FOR GETTING THIS FAR.

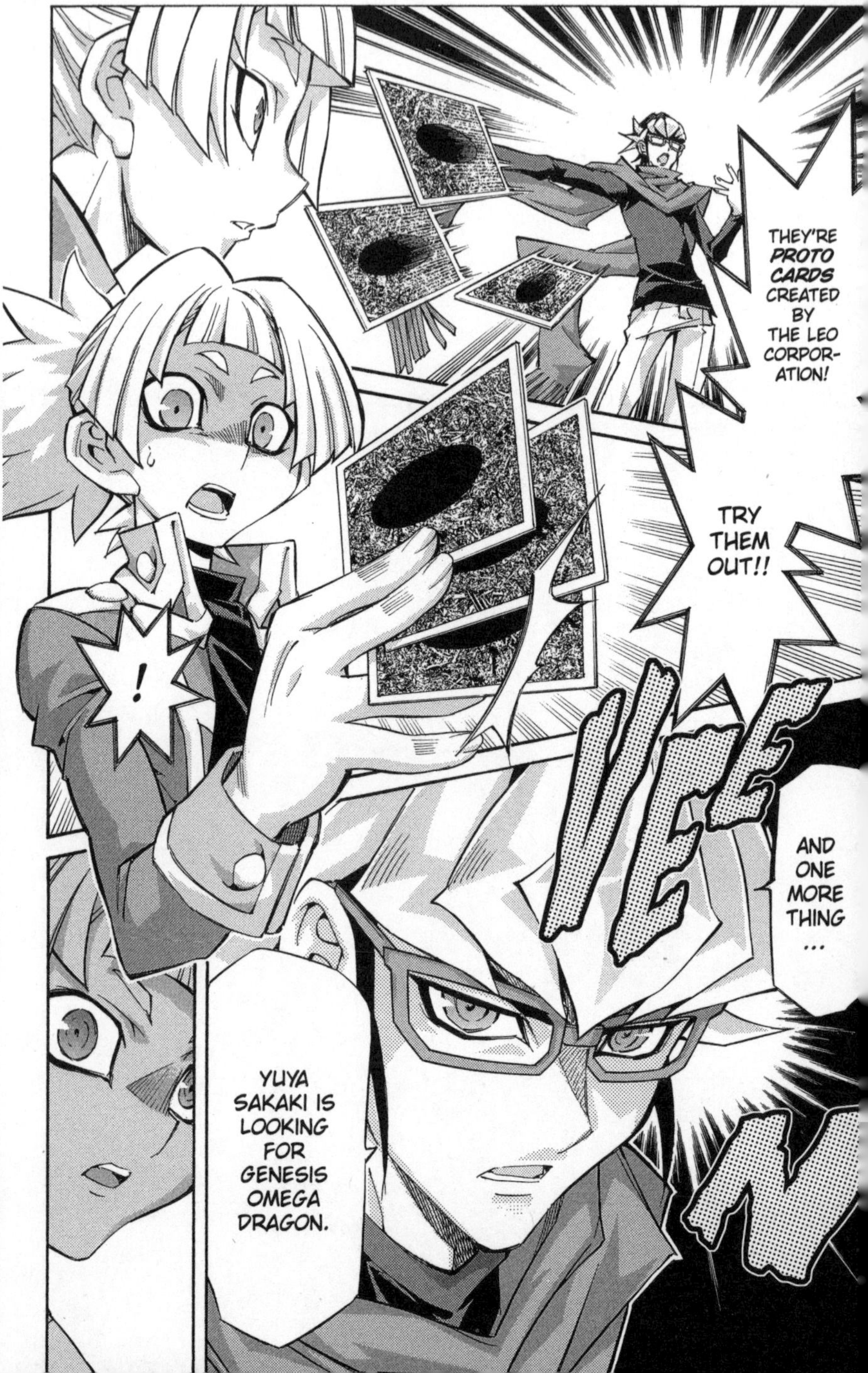
THEY'RE *PROTO CARDS* CREATED BY THE LEO CORPORATION!
TRY THEM OUT!!
!
VEE
AND ONE MORE THING...
N
YUYA SAKAKI IS LOOKING FOR GENESIS OMEGA DRAGON.

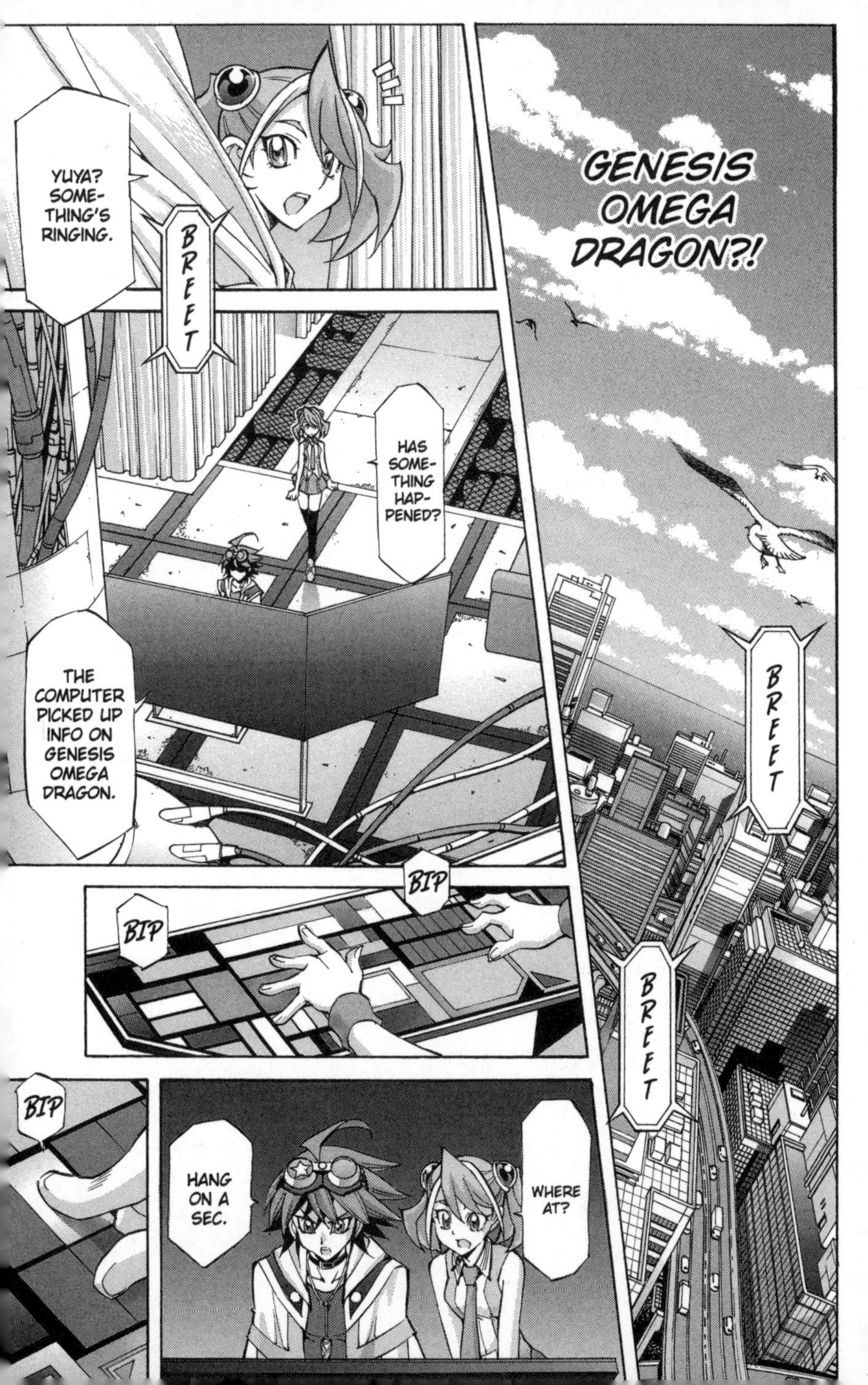

GENESIS OMEGA DRAGON?!
BREET
BREET
YUYA? SOME-THING'S RINGING.
BREET
HAS SOME-THING HAP-PENED?
THE COMPUTER PICKED UP INFO ON GENESIS OMEGA DRAGON.
BIP
BIP
WHERE AT?
HANG ON A SEC.
BIP

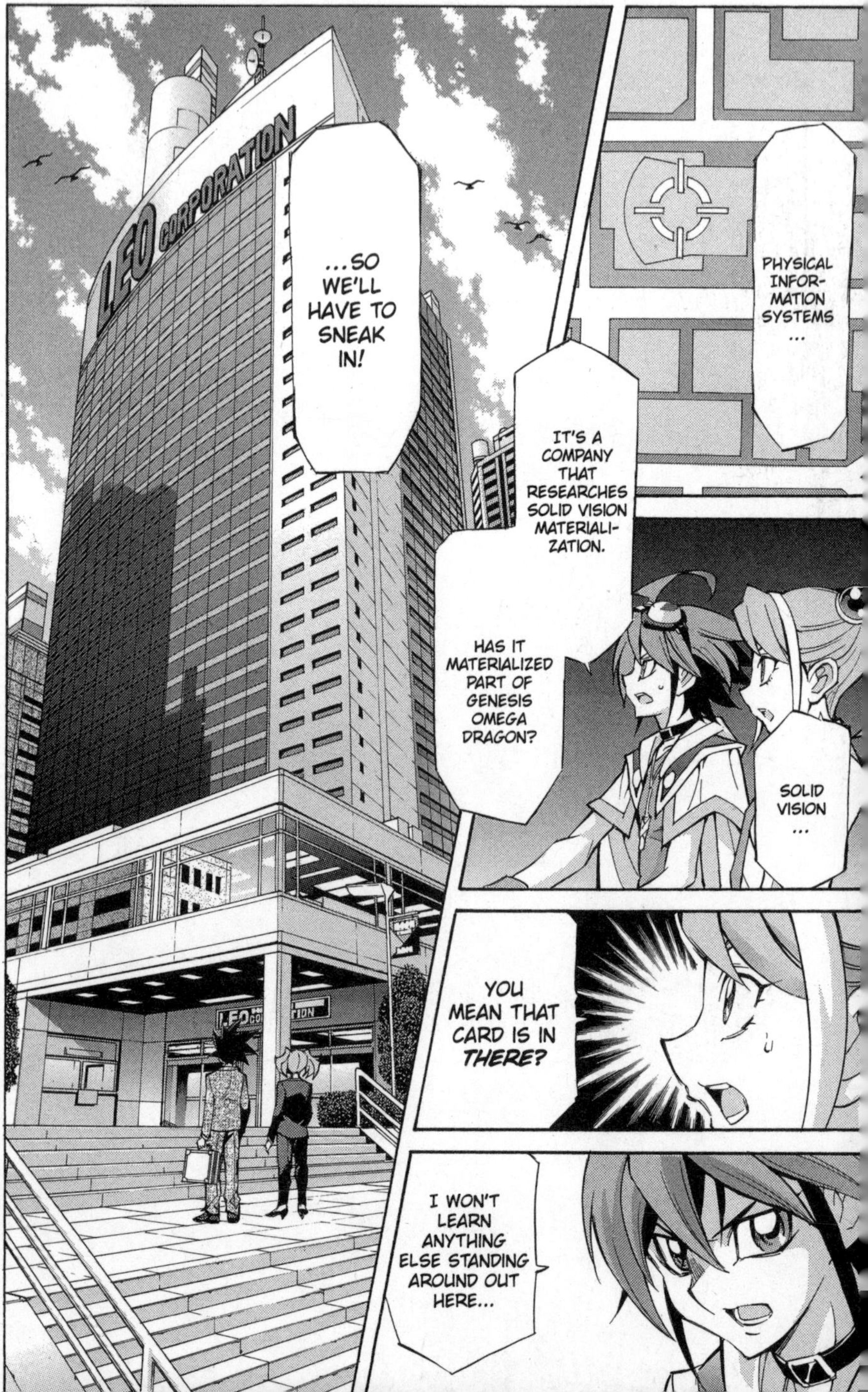
PHYSICAL INFORMATION SYSTEMS...
IT'S A COMPANY THAT RESEARCHES SOLID VISION MATERIALIZATION.
SOLID VISION...
HAS IT MATERIALIZED PART OF GENESIS OMEGA DRAGON?
YOU MEAN THAT CARD IS IN *THERE?*
I WON'T LEARN ANYTHING ELSE STANDING AROUND OUT HERE...
LEO CORPORATION
...SO WE'LL HAVE TO SNEAK IN!

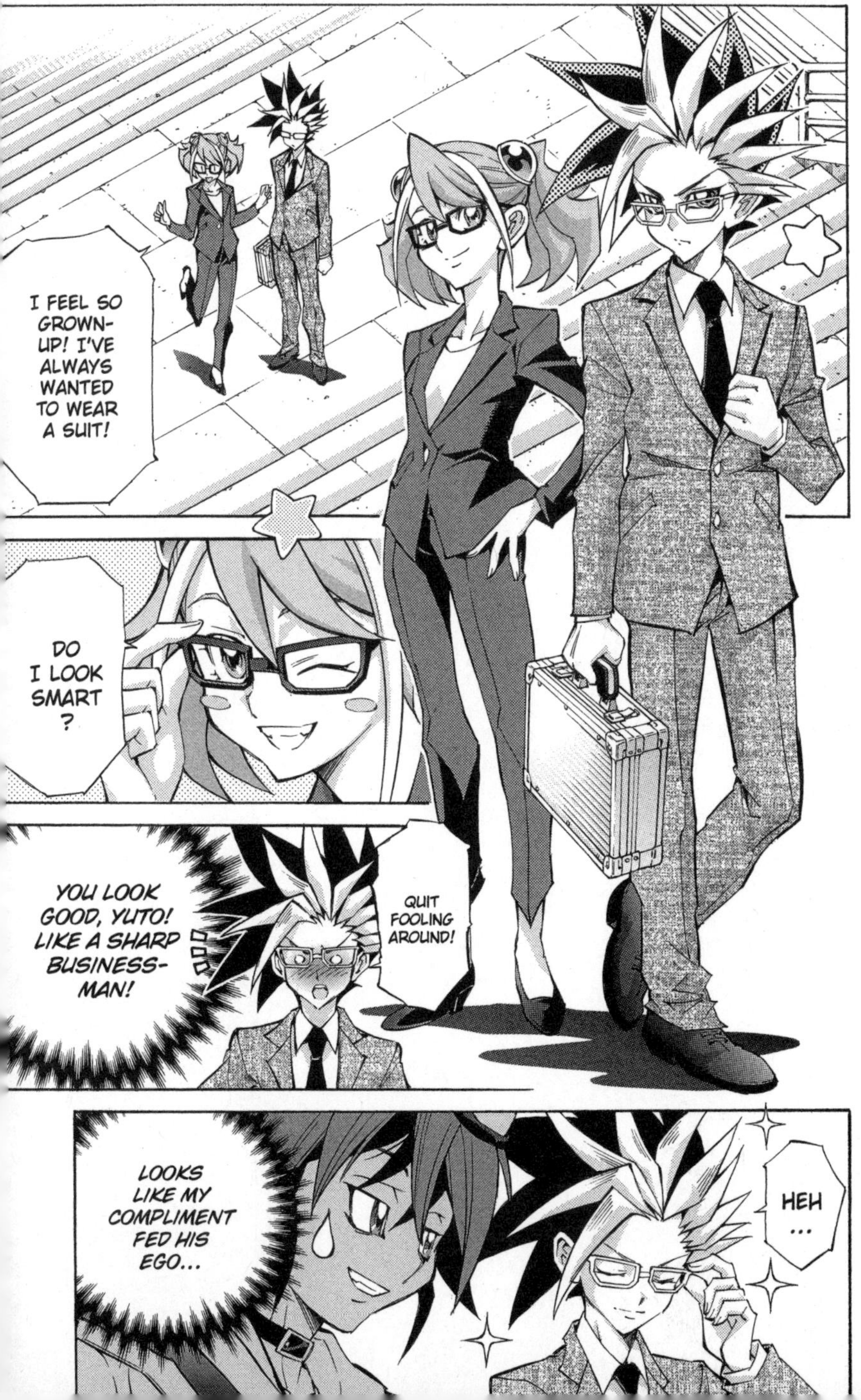

I FEEL SO GROWN-UP! I'VE ALWAYS WANTED TO WEAR A SUIT!
DO I LOOK SMART?
YOU LOOK GOOD, YUTO! LIKE A SHARP BUSINESS-MAN!
QUIT FOOLING AROUND!
HEH...
LOOKS LIKE MY COMPLIMENT FED HIS EGO...

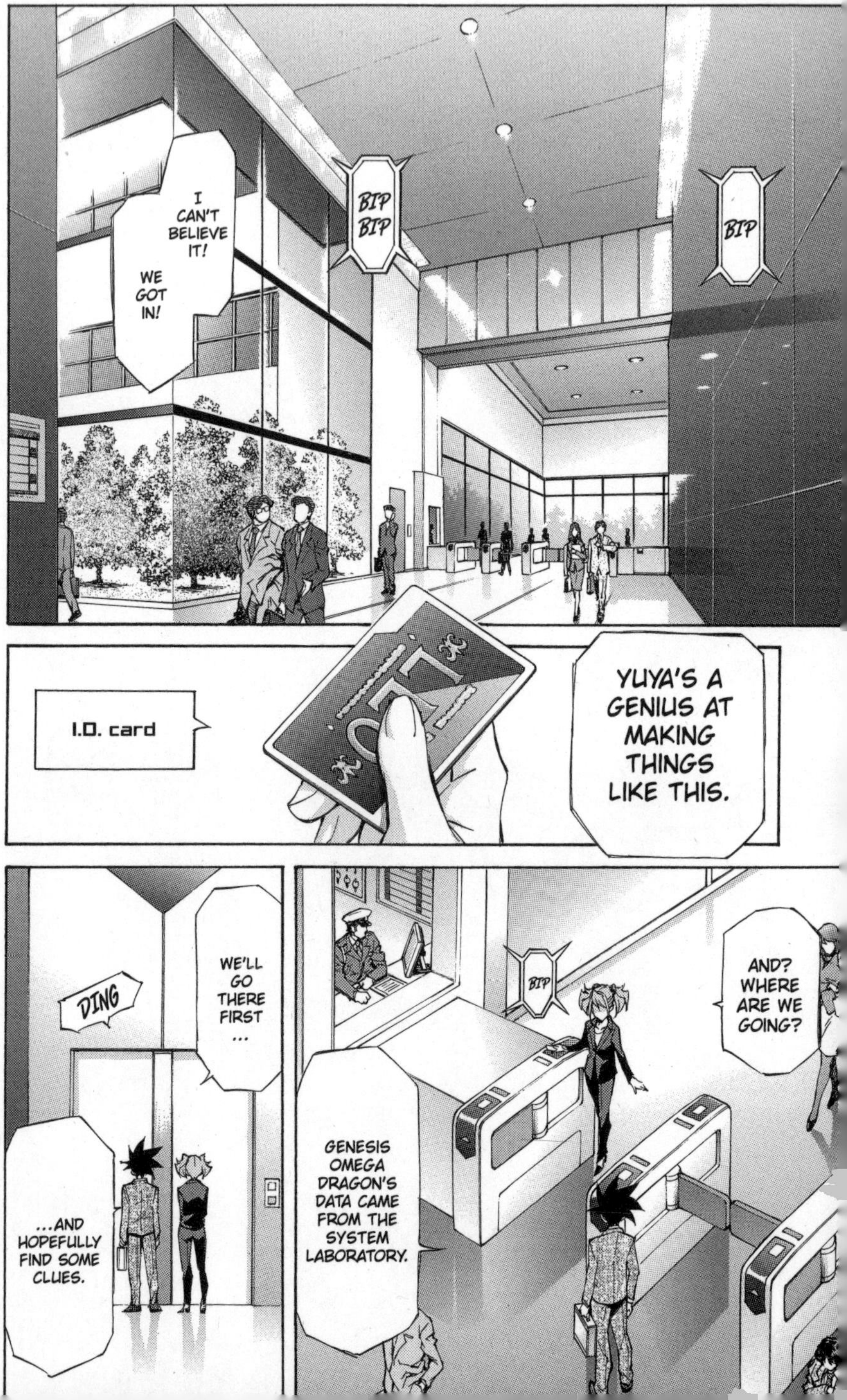
BIP
BIP BIP
I CAN'T BELIEVE IT!
WE GOT IN!
YUYA'S A GENIUS AT MAKING THINGS LIKE THIS.
I.D. card
AND? WHERE ARE WE GOING?
BIP
GENESIS OMEGA DRAGON'S DATA CAME FROM THE SYSTEM LABORATORY.
WE'LL GO THERE FIRST...
DING
...AND HOPEFULLY FIND SOME CLUES.

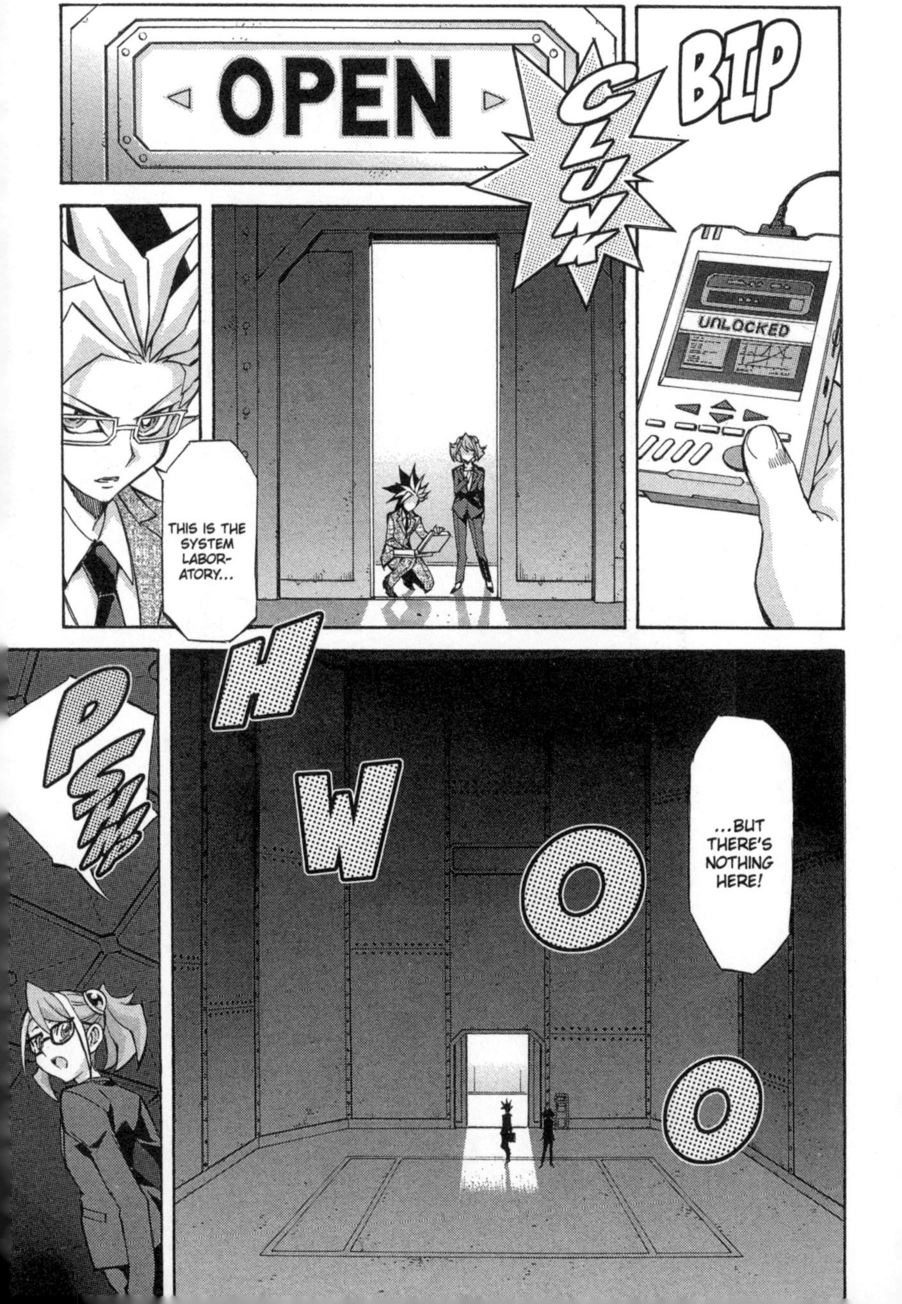
BIP
OPEN
CLUNK
UNLOCKED
THIS IS THE SYSTEM LABORATORY...
HWOOO
...BUT THERE'S NOTHING HERE!

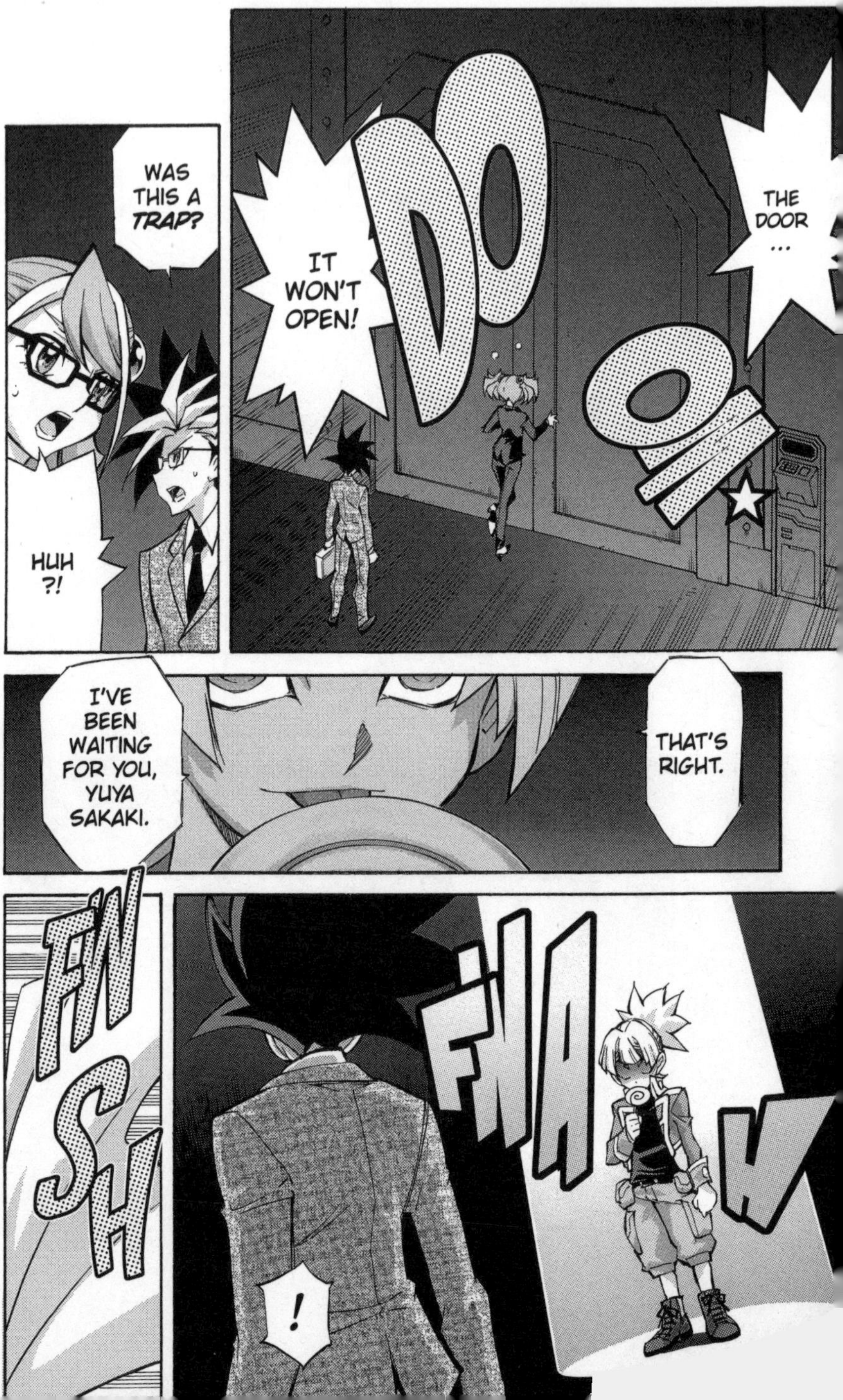
THE DOOR ...
IT WON'T OPEN!
WAS THIS A TRAP?
HUH ?!
THAT'S RIGHT.
I'VE BEEN WAITING FOR YOU, YUYA SAKAKI.
!

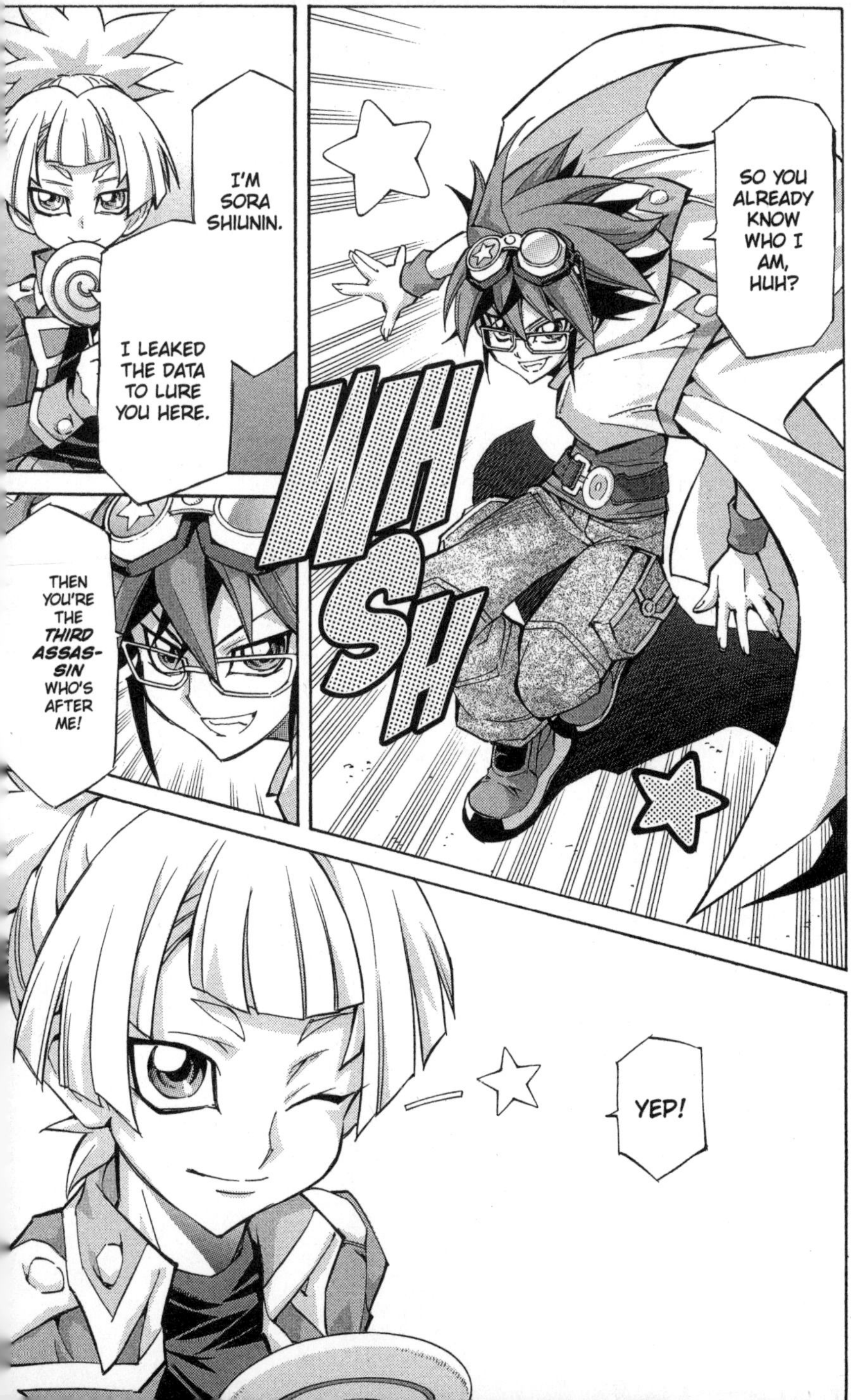
SO YOU ALREADY KNOW WHO I AM, HUH?
WHOSH
I'M SORA SHIUNIN.
I LEAKED THE DATA TO LURE YOU HERE.
THEN YOU'RE THE *THIRD ASSASSIN* WHO'S AFTER ME!
YEP!

scale 6

PRESENTING MIYOSHI SENSEI'S EARLY DESIGNS!

ARC-V CHARACTER SKETCHES

SHUN KUROSAKI

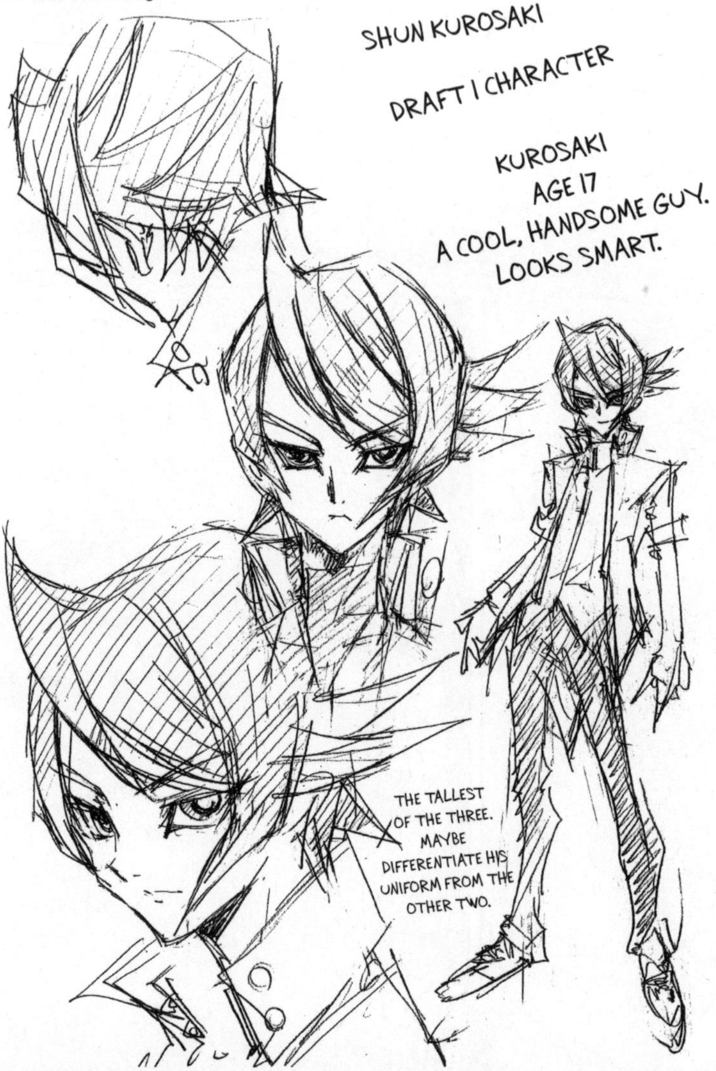
SHUN KUROSAKI
DRAFT 1 CHARACTER
KUROSAKI
AGE 17
A COOL, HANDSOME GUY.
LOOKS SMART.
THE TALLEST OF THE THREE. MAYBE DIFFERENTIATE HIS UNIFORM FROM THE OTHER TWO.

In the early designs, Kurosaki was slimmer than he is now, and he was more of the cool, handsome type. The idea that he's always hungry for a fight came up later.

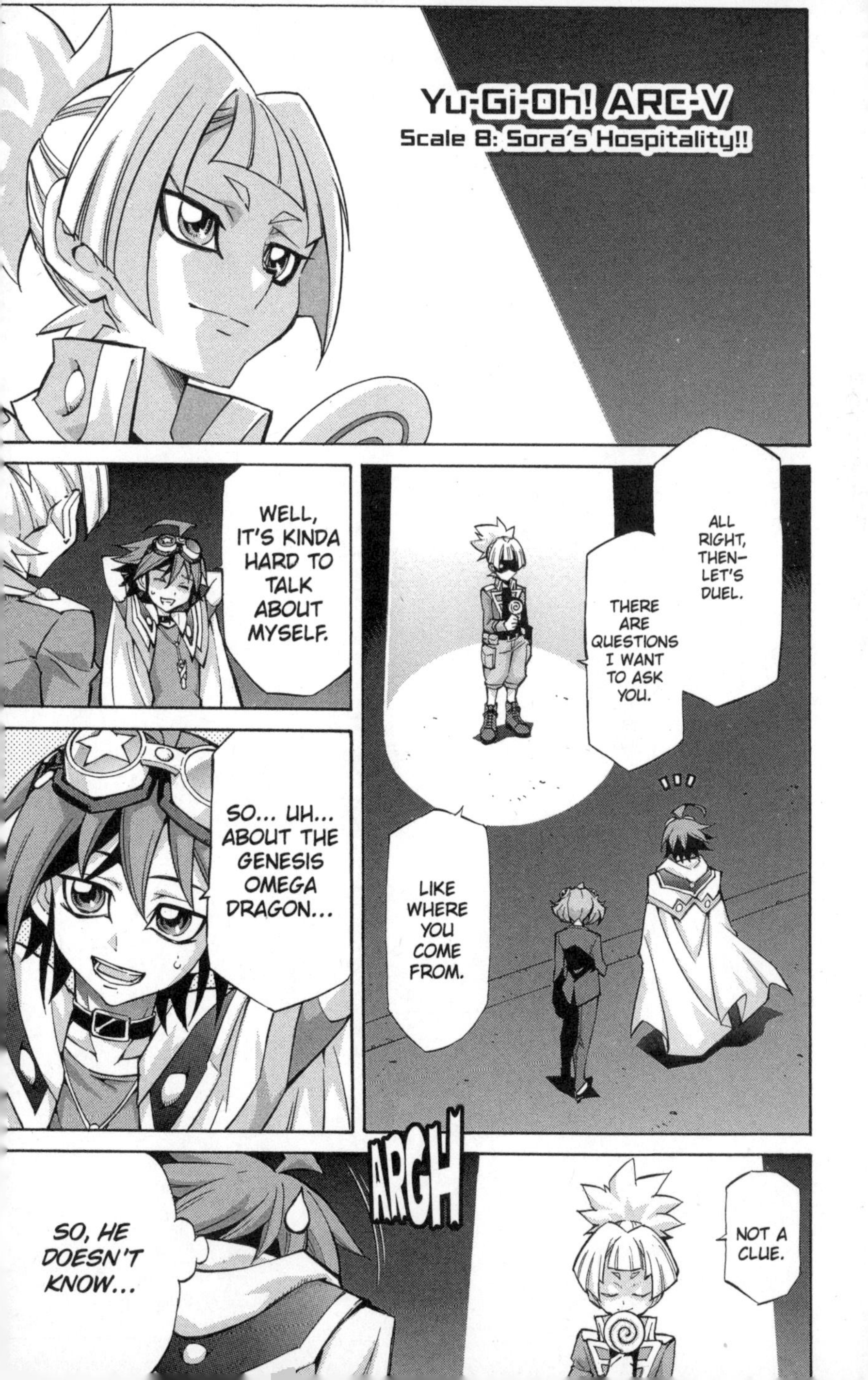
Yu-Gi-Oh! ARC-V
Scale 8: Sora's Hospitality!!
ALL RIGHT, THEN—LET'S DUEL.
THERE ARE QUESTIONS I WANT TO ASK YOU.
LIKE WHERE YOU COME FROM.
WELL, IT'S KINDA HARD TO TALK ABOUT MYSELF.
SO... UH... ABOUT THE GENESIS OMEGA DRAGON...
NOT A CLUE.
ARGH
SO, HE DOESN'T KNOW...

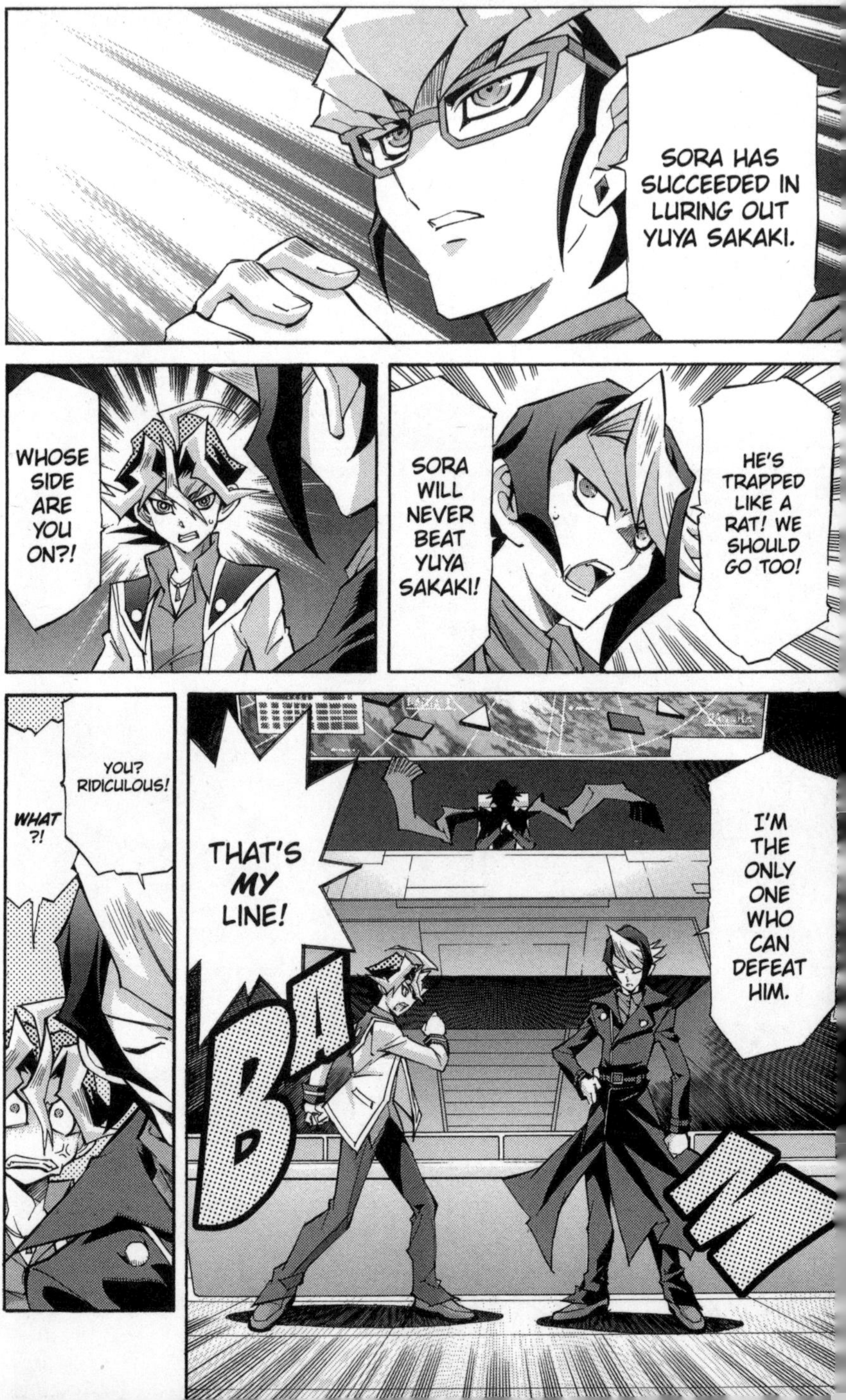
SORA HAS SUCCEEDED IN LURING OUT YUYA SAKAKI.
HE'S TRAPPED LIKE A RAT! WE SHOULD GO TOO!
SORA WILL NEVER BEAT YUYA SAKAKI!
WHOSE SIDE ARE YOU ON?!
I'M THE ONLY ONE WHO CAN DEFEAT HIM.
THAT'S *MY* LINE!
YOU? RIDICULOUS!
WHAT?!

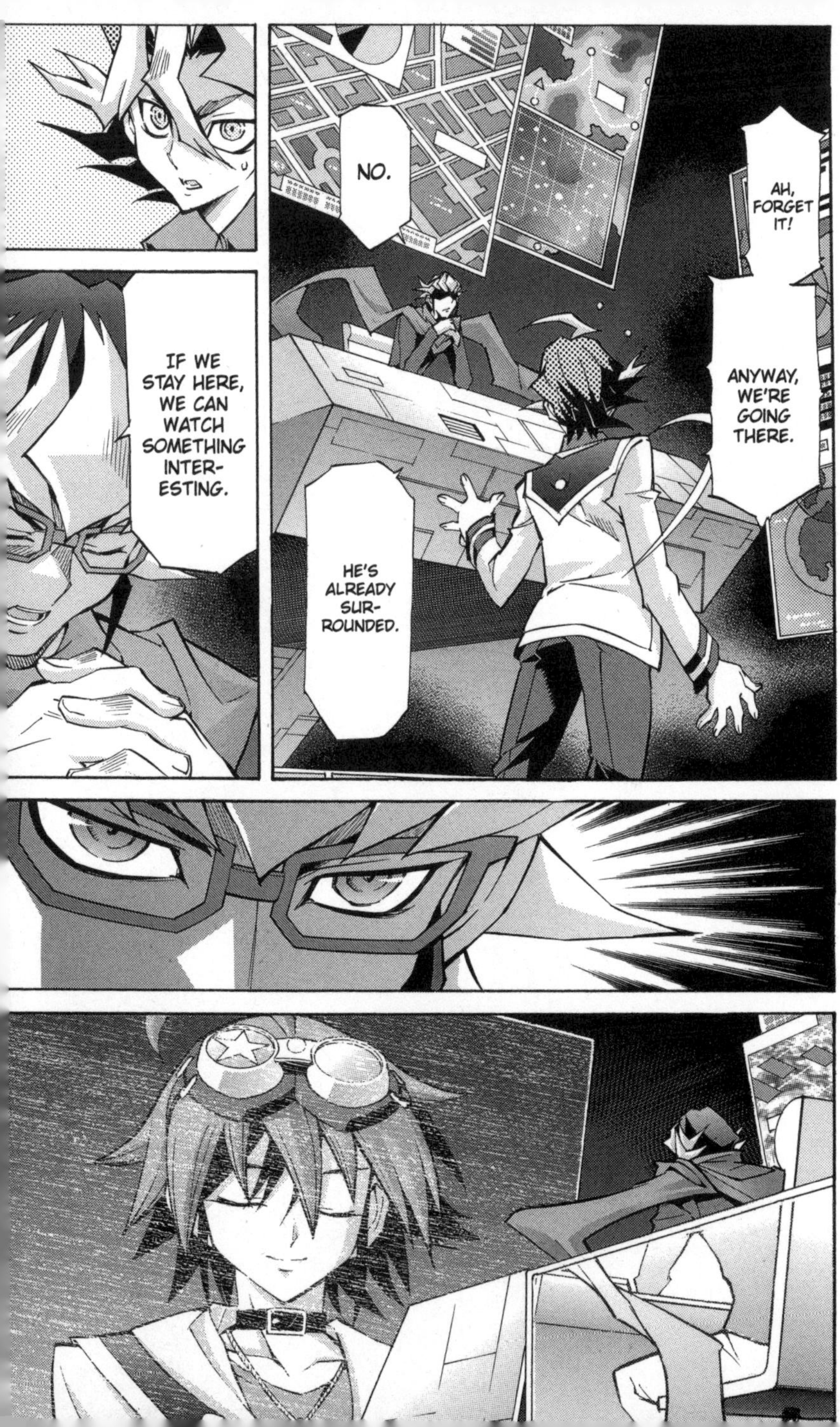
AH, FORGET IT!
ANYWAY, WE'RE GOING THERE.
NO.
HE'S ALREADY SUR-ROUNDED.
IF WE STAY HERE, WE CAN WATCH SOMETHING INTER-ESTING.

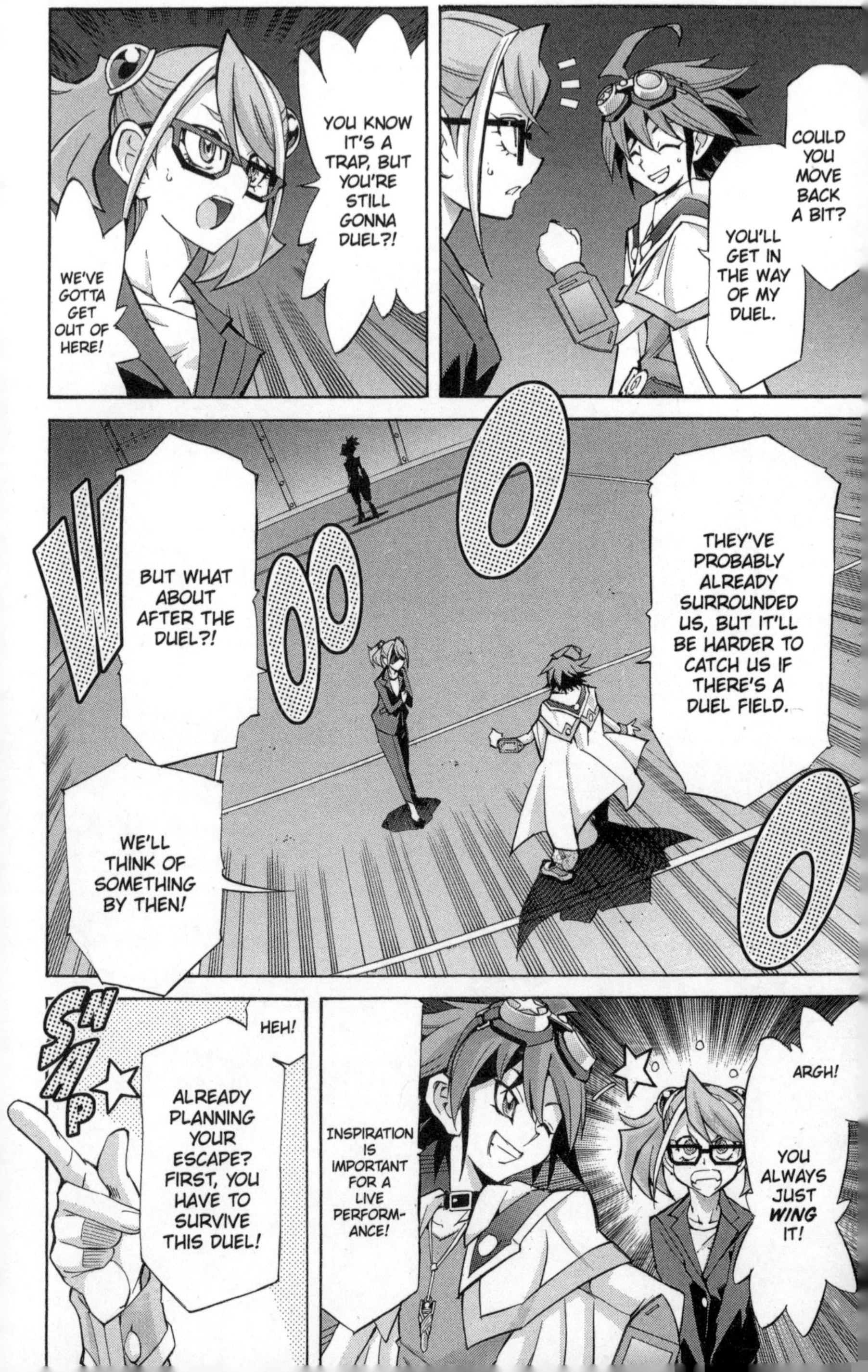
YOU KNOW IT'S A TRAP, BUT YOU'RE STILL GONNA DUEL?!
WE'VE GOTTA GET OUT OF HERE!
COULD YOU MOVE BACK A BIT?
YOU'LL GET IN THE WAY OF MY DUEL.
THEY'VE PROBABLY ALREADY SURROUNDED US, BUT IT'LL BE HARDER TO CATCH US IF THERE'S A DUEL FIELD.
WOOOO
BUT WHAT ABOUT AFTER THE DUEL?!
WE'LL THINK OF SOMETHING BY THEN!
SHAP
HEH!
ALREADY PLANNING YOUR ESCAPE? FIRST, YOU HAVE TO SURVIVE THIS DUEL!
INSPIRATION IS IMPORTANT FOR A LIVE PERFORM-ANCE!
ARGH!
YOU ALWAYS JUST WING IT!

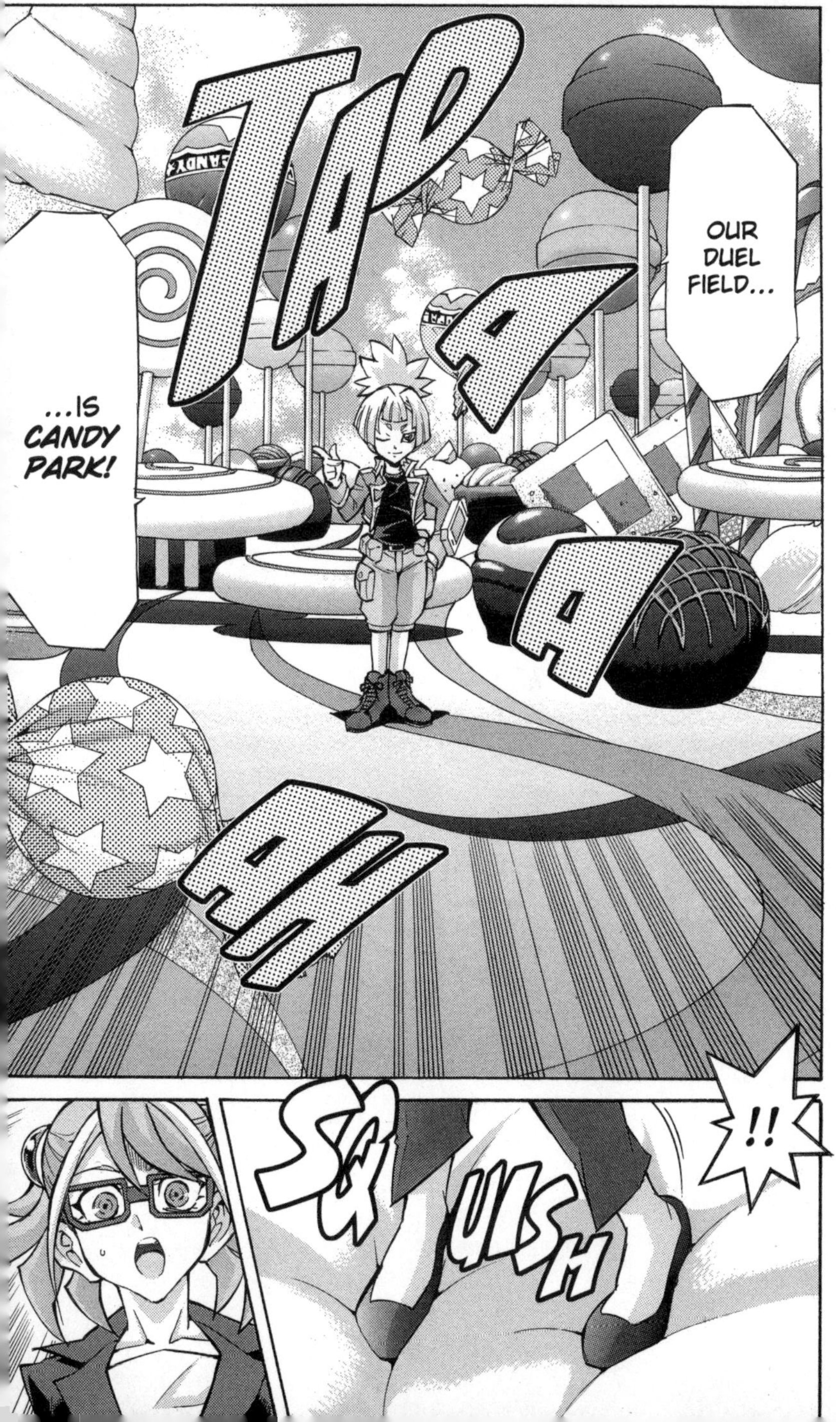
OUR DUEL FIELD...
...IS CANDY PARK!
TADAAAH
!!
SQUISH

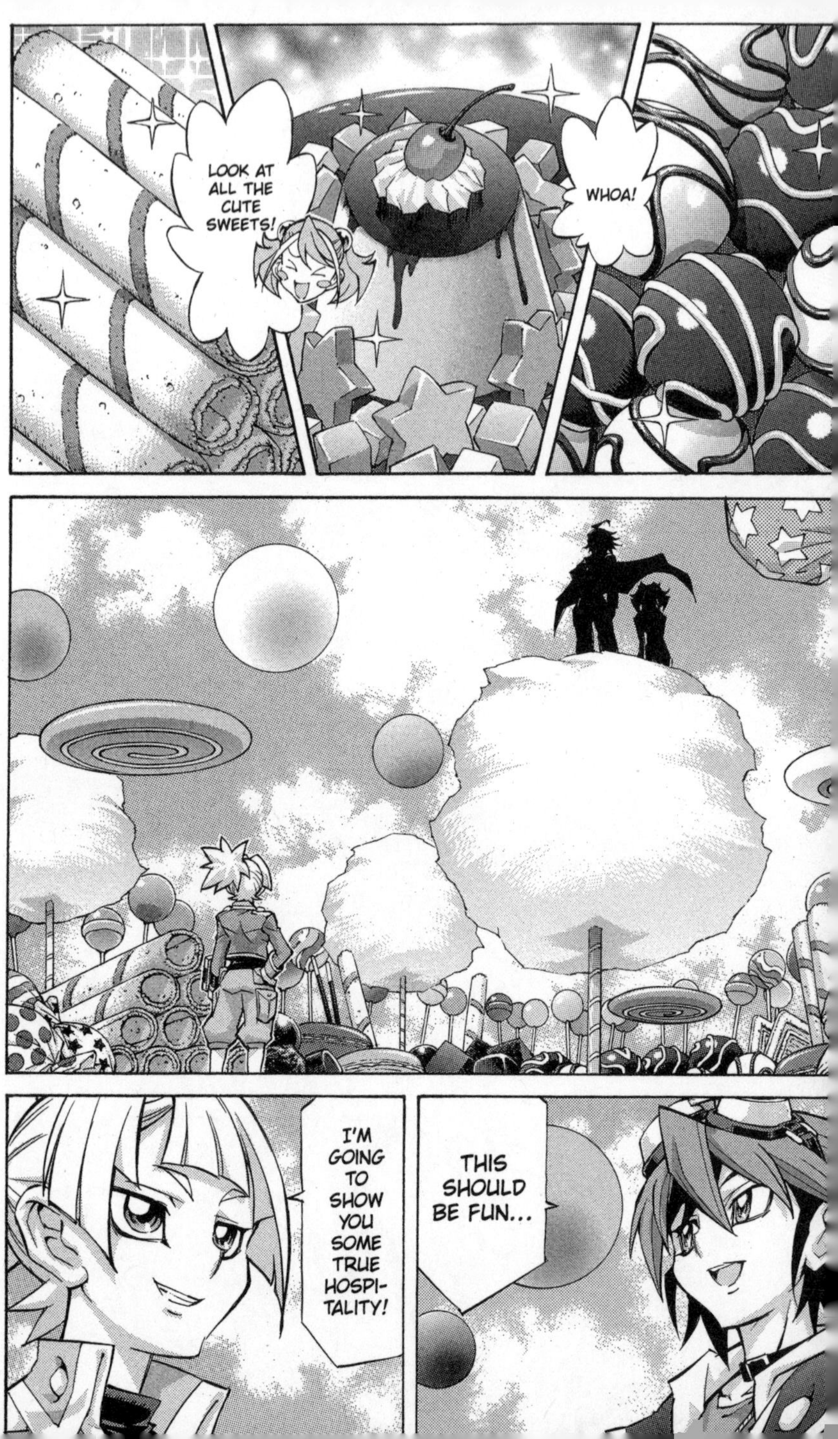
WHOA!
LOOK AT ALL THE CUTE SWEETS!
THIS SHOULD BE FUN...
I'M GOING TO SHOW YOU SOME TRUE HOSPITALITY!

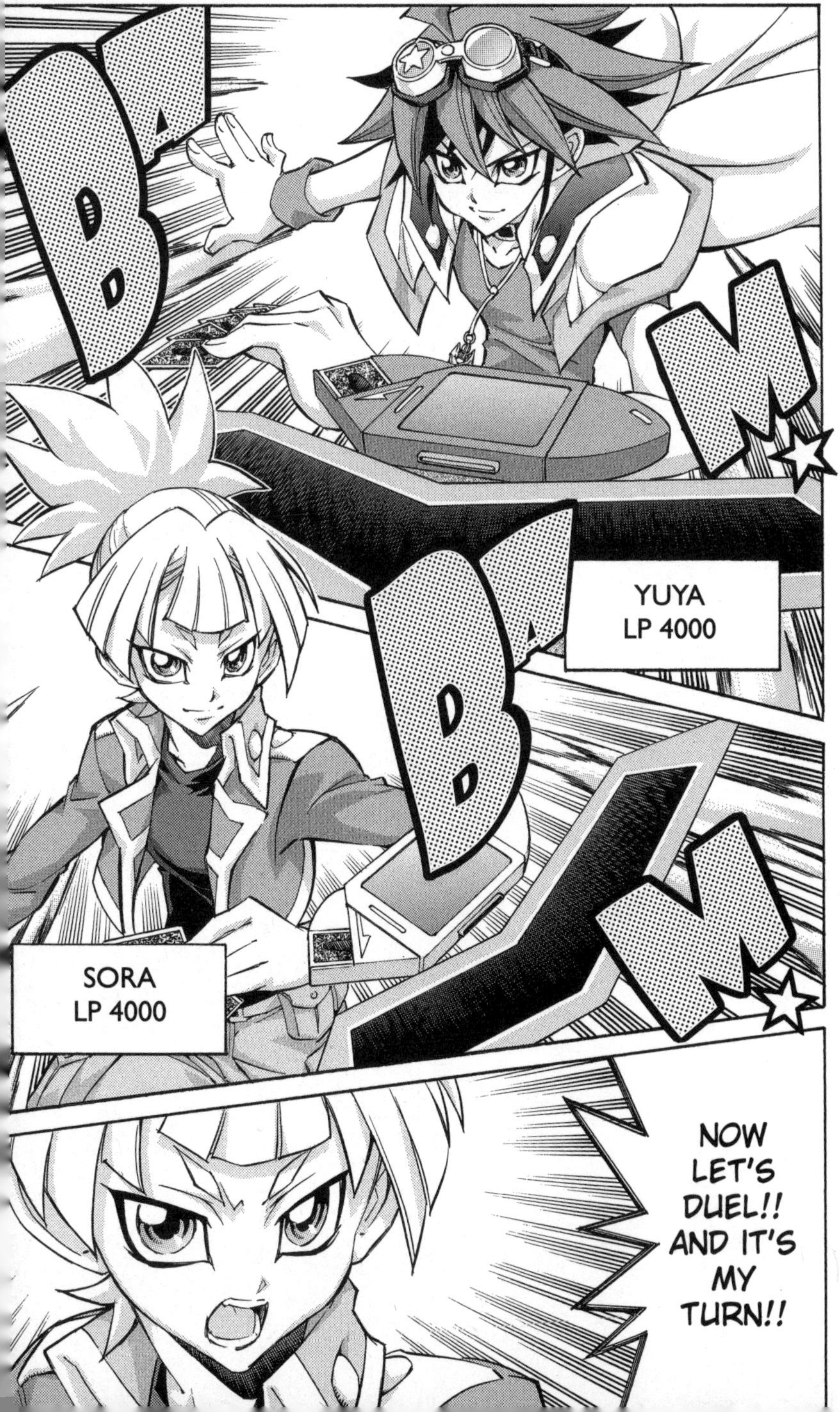
YUYA
LP 4000
SORA
LP 4000
NOW LET'S DUEL!! AND IT'S MY TURN!!

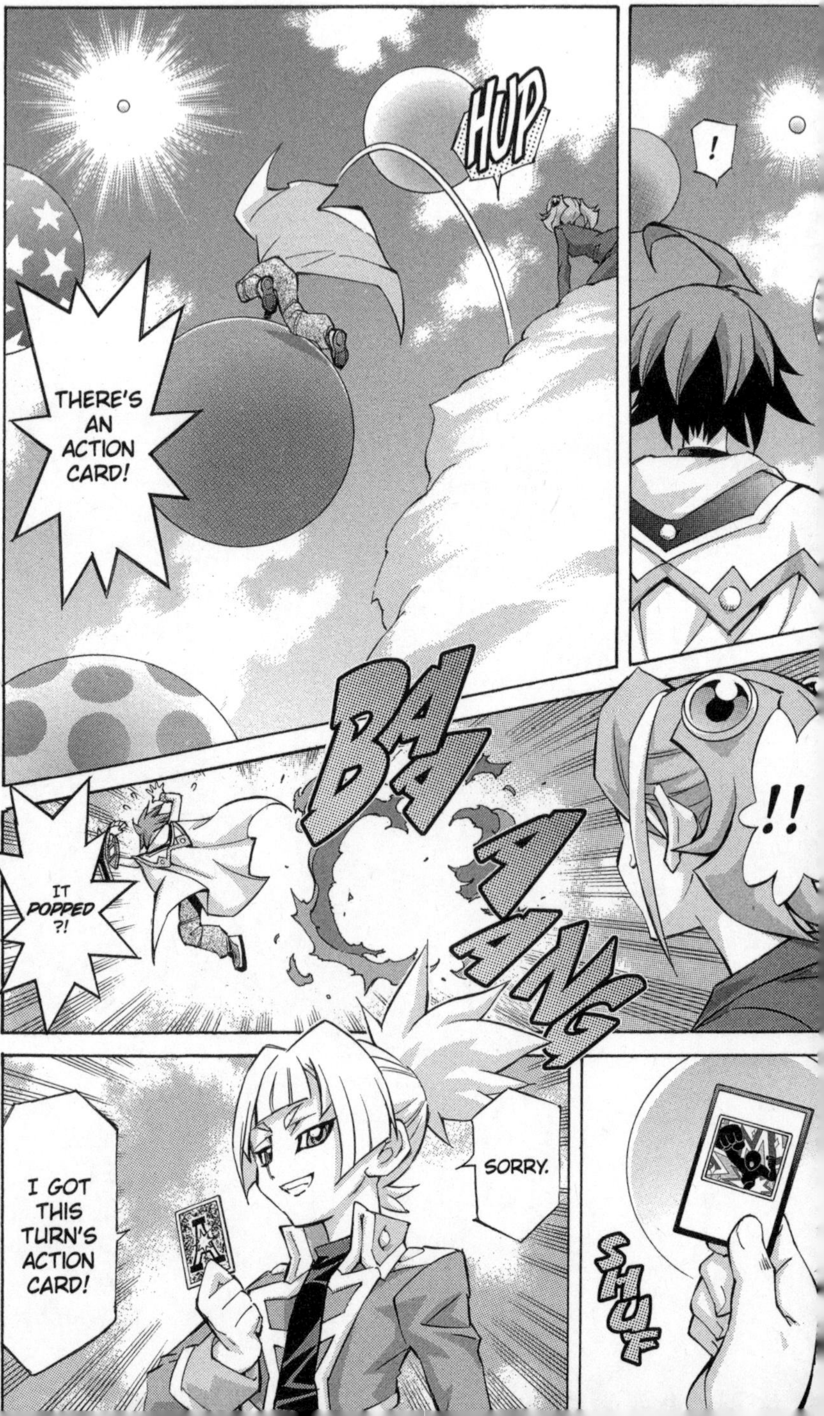
!
HUP
THERE'S AN ACTION CARD!
!!
BAAAAANG
IT POPPED?!
SHUF
SORRY.
I GOT THIS TURN'S ACTION CARD!

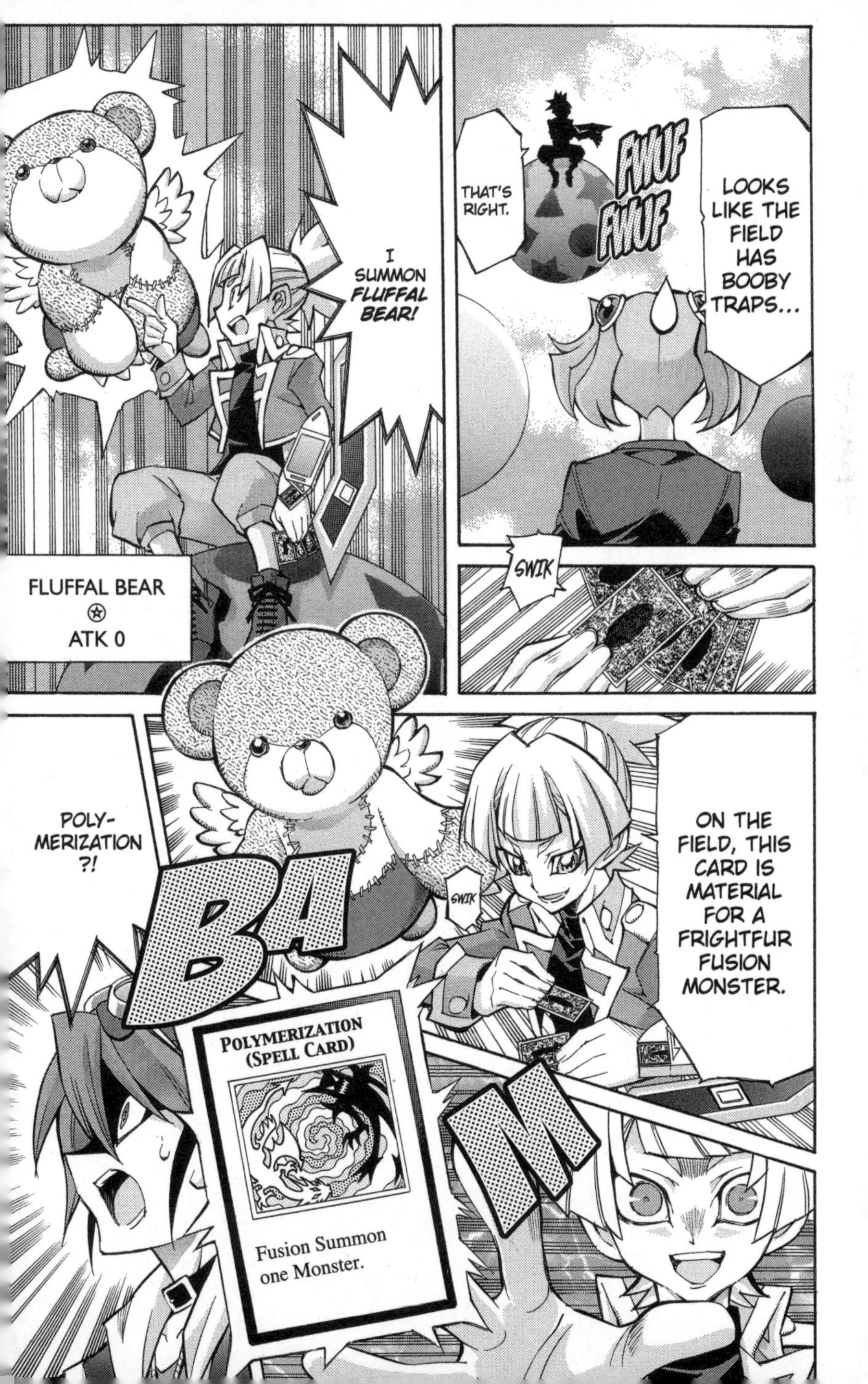
LOOKS LIKE THE FIELD HAS BOOBY TRAPS...
FWUF FWUF
THAT'S RIGHT.
SWIK
I SUMMON FLUFFAL BEAR!
FLUFFAL BEAR ☆ ATK 0
ON THE FIELD, THIS CARD IS MATERIAL FOR A FRIGHTFUR FUSION MONSTER.
SWIK
POLY-MERIZATION ?!
BAM
POLYMERIZATION (SPELL CARD)
Fusion Summon one Monster.

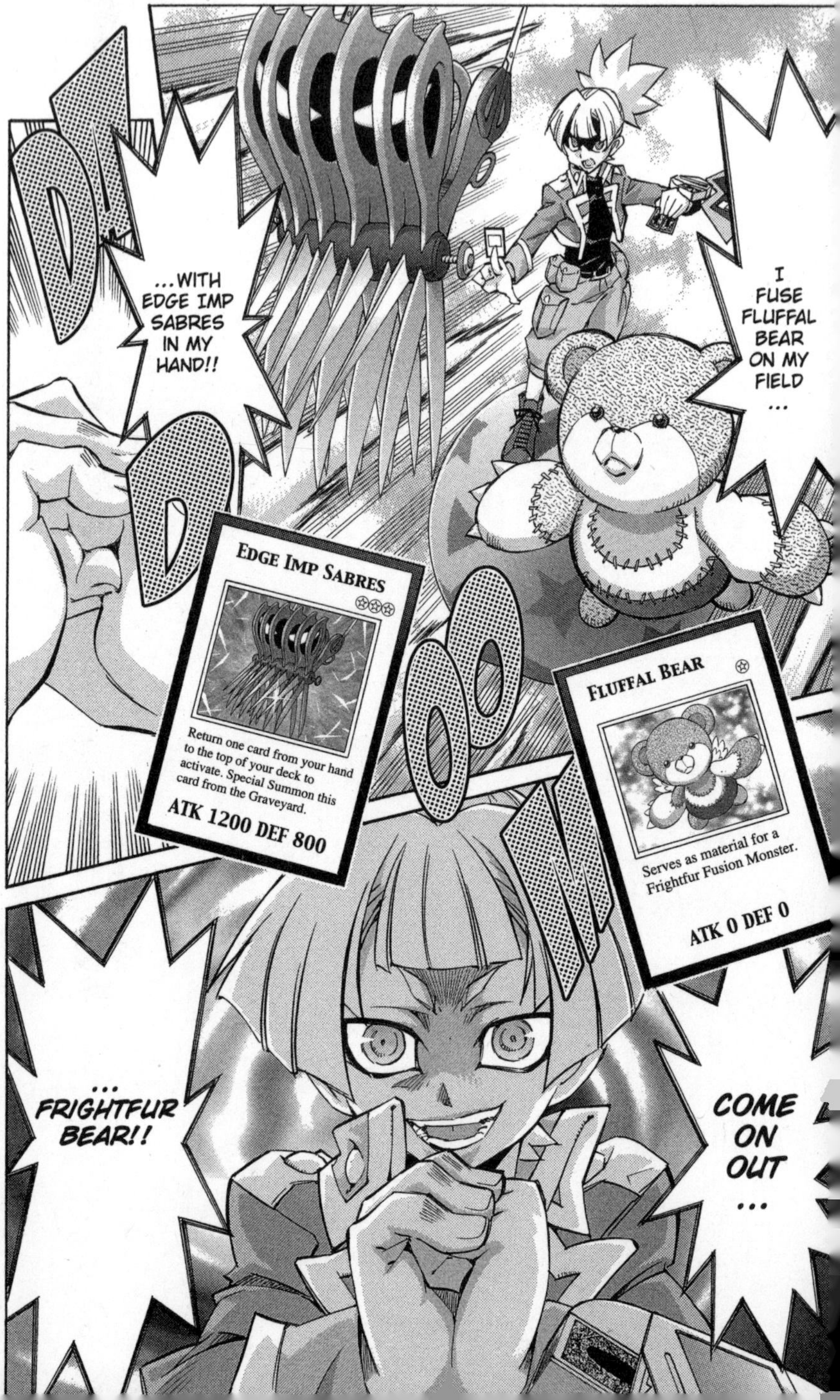
I FUSE FLUFFAL BEAR ON MY FIELD ...
...WITH EDGE IMP SABRES IN MY HAND!!
FLUFFAL BEAR
Serves as material for a Frightfur Fusion Monster.
ATK 0 DEF 0
EDGE IMP SABRES
Return one card from your hand to the top of your deck to activate. Special Summon this card from the Graveyard.
ATK 1200 DEF 800
COME ON OUT ...
... FRIGHTFUR BEAR!!

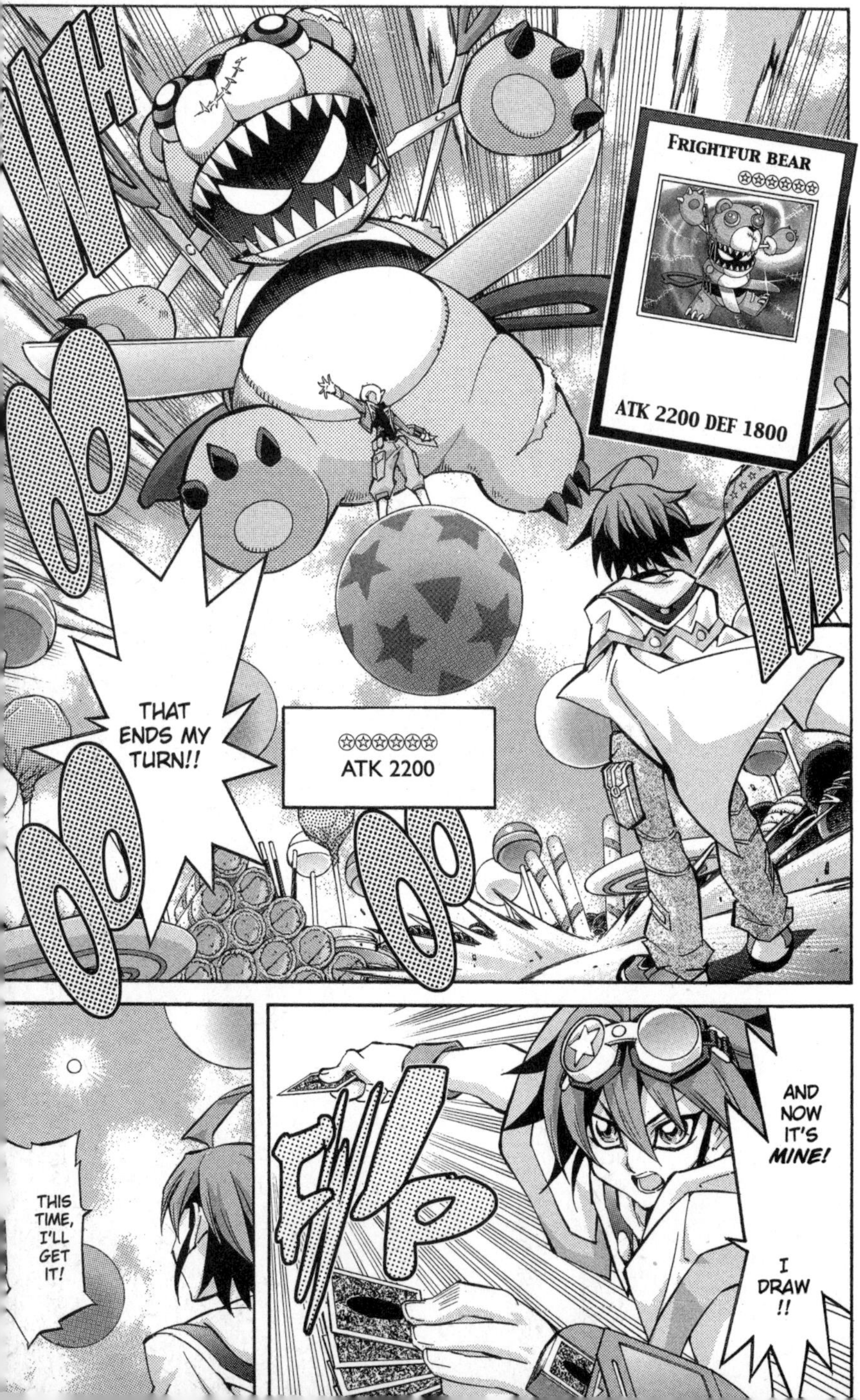
FRIGHTFUR BEAR
ATK 2200 DEF 1800
ATK 2200
THAT ENDS MY TURN!!
AND NOW IT'S MINE!
I DRAW!!
FLIP
THIS TIME, I'LL GET IT!

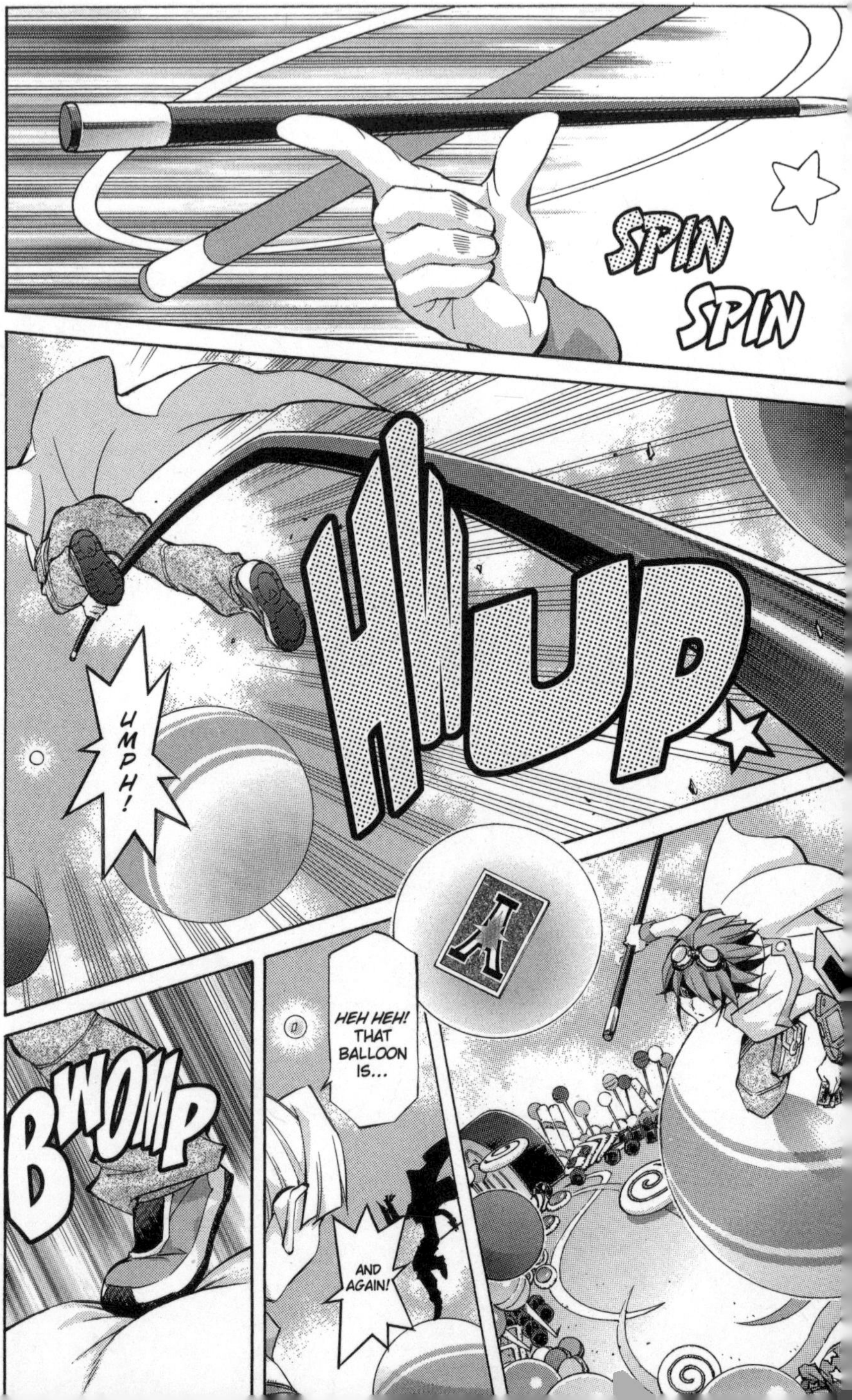
SPIN
SPIN
HWUP
UMPH!
HEH HEH! THAT BALLOON IS...
AND AGAIN!
BWOMP

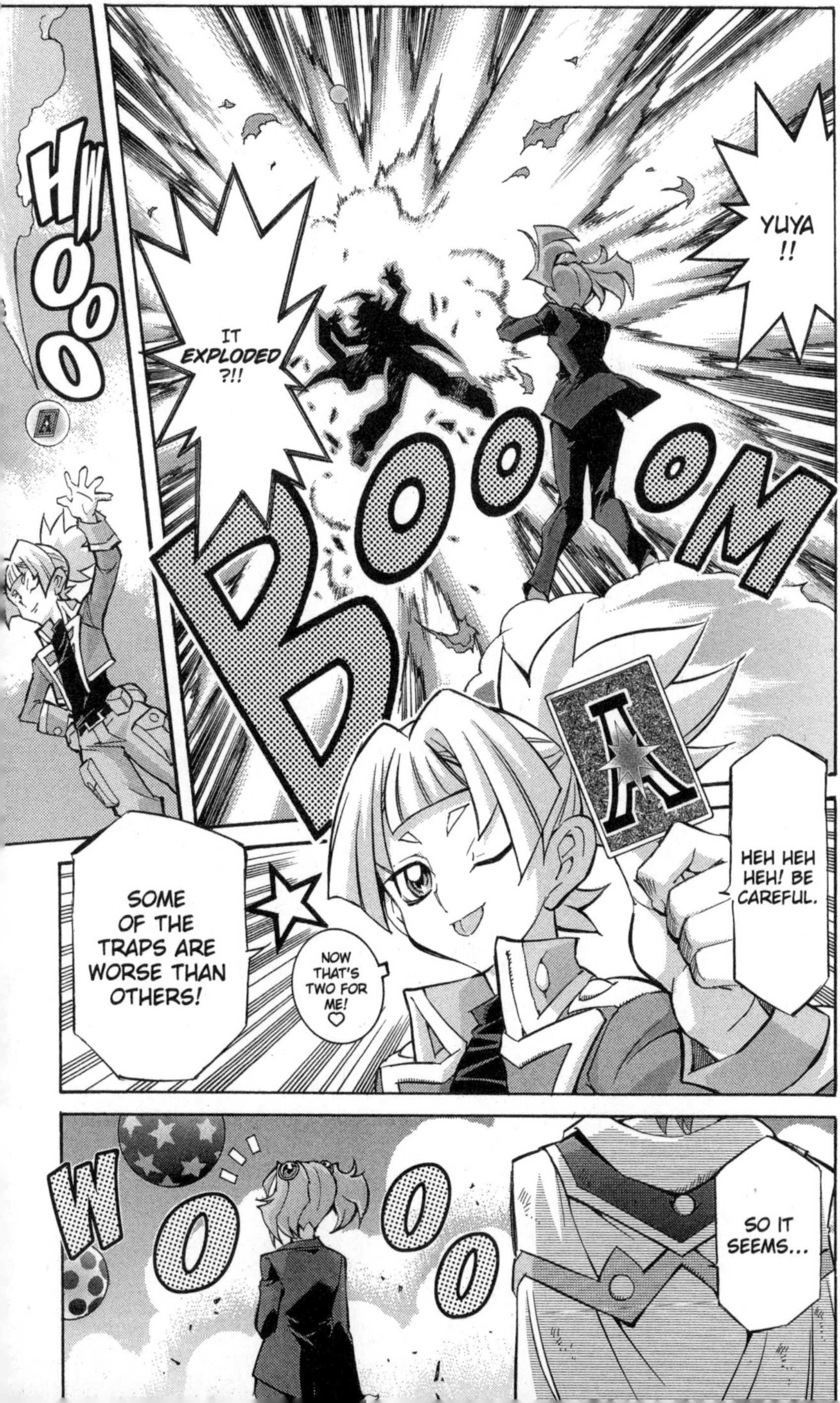
YUYA !!
IT EXPLODED ?!!
BOOOOM
HWOOO
HEH HEH HEH! BE CAREFUL.
NOW THAT'S TWO FOR ME! ♡
SOME OF THE TRAPS ARE WORSE THAN OTHERS!
SO IT SEEMS...
WOOOO

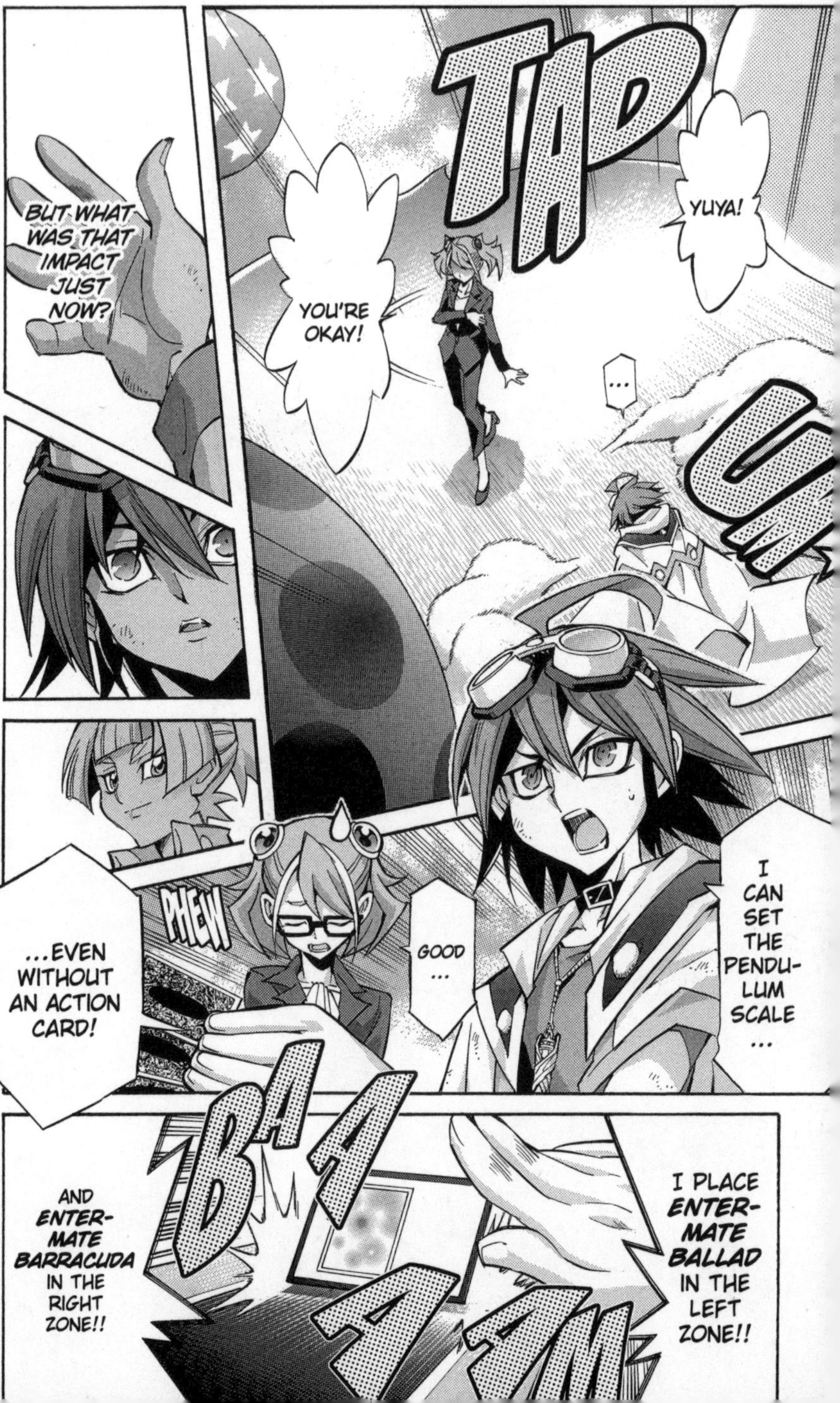
TAP
YUYA!
...
YOU'RE OKAY!
BUT WHAT WAS THAT IMPACT JUST NOW?
I CAN SET THE PENDULUM SCALE...
GOOD...
PHEW
...EVEN WITHOUT AN ACTION CARD!
I PLACE ENTERMATE BALLAD IN THE LEFT ZONE!!
AND ENTERMATE BARRACUDA IN THE RIGHT ZONE!!
BAAAM

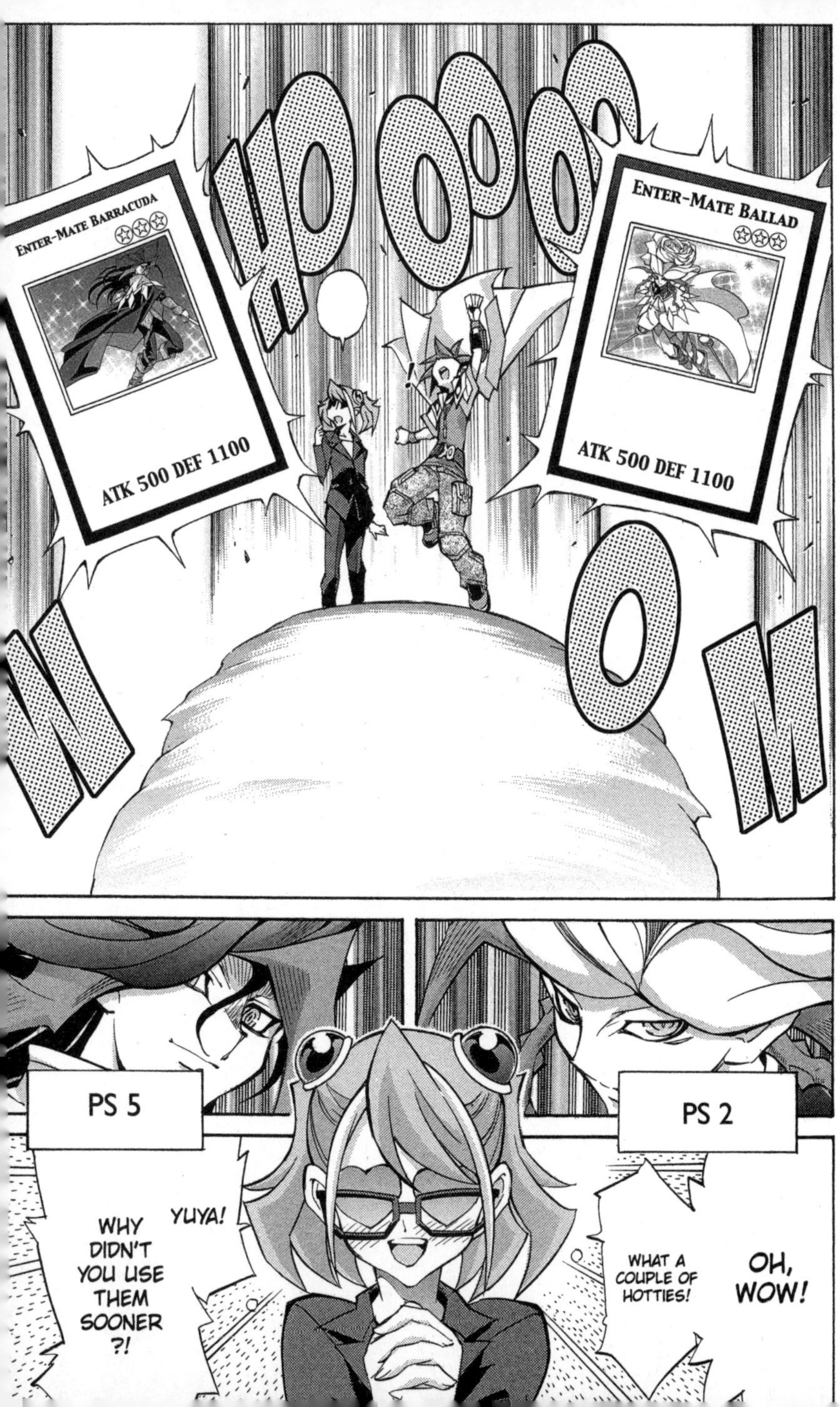
ENTER-MATE BALLAD
ATK 500 DEF 1100
WHOOOOOOOM
ENTER-MATE BARRACUDA
ATK 500 DEF 1100
PS 2
OH, WOW!
WHAT A COUPLE OF HOTTIES!
PS 5
YUYA!
WHY DIDN'T YOU USE THEM SOONER?!

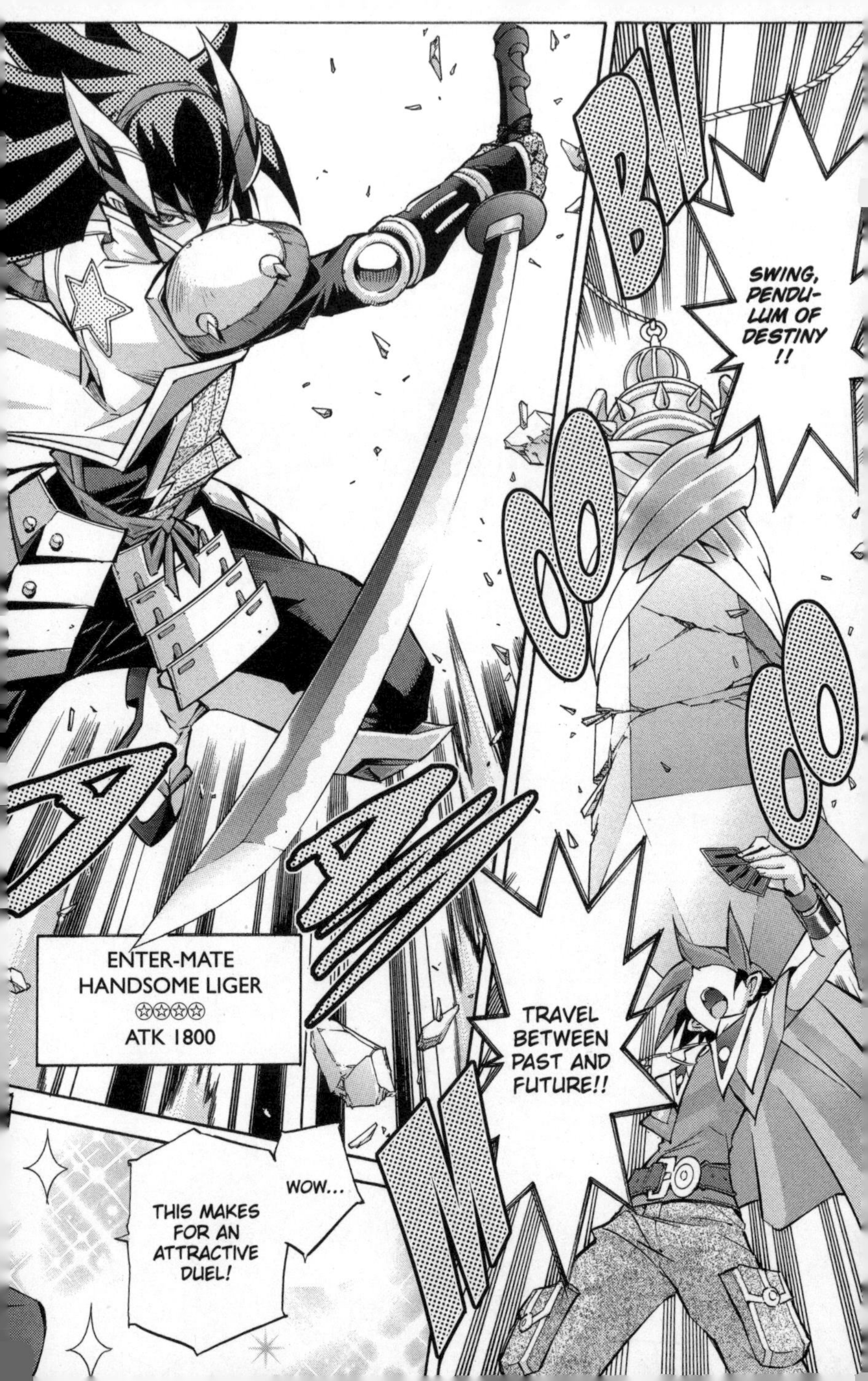
SWING, PENDULUM OF DESTINY!!
TRAVEL BETWEEN PAST AND FUTURE!!
ENTER-MATE HANDSOME LIGER
ATK 1800
WOW...
THIS MAKES FOR AN ATTRACTIVE DUEL!

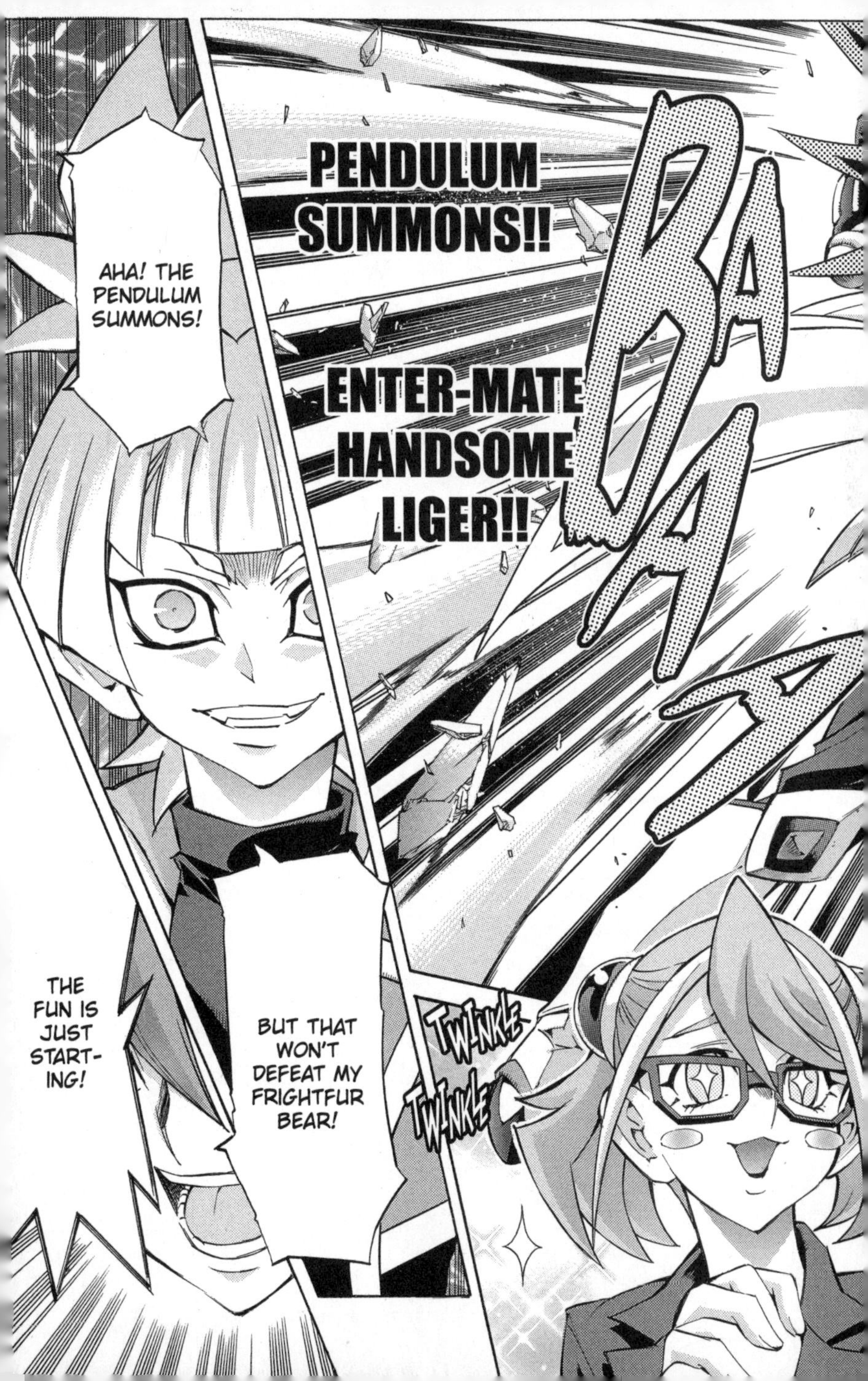
PENDULUM SUMMONS!!
ENTER-MATE HANDSOME LIGER!!
BAAA
AHA! THE PENDULUM SUMMONS!
TWINKLE
TWINKLE
BUT THAT WON'T DEFEAT MY FRIGHTFUR BEAR!
THE FUN IS JUST START-ING!

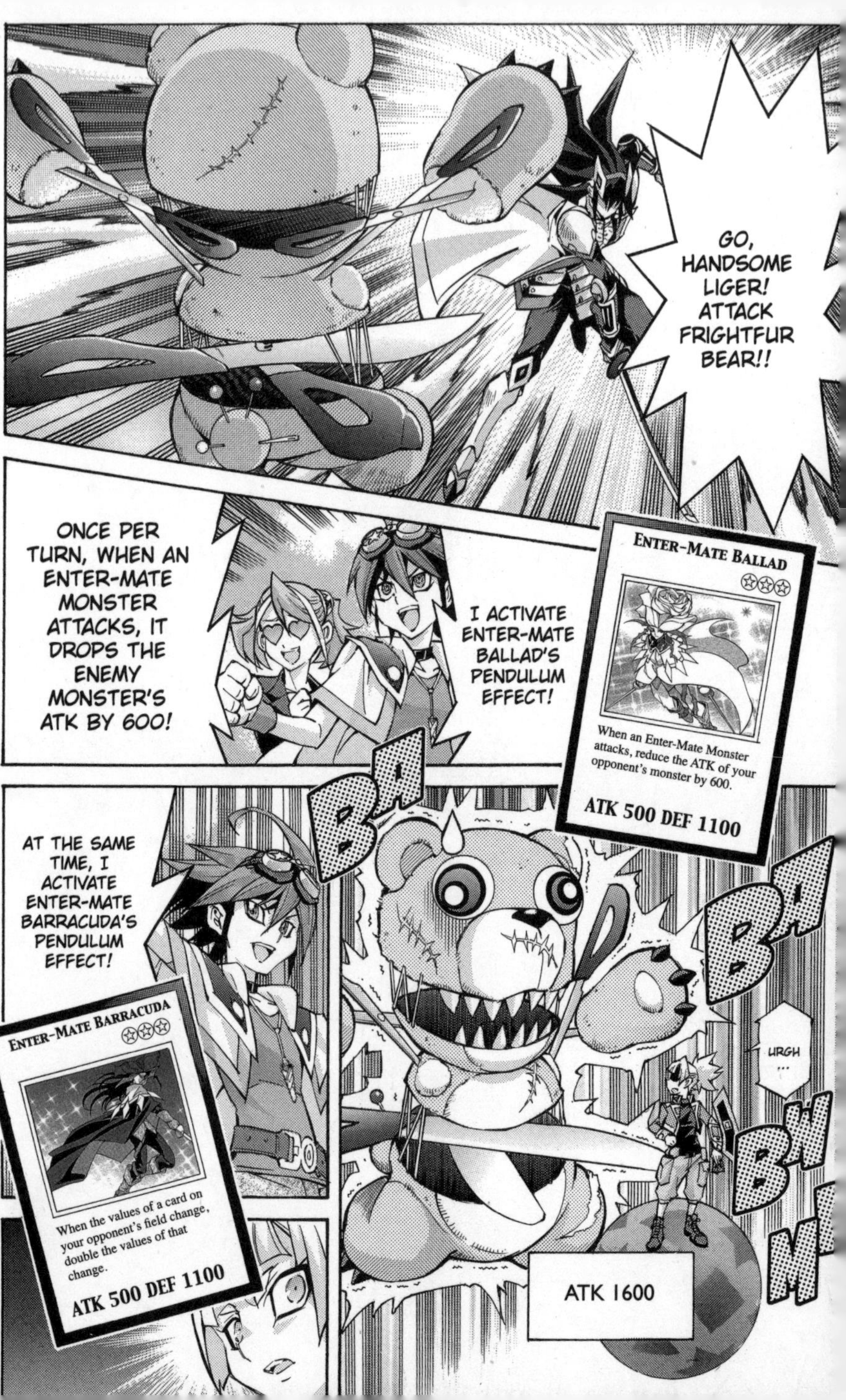
GO, HANDSOME LIGER! ATTACK FRIGHTFUR BEAR!!
ENTER-MATE BALLAD
When an Enter-Mate Monster attacks, reduce the ATK of your opponent's monster by 600.
ATK 500 DEF 1100
I ACTIVATE ENTER-MATE BALLAD'S PENDULUM EFFECT!
ONCE PER TURN, WHEN AN ENTER-MATE MONSTER ATTACKS, IT DROPS THE ENEMY MONSTER'S ATK BY 600!
BA
BA
URGH...
BWM
ATK 1600
AT THE SAME TIME, I ACTIVATE ENTER-MATE BARRACUDA'S PENDULUM EFFECT!
ENTER-MATE BARRACUDA
When the values of a card on your opponent's field change, double the values of that change.
ATK 500 DEF 1100

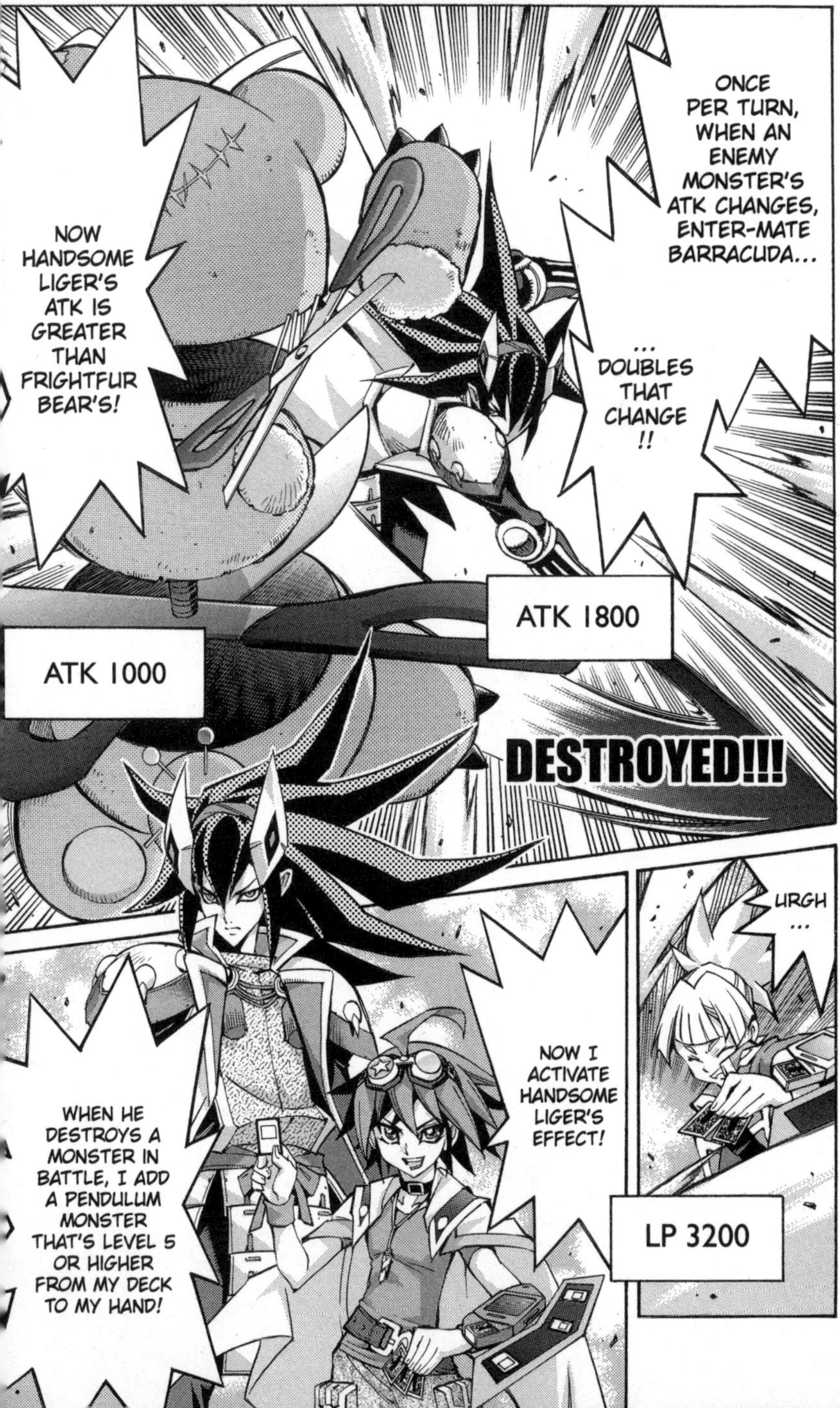
ONCE PER TURN, WHEN AN ENEMY MONSTER'S ATK CHANGES, ENTER-MATE BARRACUDA...
...DOUBLES THAT CHANGE!!
NOW HANDSOME LIGER'S ATK IS GREATER THAN FRIGHTFUR BEAR'S!
ATK 1800
ATK 1000
DESTROYED!!!
URGH...
LP 3200
NOW I ACTIVATE HANDSOME LIGER'S EFFECT!
WHEN HE DESTROYS A MONSTER IN BATTLE, I ADD A PENDULUM MONSTER THAT'S LEVEL 5 OR HIGHER FROM MY DECK TO MY HAND!

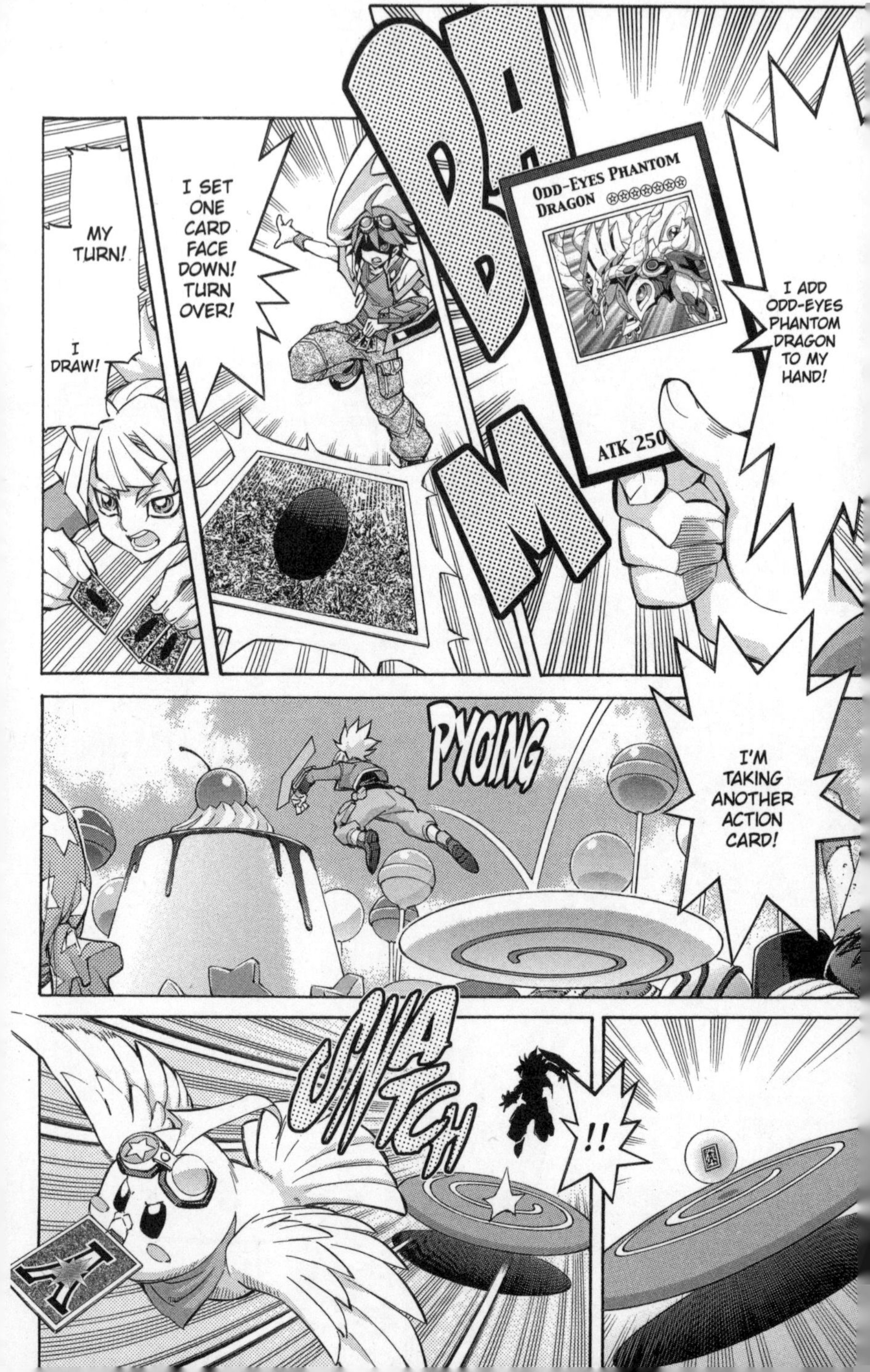
BAM
ODD-EYES PHANTOM DRAGON
ATK 250
I ADD ODD-EYES PHANTOM DRAGON TO MY HAND!
I SET ONE CARD FACE DOWN! TURN OVER!
MY TURN!
I DRAW!
I'M TAKING ANOTHER ACTION CARD!
PYOING
!!
SNATCH

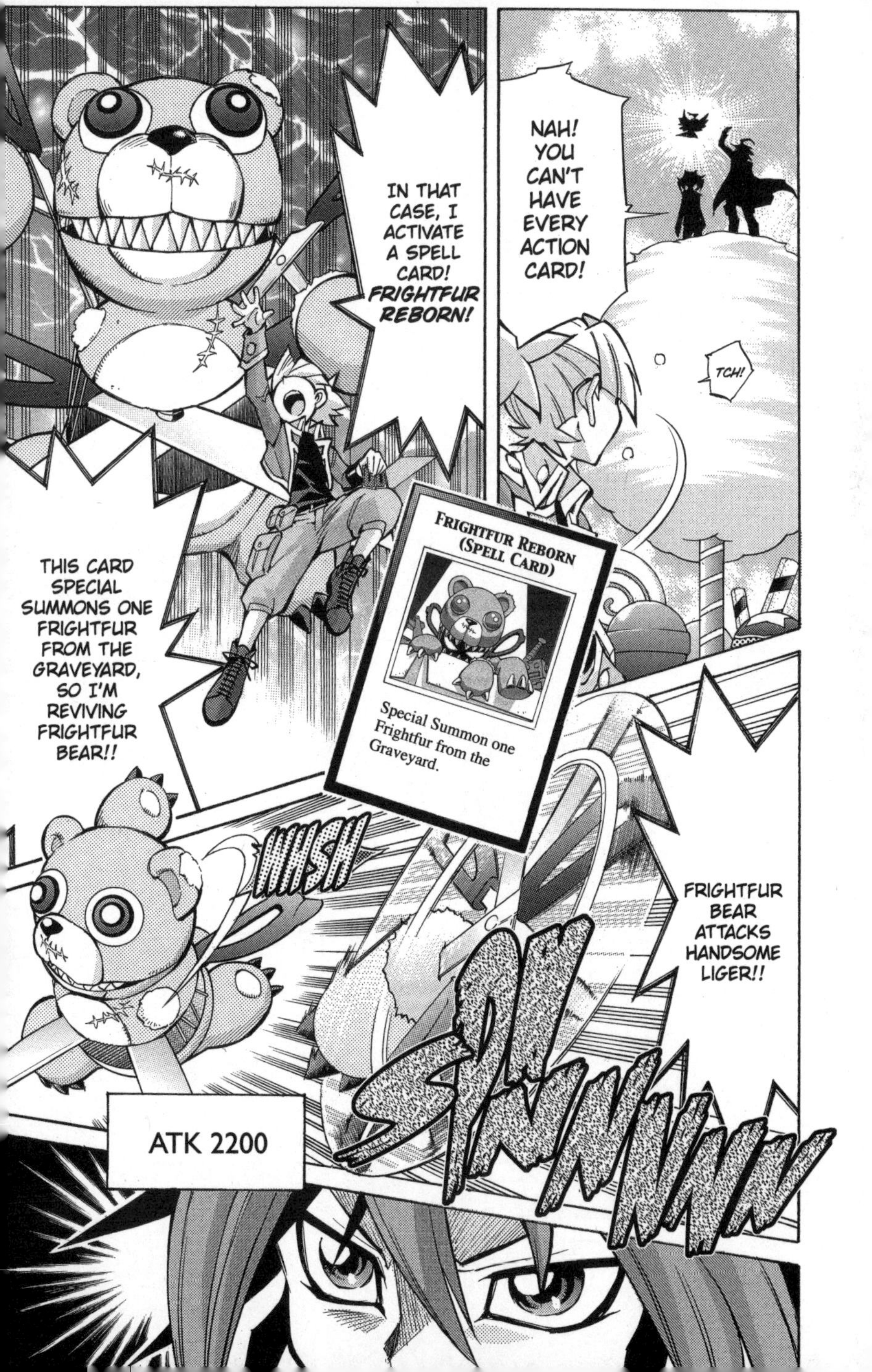
NAH! YOU CAN'T HAVE EVERY ACTION CARD!
TCH!
IN THAT CASE, I ACTIVATE A SPELL CARD! FRIGHTFUR REBORN!
FRIGHTFUR REBORN (SPELL CARD)
Special Summon one Frightfur from the Graveyard.
THIS CARD SPECIAL SUMMONS ONE FRIGHTFUR FROM THE GRAVEYARD, SO I'M REVIVING FRIGHTFUR BEAR!!
FRIGHTFUR BEAR ATTACKS HANDSOME LIGER!!
WHSH
ATK 2200

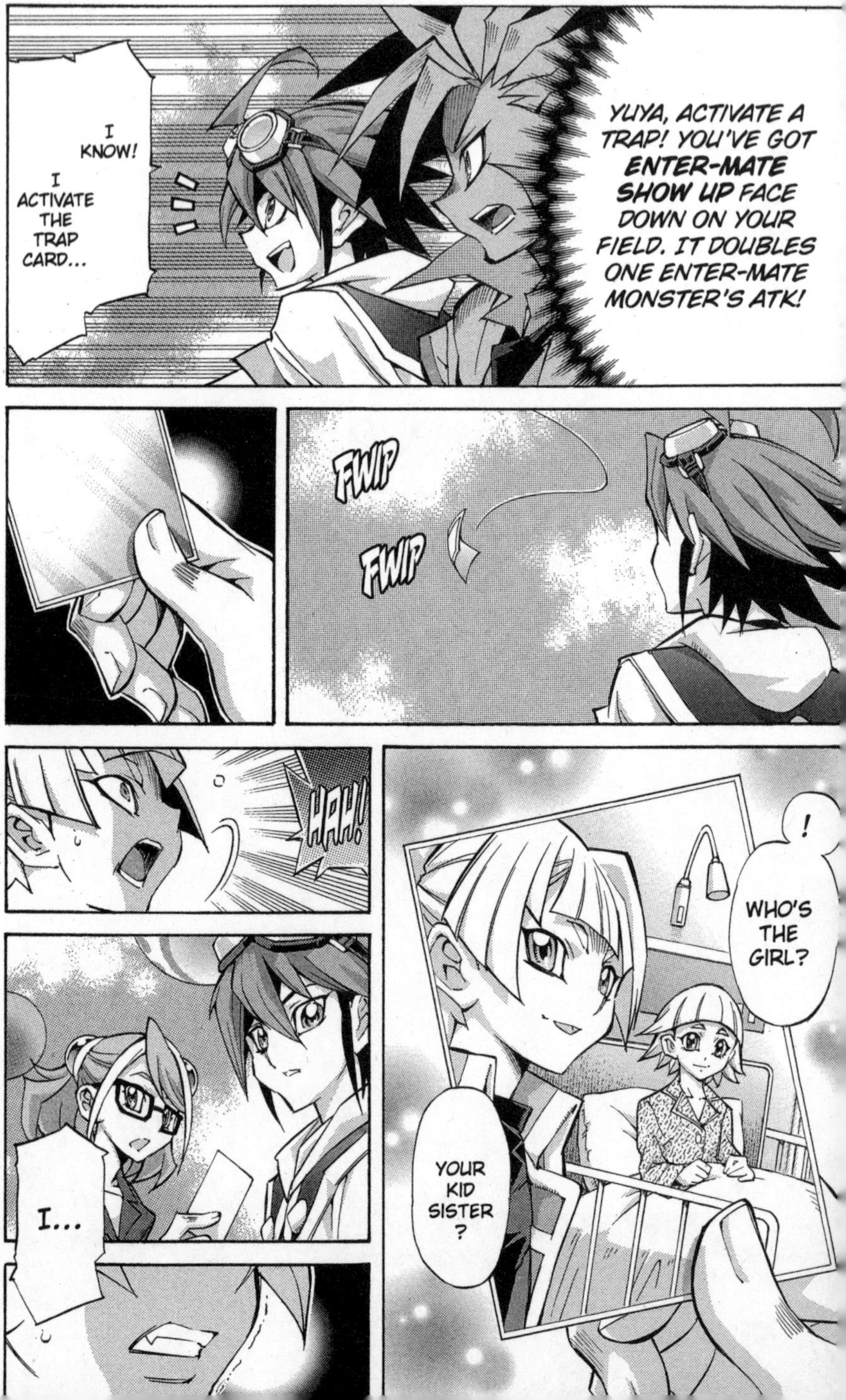
YUYA, ACTIVATE A TRAP! YOU'VE GOT **ENTER-MATE SHOW UP** FACE DOWN ON YOUR FIELD. IT DOUBLES ONE ENTER-MATE MONSTER'S ATK!
I KNOW!
I ACTIVATE THE TRAP CARD...
FWIP
FWIP
!
WHO'S THE GIRL?
YOUR KID SISTER?
HAH!
I...

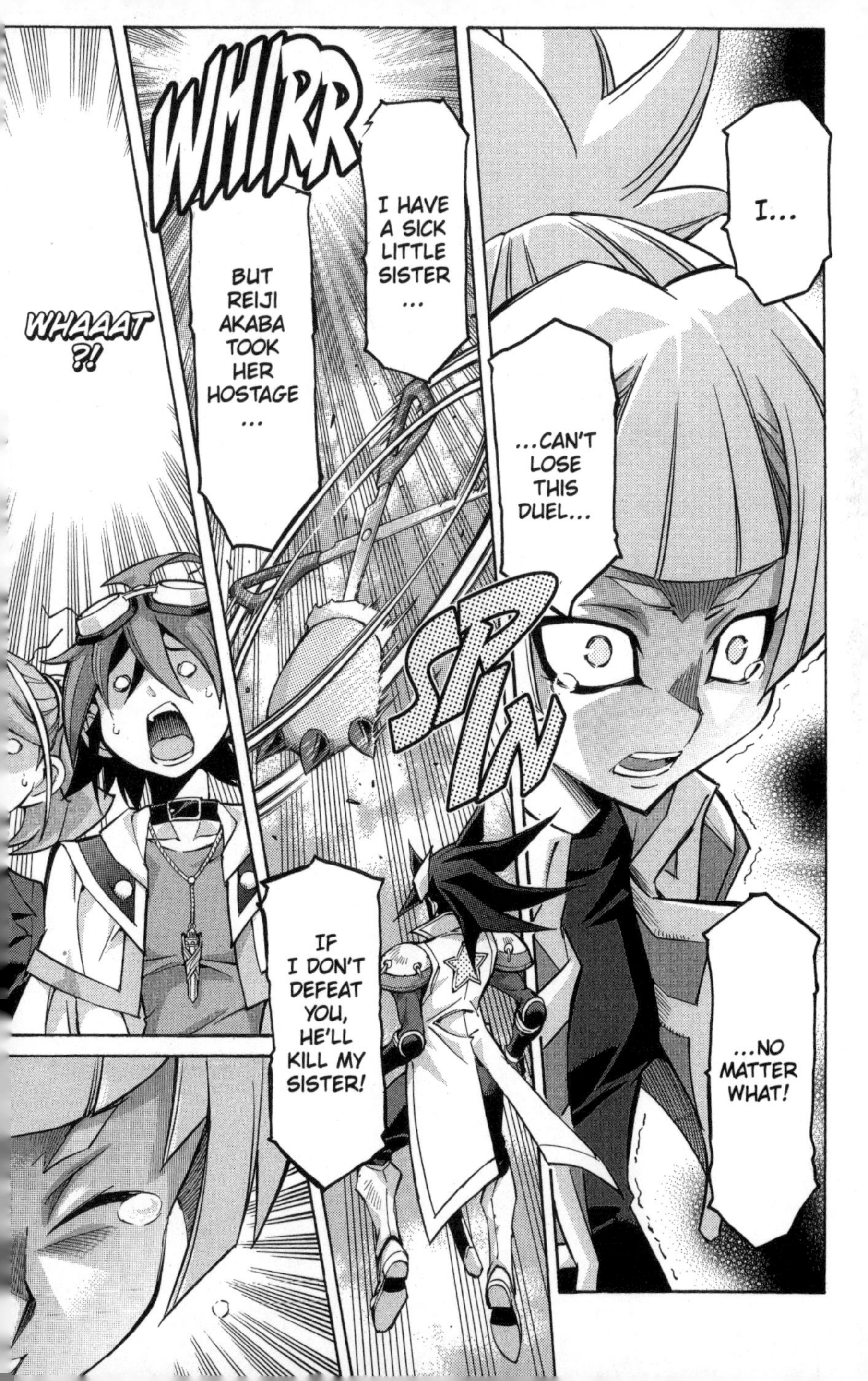
I...
...CAN'T LOSE THIS DUEL...
SPIN
...NO MATTER WHAT!
WHIRR
I HAVE A SICK LITTLE SISTER ...
BUT REIJI AKABA TOOK HER HOSTAGE ...
IF I DON'T DEFEAT YOU, HE'LL KILL MY SISTER!
WHAAAT ?!

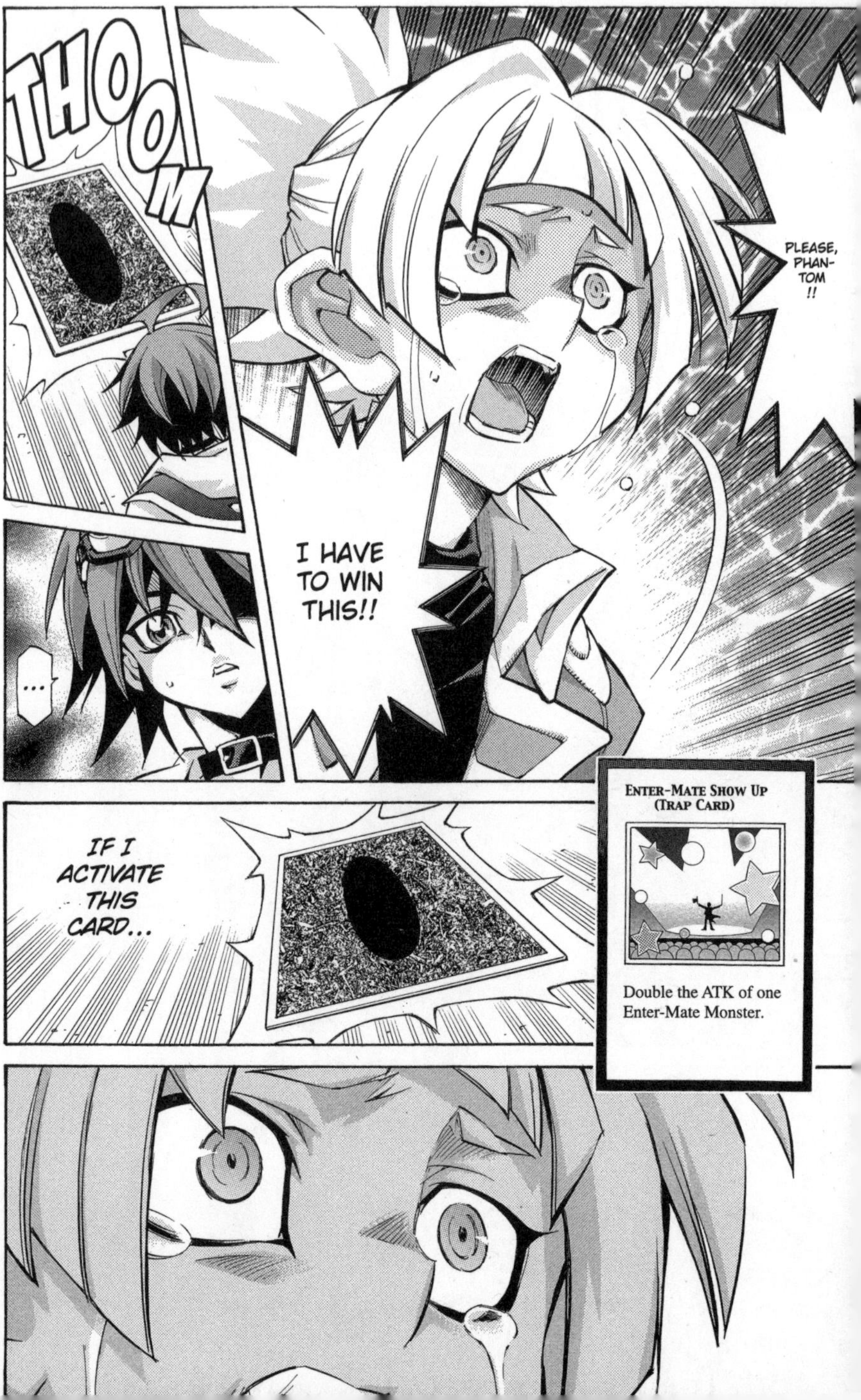
PLEASE, PHAN-TOM !!
I HAVE TO WIN THIS!!
THOOM
...
ENTER-MATE SHOW UP (TRAP CARD)
Double the ATK of one Enter-Mate Monster.
IF I ACTIVATE THIS CARD...

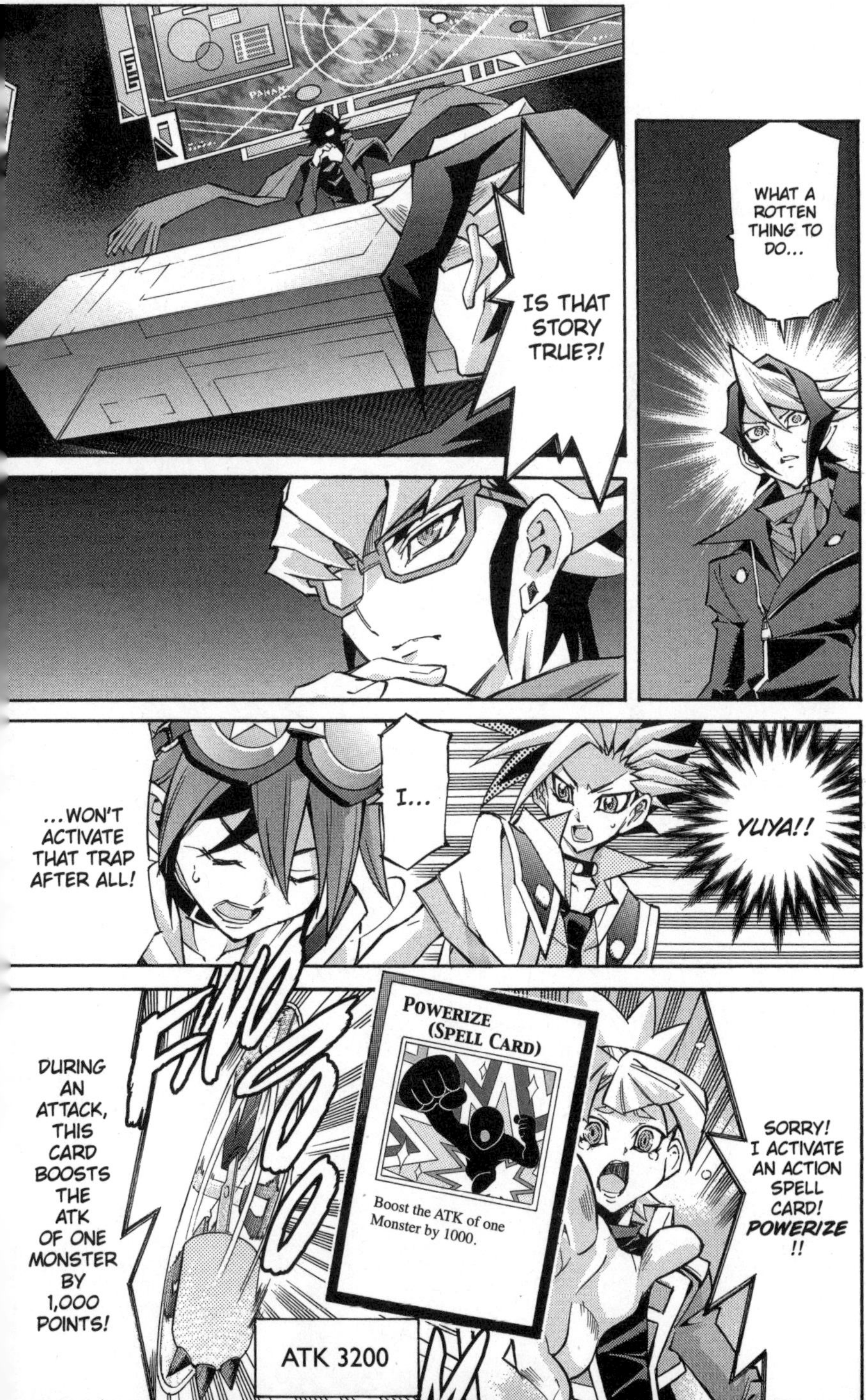
WHAT A ROTTEN THING TO DO...
IS THAT STORY TRUE?!
YUYA!!
I...
...WON'T ACTIVATE THAT TRAP AFTER ALL!
SORRY! I ACTIVATE AN ACTION SPELL CARD! POWERIZE!!
POWERIZE (SPELL CARD)
Boost the ATK of one Monster by 1000.
DURING AN ATTACK, THIS CARD BOOSTS THE ATK OF ONE MONSTER BY 1,000 POINTS!
ATK 3200

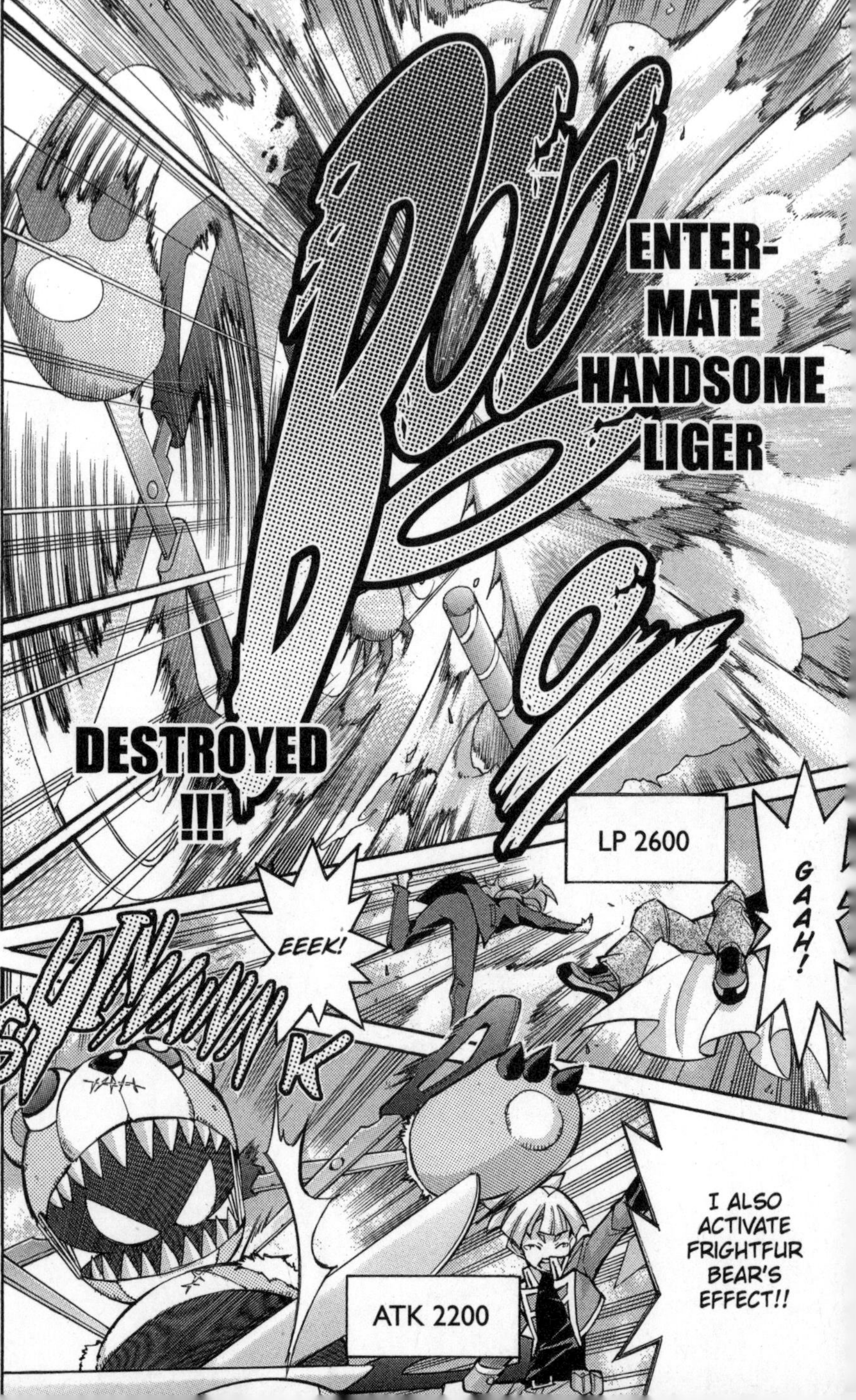
ENTER-MATE HANDSOME LIGER
DESTROYED !!!
GAAH!
LP 2600
EEEK!
I ALSO ACTIVATE FRIGHTFUR BEAR'S EFFECT!!
ATK 2200

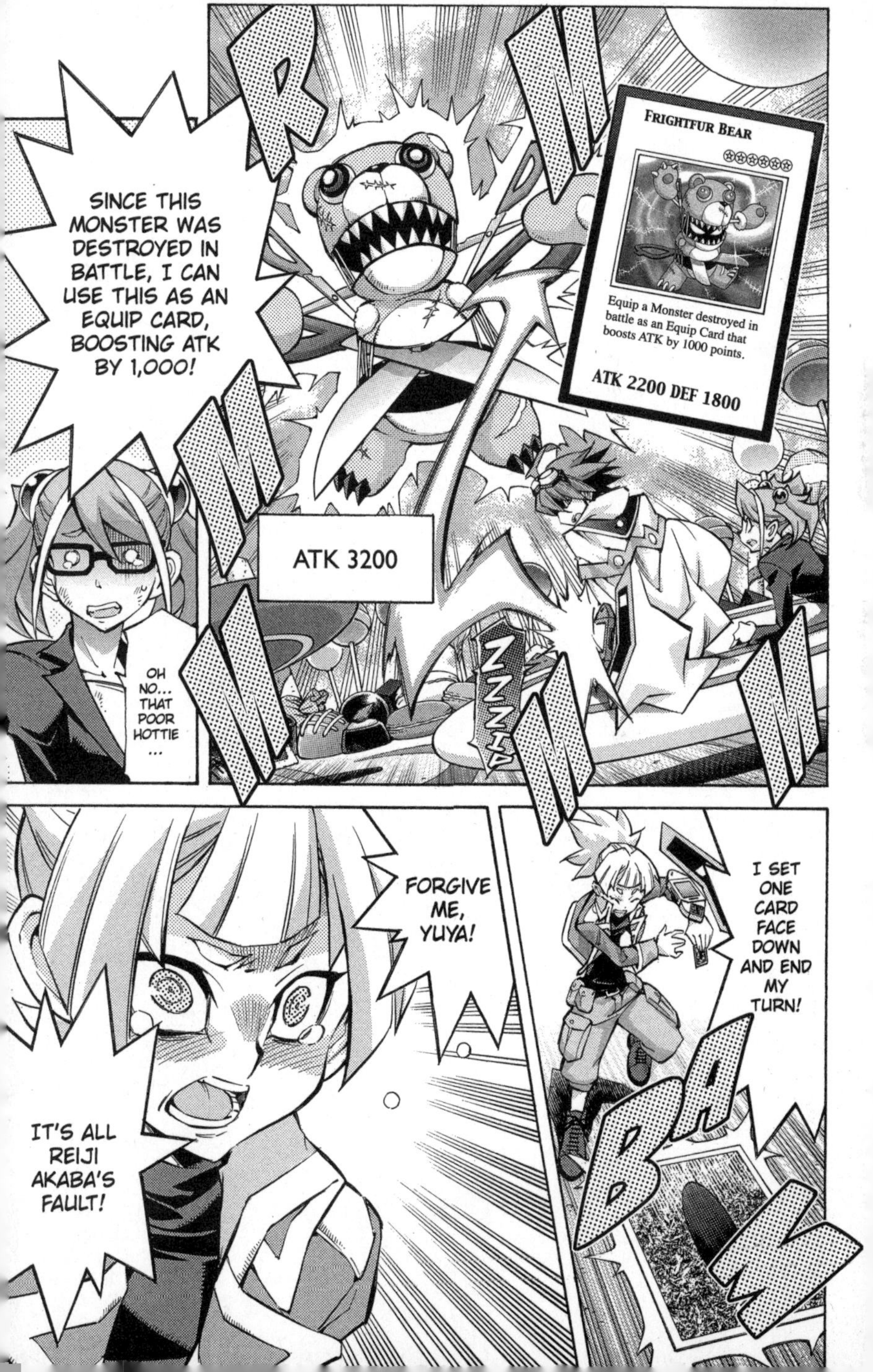
FRIGHTFUR BEAR
Equip a Monster destroyed in battle as an Equip Card that boosts ATK by 1000 points.
ATK 2200 DEF 1800
SINCE THIS MONSTER WAS DESTROYED IN BATTLE, I CAN USE THIS AS AN EQUIP CARD, BOOSTING ATK BY 1,000!
ATK 3200
ZZZIP
OH NO... THAT POOR HOTTIE ...
I SET ONE CARD FACE DOWN AND END MY TURN!
BAM
FORGIVE ME, YUYA!
IT'S ALL REIJI AKABA'S FAULT!

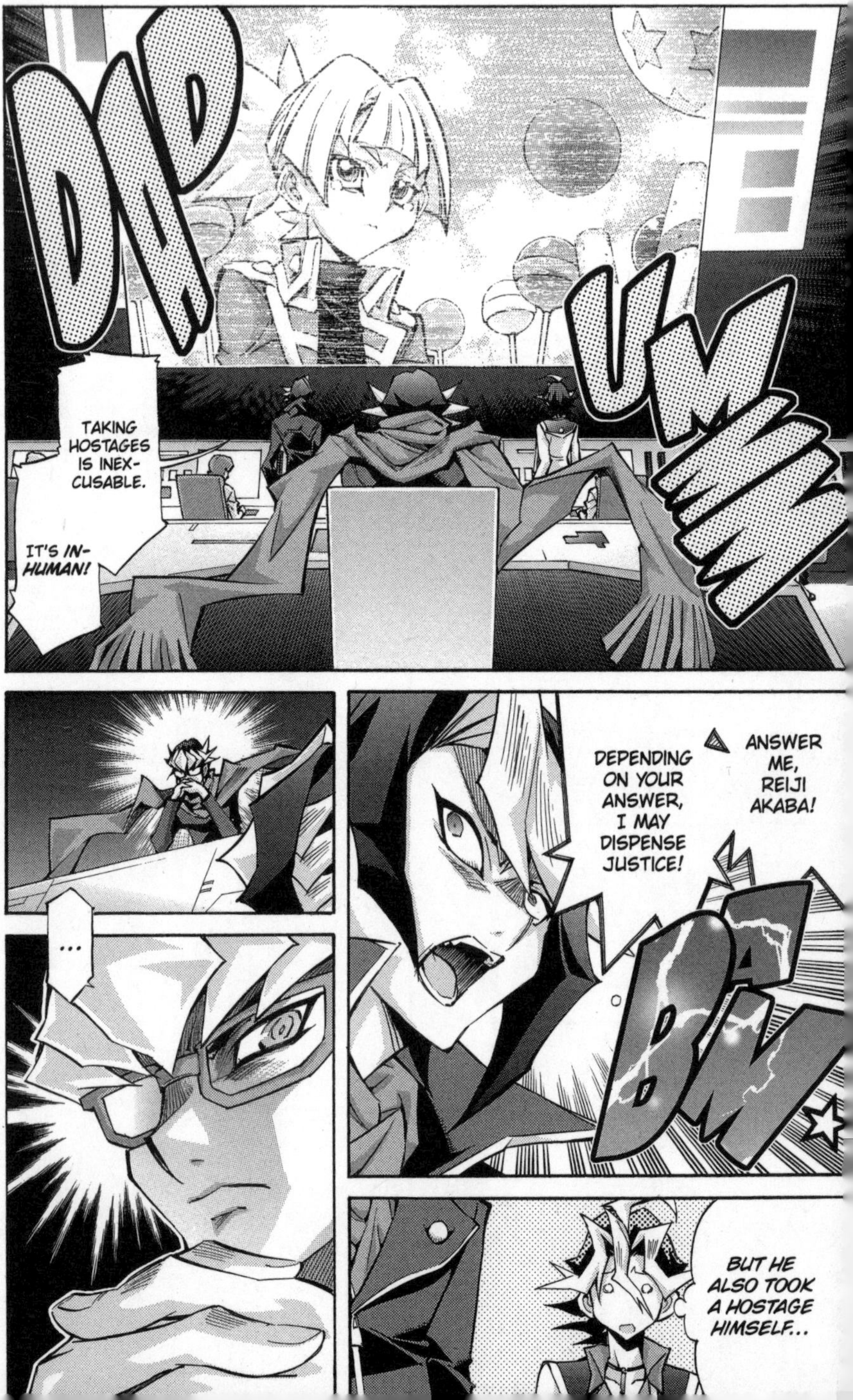
UMMM
DAP
TAKING HOSTAGES IS INEXCUSABLE.
IT'S IN-HUMAN!
ANSWER ME, REIJI AKABA!
DEPENDING ON YOUR ANSWER, I MAY DISPENSE JUSTICE!
BAM
...
BUT HE ALSO TOOK A HOSTAGE HIMSELF...

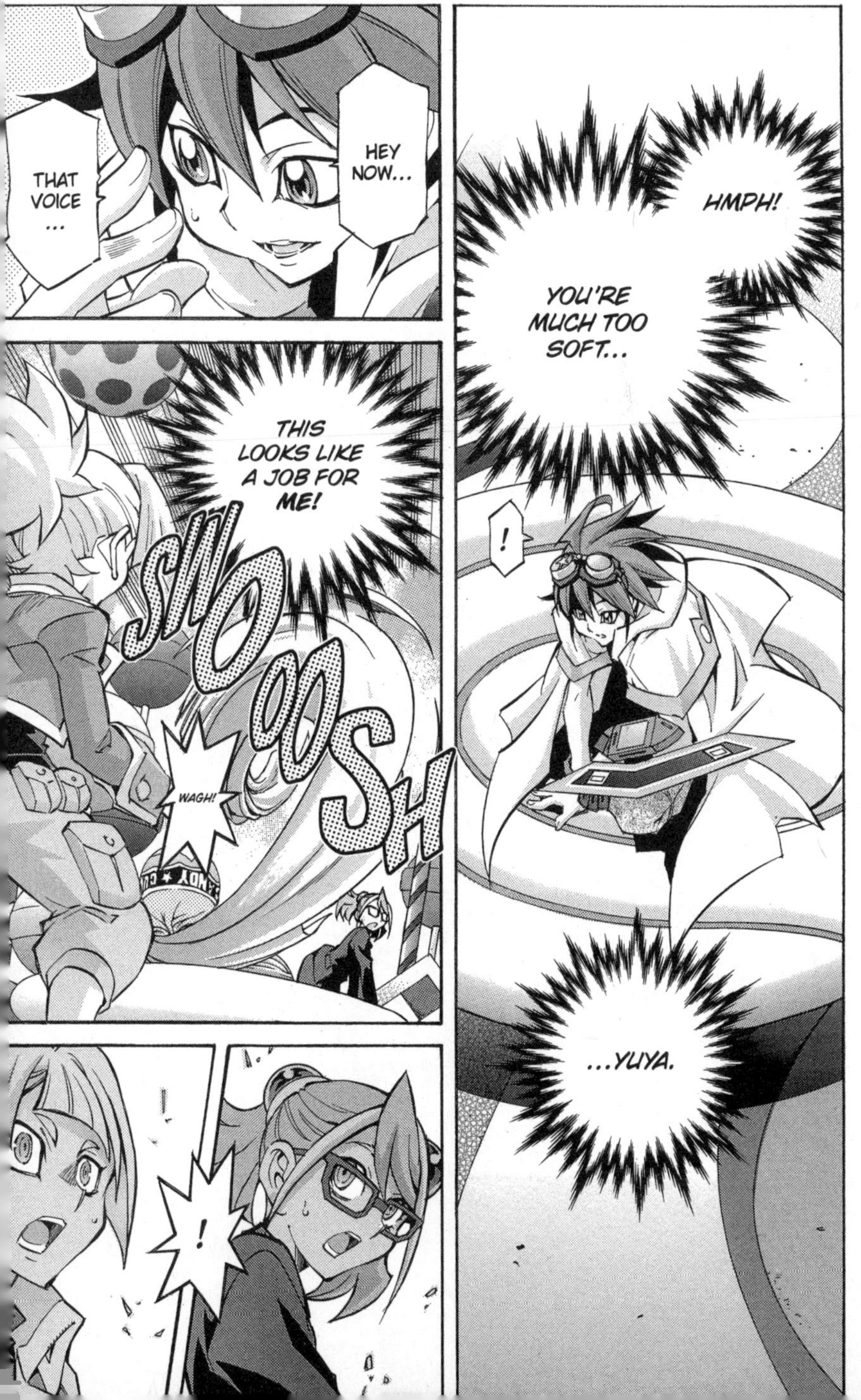
HMPH!
YOU'RE MUCH TOO SOFT...
!
...YUYA.
HEY NOW...
THAT VOICE ...
THIS LOOKS LIKE A JOB FOR ME!
SHOOOSH
WAGH!
!
!

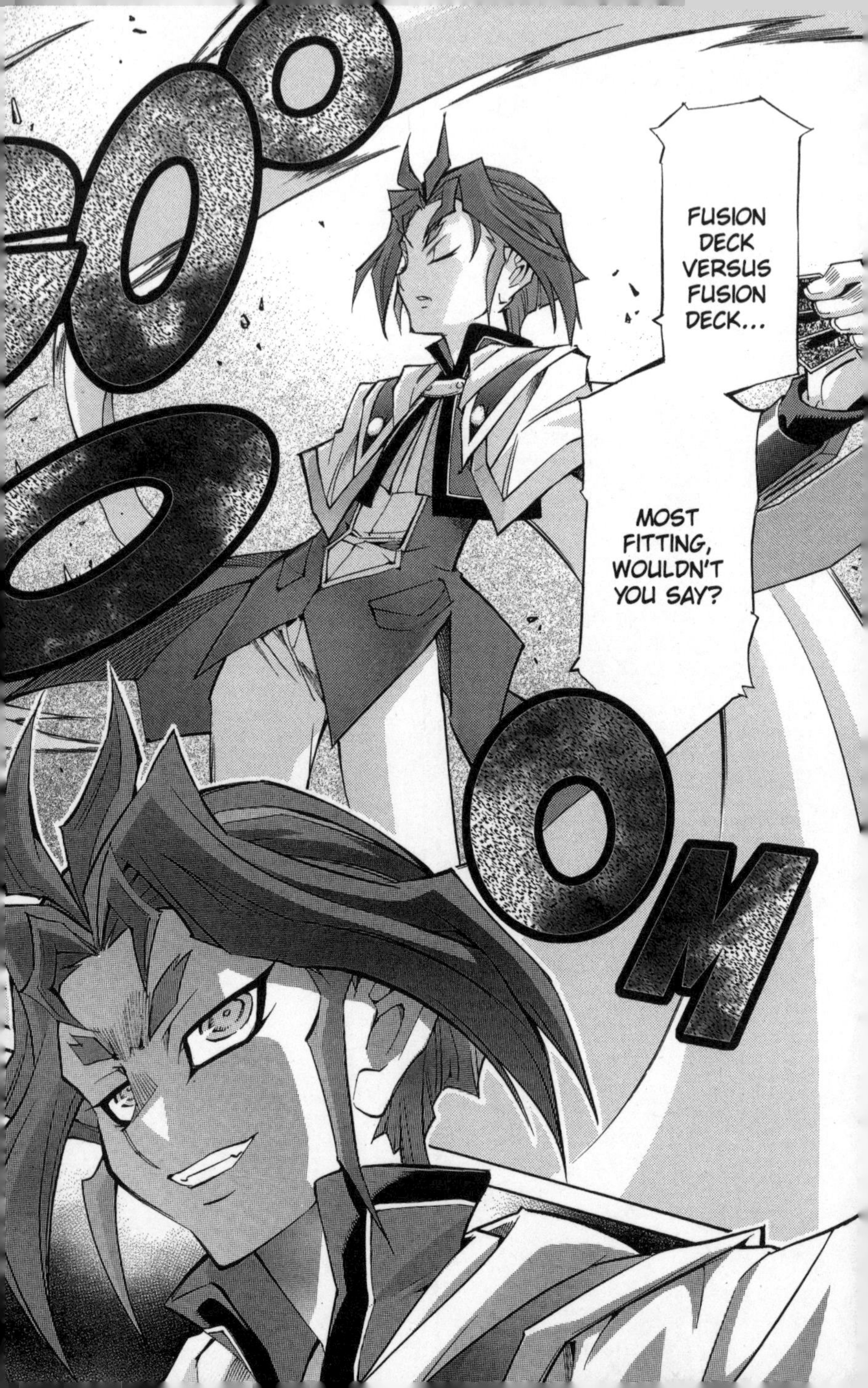
FUSION DECK VERSUS FUSION DECK...
MOST FITTING, WOULDN'T YOU SAY?
OOOOOM

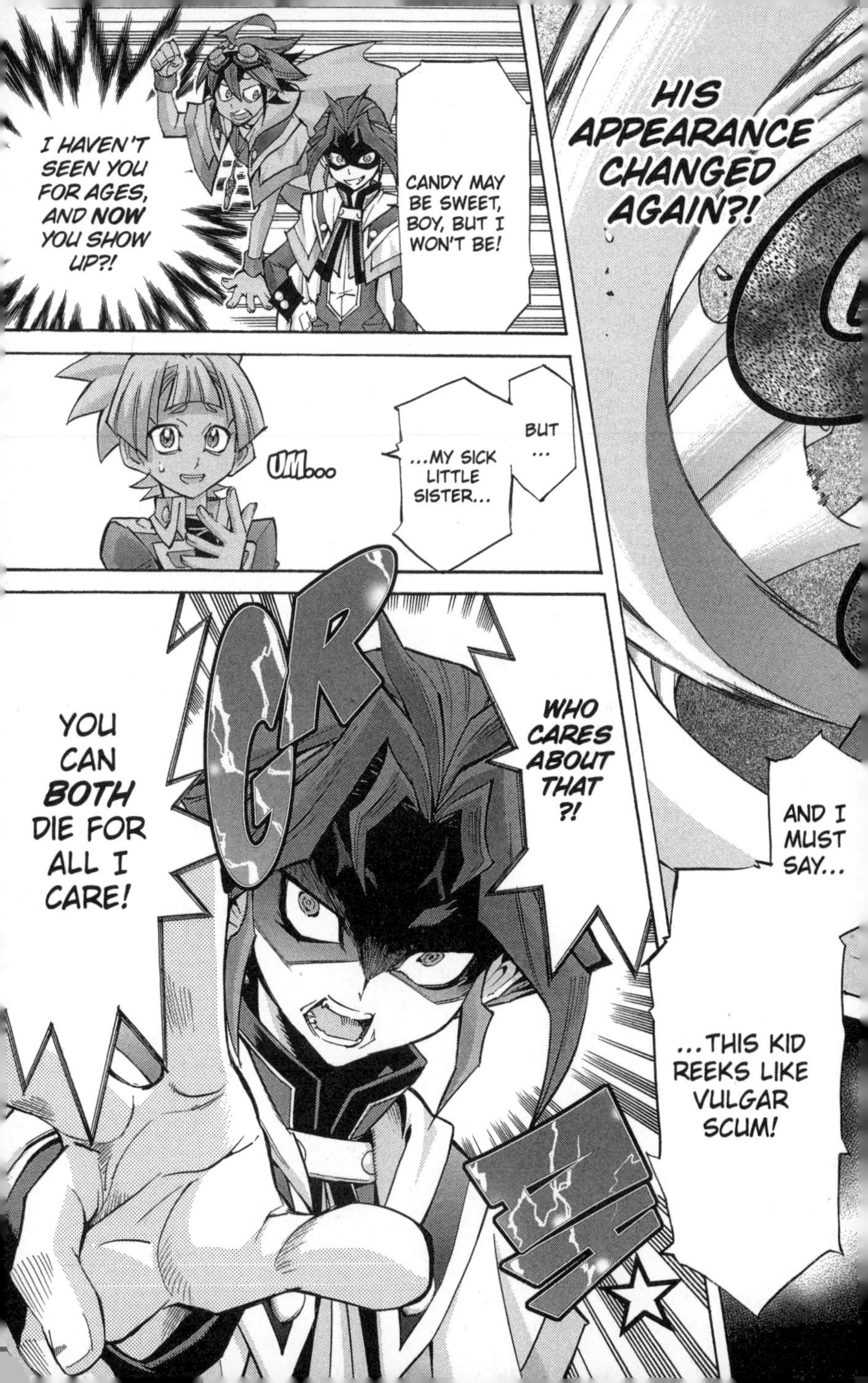
HIS APPEARANCE CHANGED AGAIN?!
AND I MUST SAY...
...THIS KID REEKS LIKE VULGAR SCUM!
CANDY MAY BE SWEET, BOY, BUT I WON'T BE!
I HAVEN'T SEEN YOU FOR AGES, AND NOW YOU SHOW UP?!
BUT ...
...MY SICK LITTLE SISTER...
UM...
WHO CARES ABOUT THAT?!
YOU CAN BOTH DIE FOR ALL I CARE!

ARC-V CHARACTER SKETCHES

SORA SHIUNIN

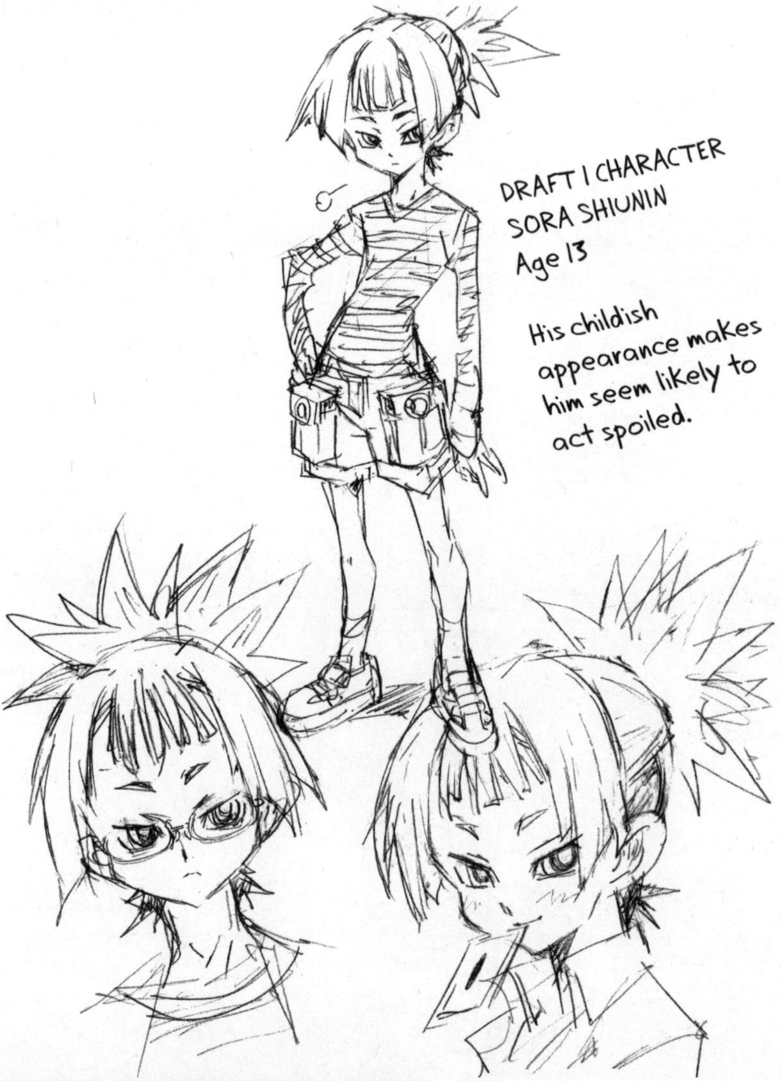
DRAFT 1 CHARACTER
SORA SHIUNIN
Age 13
His childish appearance makes him seem likely to act spoiled.

Sora's hairstyle and atmosphere haven't changed much since his early designs. About the only difference is that his clothes are more casual now. That drawing of him with glasses is rare!

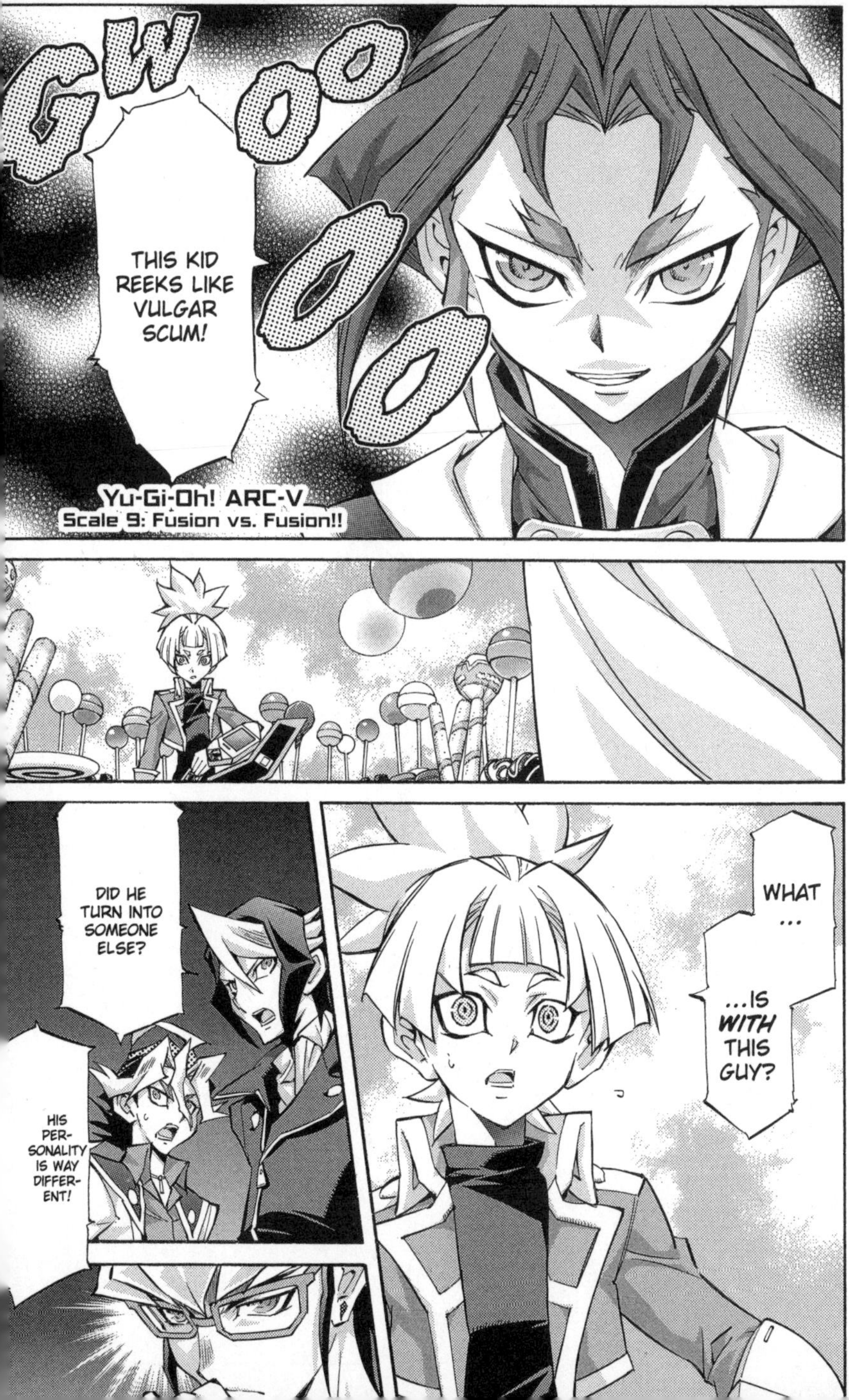
GWOOOOO
THIS KID REEKS LIKE VULGAR SCUM!
Yu-Gi-Oh! ARC-V
Scale 9: Fusion vs. Fusion!!
WHAT ...
...IS *WITH* THIS GUY?
DID HE TURN INTO SOMEONE ELSE?
HIS PER-SONALITY IS WAY DIFFER-ENT!

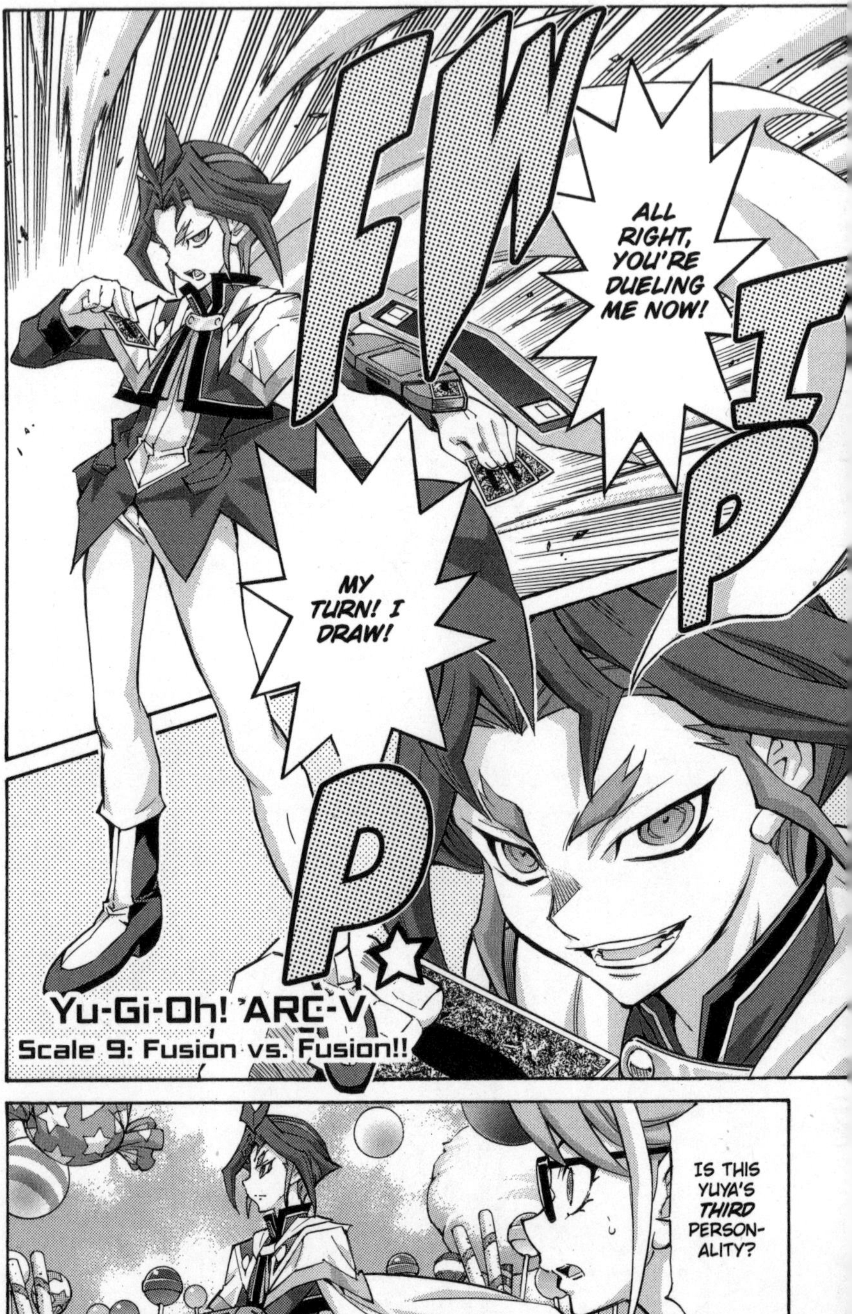

ALL RIGHT, YOU'RE DUELING ME NOW!
FWIP
MY TURN! I DRAW!
P
Yu-Gi-Oh! ARC-V
Scale 9: Fusion vs. Fusion!!
IS THIS YUYA'S *THIRD* PERSON-ALITY?

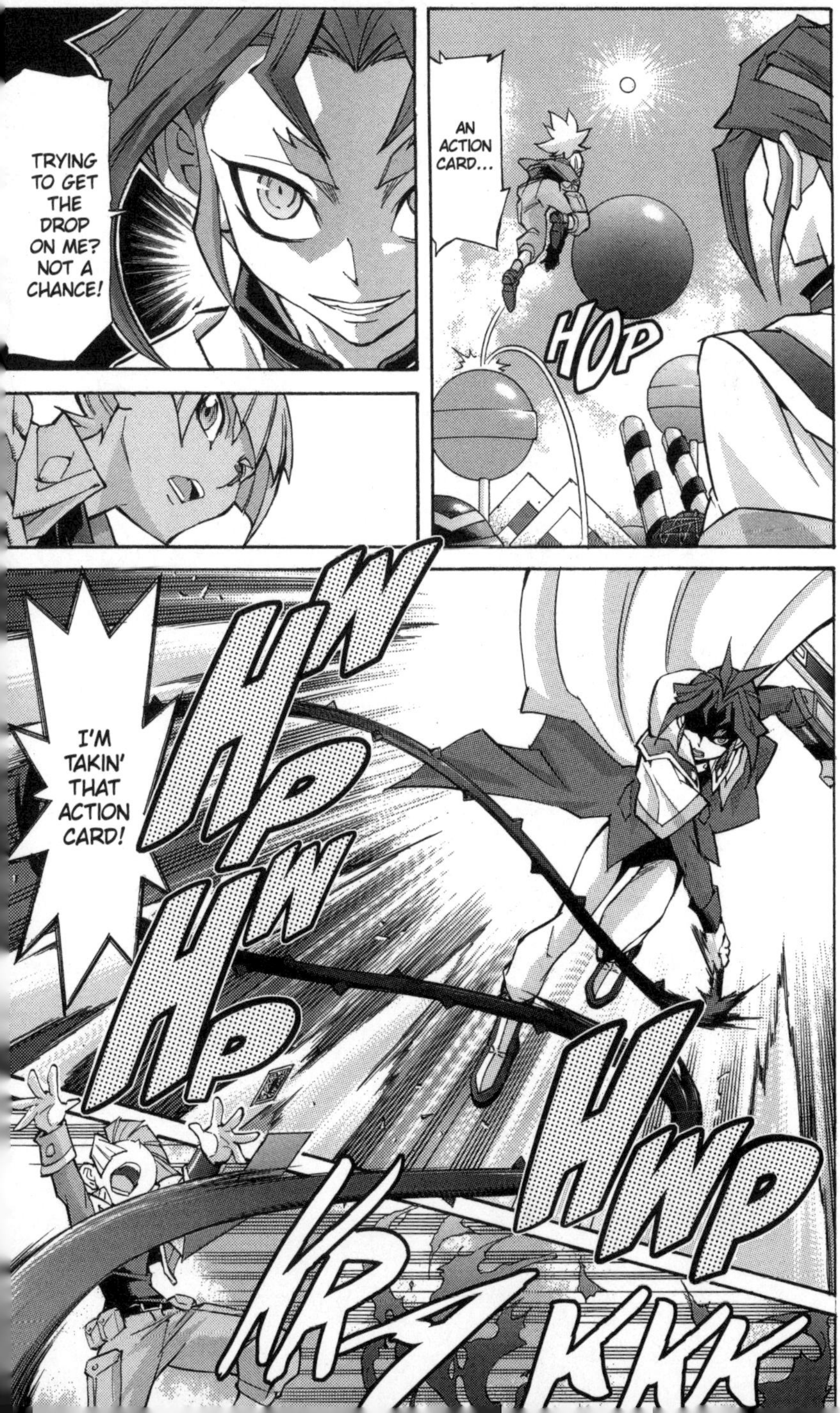
AN ACTION CARD...
HOP
TRYING TO GET THE DROP ON ME? NOT A CHANCE!
I'M TAKIN' THAT ACTION CARD!

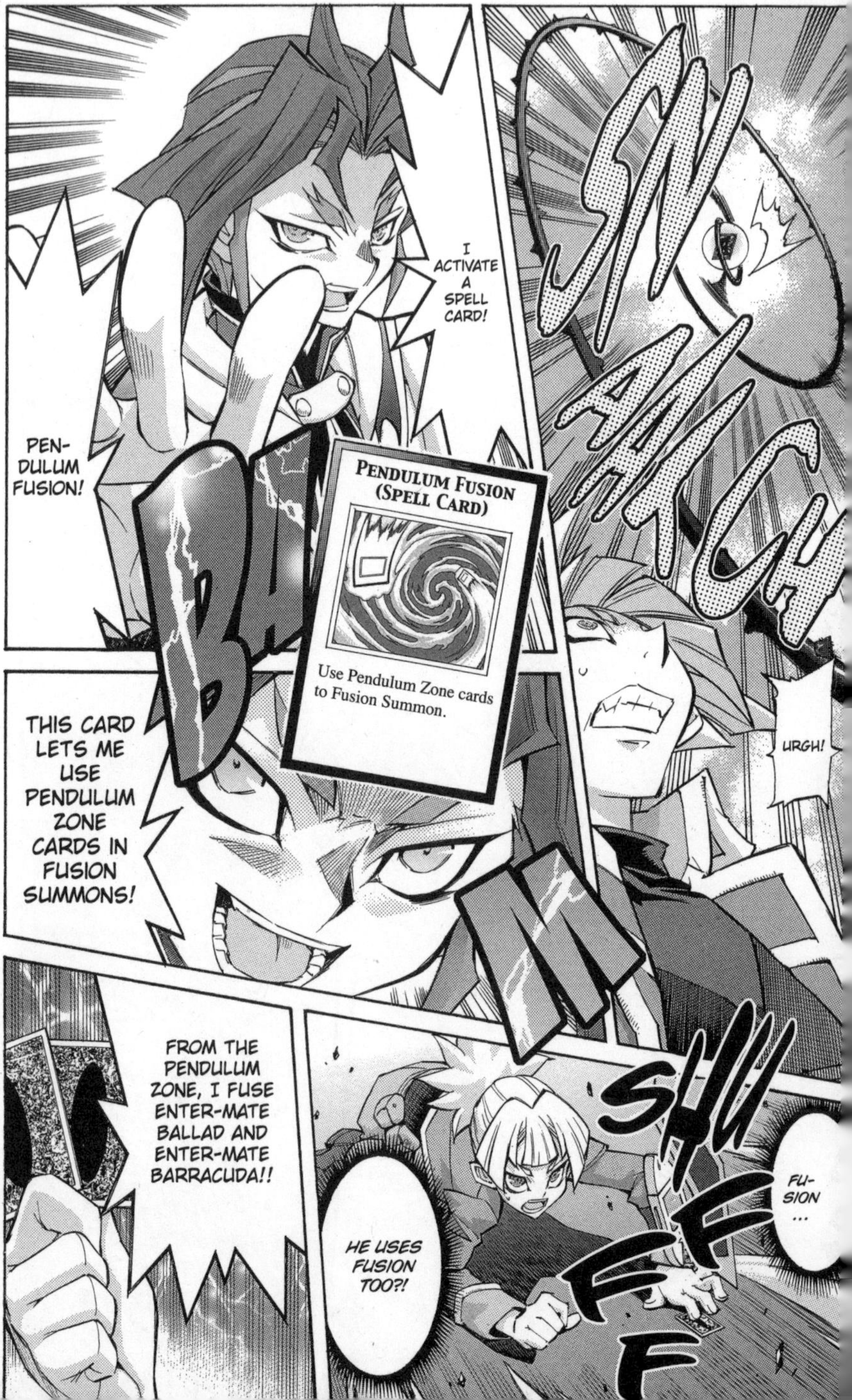
SNAAACH
URGH!
I ACTIVATE A SPELL CARD!
PEN-DULUM FUSION!
BAM
PENDULUM FUSION (SPELL CARD)
Use Pendulum Zone cards to Fusion Summon.
THIS CARD LETS ME USE PENDULUM ZONE CARDS IN FUSION SUMMONS!
SHUFFF
FU-SION...
HE USES FUSION TOO?!
FROM THE PENDULUM ZONE, I FUSE ENTER-MATE BALLAD AND ENTER-MATE BARRACUDA!!

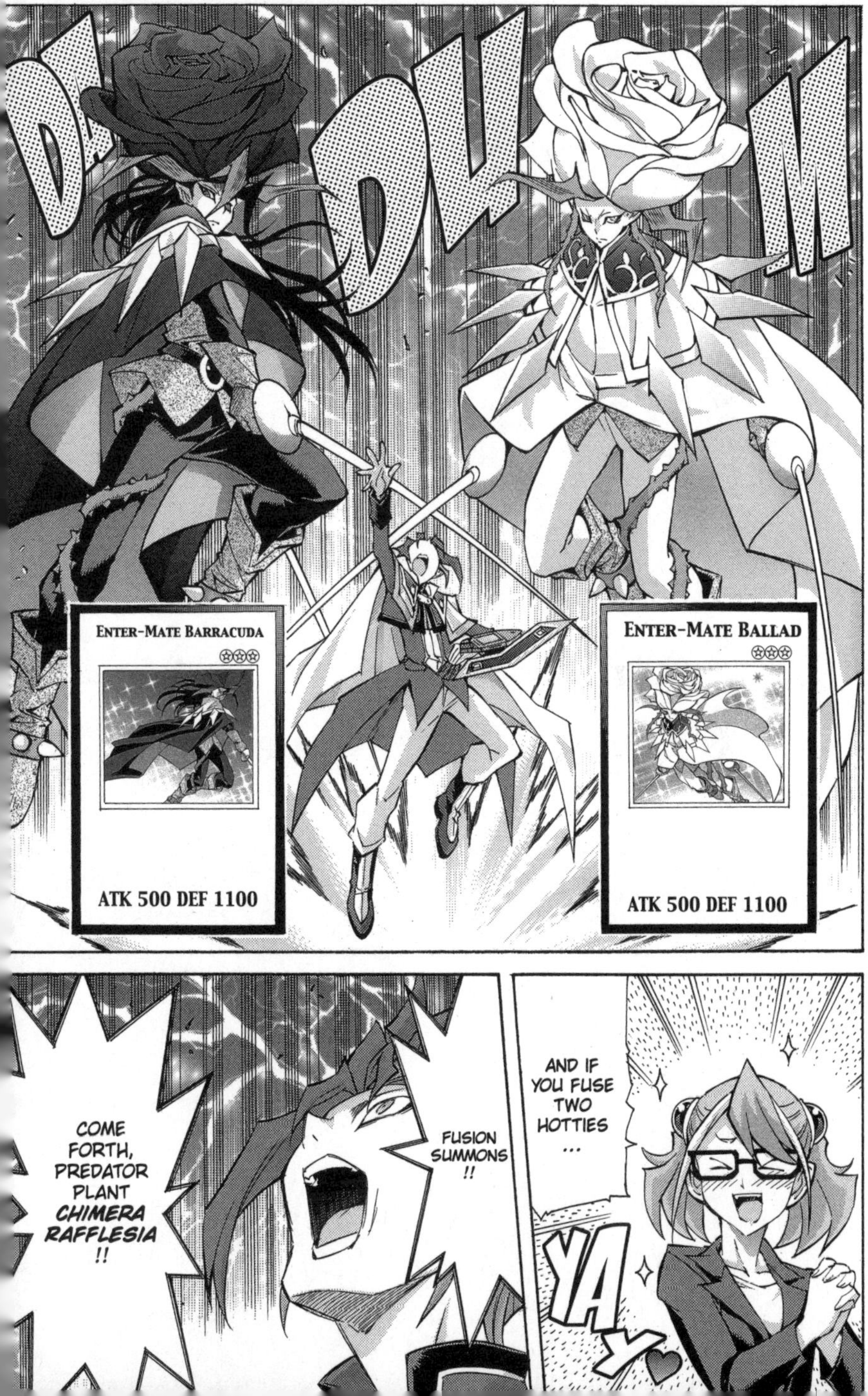
DADUM
ENTER-MATE BALLAD
ATK 500 DEF 1100
ENTER-MATE BARRACUDA
ATK 500 DEF 1100
AND IF YOU FUSE TWO HOTTIES ...
YAY
FUSION SUMMONS !!
COME FORTH, PREDATOR PLANT CHIMERA RAFFLESIA !!

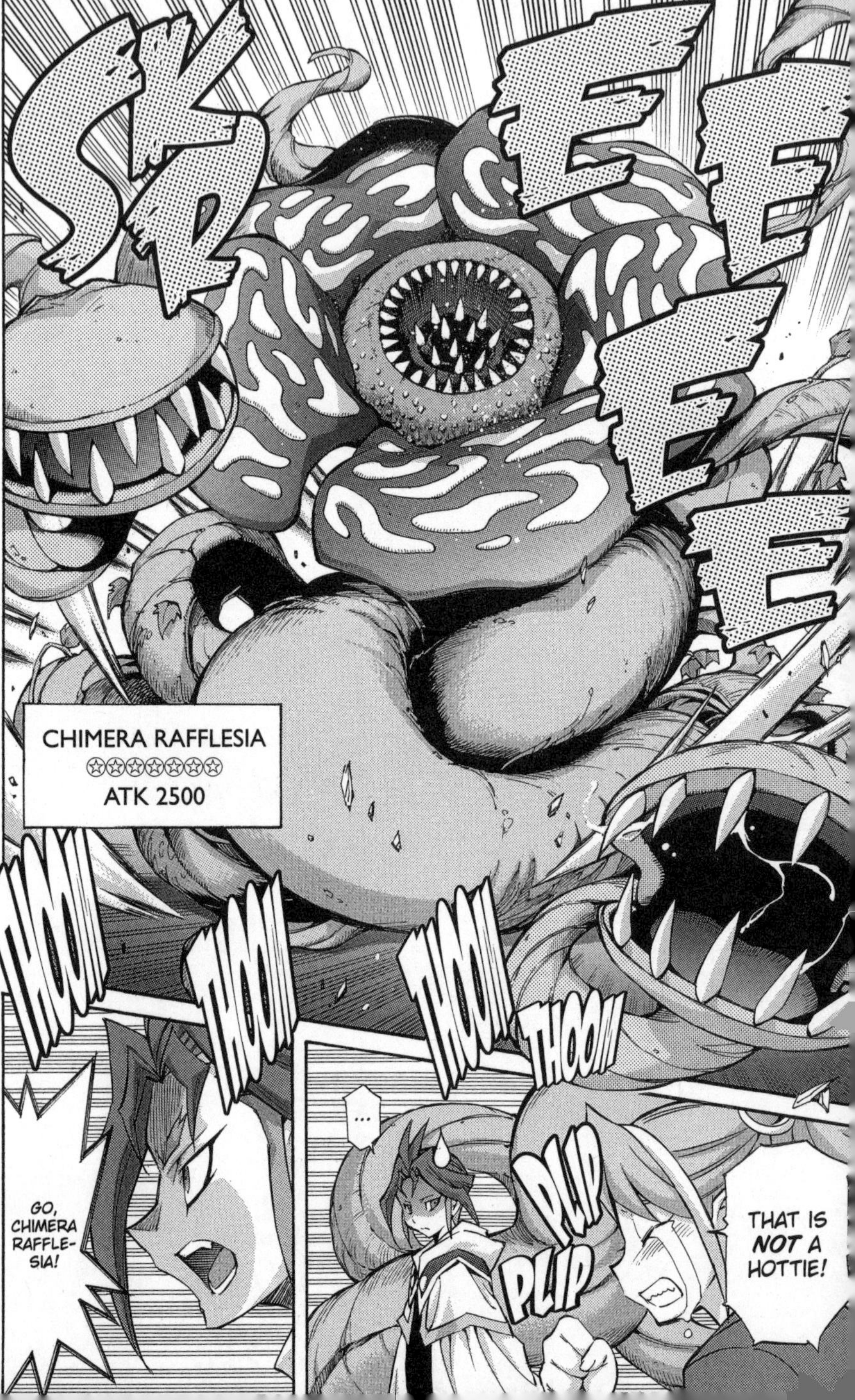
SKREEEEE
CHIMERA RAFFLESIA
ATK 2500
THOOM
THOOM
THOOM
THOOM
...
PLIP
PLIP
THAT IS *NOT* A HOTTIE!
GO, CHIMERA RAFFLE-SIA!

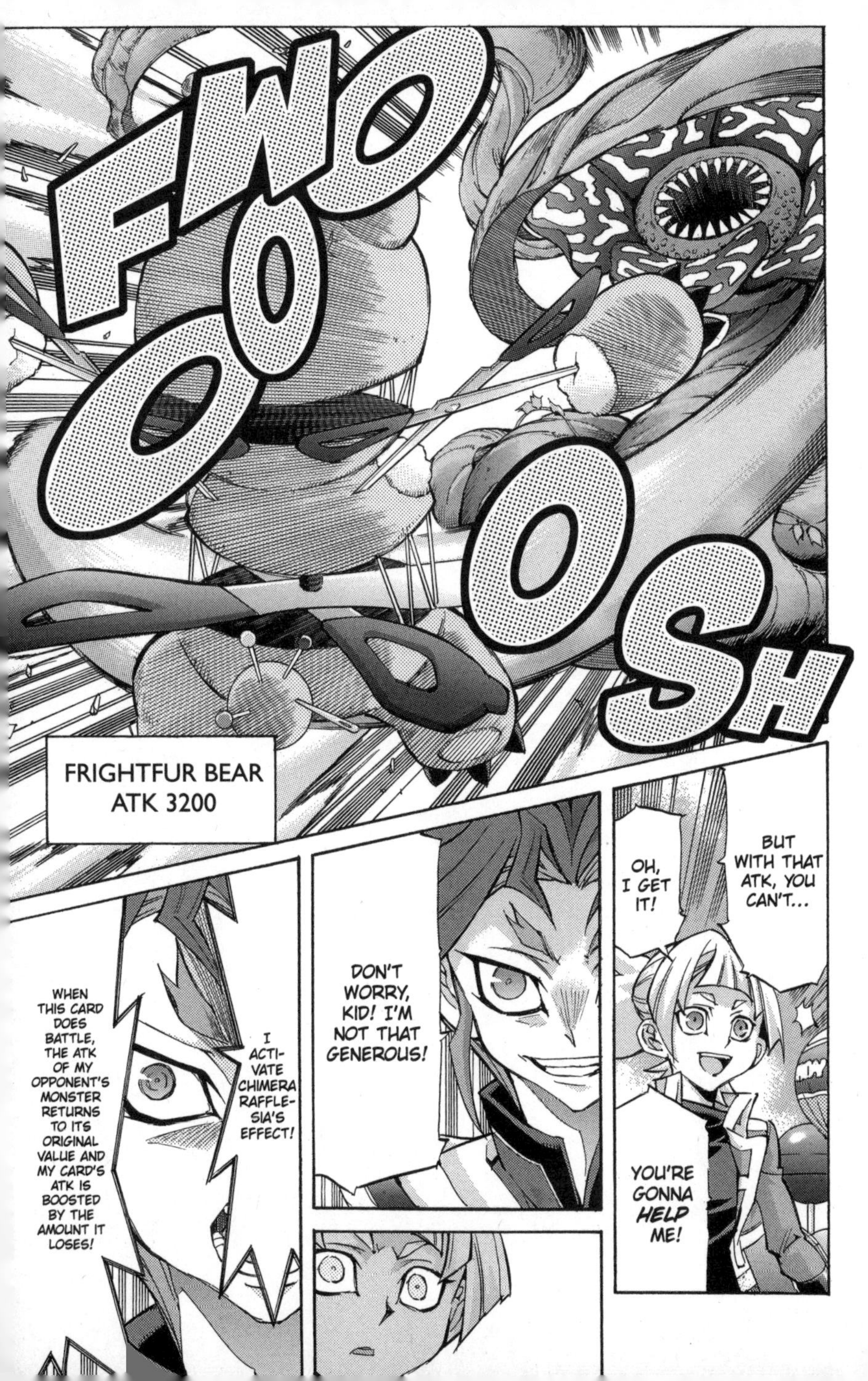
FWOOOOOSH
FRIGHTFUR BEAR ATK 3200
BUT WITH THAT ATK, YOU CAN'T...
OH, I GET IT!
YOU'RE GONNA HELP ME!
DON'T WORRY, KID! I'M NOT THAT GENEROUS!
I ACTI-VATE CHIMERA RAFFLE-SIA'S EFFECT!
WHEN THIS CARD DOES BATTLE, THE ATK OF MY OPPONENT'S MONSTER RETURNS TO ITS ORIGINAL VALUE AND MY CARD'S ATK IS BOOSTED BY THE AMOUNT IT LOSES!

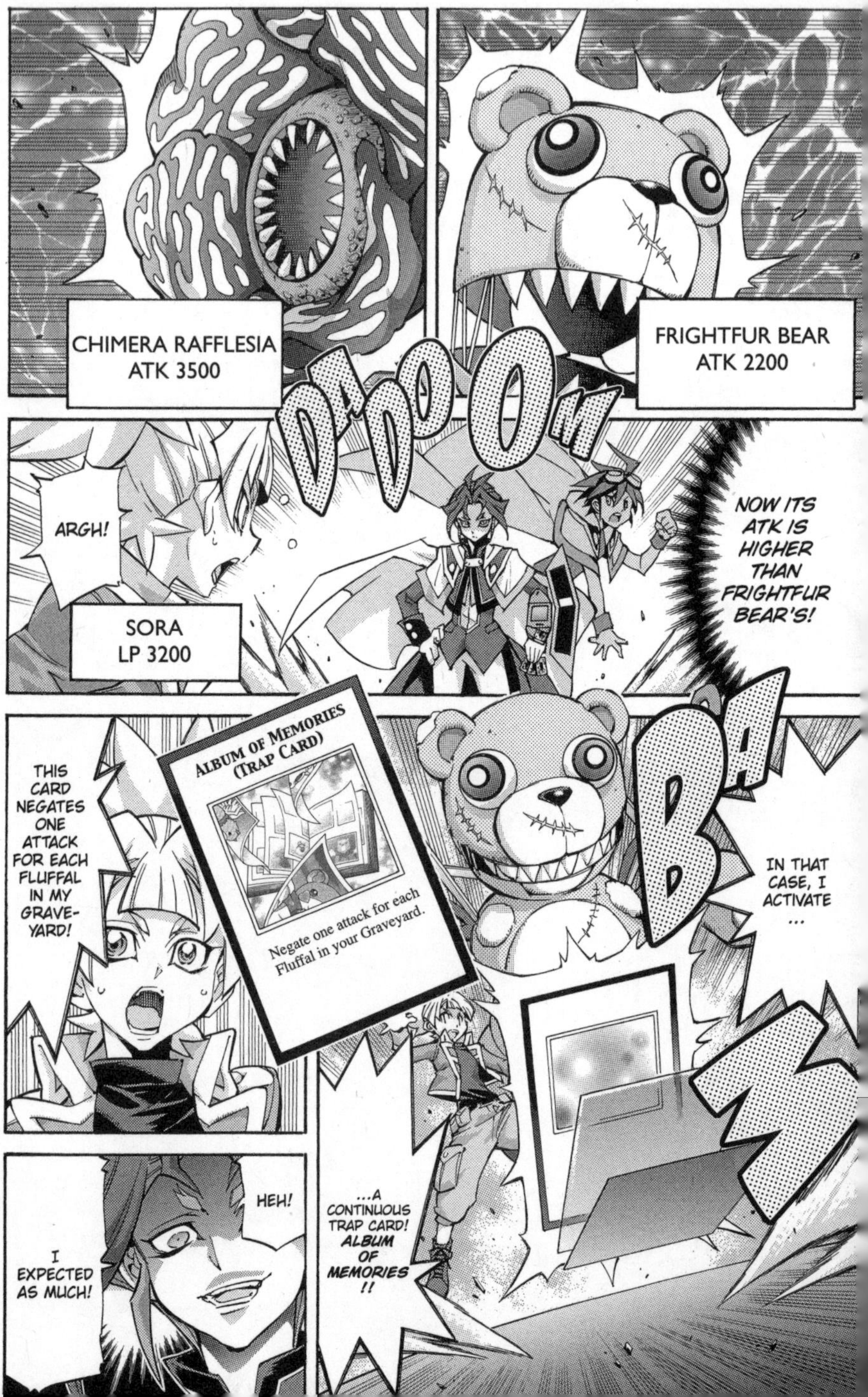
FRIGHTFUR BEAR
ATK 2200
CHIMERA RAFFLESIA
ATK 3500
DADOOOM
NOW ITS ATK IS HIGHER THAN FRIGHTFUR BEAR'S!
ARGH!
SORA
LP 3200
BA
IN THAT CASE, I ACTIVATE ...
...A CONTINUOUS TRAP CARD! ALBUM OF MEMORIES!!
ALBUM OF MEMORIES
(TRAP CARD)
Negate one attack for each Fluffal in your Graveyard.
THIS CARD NEGATES ONE ATTACK FOR EACH FLUFFAL IN MY GRAVE-YARD!
HEH!
I EXPECTED AS MUCH!

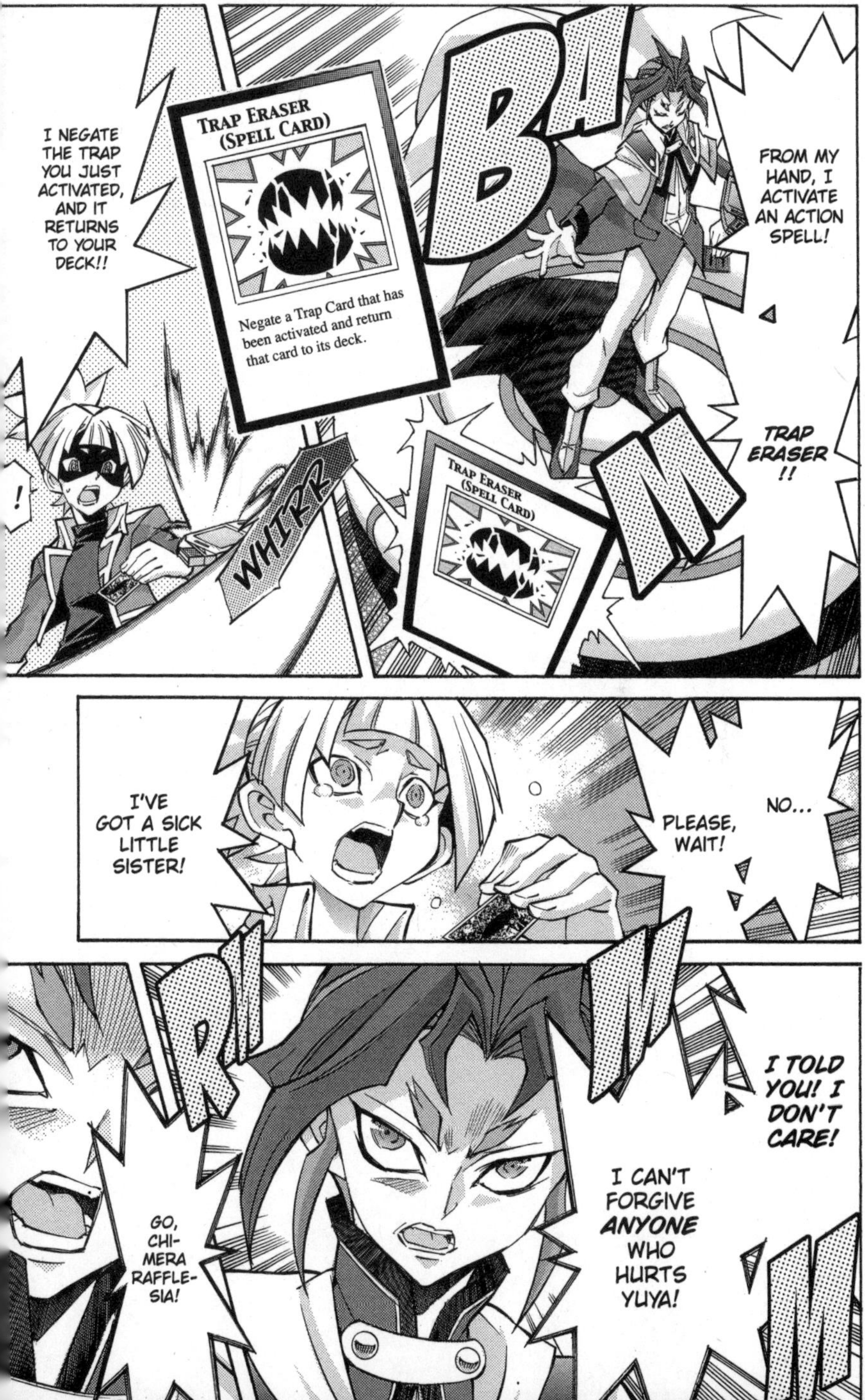
BAM
FROM MY HAND, I ACTIVATE AN ACTION SPELL!
TRAP ERASER!!
TRAP ERASER (SPELL CARD)
Negate a Trap Card that has been activated and return that card to its deck.
TRAP ERASER (SPELL CARD)
I NEGATE THE TRAP YOU JUST ACTIVATED, AND IT RETURNS TO YOUR DECK!!
WHIRR
!
NO...
PLEASE, WAIT!
I'VE GOT A SICK LITTLE SISTER!
I TOLD YOU! I DON'T CARE!
I CAN'T FORGIVE ANYONE WHO HURTS YUYA!
GO, CHIMERA RAFFLESIA!

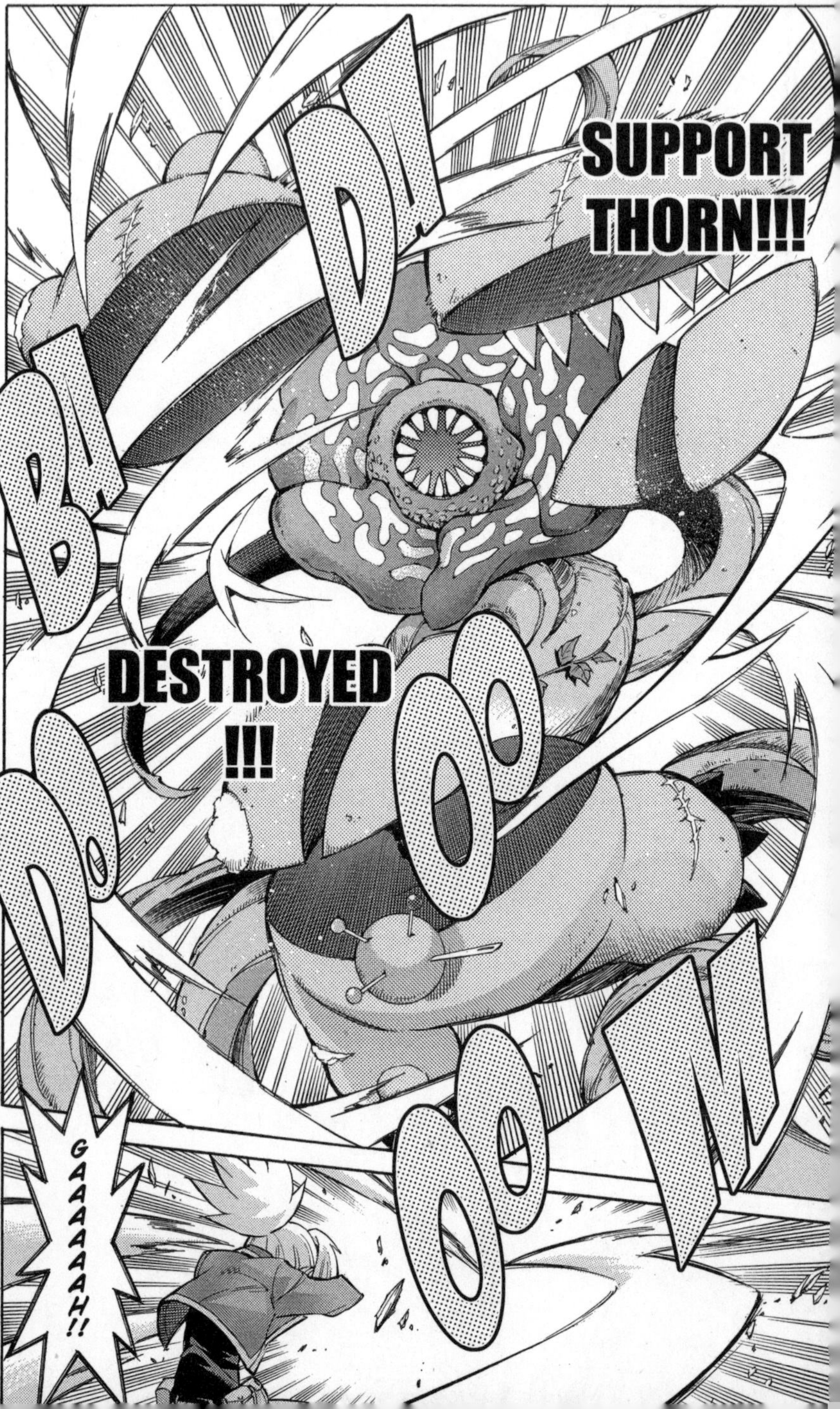
SUPPORT THORN!!!
DESTROYED !!!
GAAAAAAH!!

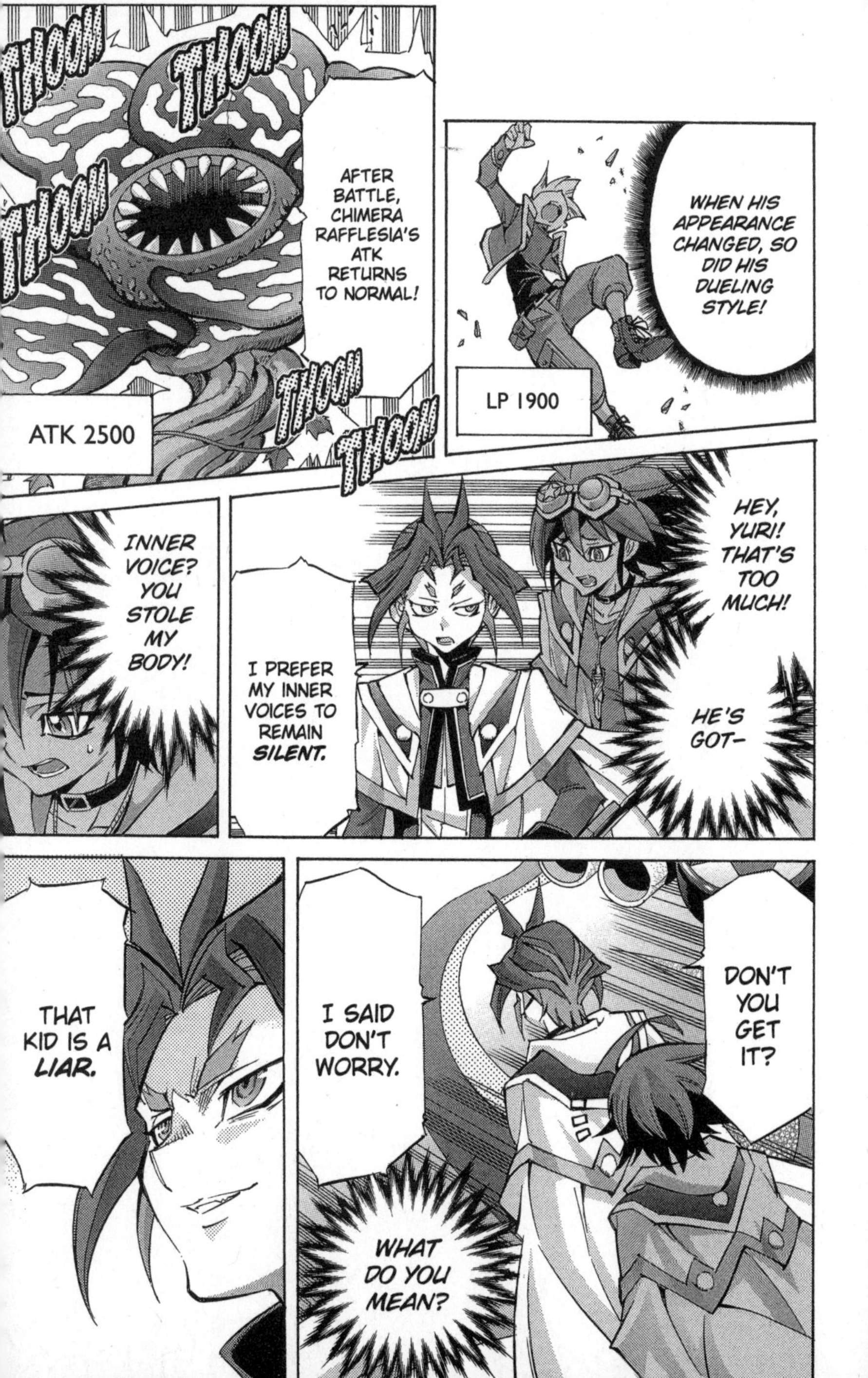
WHEN HIS APPEARANCE CHANGED, SO DID HIS DUELING STYLE!
LP 1900
THOOM THOOM THOOM
AFTER BATTLE, CHIMERA RAFFLESIA'S ATK RETURNS TO NORMAL!
THOOM THOOM
ATK 2500
HEY, YURI! THAT'S TOO MUCH!
HE'S GOT-
I PREFER MY INNER VOICES TO REMAIN *SILENT.*
INNER VOICE? YOU STOLE MY BODY!
DON'T YOU GET IT?
I SAID DON'T WORRY.
WHAT DO YOU MEAN?
THAT KID IS A *LIAR.*

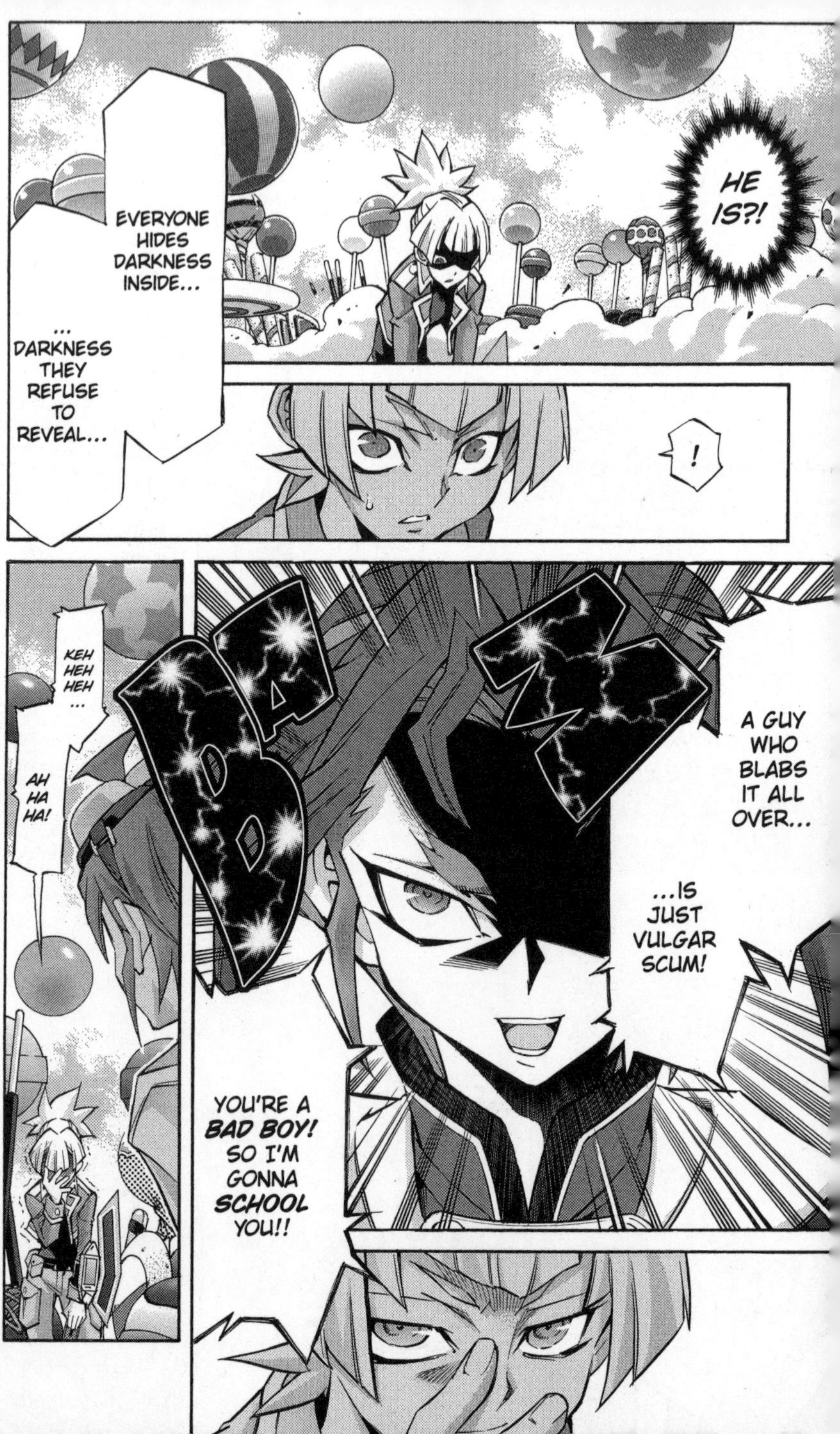
HE IS?!
EVERYONE HIDES DARKNESS INSIDE...
!
... DARKNESS THEY REFUSE TO REVEAL...
BAM
A GUY WHO BLABS IT ALL OVER...
...IS JUST VULGAR SCUM!
YOU'RE A *BAD BOY!* SO I'M GONNA *SCHOOL* YOU!!
KEH HEH HEH ...
AH HA HA!

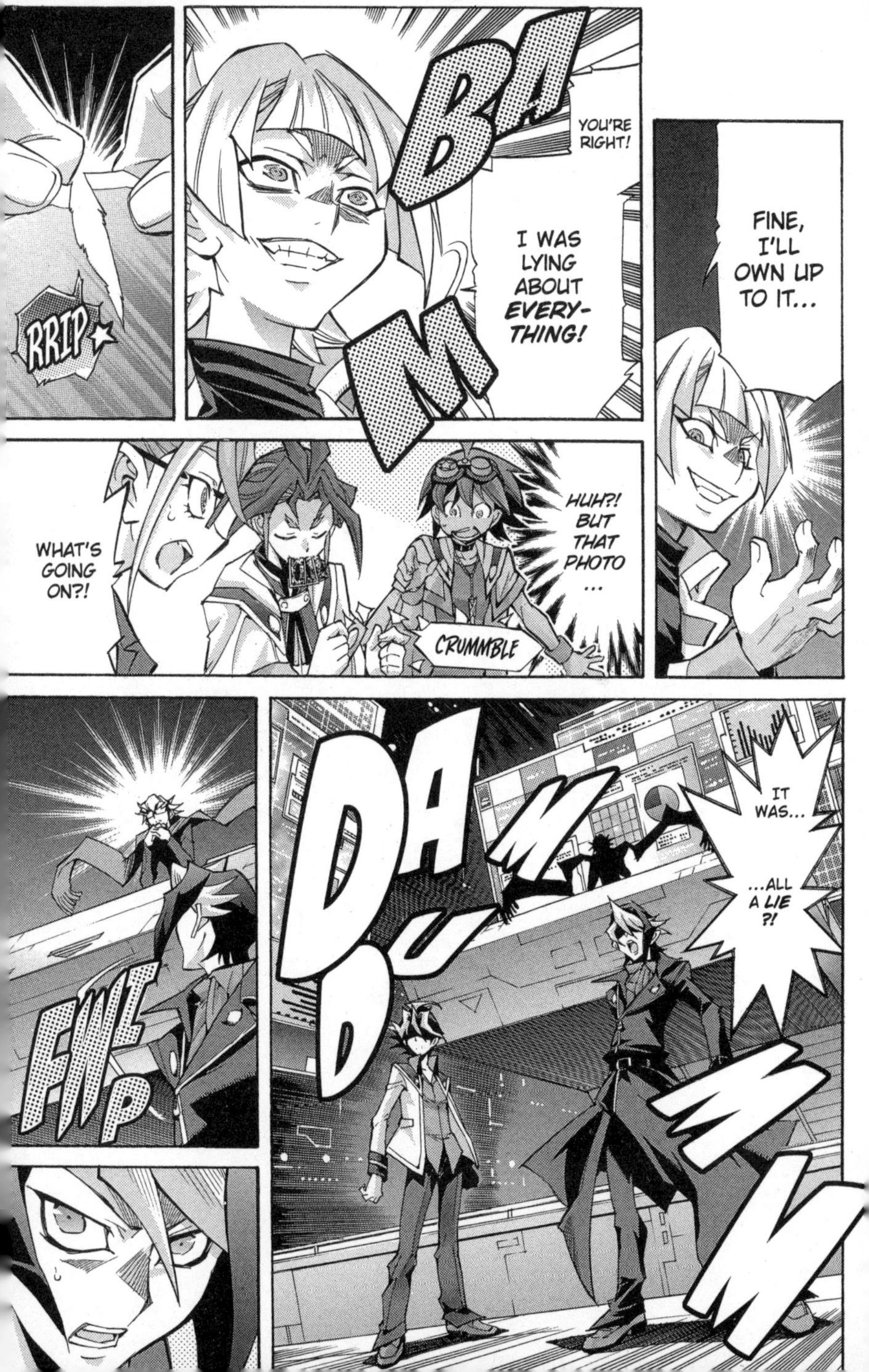
FINE, I'LL OWN UP TO IT...
YOU'RE RIGHT!
I WAS LYING ABOUT *EVERYTHING!*
BAM
RRIP
HUH?! BUT THAT PHOTO...
CRUMMBLE
WHAT'S GOING ON?!
IT WAS...
...ALL A *LIE*?!
FWIP

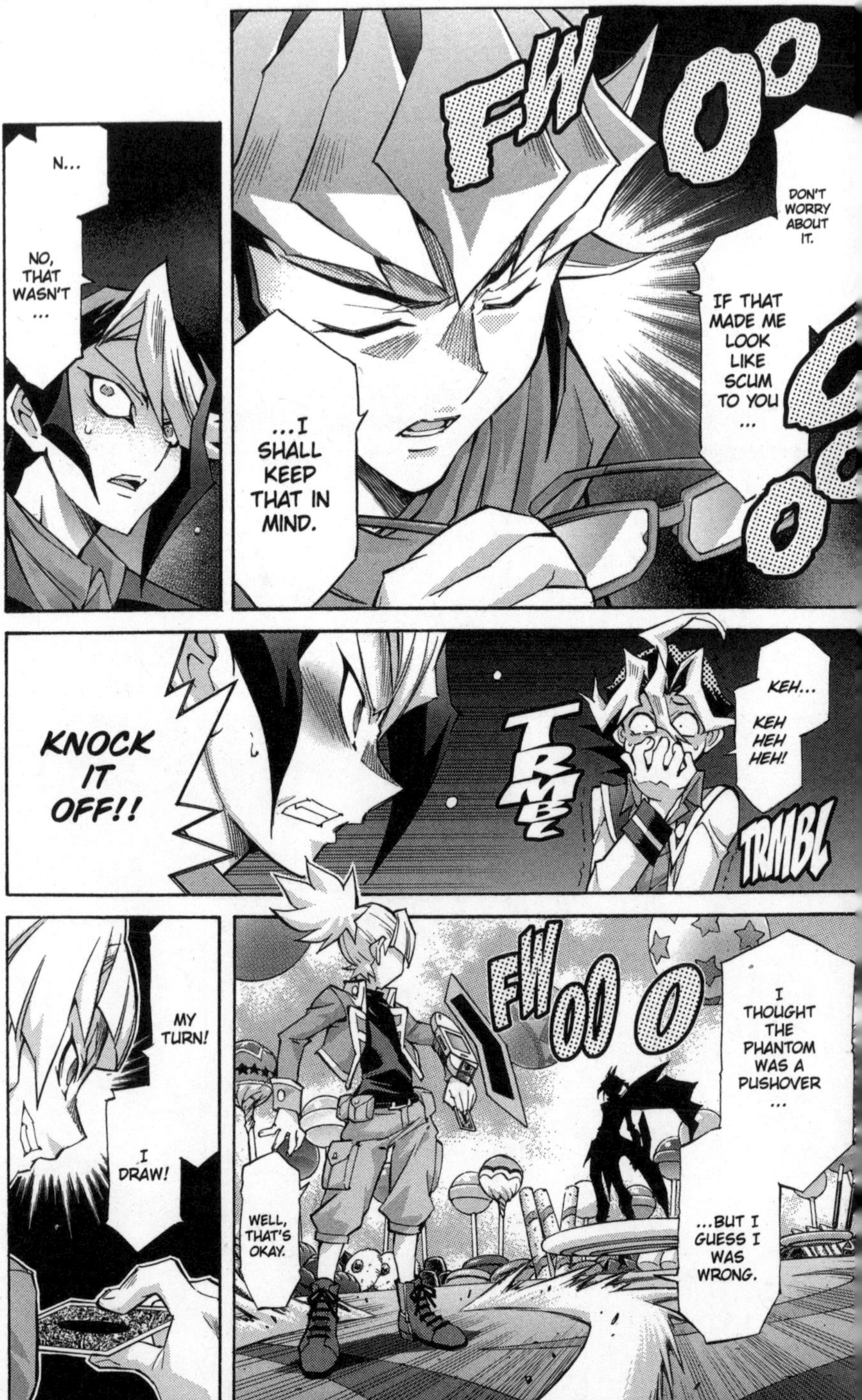
FWOOO
DON'T WORRY ABOUT IT.
IF THAT MADE ME LOOK LIKE SCUM TO YOU ...
...I SHALL KEEP THAT IN MIND.
N...
NO, THAT WASN'T ...
KEH...
KEH HEH HEH!
TRMBL
TRMBL
KNOCK IT OFF!!
FWOOO
I THOUGHT THE PHANTOM WAS A PUSHOVER ...
...BUT I GUESS I WAS WRONG.
WELL, THAT'S OKAY.
MY TURN!
I DRAW!

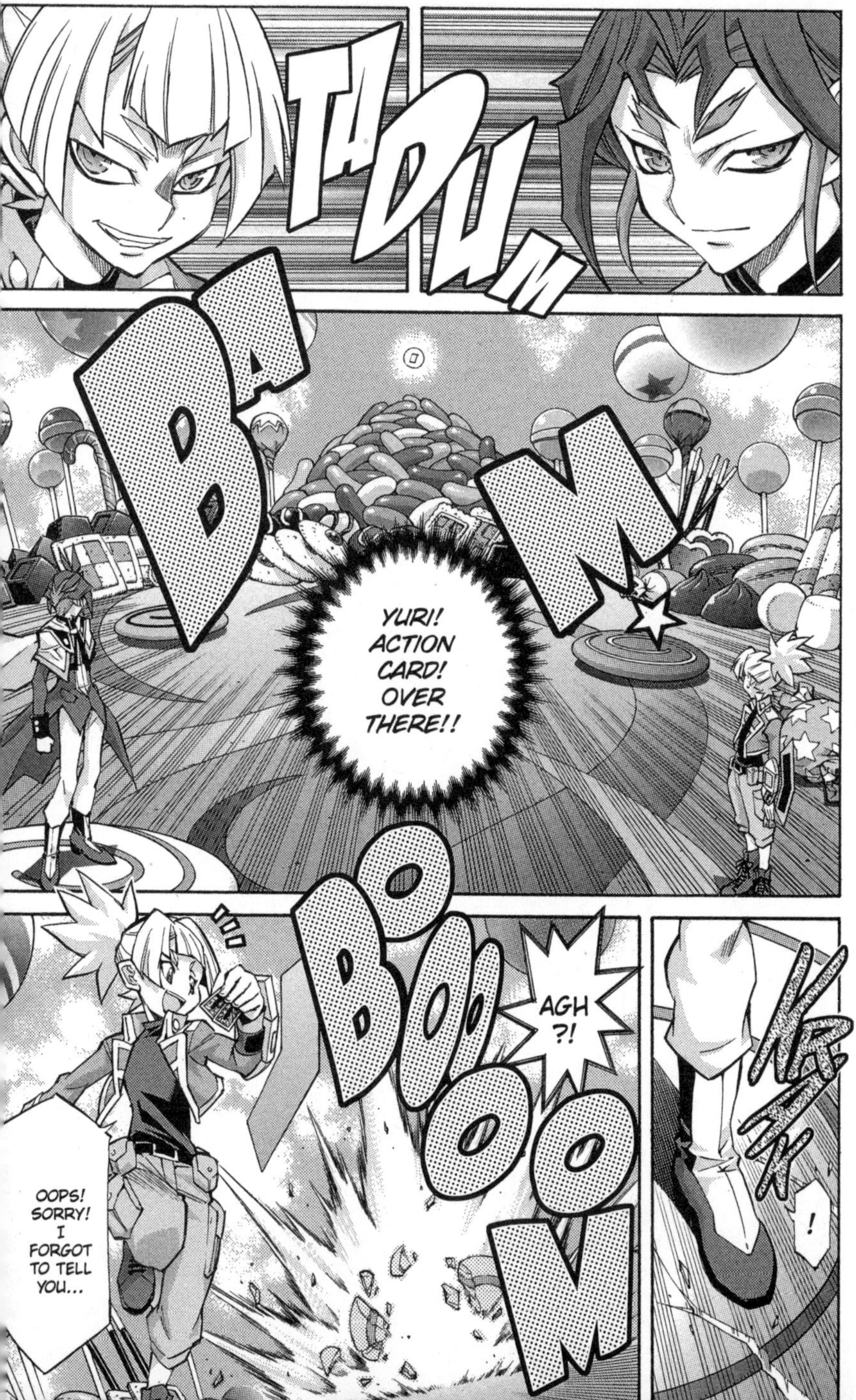
TA-DUM
BAM
YURI! ACTION CARD! OVER THERE!!
!
AGH ?!
BOOOOOM
OOPS! SORRY! I FORGOT TO TELL YOU...

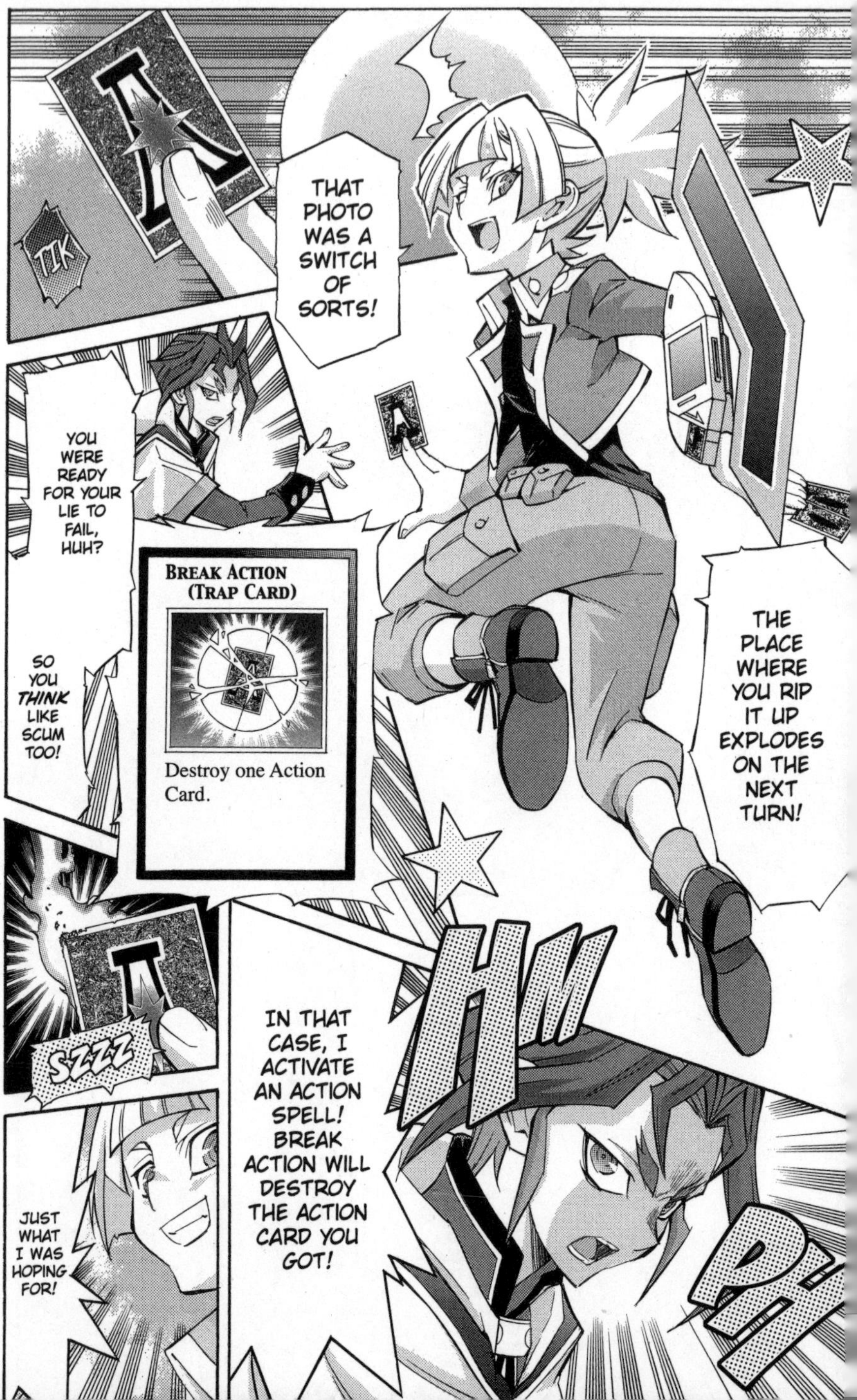
THAT PHOTO WAS A SWITCH OF SORTS!
THE PLACE WHERE YOU RIP IT UP EXPLODES ON THE NEXT TURN!
TIK
YOU WERE READY FOR YOUR LIE TO FAIL, HUH?
SO YOU *THINK* LIKE SCUM TOO!
HM
IN THAT CASE, I ACTIVATE AN ACTION SPELL! BREAK ACTION WILL DESTROY THE ACTION CARD YOU GOT!
BREAK ACTION (TRAP CARD)
Destroy one Action Card.
SZZZ
JUST WHAT I WAS HOPING FOR!

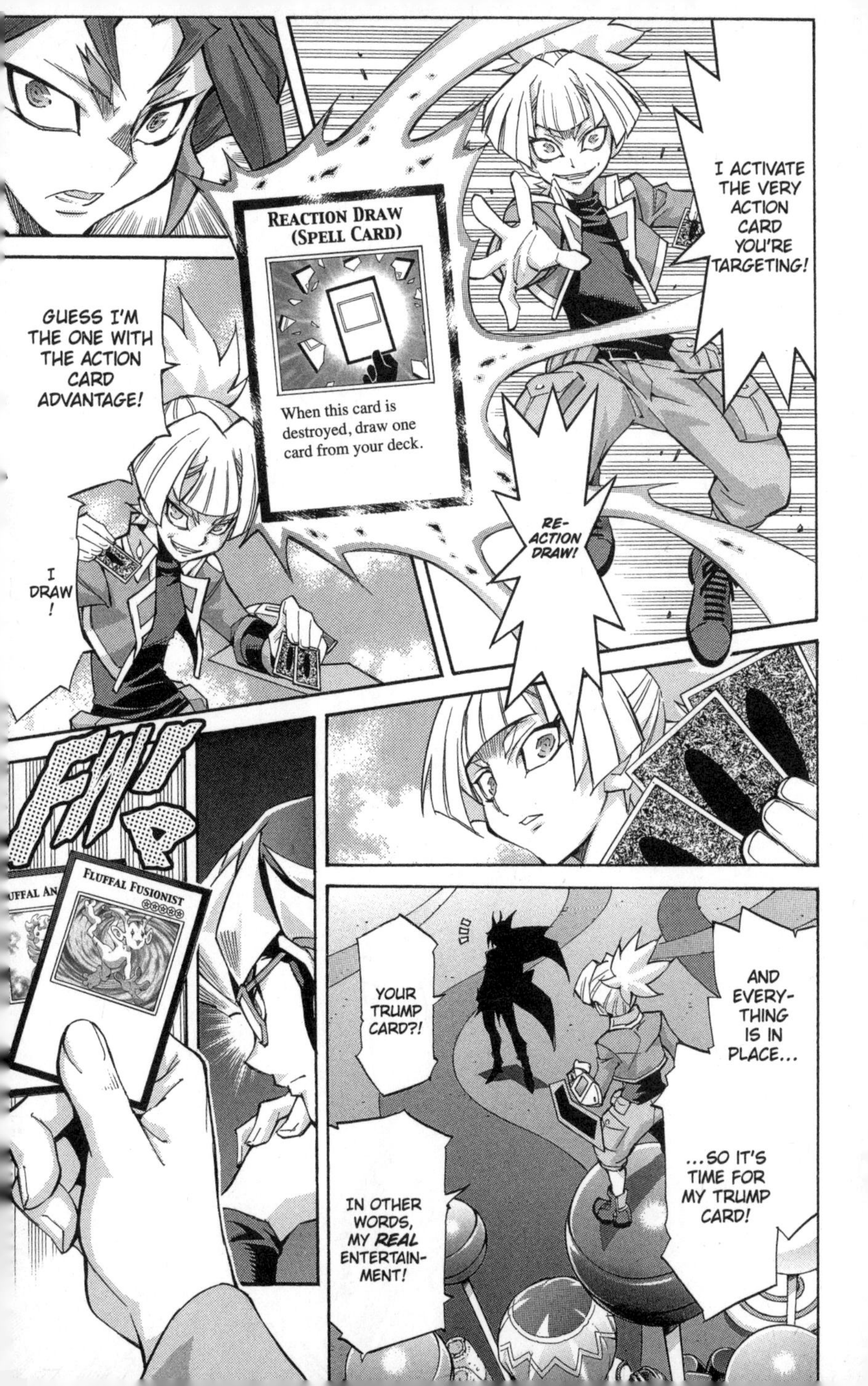
I ACTIVATE THE VERY ACTION CARD YOU'RE TARGETING!
REACTION DRAW (SPELL CARD)
When this card is destroyed, draw one card from your deck.
RE-ACTION DRAW!
GUESS I'M THE ONE WITH THE ACTION CARD ADVANTAGE!
I DRAW!
FW!
FLUFFAL FUSIONIST
AND EVERYTHING IS IN PLACE...
...SO IT'S TIME FOR MY TRUMP CARD!
YOUR TRUMP CARD?!
IN OTHER WORDS, MY REAL ENTERTAINMENT!

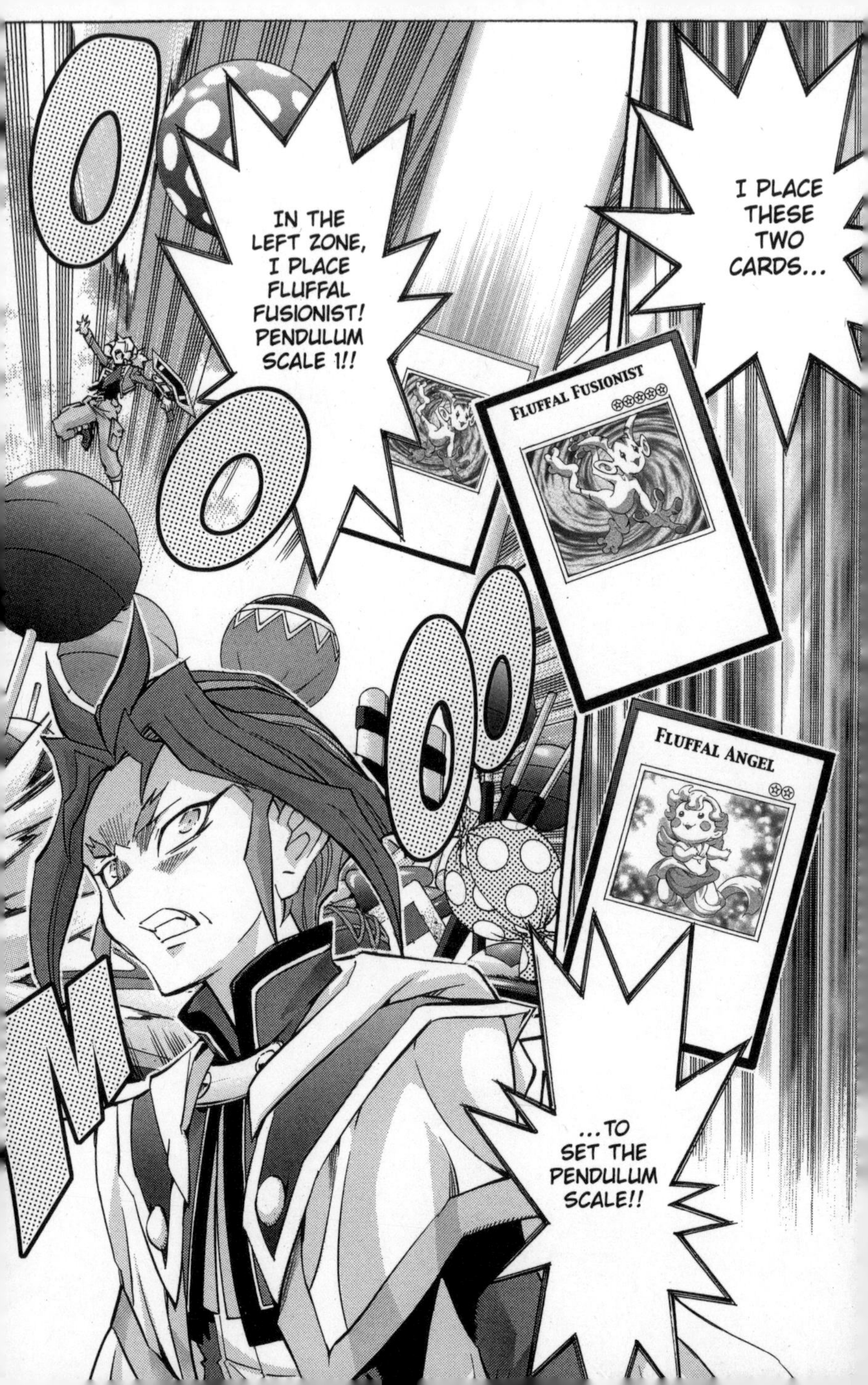
I PLACE THESE TWO CARDS...
IN THE LEFT ZONE, I PLACE FLUFFAL FUSIONIST! PENDULUM SCALE 1!!
FLUFFAL FUSIONIST
FLUFFAL ANGEL
...TO SET THE PENDULUM SCALE!!

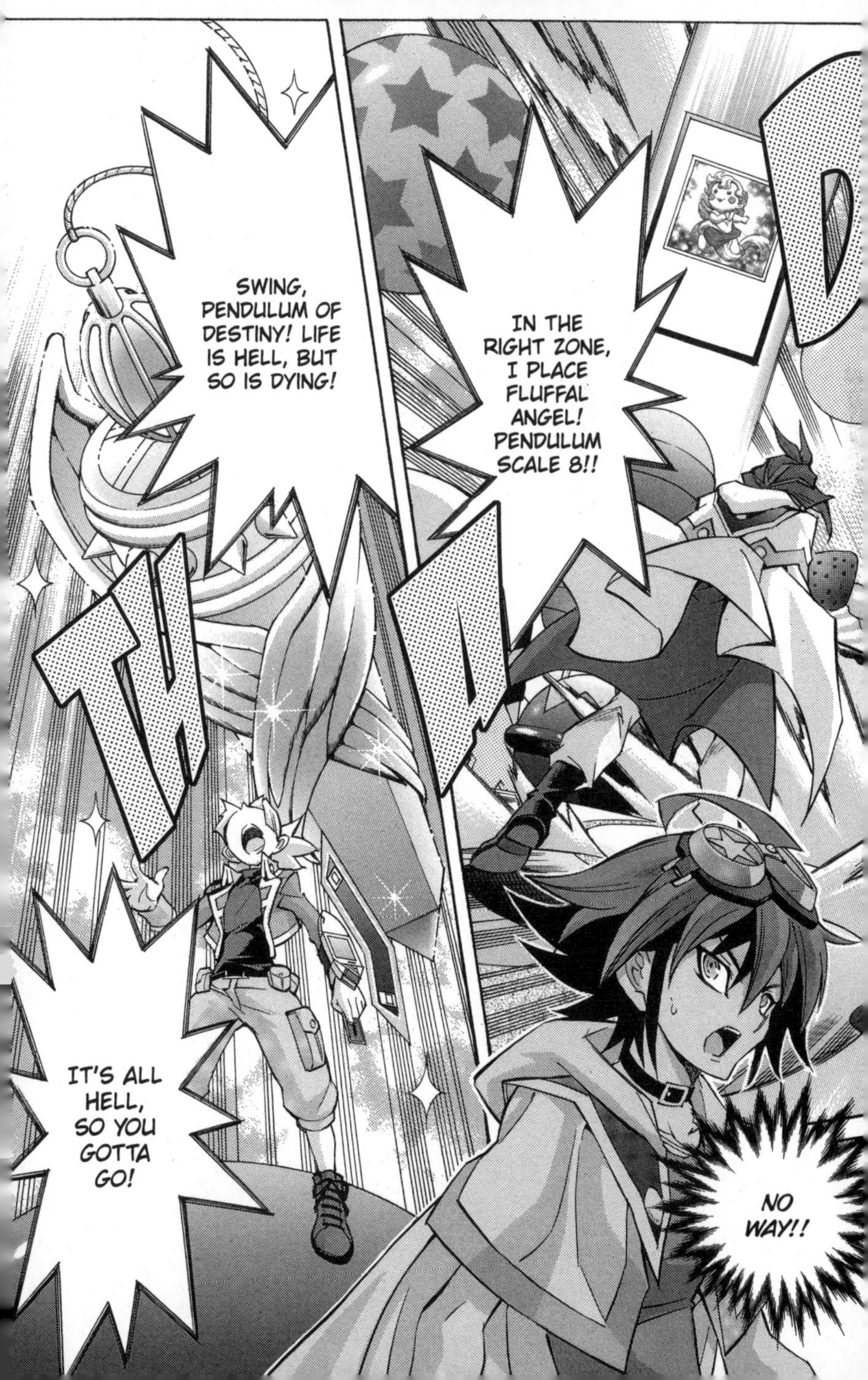
IN THE RIGHT ZONE, I PLACE FLUFFAL ANGEL! PENDULUM SCALE 8!!
SWING, PENDULUM OF DESTINY! LIFE IS HELL, BUT SO IS DYING!
NO WAY!!
IT'S ALL HELL, SO YOU GOTTA GO!

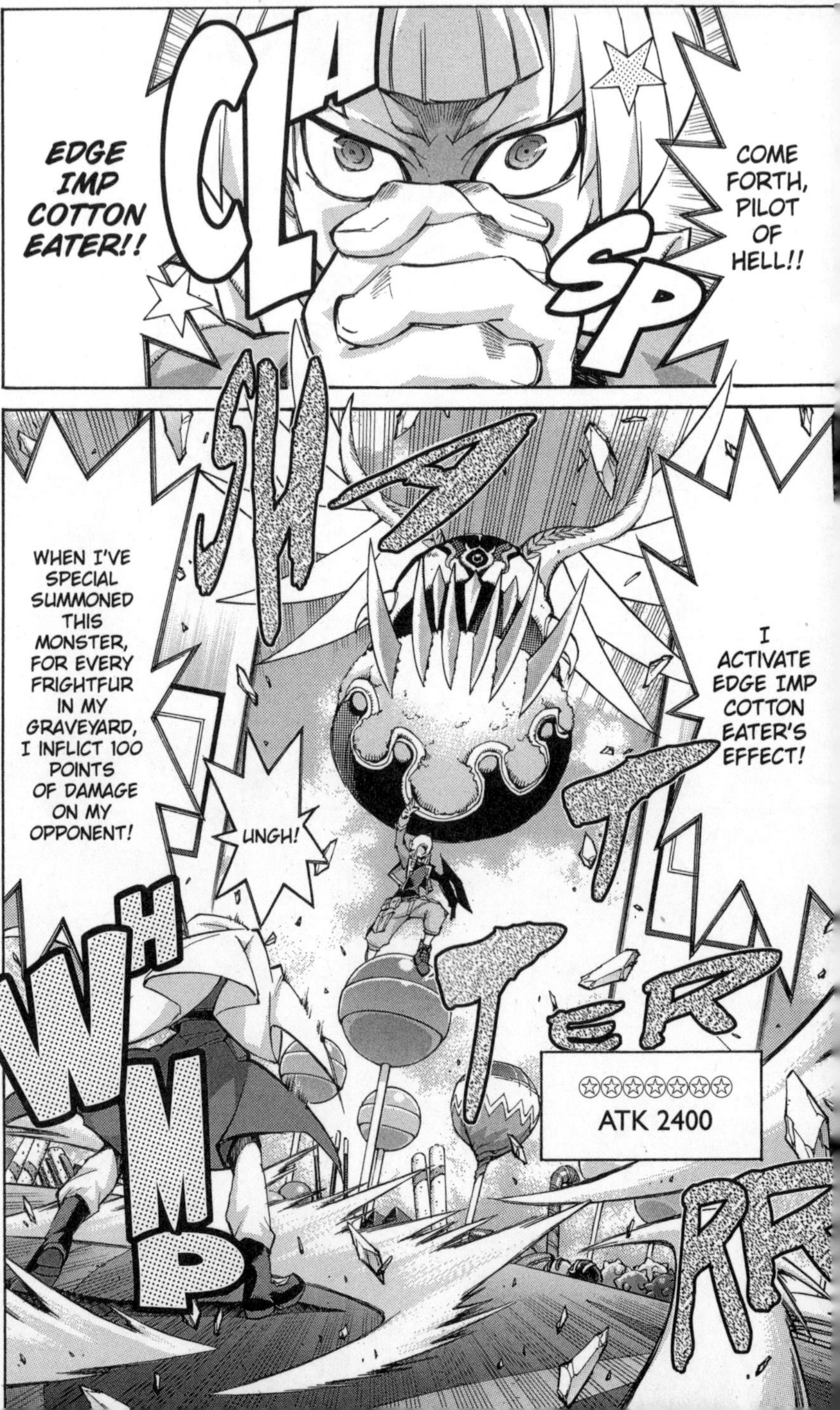
COME FORTH, PILOT OF HELL!!
EDGE IMP COTTON EATER!!
I ACTIVATE EDGE IMP COTTON EATER'S EFFECT!
WHEN I'VE SPECIAL SUMMONED THIS MONSTER, FOR EVERY FRIGHTFUR IN MY GRAVEYARD, I INFLICT 100 POINTS OF DAMAGE ON MY OPPONENT!
UNGH!
ATK 2400
WHMP

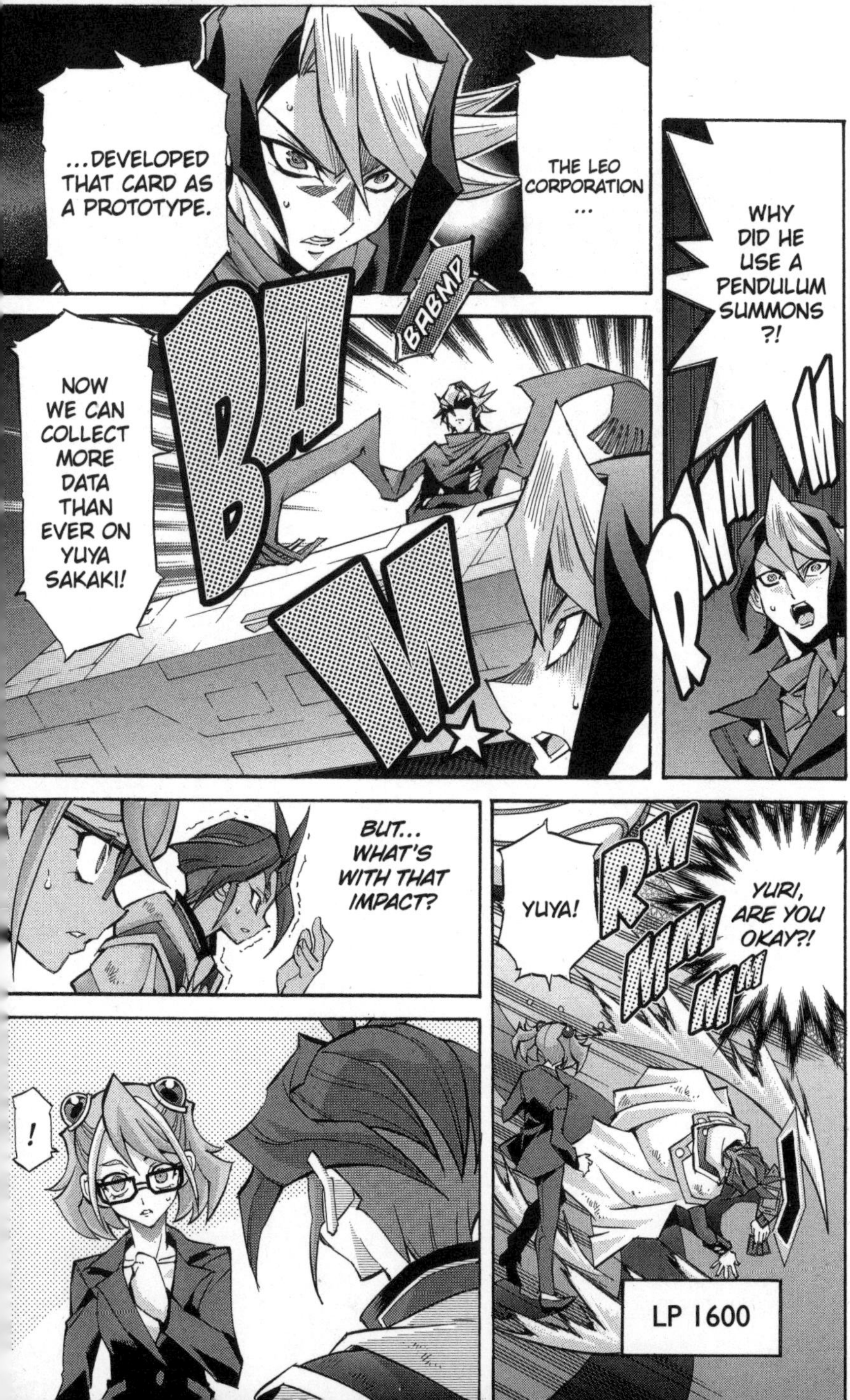
WHY DID HE USE A PENDULUM SUMMONS?!
RMMMM
THE LEO CORPORATION...
...DEVELOPED THAT CARD AS A PROTOTYPE.
BABMP
BAM!
NOW WE CAN COLLECT MORE DATA THAN EVER ON YUYA SAKAKI!
YURI, ARE YOU OKAY?!
RMMMM...
YUYA!
LP 1600
BUT... WHAT'S WITH THAT IMPACT?
!

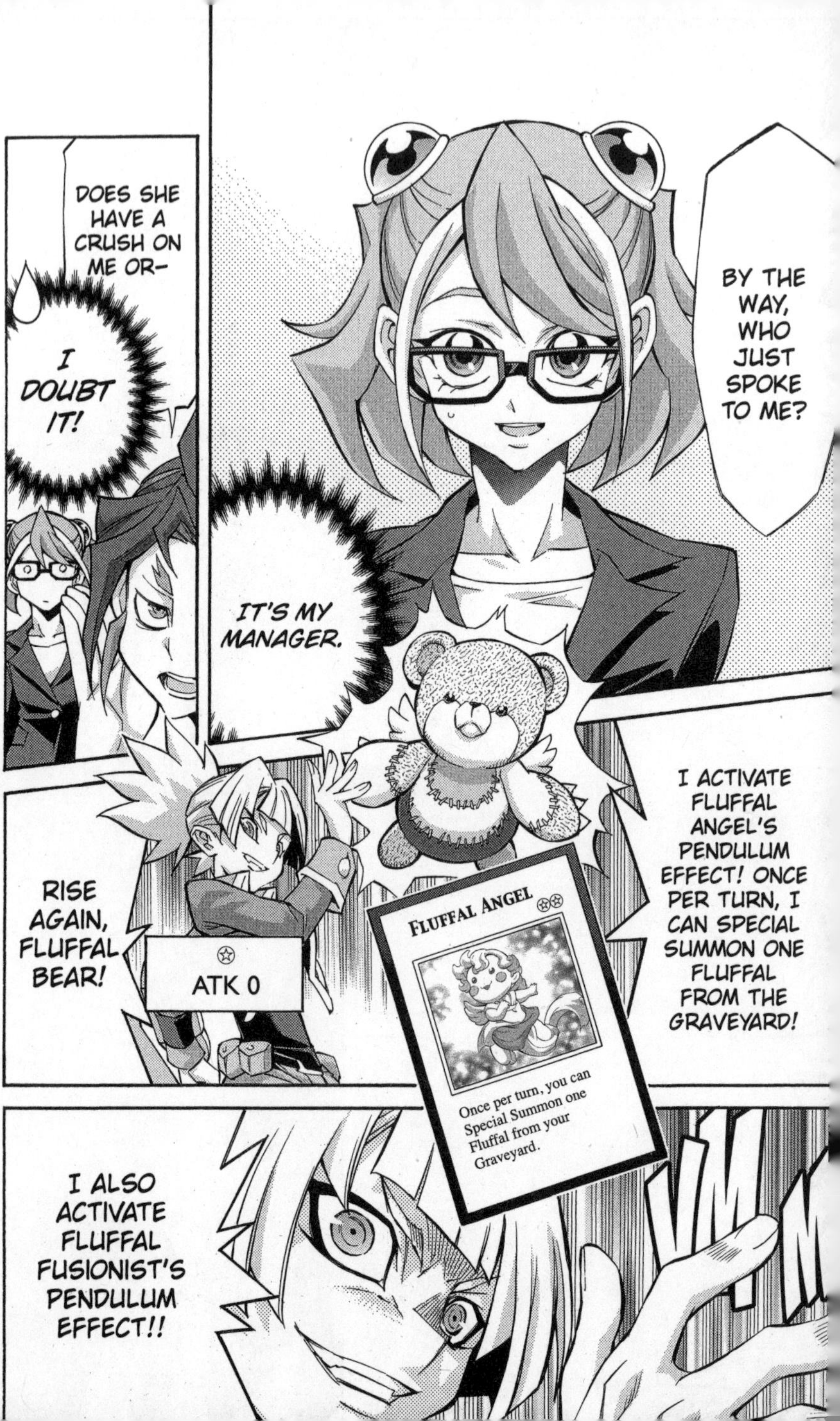
BY THE WAY, WHO JUST SPOKE TO ME?
IT'S MY MANAGER.
DOES SHE HAVE A CRUSH ON ME OR–
I DOUBT IT!
I ACTIVATE FLUFFAL ANGEL'S PENDULUM EFFECT! ONCE PER TURN, I CAN SPECIAL SUMMON ONE FLUFFAL FROM THE GRAVEYARD!
FLUFFAL ANGEL
Once per turn, you can Special Summon one Fluffal from your Graveyard.
RISE AGAIN, FLUFFAL BEAR!
ATK 0
I ALSO ACTIVATE FLUFFAL FUSIONIST'S PENDULUM EFFECT!!

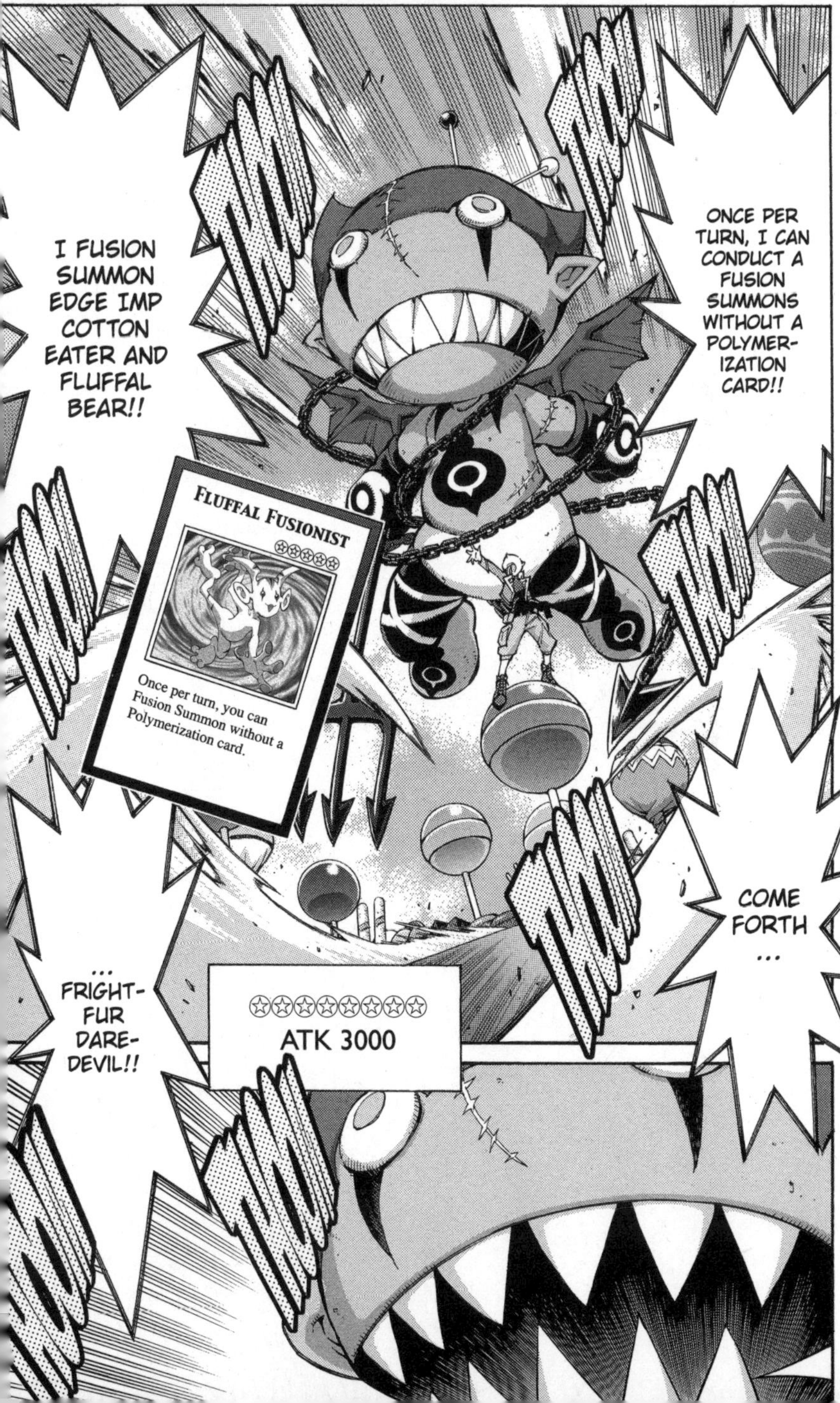
ONCE PER TURN, I CAN CONDUCT A FUSION SUMMONS WITHOUT A POLYMER-IZATION CARD!!
I FUSION SUMMON EDGE IMP COTTON EATER AND FLUFFAL BEAR!!
FLUFFAL FUSIONIST
Once per turn, you can Fusion Summon without a Polymerization card.
COME FORTH ...
... FRIGHT-FUR DARE-DEVIL!!
ATK 3000

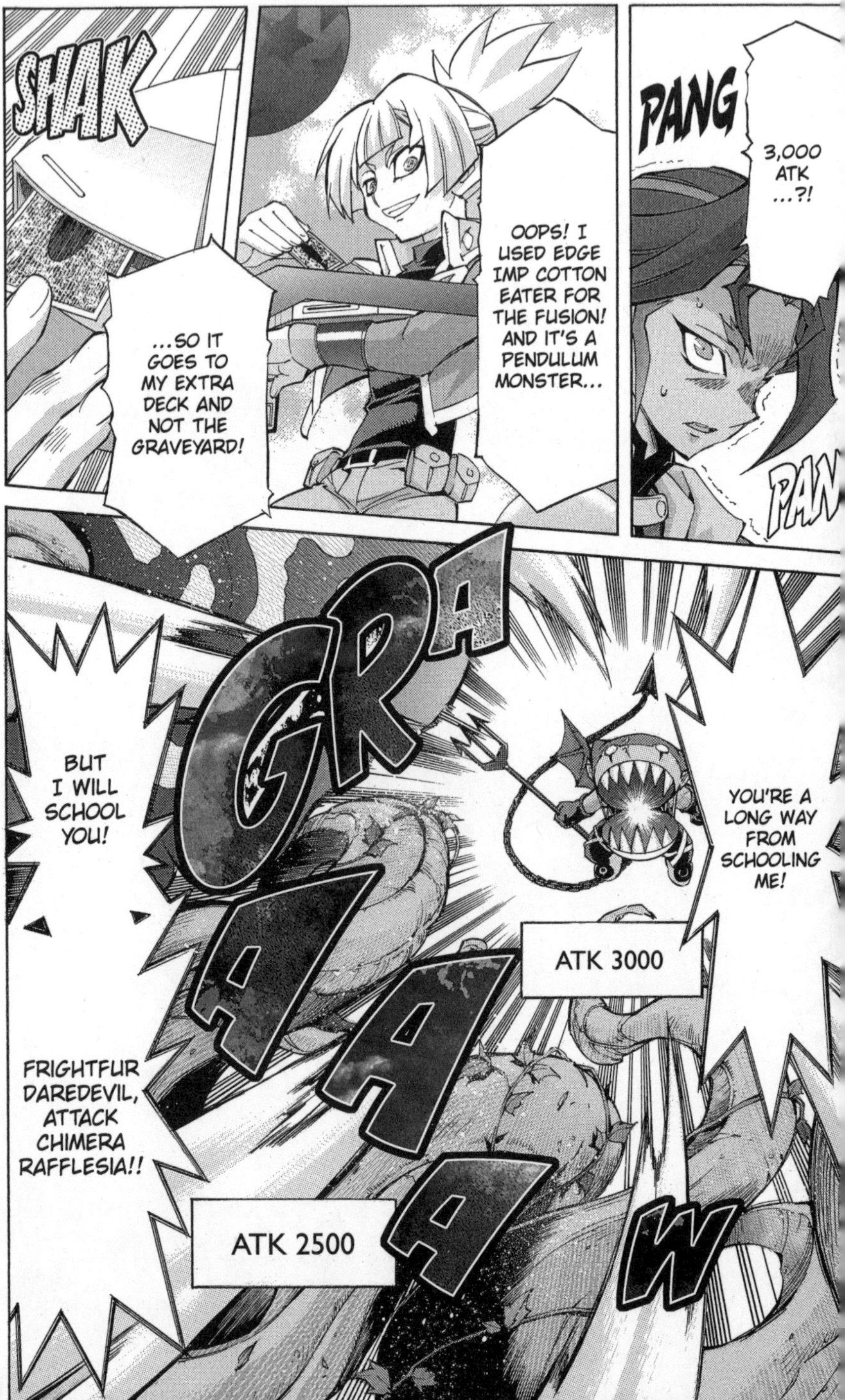
PANG
3,000 ATK ...?!
PAN
OOPS! I USED EDGE IMP COTTON EATER FOR THE FUSION! AND IT'S A PENDULUM MONSTER...
...SO IT GOES TO MY EXTRA DECK AND NOT THE GRAVEYARD!
SHAK
YOU'RE A LONG WAY FROM SCHOOLING ME!
GRAAAAW
ATK 3000
BUT I WILL SCHOOL YOU!
FRIGHTFUR DAREDEVIL, ATTACK CHIMERA RAFFLESIA!!
ATK 2500

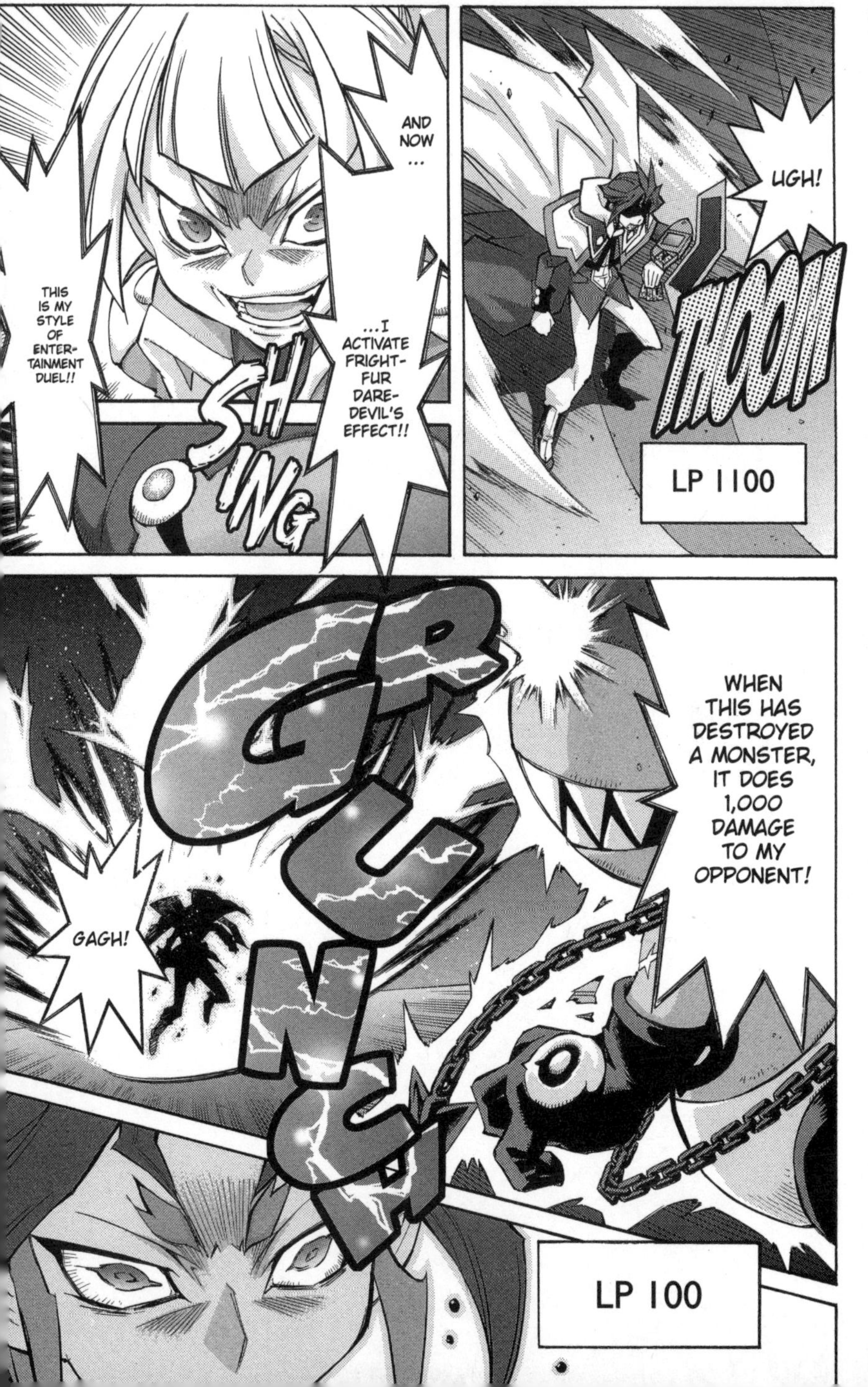

UGH!
THOOM
LP 1100
AND NOW ...
...I ACTIVATE FRIGHT-FUR DARE-DEVIL'S EFFECT!!
THIS IS MY STYLE OF ENTER-TAINMENT DUEL!!
SHING
WHEN THIS HAS DESTROYED A MONSTER, IT DOES 1,000 DAMAGE TO MY OPPONENT!
GAGH!
LP 100

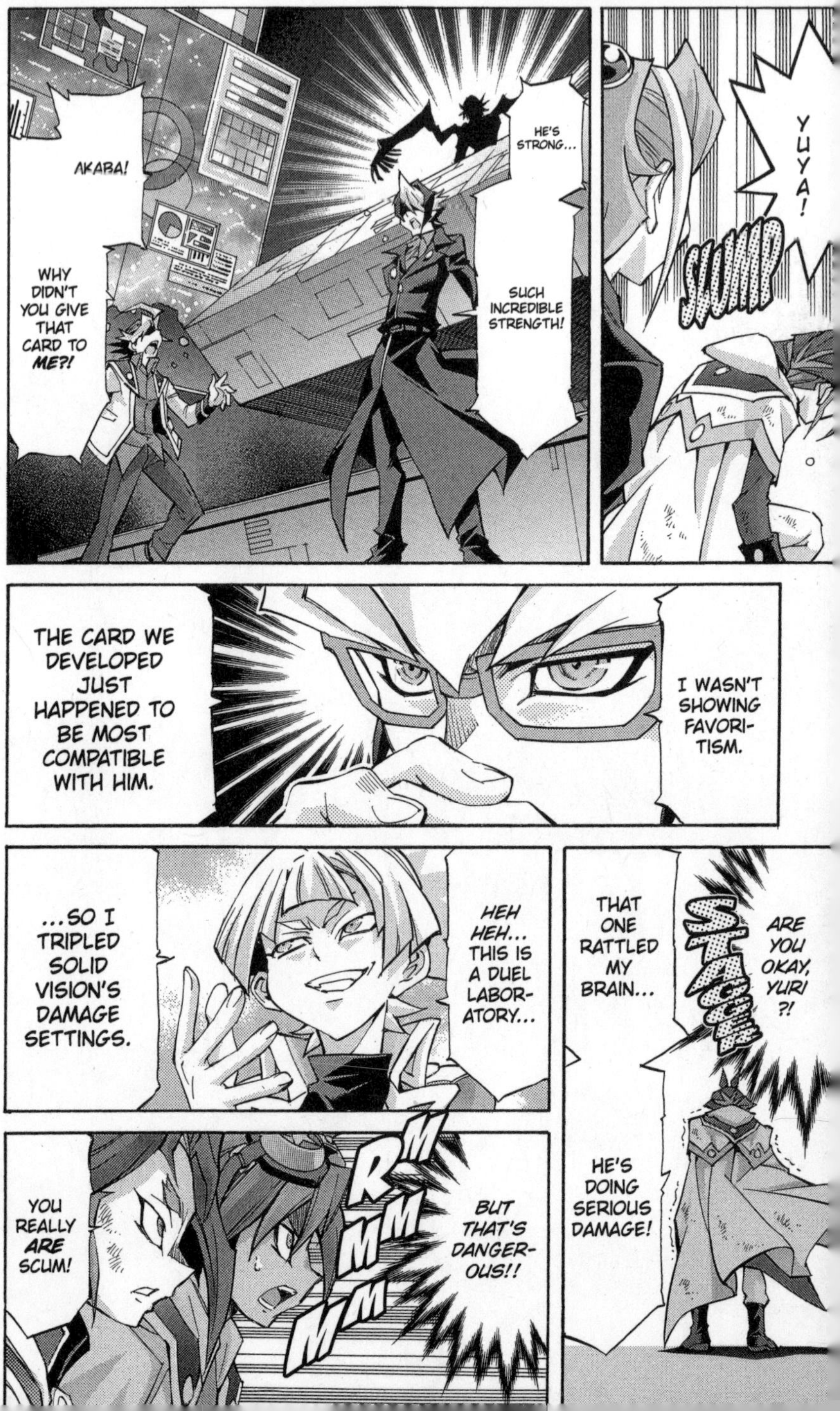
YUYA!
SLUMP
HE'S STRONG...
SUCH INCREDIBLE STRENGTH!
AKABA!
WHY DIDN'T YOU GIVE THAT CARD TO ME?!
I WASN'T SHOWING FAVORITISM.
THE CARD WE DEVELOPED JUST HAPPENED TO BE MOST COMPATIBLE WITH HIM.
ARE YOU OKAY, YURI?!
THAT ONE RATTLED MY BRAIN...
HE'S DOING SERIOUS DAMAGE!
HEH HEH... THIS IS A DUEL LABORATORY...
...SO I TRIPLED SOLID VISION'S DAMAGE SETTINGS.
BUT THAT'S DANGEROUS!!
YOU REALLY ARE SCUM!

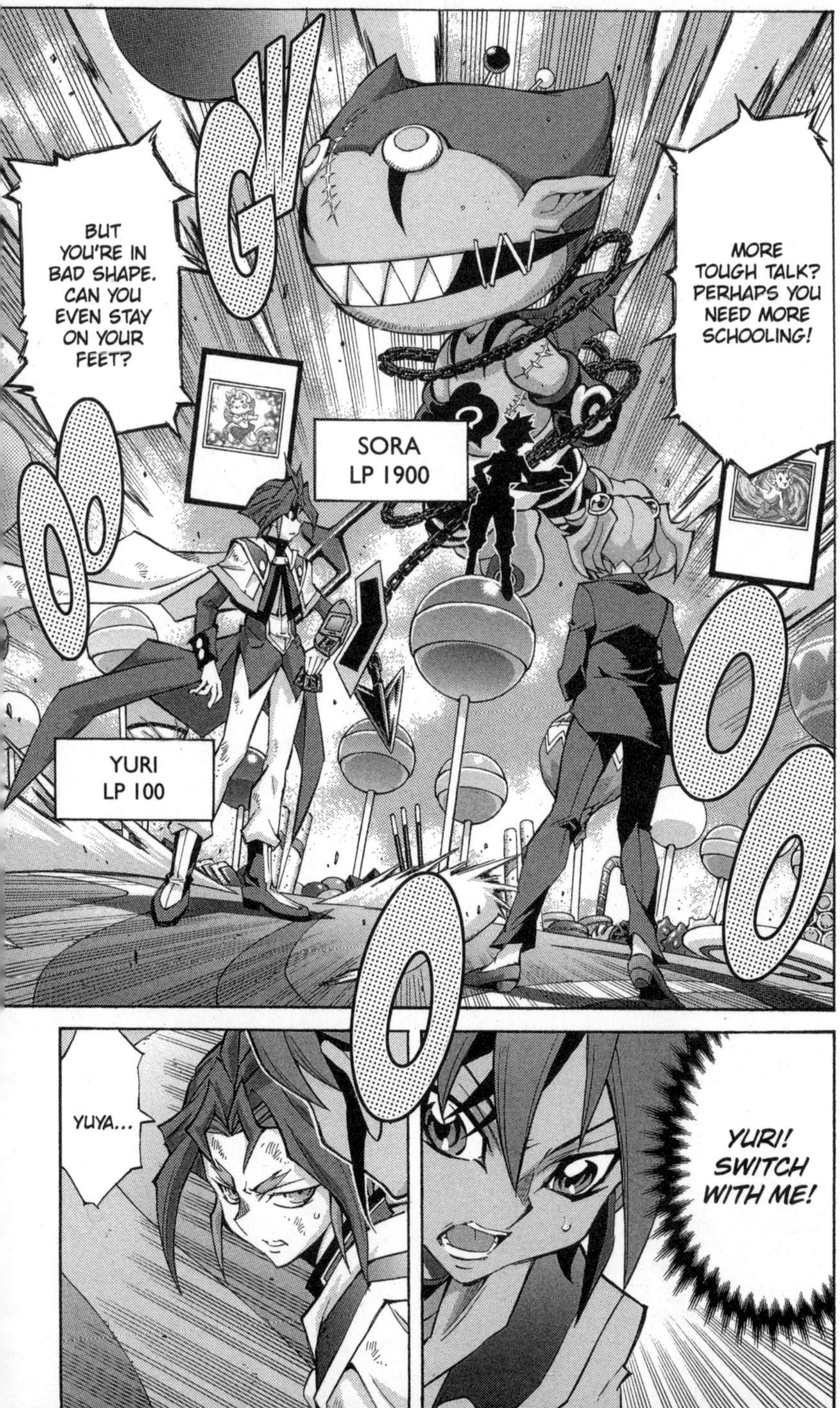
MORE TOUGH TALK? PERHAPS YOU NEED MORE SCHOOLING!
BUT YOU'RE IN BAD SHAPE. CAN YOU EVEN STAY ON YOUR FEET?
SORA
LP 1900
YURI
LP 100
YURI! SWITCH WITH ME!
YUYA...

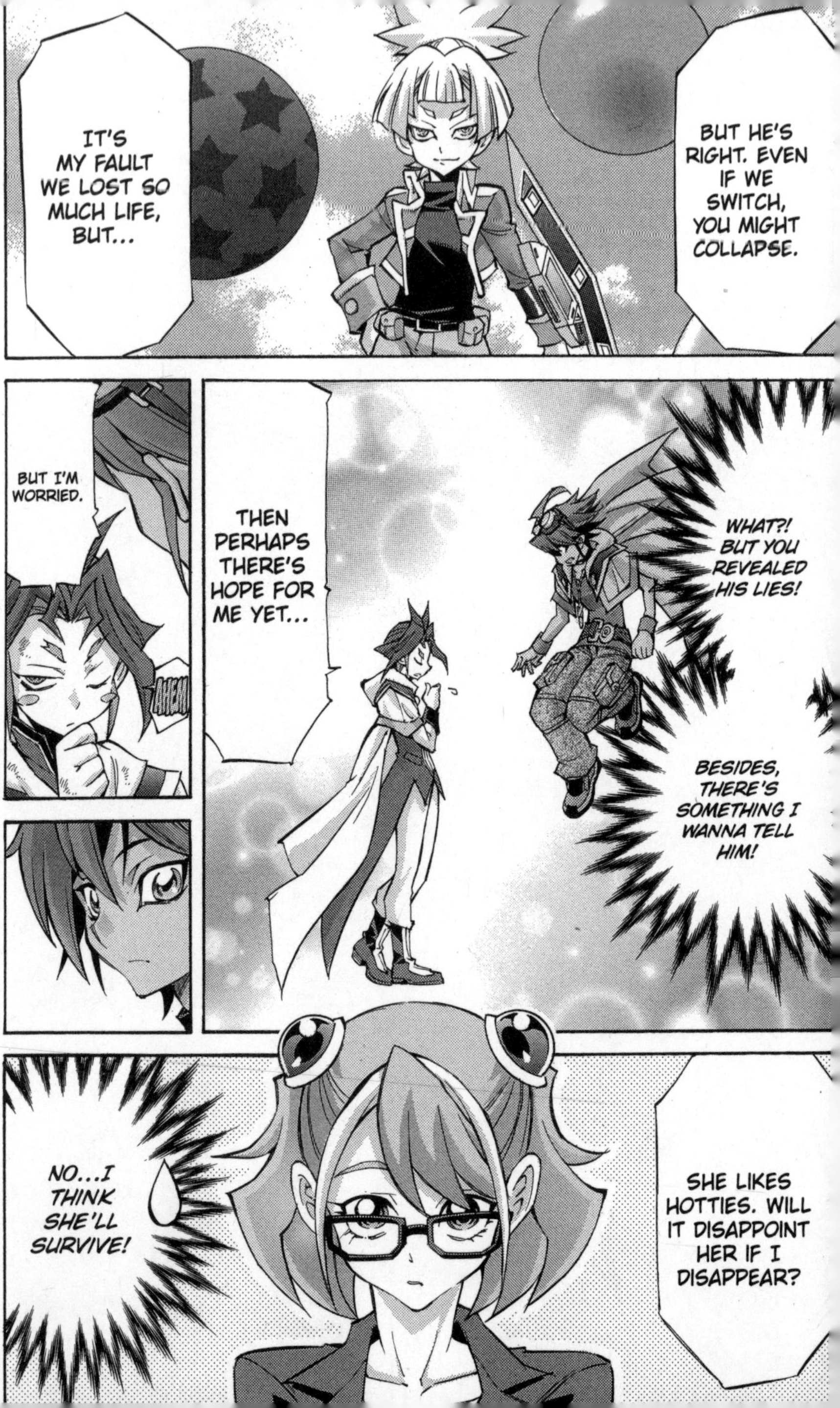
BUT HE'S RIGHT. EVEN IF WE SWITCH, YOU MIGHT COLLAPSE.
IT'S MY FAULT WE LOST SO MUCH LIFE, BUT...
WHAT?! BUT YOU REVEALED HIS LIES!
BESIDES, THERE'S SOMETHING I WANNA TELL HIM!
THEN PERHAPS THERE'S HOPE FOR ME YET...
BUT I'M WORRIED.
AHEM
SHE LIKES HOTTIES. WILL IT DISAPPOINT HER IF I DISAPPEAR?
NO...I THINK SHE'LL SURVIVE!

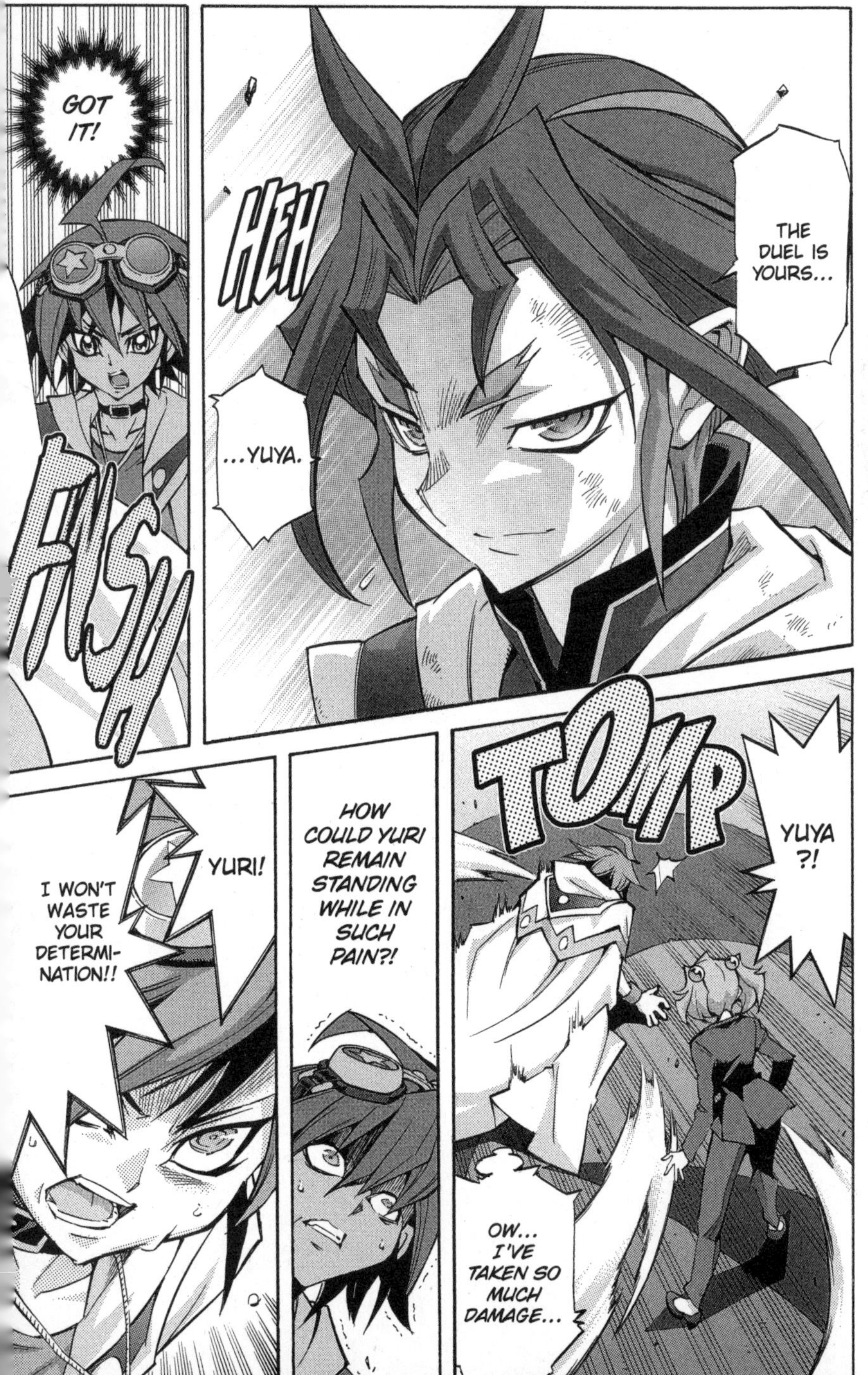
THE DUEL IS YOURS...
HEH
...YUYA.
GOT IT!
YUYA ?!
OW... I'VE TAKEN SO MUCH DAMAGE...
HOW COULD YURI REMAIN STANDING WHILE IN SUCH PAIN?!
YURI!
I WON'T WASTE YOUR DETERMINATION!!

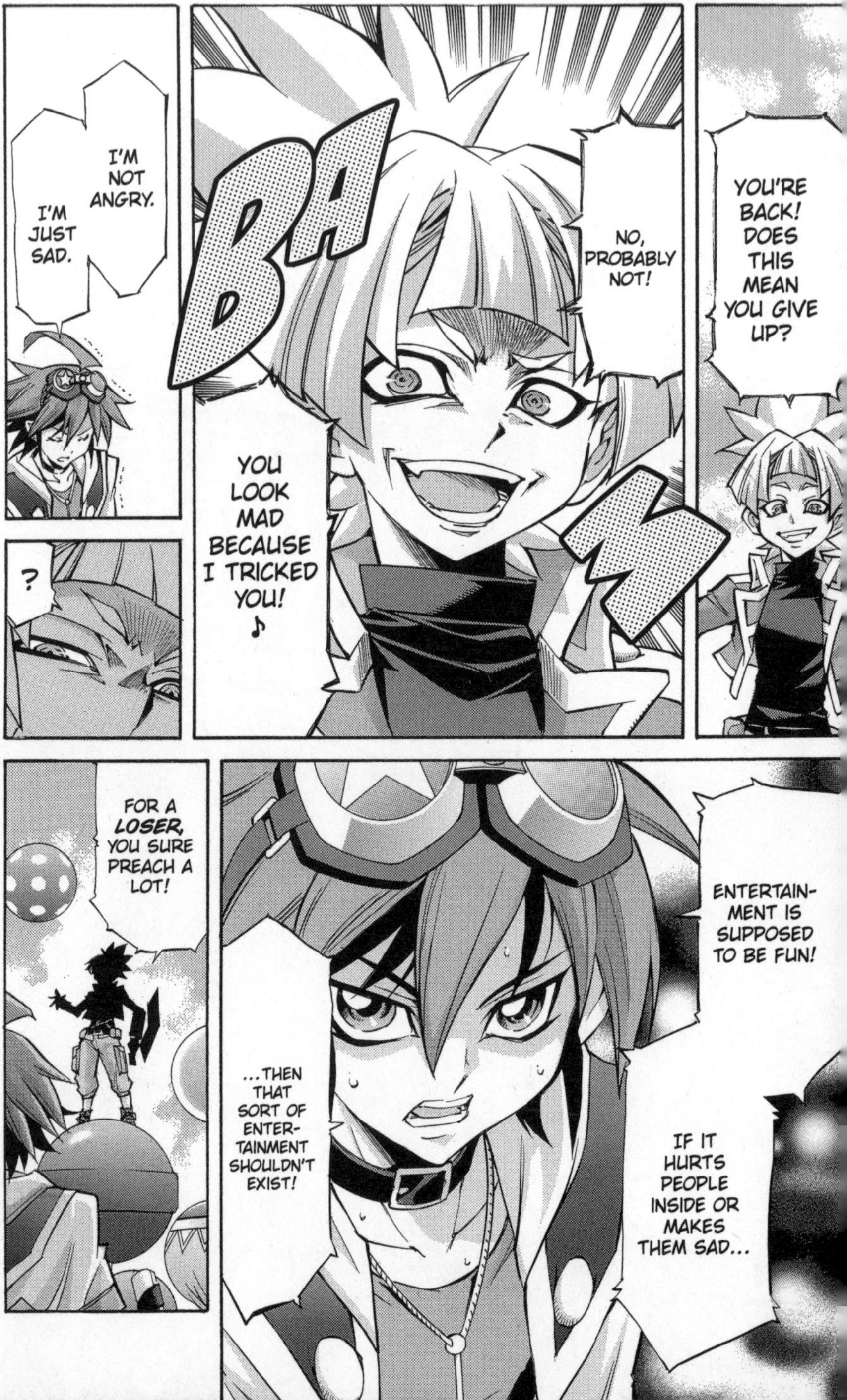

YOU'RE BACK! DOES THIS MEAN YOU GIVE UP?
NO, PROBABLY NOT!
BA
M
YOU LOOK MAD BECAUSE I TRICKED YOU! ♪
I'M NOT ANGRY.
I'M JUST SAD.
?
ENTERTAINMENT IS SUPPOSED TO BE FUN!
IF IT HURTS PEOPLE INSIDE OR MAKES THEM SAD...
...THEN THAT SORT OF ENTERTAINMENT SHOULDN'T EXIST!
FOR A *LOSER*, YOU SURE PREACH A LOT!

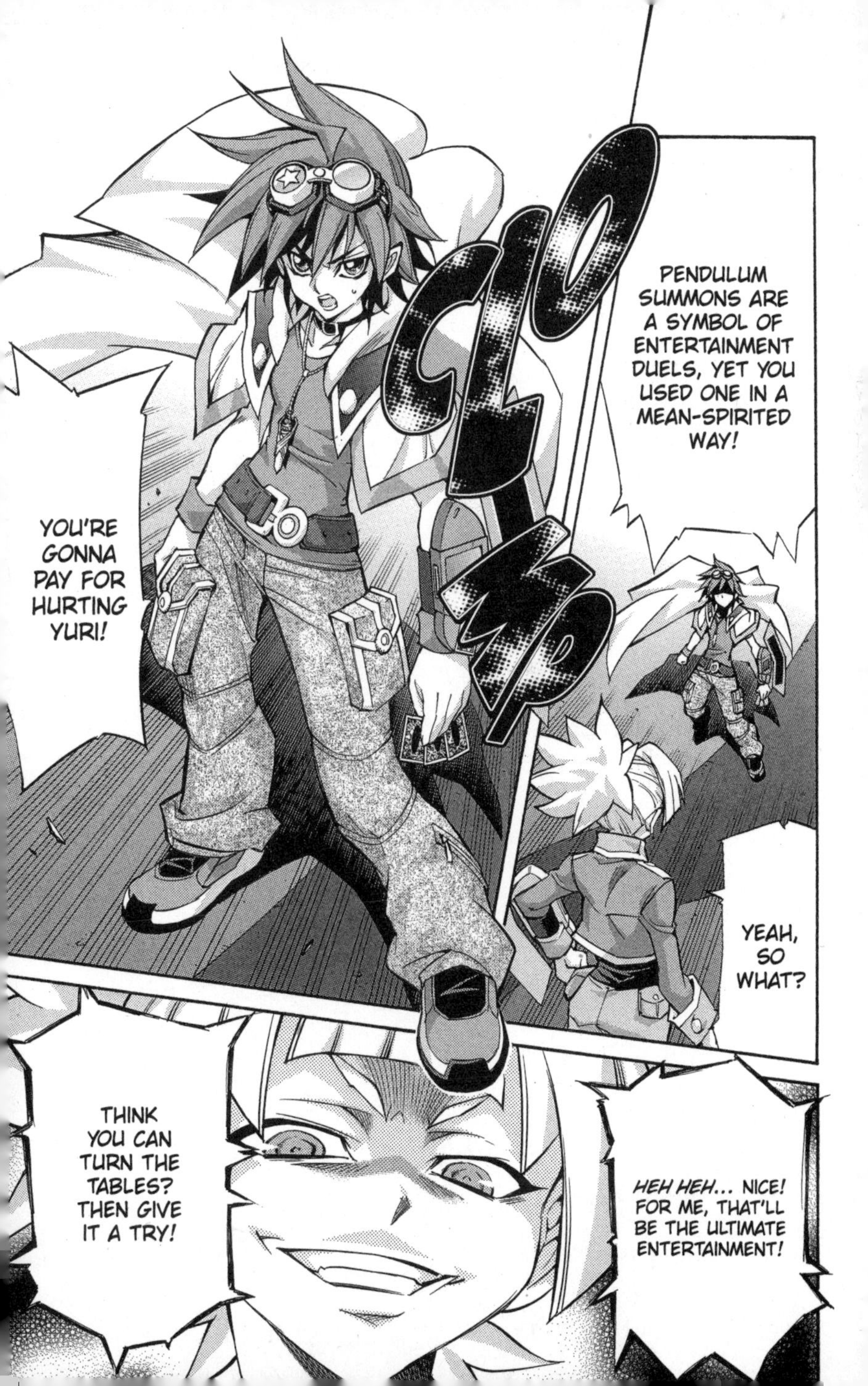
PENDULUM SUMMONS ARE A SYMBOL OF ENTERTAINMENT DUELS, YET YOU USED ONE IN A MEAN-SPIRITED WAY!
CLOMP
YOU'RE GONNA PAY FOR HURTING YURI!
YEAH, SO WHAT?
HEH HEH... NICE! FOR ME, THAT'LL BE THE ULTIMATE ENTERTAINMENT!
THINK YOU CAN TURN THE TABLES? THEN GIVE IT A TRY!

YURI

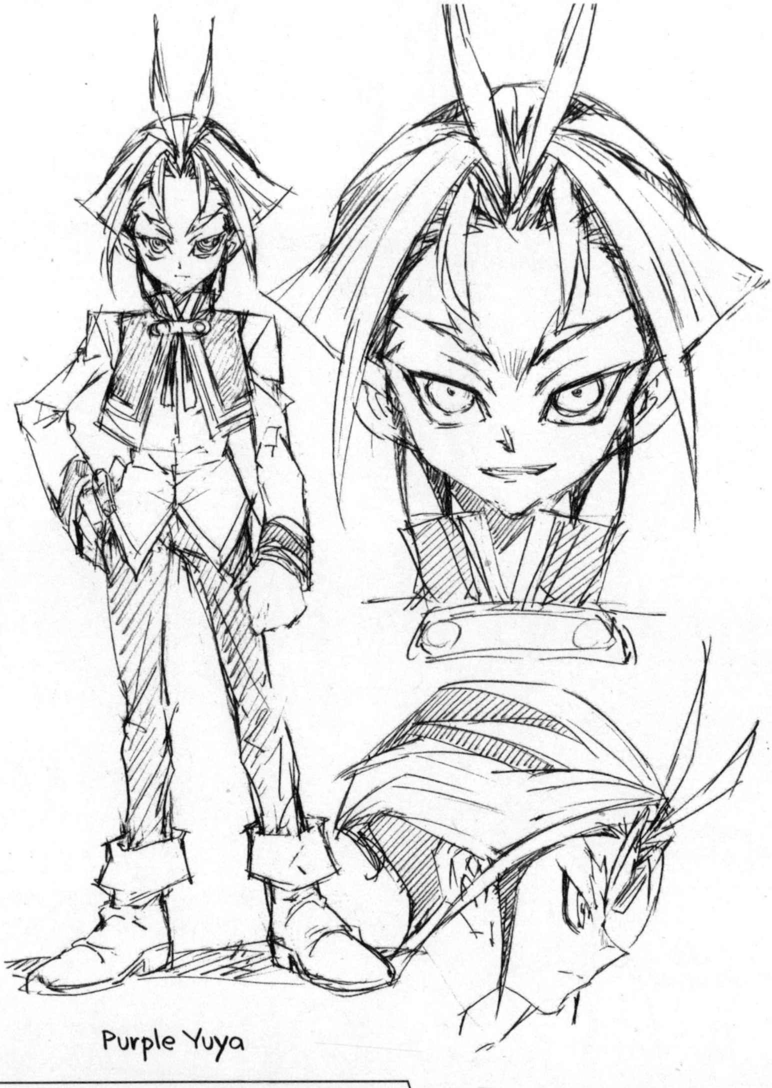
Purple Yuya

Here's Yuri, who entered the story as Yuya's third personality. His design hasn't changed much since early on. Was his ability to spot "vulgar scum" there from the beginning too?

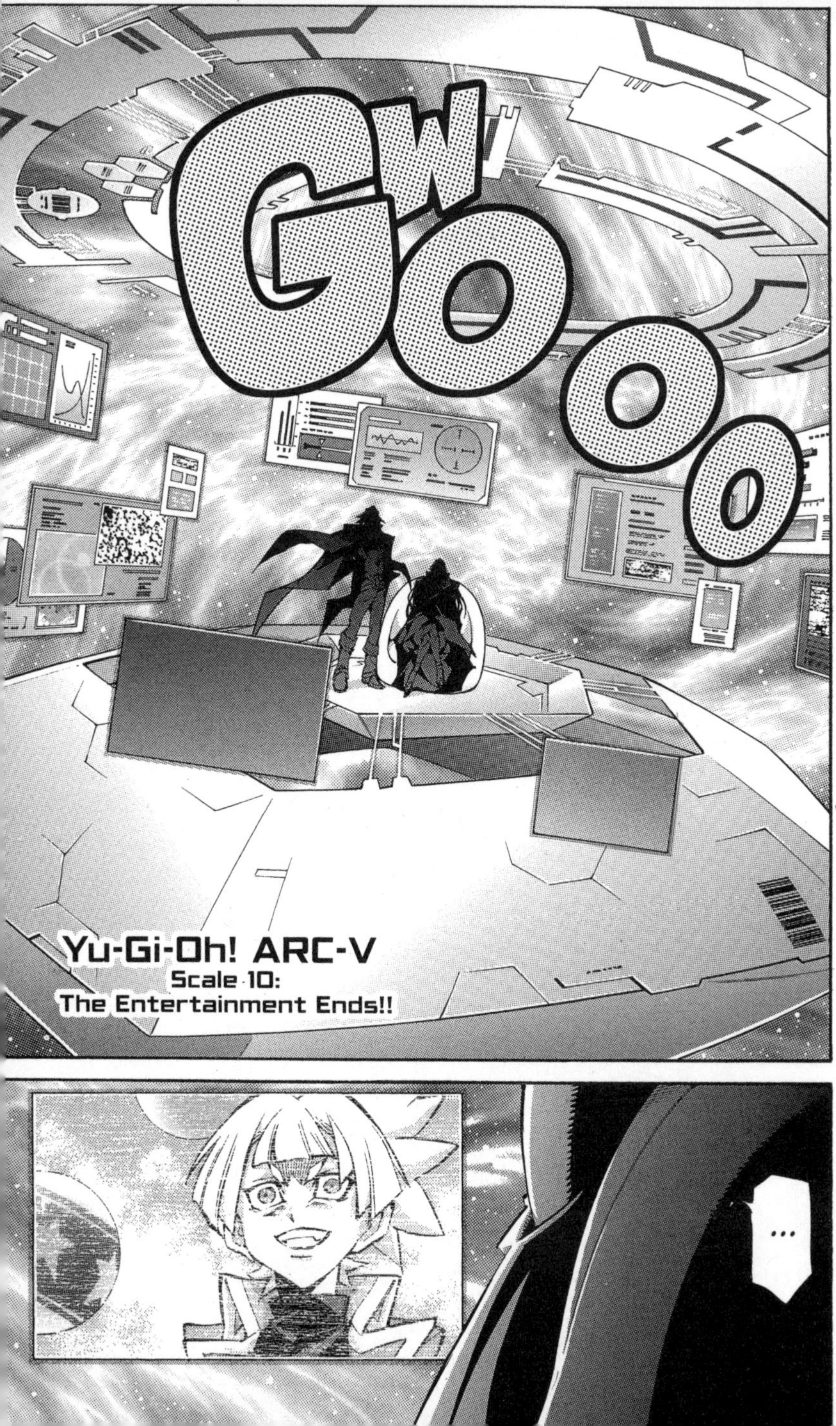
GWOOOOO
Yu-Gi-Oh! ARC-V
Scale 10:
The Entertainment Ends!!
...

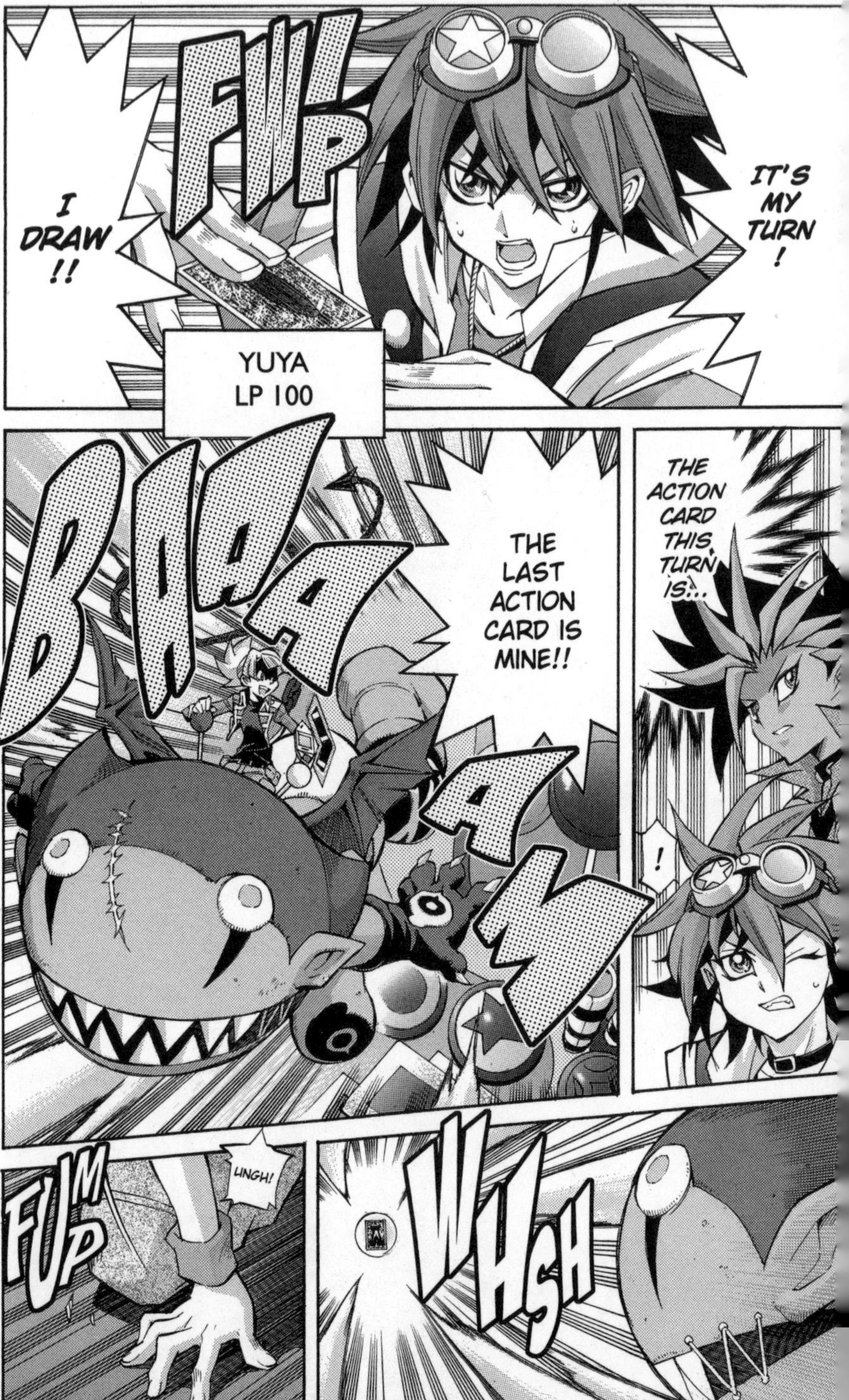
IT'S MY TURN!
FWIP
I DRAW!!
YUYA
LP 100
THE ACTION CARD THIS TURN IS...
THE LAST ACTION CARD IS MINE!!
WHSH
UNGH!
FUMP

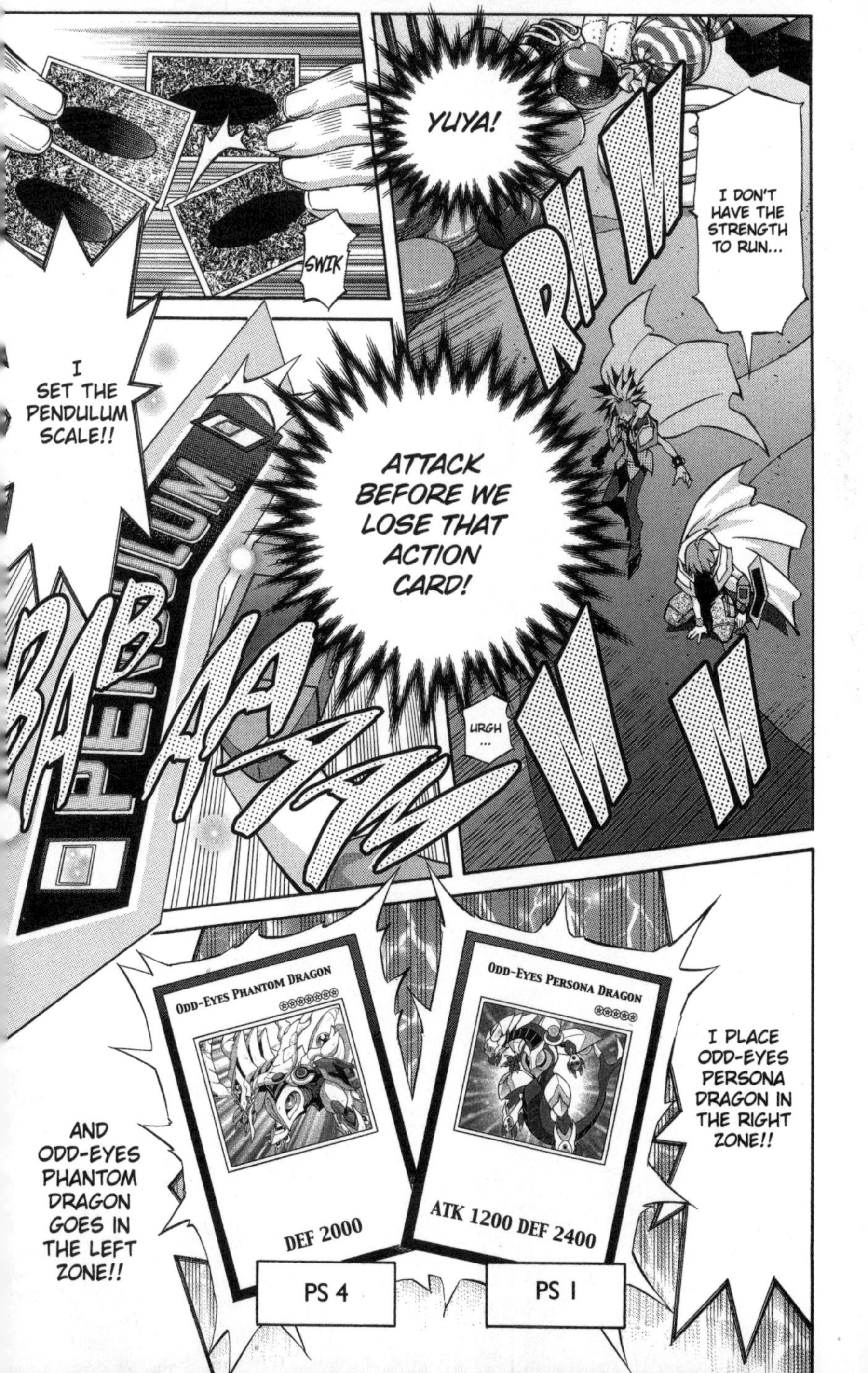
YUYA!
I DON'T HAVE THE STRENGTH TO RUN...
ATTACK BEFORE WE LOSE THAT ACTION CARD!
URGH ...
SWIK
I SET THE PENDULUM SCALE!!
PENDULUM
I PLACE ODD-EYES PERSONA DRAGON IN THE RIGHT ZONE!!
ODD-EYES PERSONA DRAGON
ATK 1200 DEF 2400
PS 1
ODD-EYES PHANTOM DRAGON
DEF 2000
PS 4
AND ODD-EYES PHANTOM DRAGON GOES IN THE LEFT ZONE!!

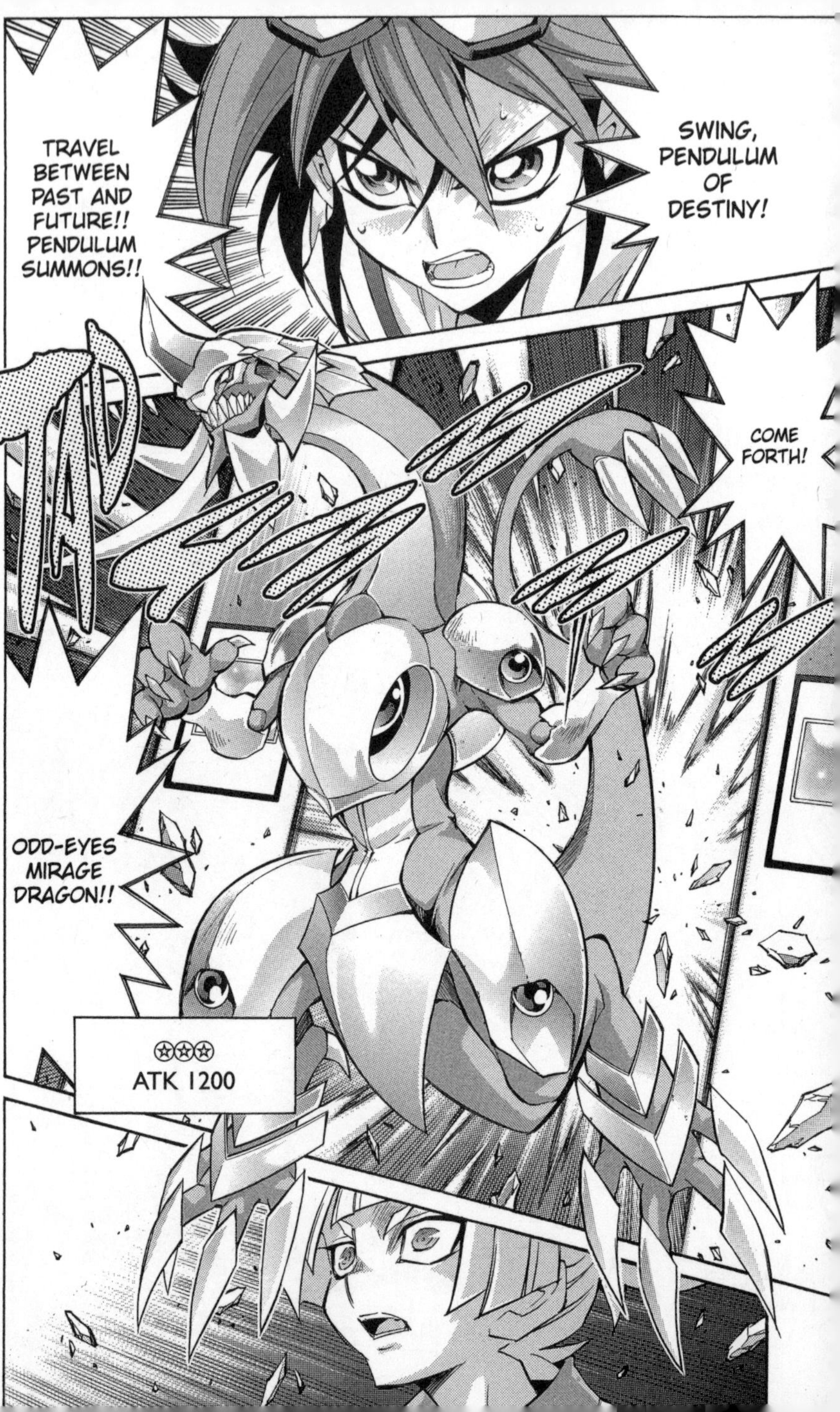
SWING, PENDULUM OF DESTINY!
TRAVEL BETWEEN PAST AND FUTURE!! PENDULUM SUMMONS!!
COME FORTH!
TAP
ODD-EYES MIRAGE DRAGON!!
ATK 1200

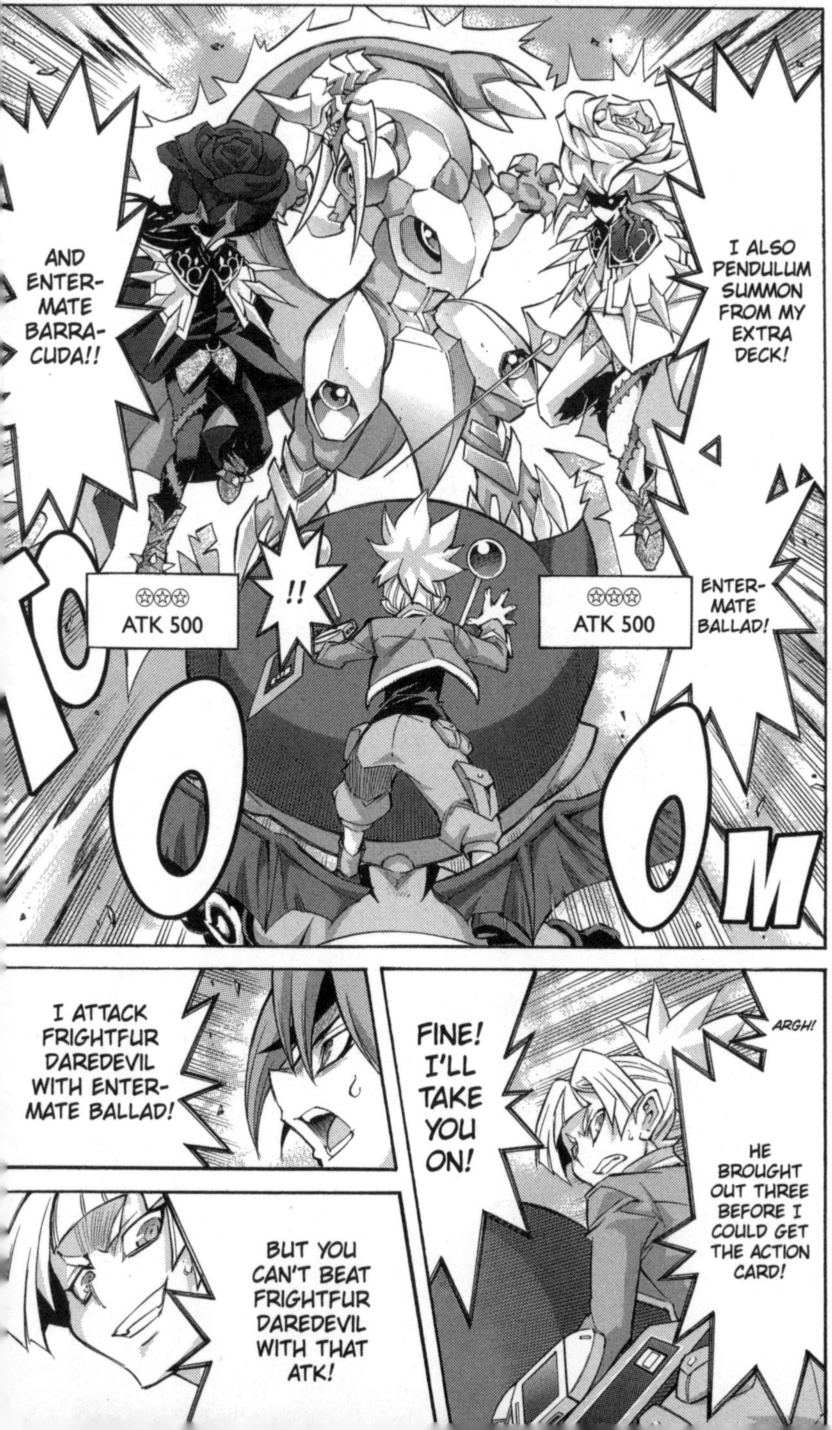
I ALSO PENDULUM SUMMON FROM MY EXTRA DECK!
ENTER-MATE BALLAD!
ATK 500
!!
ATK 500
AND ENTER-MATE BARRACUDA!!
ARGH!
FINE! I'LL TAKE YOU ON!
HE BROUGHT OUT THREE BEFORE I COULD GET THE ACTION CARD!
I ATTACK FRIGHTFUR DAREDEVIL WITH ENTER-MATE BALLAD!
BUT YOU CAN'T BEAT FRIGHTFUR DAREDEVIL WITH THAT ATK!

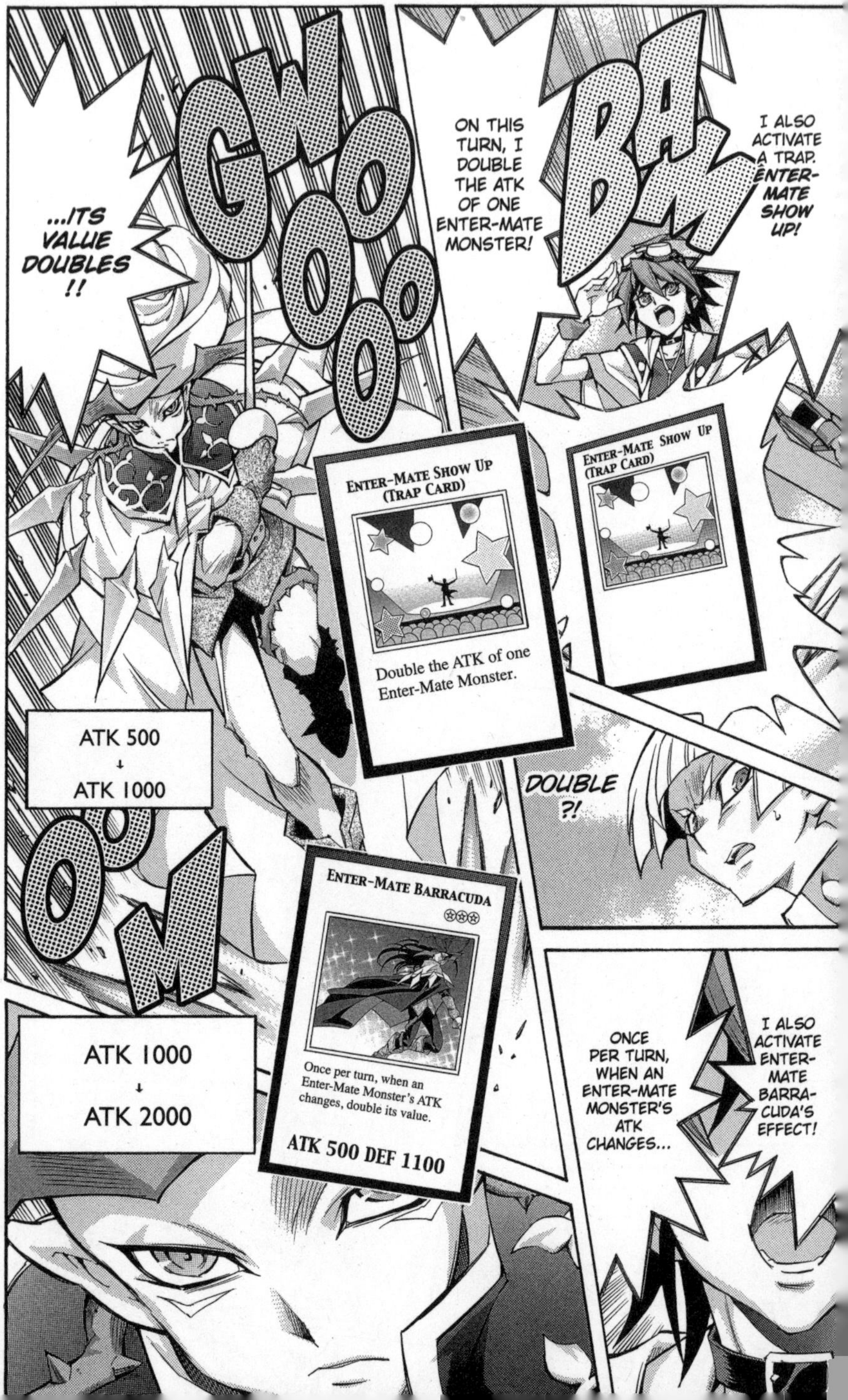
BAM
I ALSO ACTIVATE A TRAP. ENTER-MATE SHOW UP!
ON THIS TURN, I DOUBLE THE ATK OF ONE ENTER-MATE MONSTER!
ENTER-MATE SHOW UP (TRAP CARD)
ENTER-MATE SHOW UP (TRAP CARD)
Double the ATK of one Enter-Mate Monster.
DOUBLE ?!
I ALSO ACTIVATE ENTER-MATE BARRACUDA'S EFFECT!
ONCE PER TURN, WHEN AN ENTER-MATE MONSTER'S ATK CHANGES...
...ITS VALUE DOUBLES !!
GWOOOOOOOOM
ATK 500 ↓ ATK 1000
ENTER-MATE BARRACUDA
Once per turn, when an Enter-Mate Monster's ATK changes, double its value.
ATK 500 DEF 1100
ATK 1000 ↓ ATK 2000

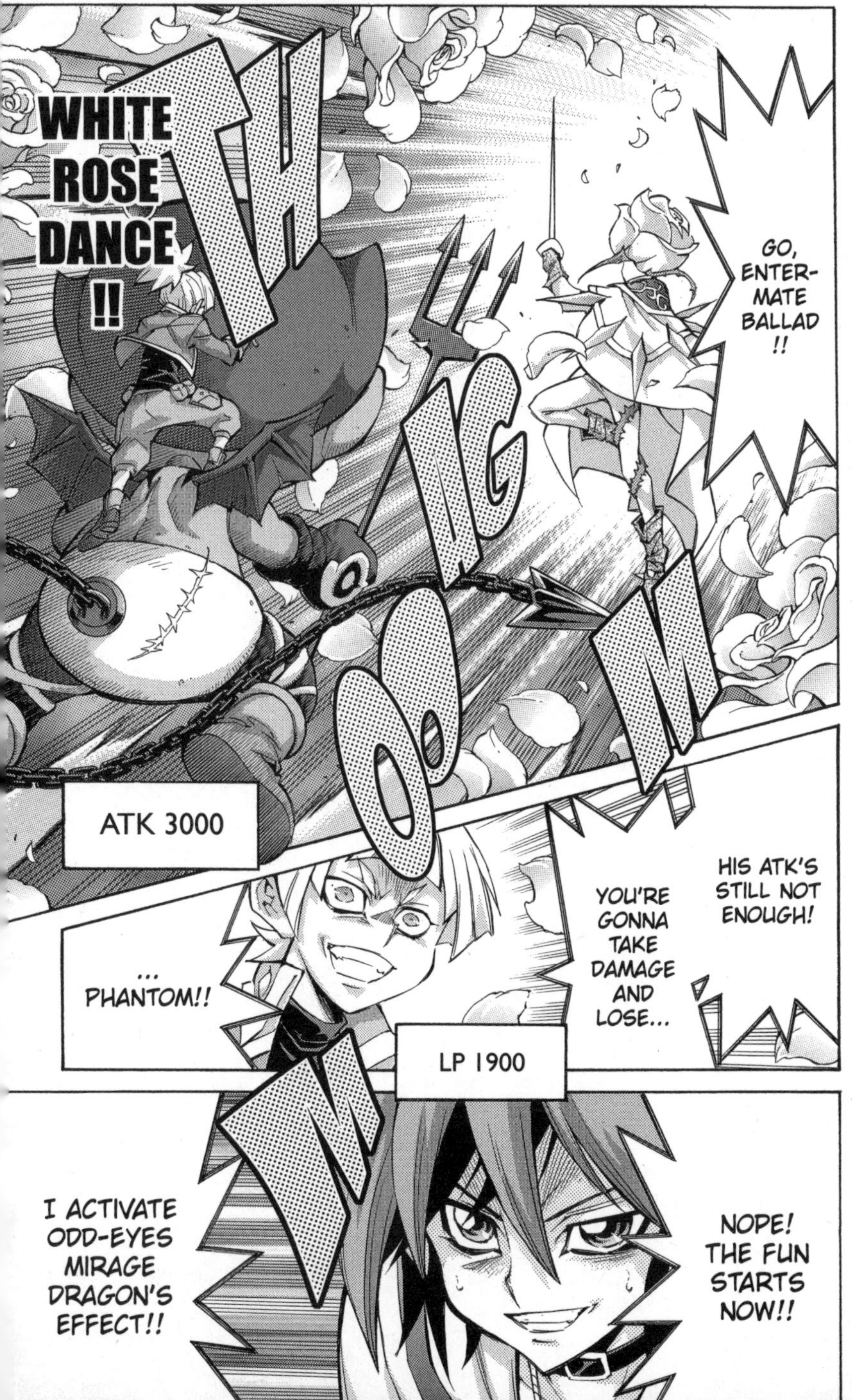

GO, ENTER-MATE BALLAD!!
WHITE ROSE DANCE!!
ATK 3000
HIS ATK'S STILL NOT ENOUGH!
YOU'RE GONNA TAKE DAMAGE AND LOSE...
... PHANTOM!!
LP 1900
NOPE! THE FUN STARTS NOW!!
I ACTIVATE ODD-EYES MIRAGE DRAGON'S EFFECT!!

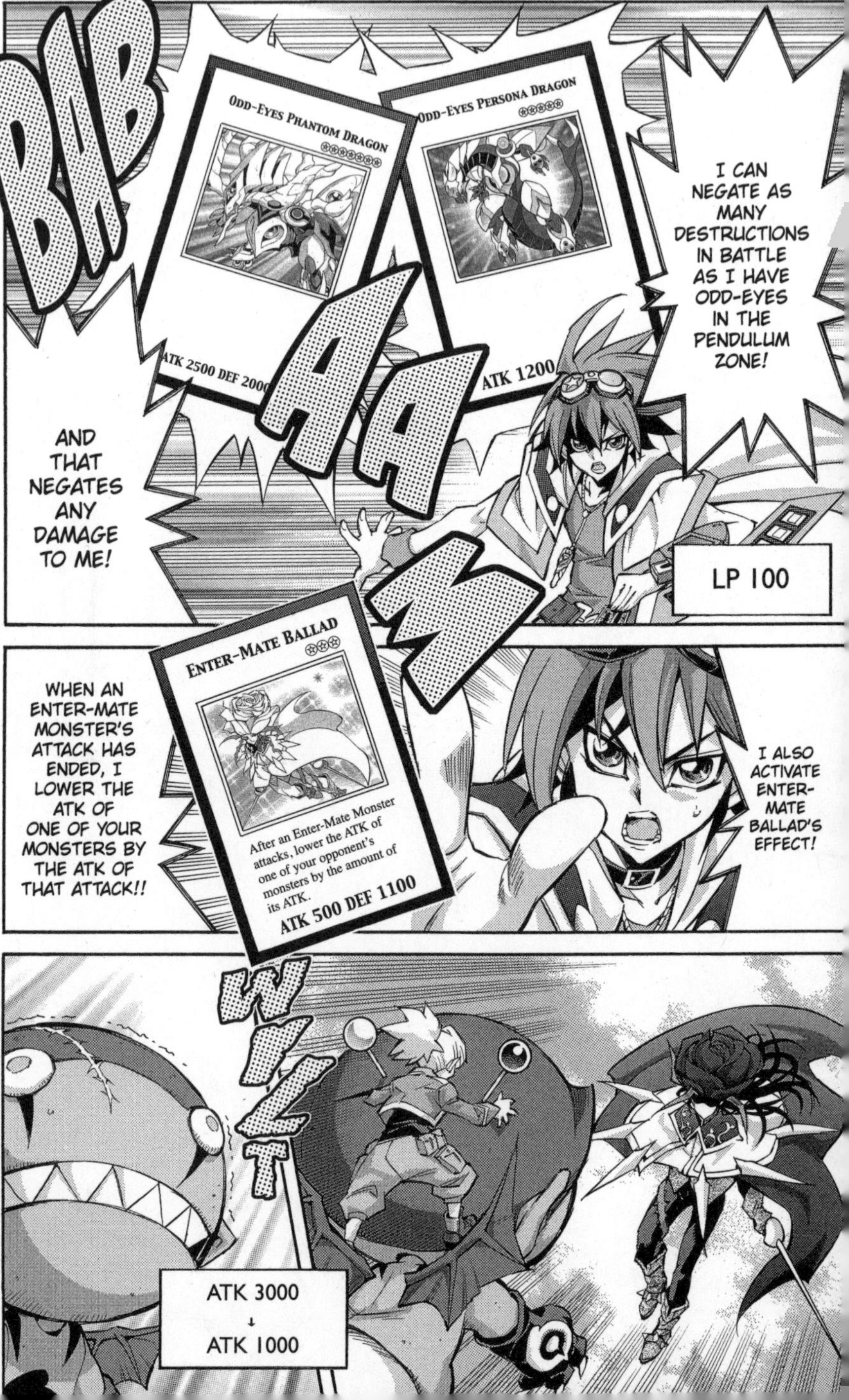
I CAN NEGATE AS MANY DESTRUCTIONS IN BATTLE AS I HAVE ODD-EYES IN THE PENDULUM ZONE!
ODD-EYES PERSONA DRAGON
ATK 1200
ODD-EYES PHANTOM DRAGON
ATK 2500 DEF 2000
BAB
AAM
AND THAT NEGATES ANY DAMAGE TO ME!
LP 100
I ALSO ACTIVATE ENTER-MATE BALLAD'S EFFECT!
ENTER-MATE BALLAD
After an Enter-Mate Monster attacks, lower the ATK of one of your opponent's monsters by the amount of its ATK.
ATK 500 DEF 1100
WHEN AN ENTER-MATE MONSTER'S ATTACK HAS ENDED, I LOWER THE ATK OF ONE OF YOUR MONSTERS BY THE ATK OF THAT ATTACK!!
WIZT
ATK 3000
↓
ATK 1000

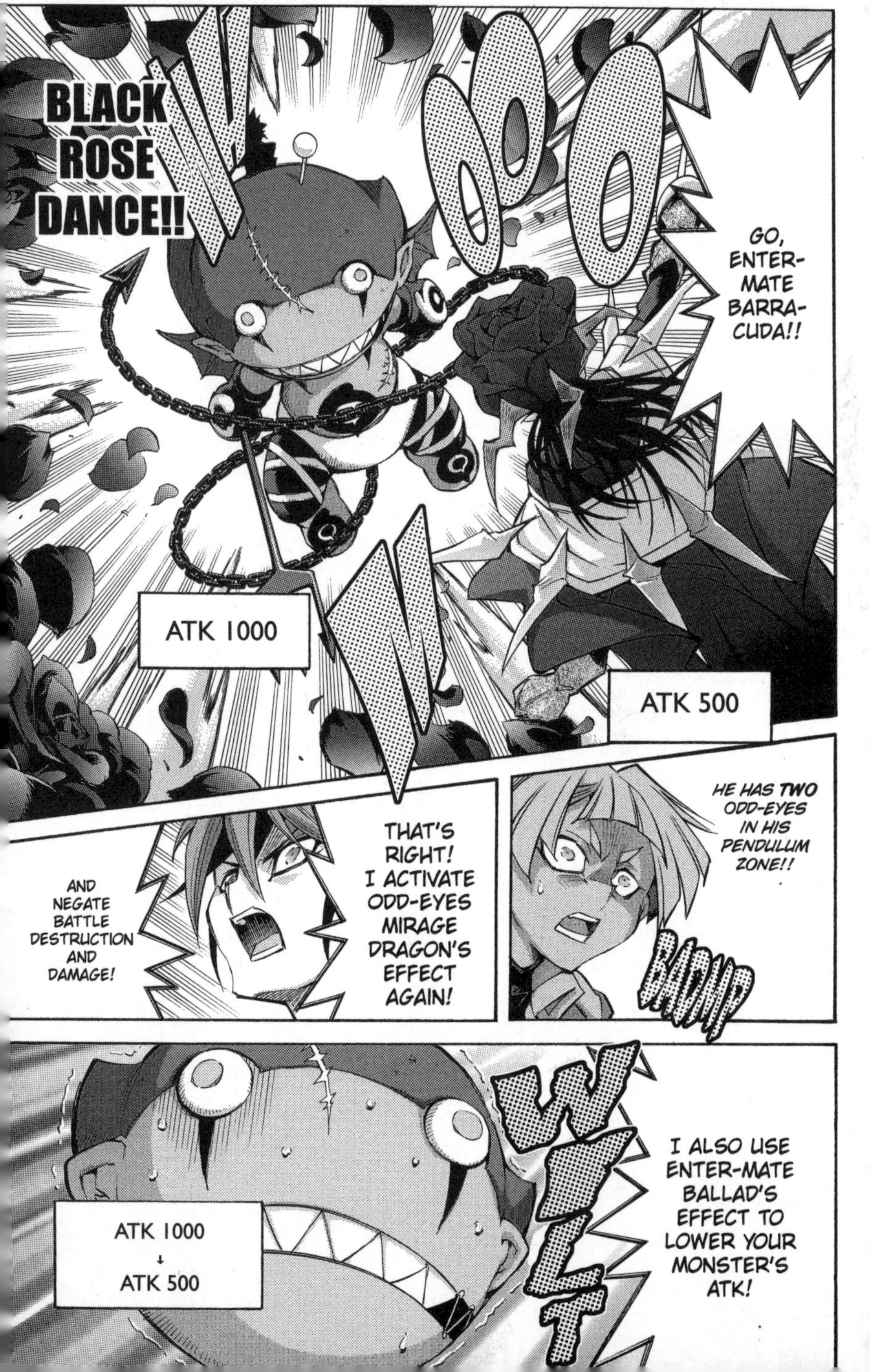
GO, ENTER-MATE BARRACUDA!!
BLACK ROSE DANCE!!
ATK 1000
ATK 500
HE HAS **TWO** ODD-EYES IN HIS PENDULUM ZONE!!
BADUMP
THAT'S RIGHT! I ACTIVATE ODD-EYES MIRAGE DRAGON'S EFFECT AGAIN!
AND NEGATE BATTLE DESTRUCTION AND DAMAGE!
I ALSO USE ENTER-MATE BALLAD'S EFFECT TO LOWER YOUR MONSTER'S ATK!
WILT
ATK 1000 ↓ ATK 500

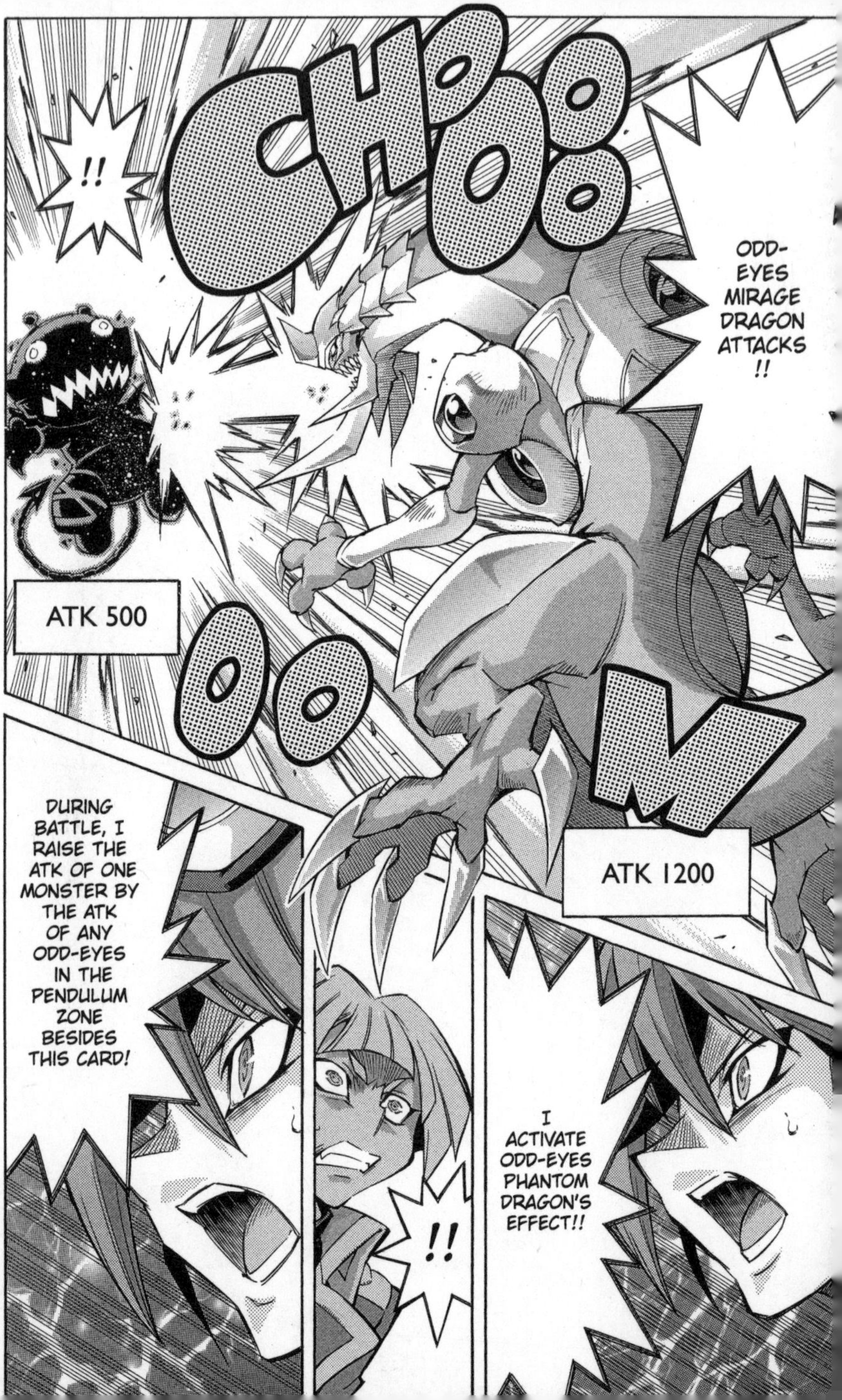
ODD-EYES MIRAGE DRAGON ATTACKS!!
CHOOOO
!!
ATK 500
OOM
ATK 1200
I ACTIVATE ODD-EYES PHANTOM DRAGON'S EFFECT!!
!!
DURING BATTLE, I RAISE THE ATK OF ONE MONSTER BY THE ATK OF ANY ODD-EYES IN THE PENDULUM ZONE BESIDES THIS CARD!

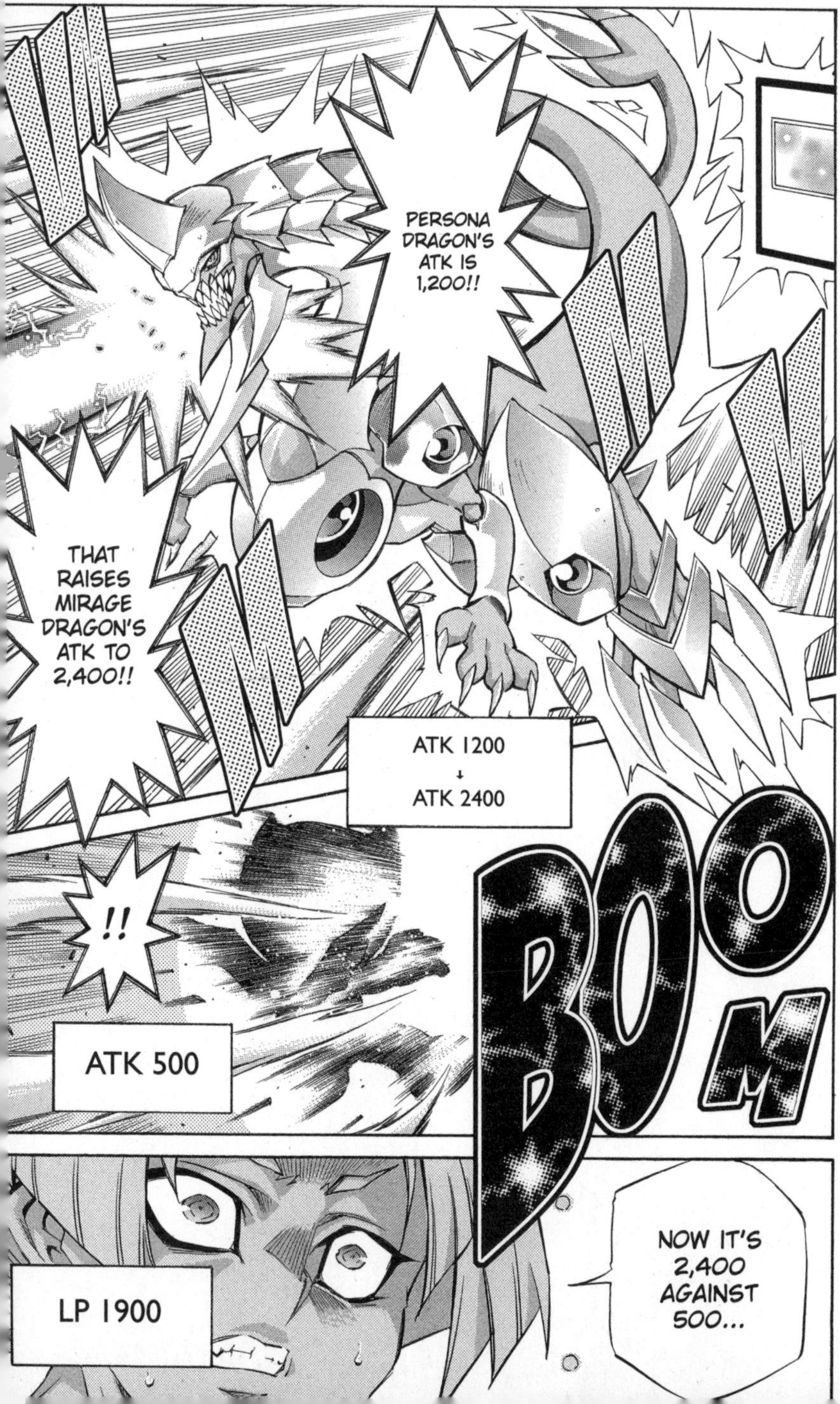
PERSONA DRAGON'S ATK IS 1,200!!
THAT RAISES MIRAGE DRAGON'S ATK TO 2,400!!
ATK 1200 ↓ ATK 2400
BOOM
!!
ATK 500
NOW IT'S 2,400 AGAINST 500...
LP 1900

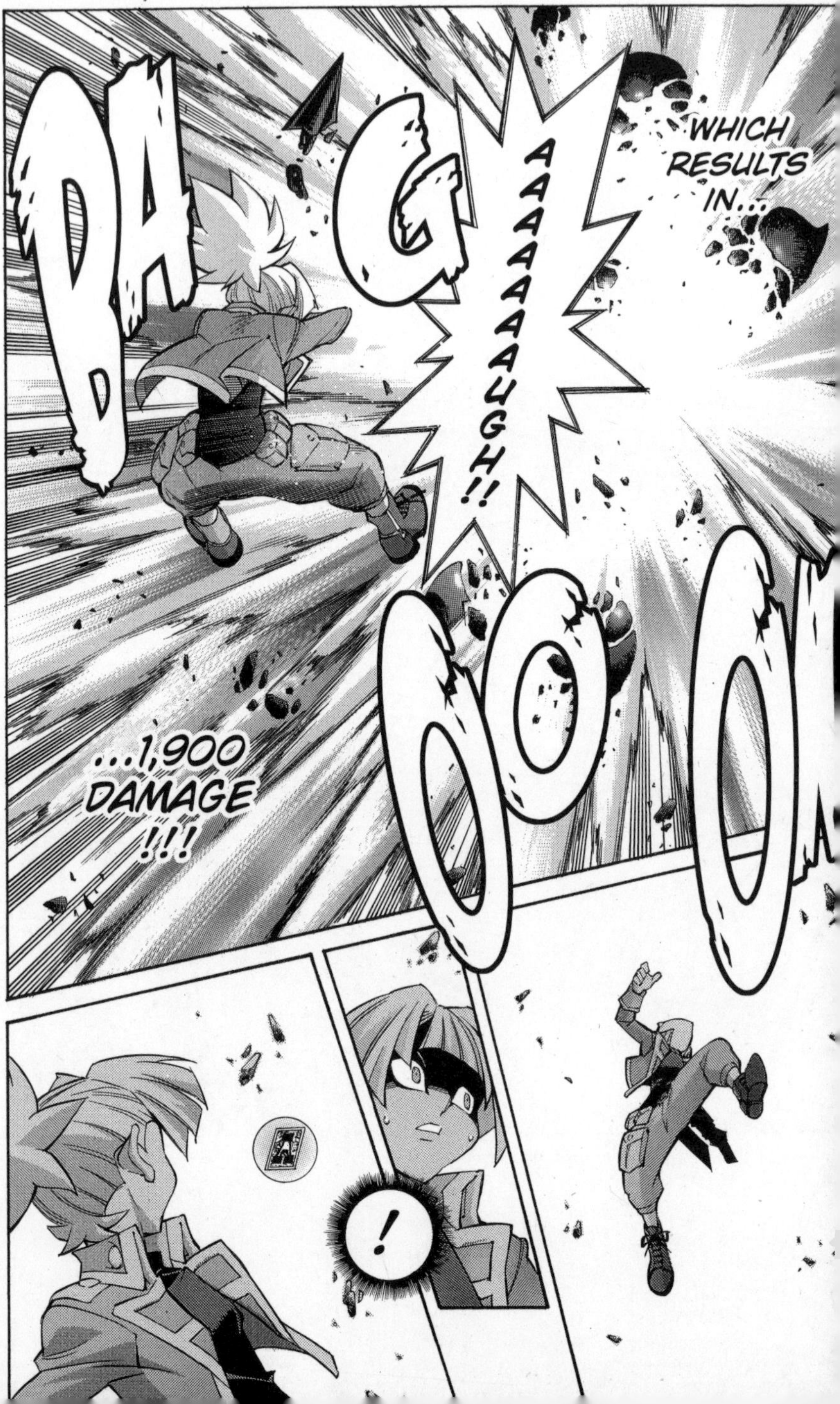
WHICH RESULTS IN...
DA G
AAAAAAAUGH!!
...1,900 DAMAGE !!!
!

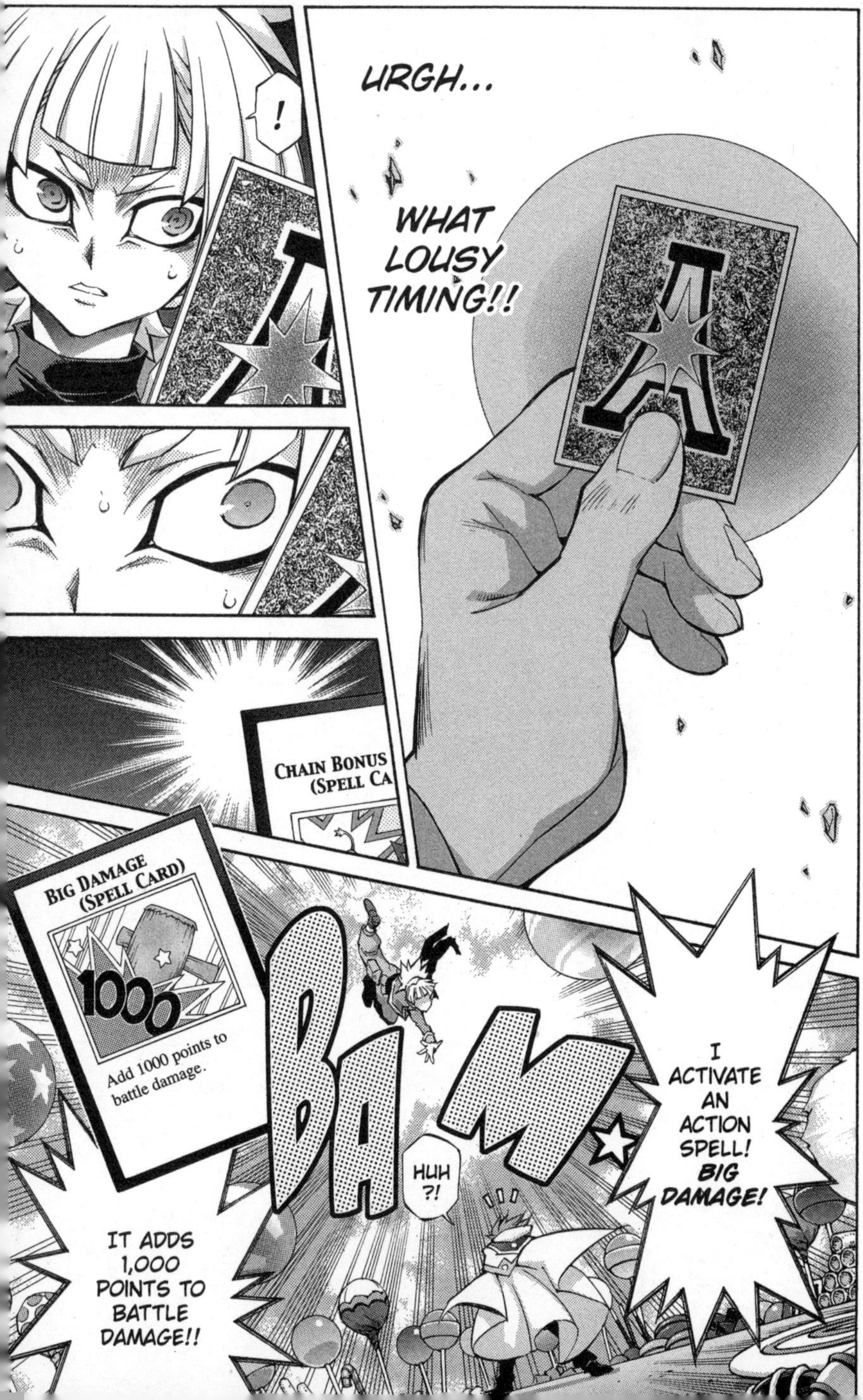
URGH...
WHAT LOUSY TIMING!!
!
CHAIN BONUS (SPELL CA
I ACTIVATE AN ACTION SPELL! BIG DAMAGE!
BAM
HUH ?!
BIG DAMAGE (SPELL CARD)
1000
Add 1000 points to battle damage.
IT ADDS 1,000 POINTS TO BATTLE DAMAGE!!

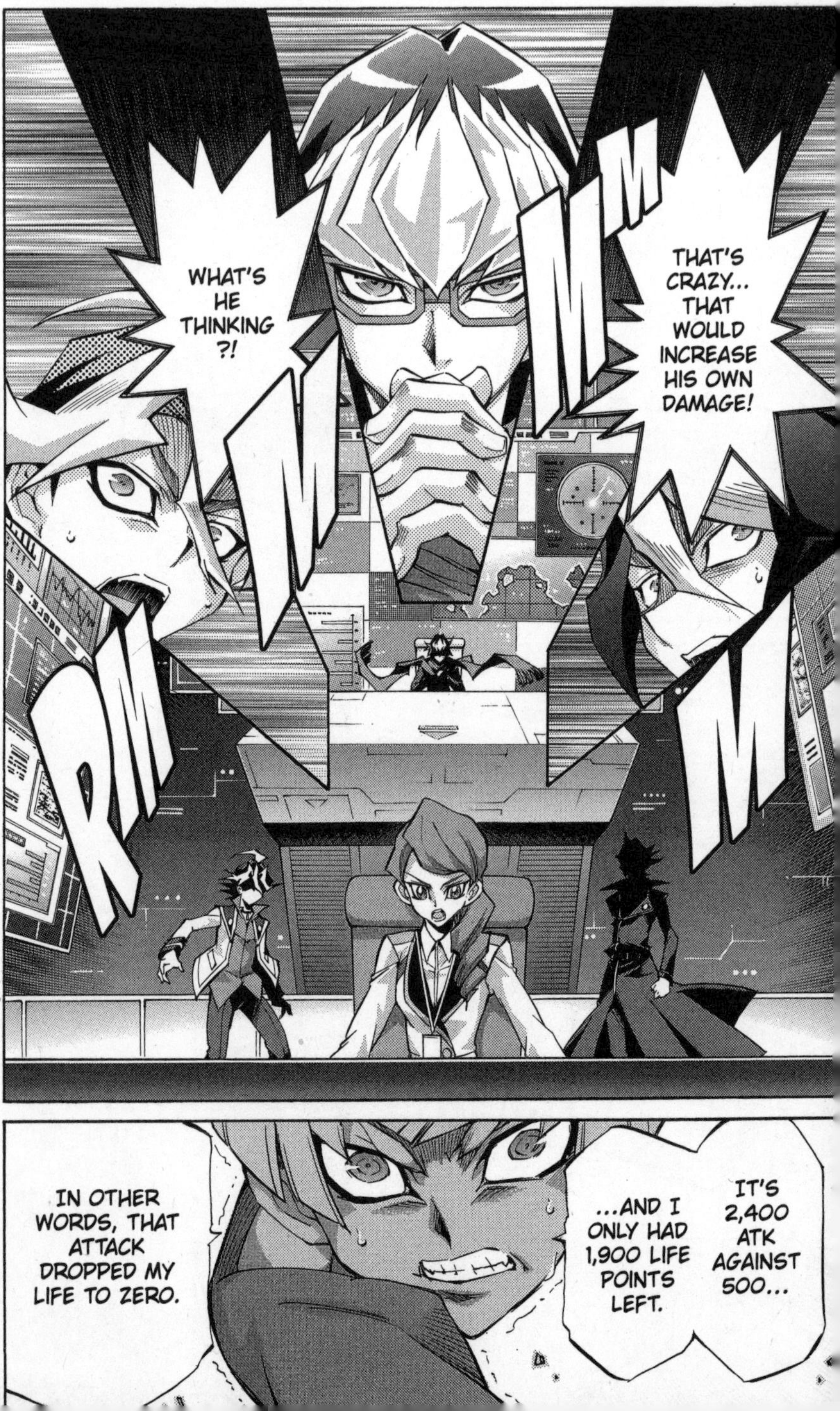
THAT'S CRAZY... THAT WOULD INCREASE HIS OWN DAMAGE!
WHAT'S HE THINKING ?!
IT'S 2,400 ATK AGAINST 500...
...AND I ONLY HAD 1,900 LIFE POINTS LEFT.
IN OTHER WORDS, THAT ATTACK DROPPED MY LIFE TO ZERO.

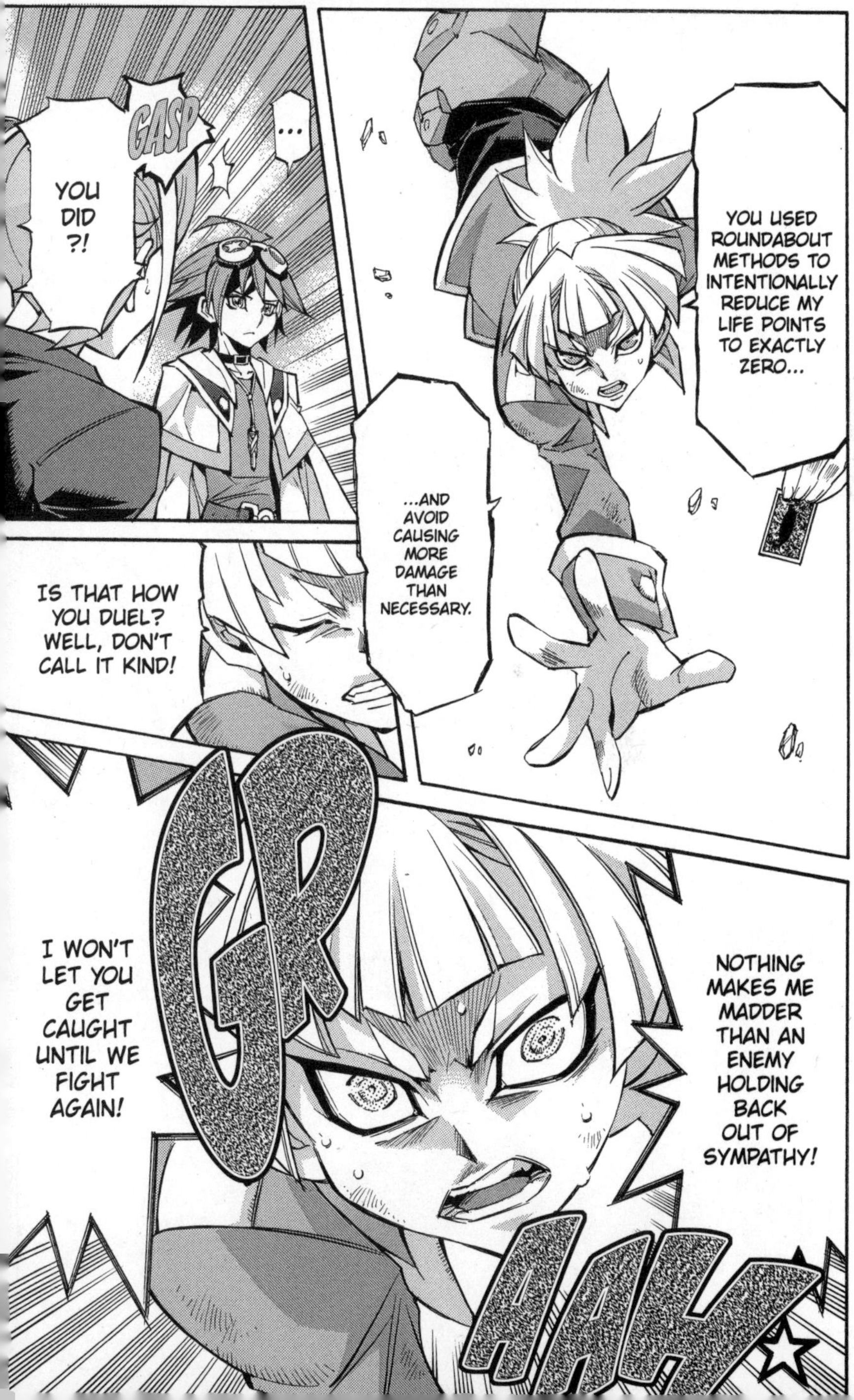
YOU USED ROUNDABOUT METHODS TO INTENTIONALLY REDUCE MY LIFE POINTS TO EXACTLY ZERO...
...AND AVOID CAUSING MORE DAMAGE THAN NECESSARY.
...
GASP
YOU DID ?!
IS THAT HOW YOU DUEL? WELL, DON'T CALL IT KIND!
NOTHING MAKES ME MADDER THAN AN ENEMY HOLDING BACK OUT OF SYMPATHY!
I WON'T LET YOU GET CAUGHT UNTIL WE FIGHT AGAIN!
GR
AAH

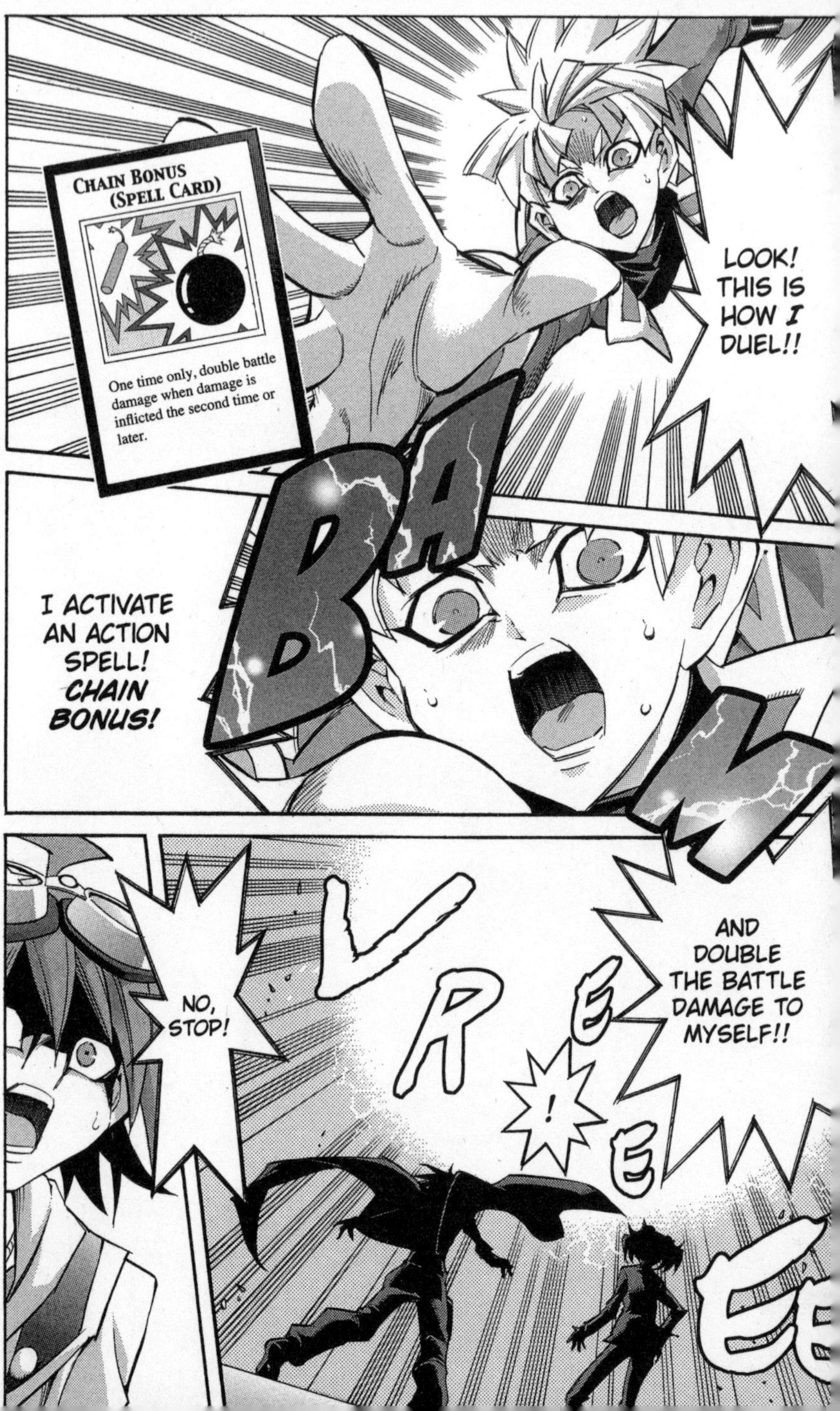
LOOK! THIS IS HOW *I* DUEL!!
CHAIN BONUS (SPELL CARD)
One time only, double battle damage when damage is inflicted the second time or later.
BAM
I ACTIVATE AN ACTION SPELL! *CHAIN BONUS!*
AND DOUBLE THE BATTLE DAMAGE TO MYSELF!!
VREE
!
NO, STOP!

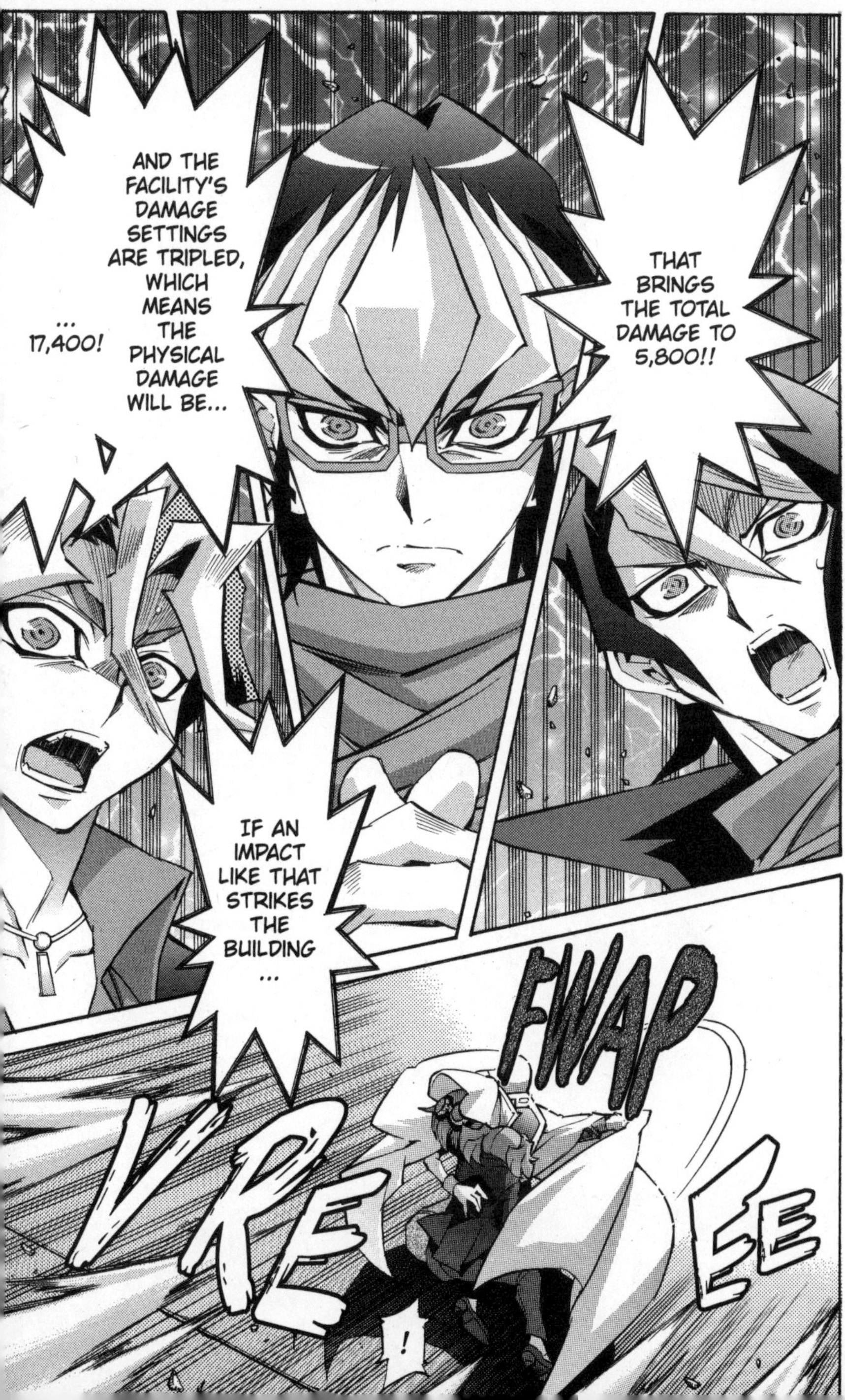
THAT BRINGS THE TOTAL DAMAGE TO 5,800!!
AND THE FACILITY'S DAMAGE SETTINGS ARE TRIPLED, WHICH MEANS THE PHYSICAL DAMAGE WILL BE...
... 17,400!
IF AN IMPACT LIKE THAT STRIKES THE BUILDING ...
FWAP
VREEE
!

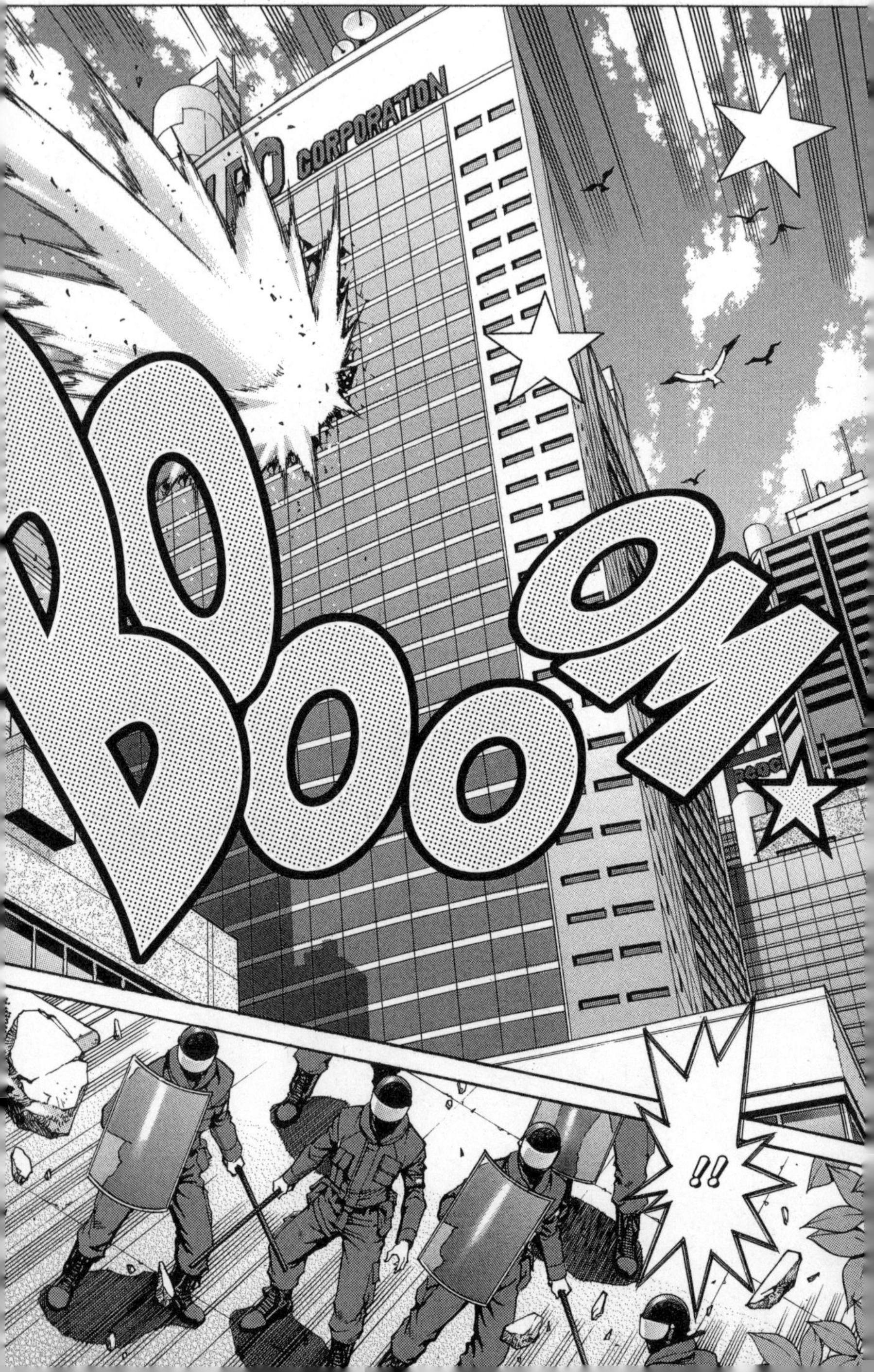
CORPORATION
BOOOM
!!

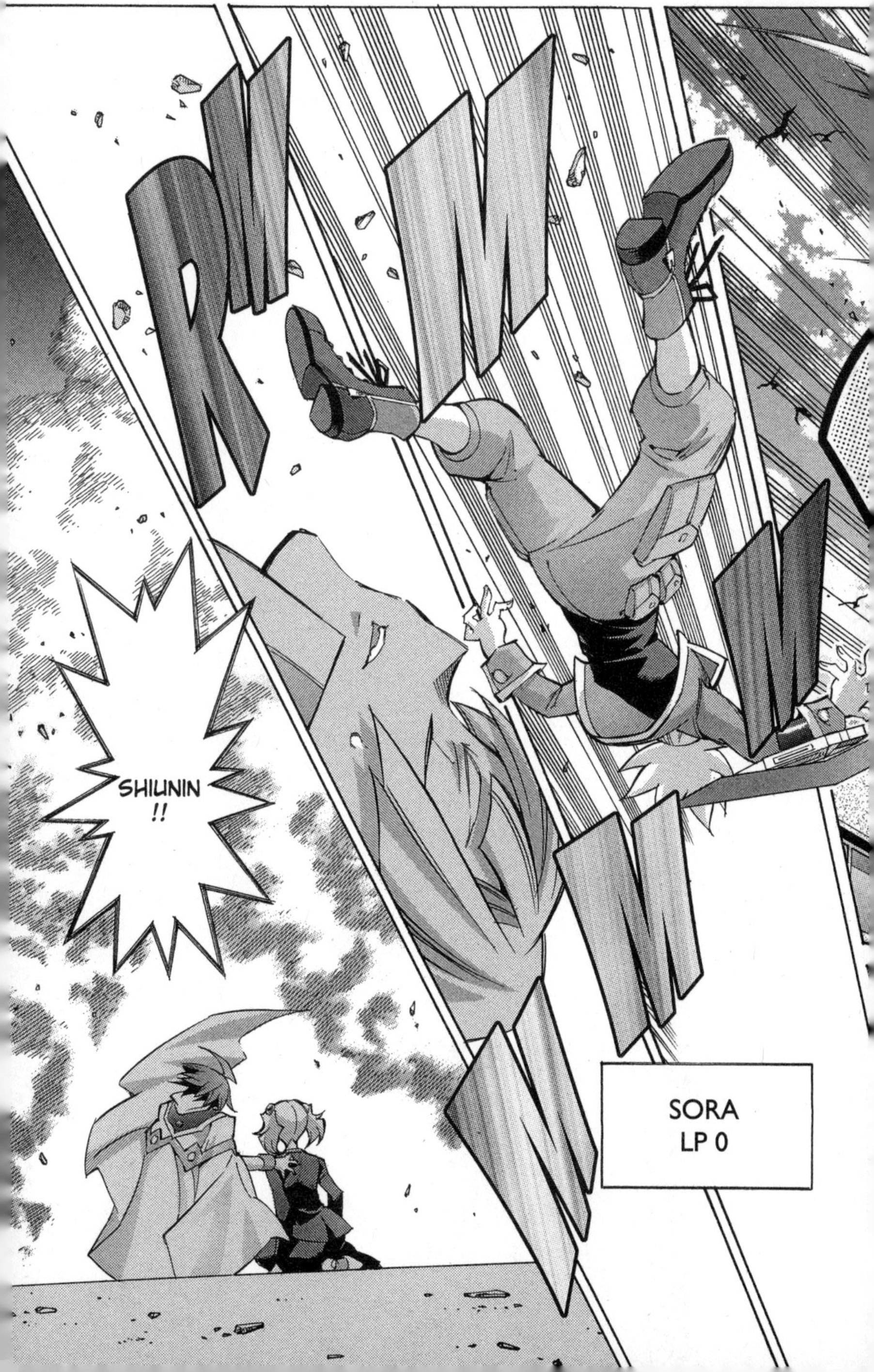
SHIUNIN !!
SORA LP 0

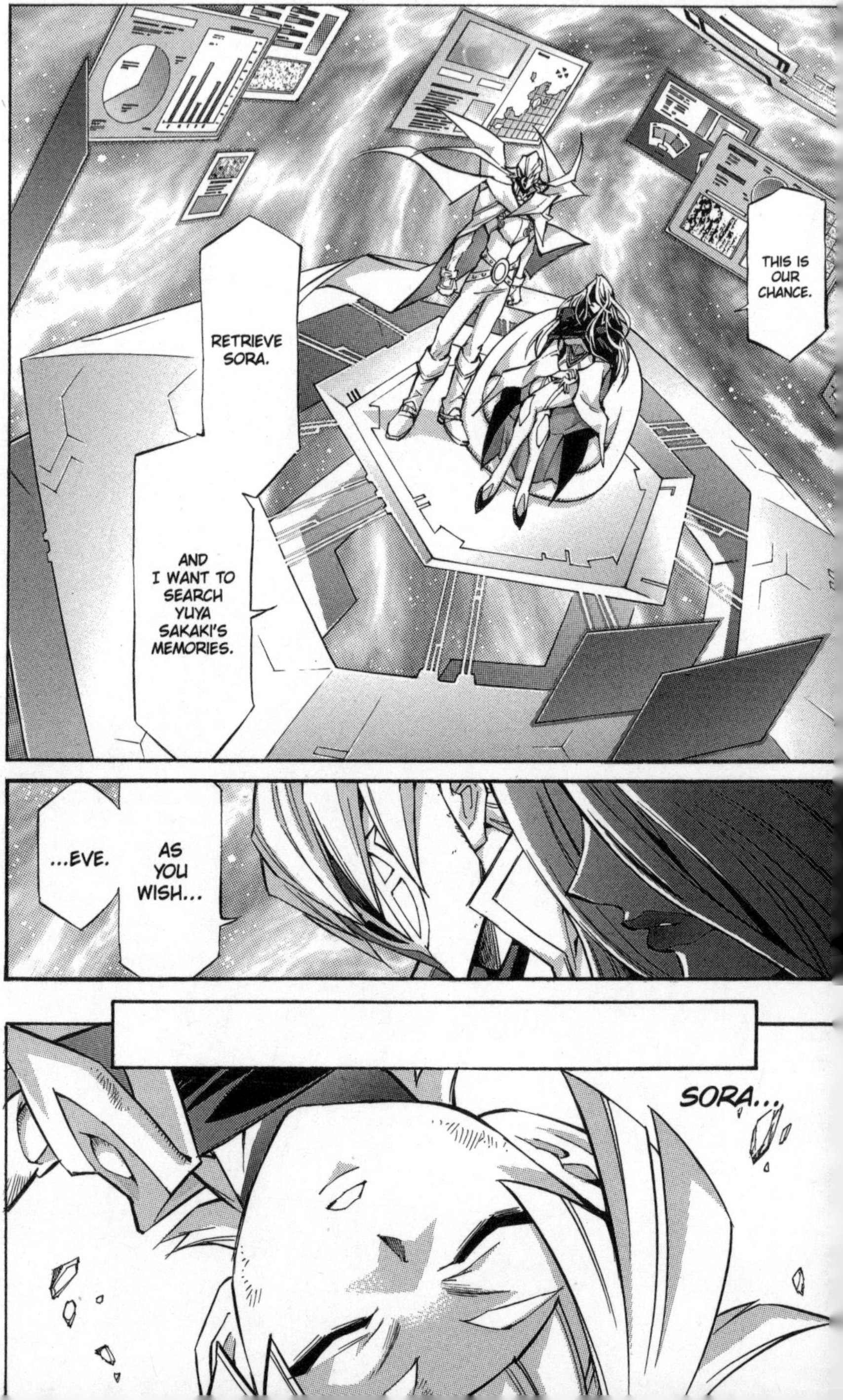
THIS IS OUR CHANCE.
RETRIEVE SORA.
AND I WANT TO SEARCH YUYA SAKAKI'S MEMORIES.
AS YOU WISH...
...EVE.
SORA...

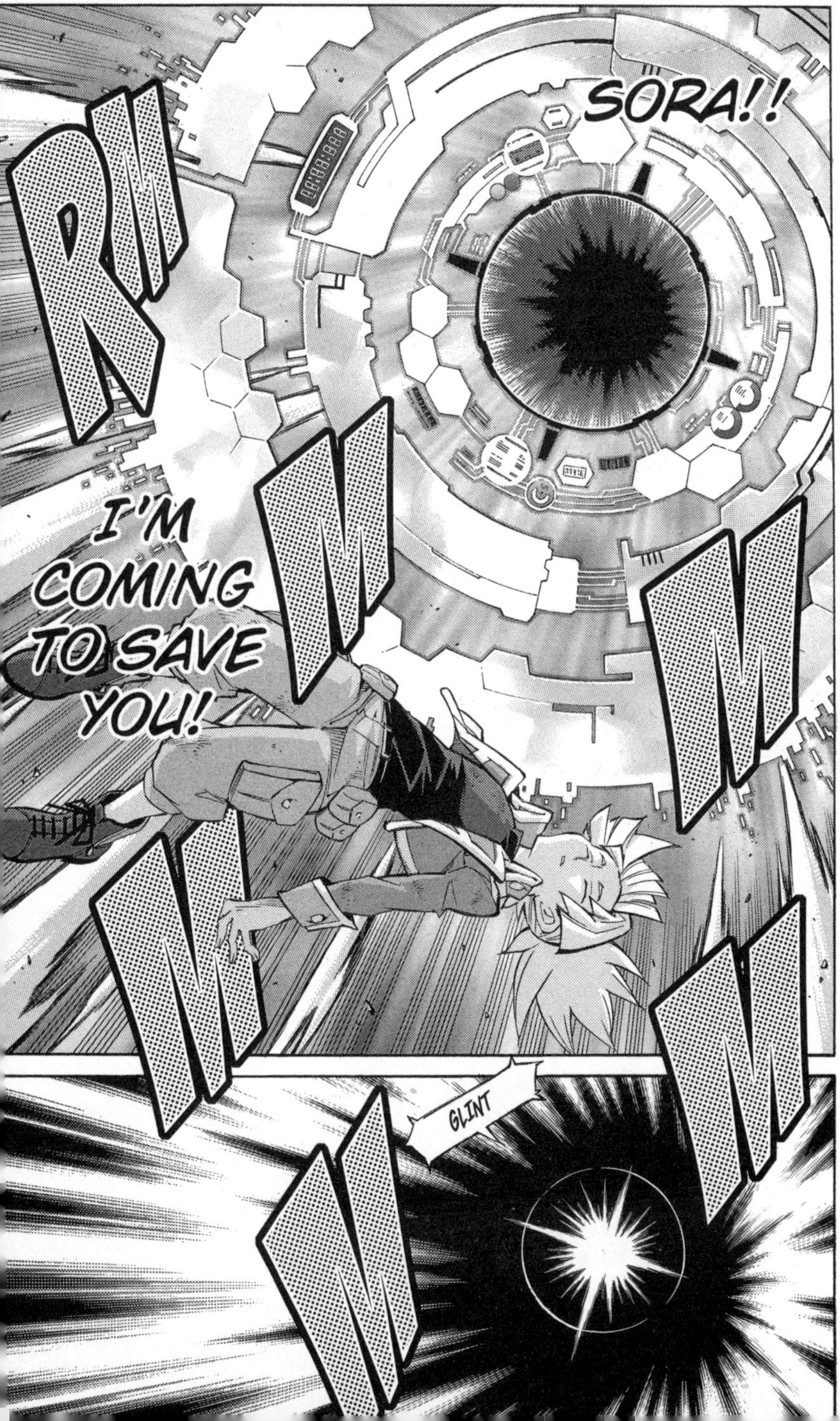
SORA!!
I'M COMING TO SAVE YOU!
GLINT

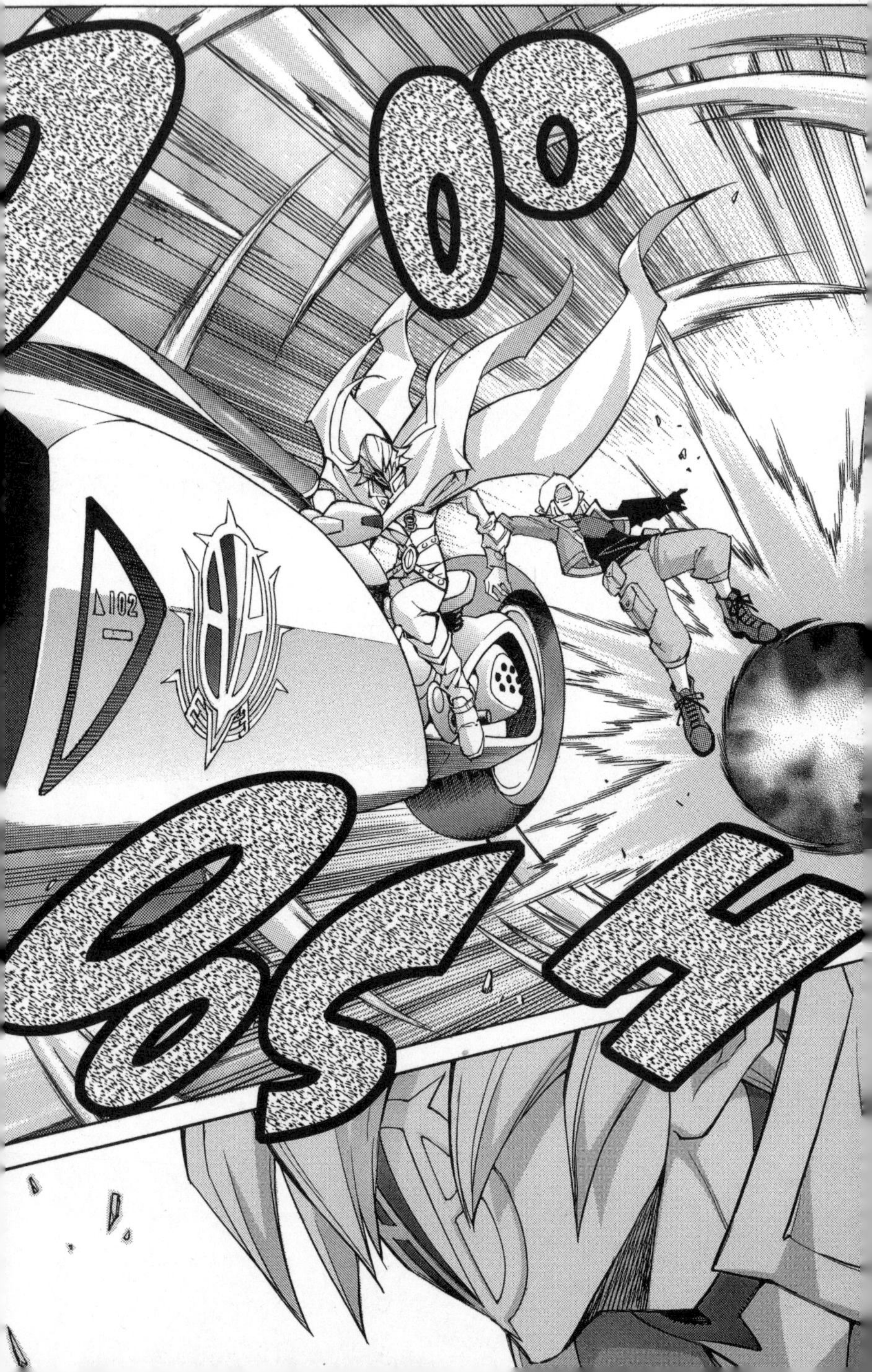
102

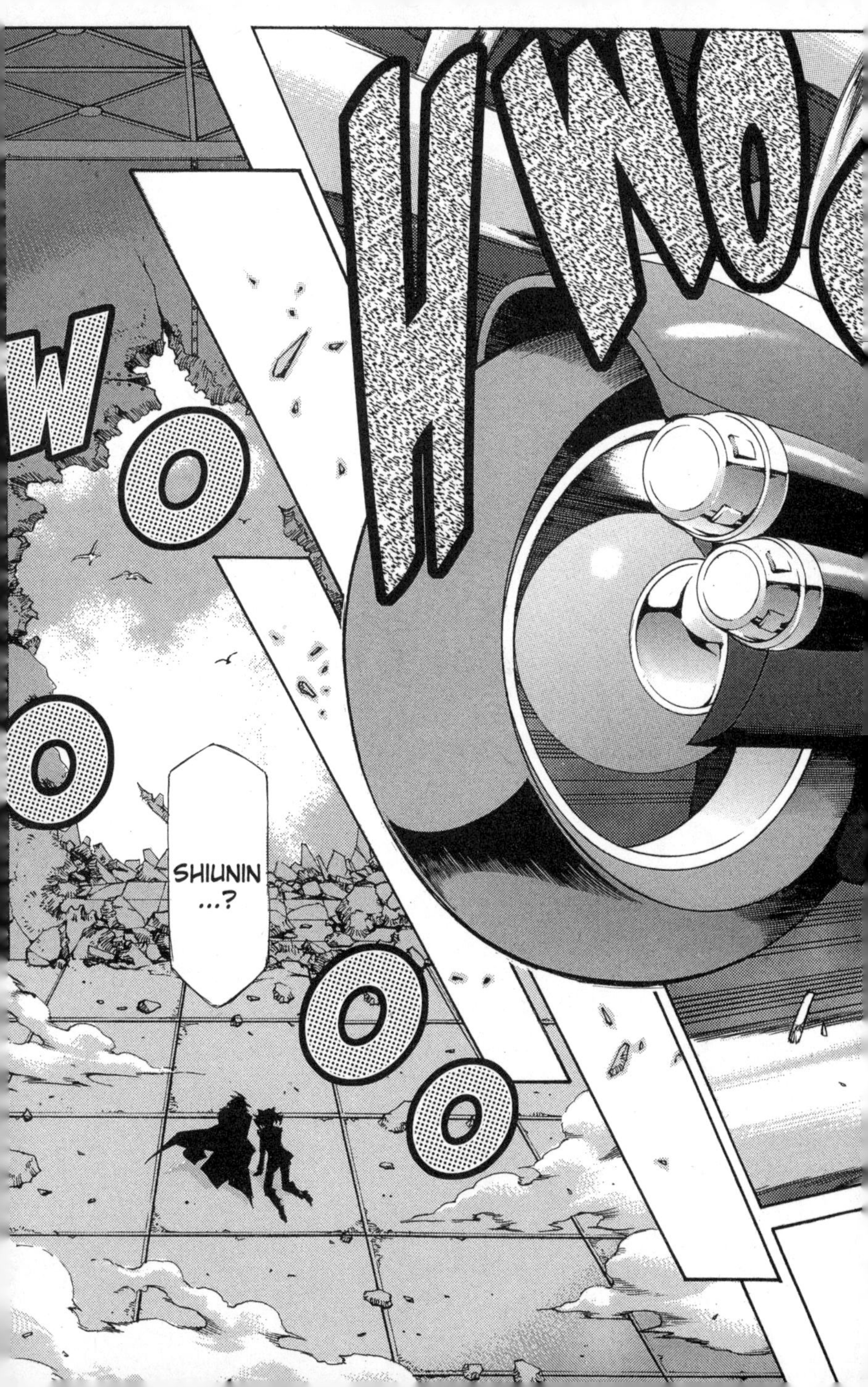
SHIUNIN ...?

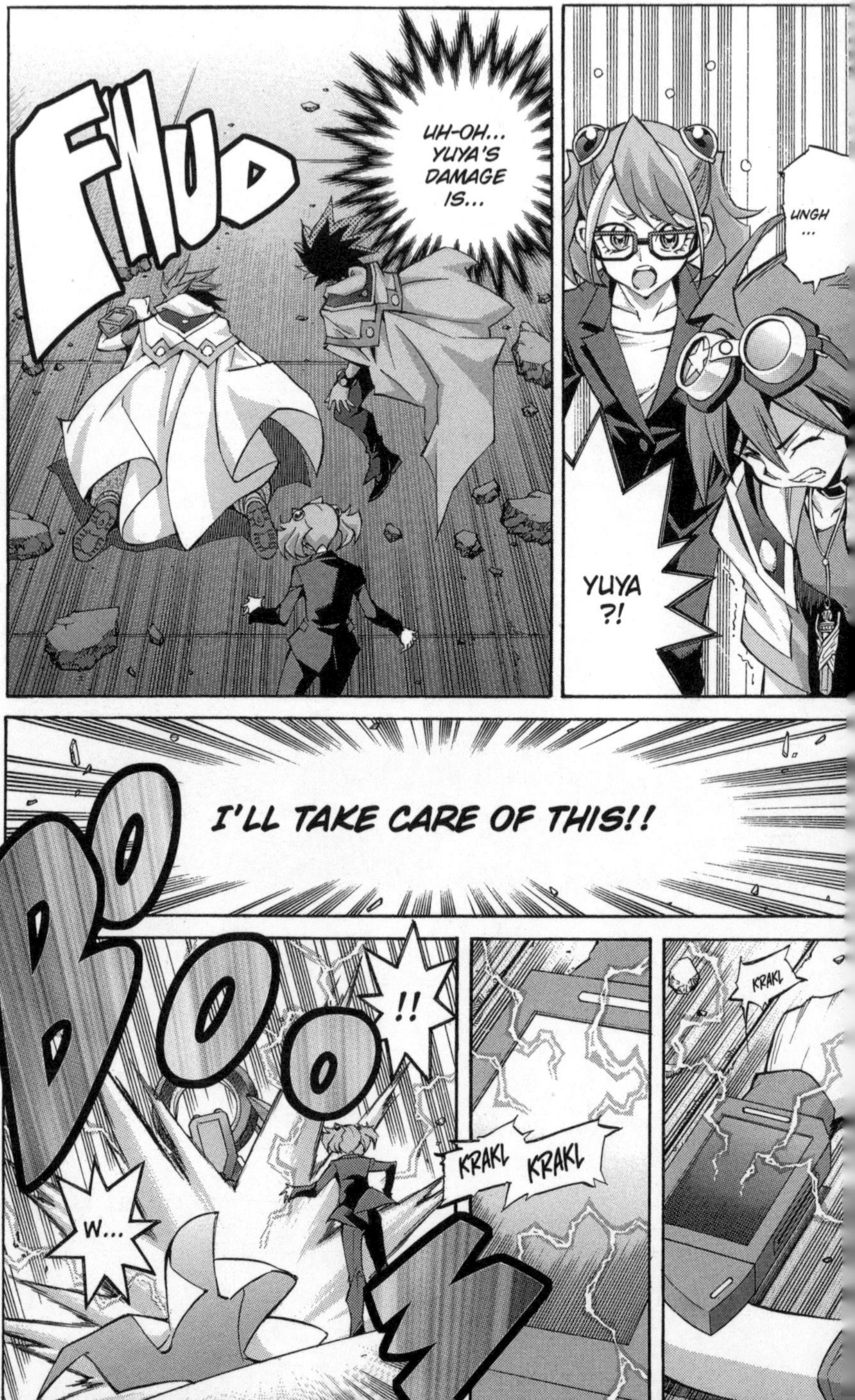
UNGH...
YUYA?!
UH-OH... YUYA'S DAMAGE IS...
FWUD
I'LL TAKE CARE OF THIS!!
BOOOM
KRAKL
!!
KRAKL KRAKL
W...

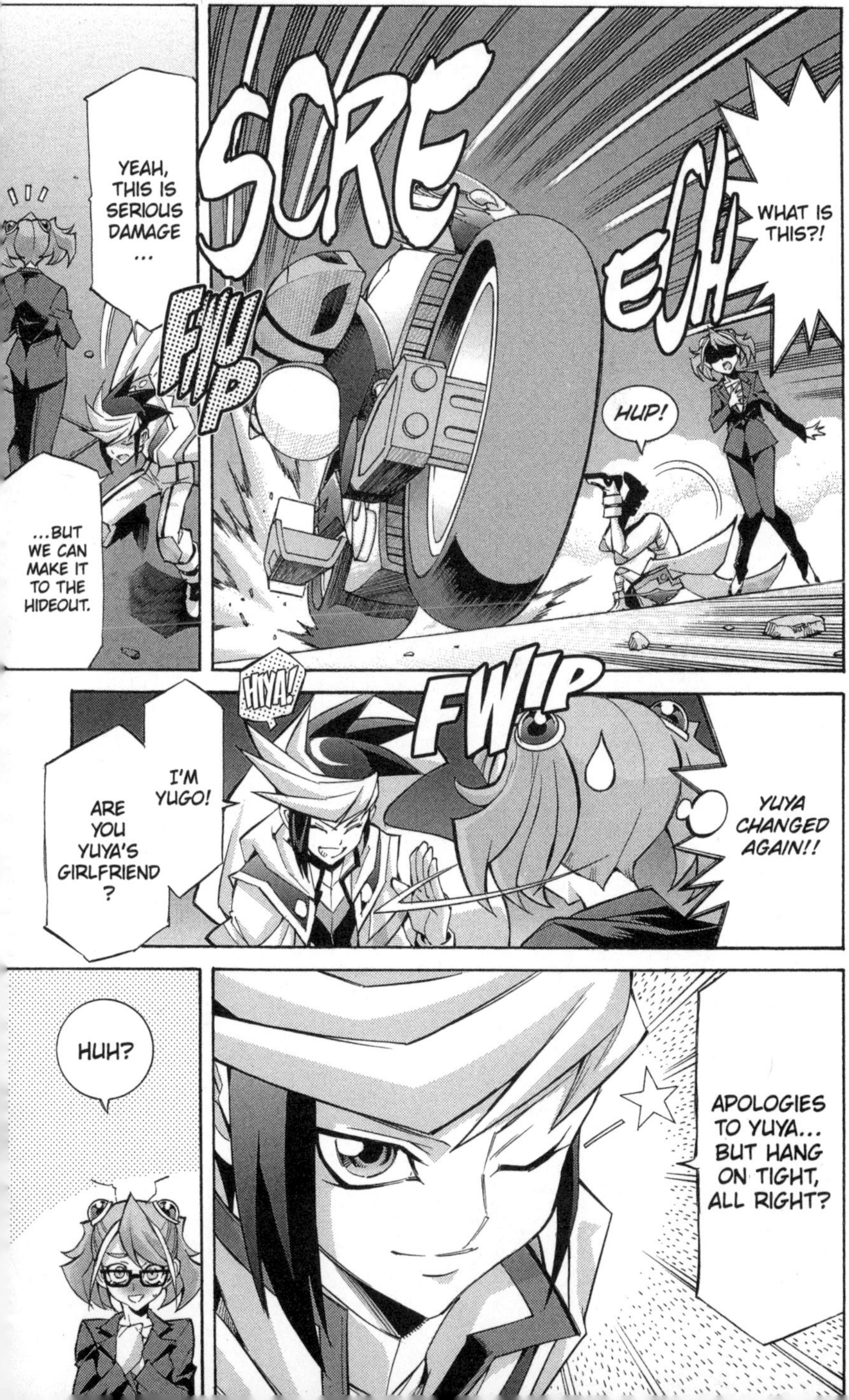
SCREECH
WHAT IS THIS?!
HUP!
FWIP
YEAH, THIS IS SERIOUS DAMAGE...
...BUT WE CAN MAKE IT TO THE HIDEOUT.
YUYA CHANGED AGAIN!!
FW!P
HIYA!
I'M YUGO!
ARE YOU YUYA'S GIRLFRIEND?
APOLOGIES TO YUYA... BUT HANG ON TIGHT, ALL RIGHT?
HUH?

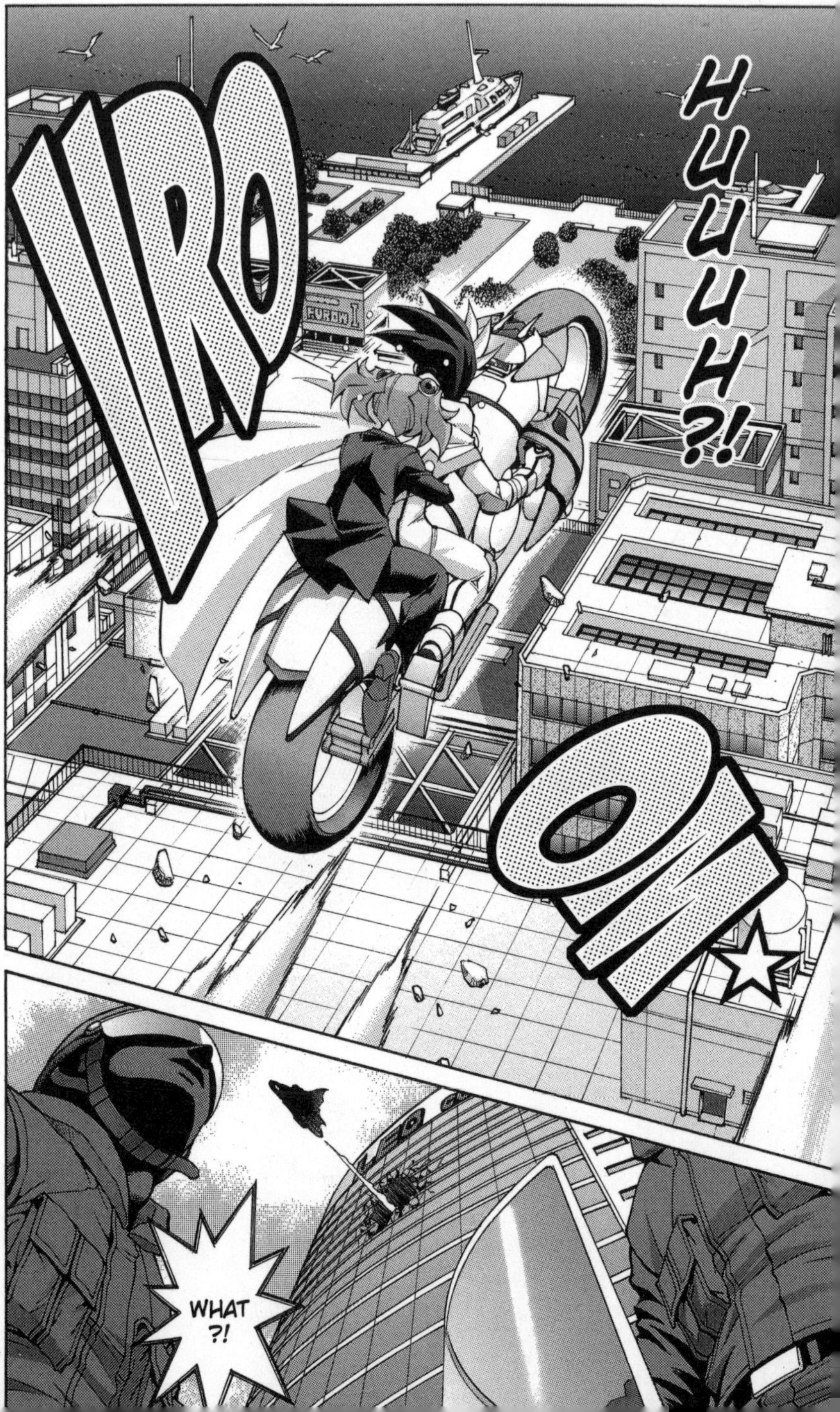
HUUUH?!
VRO
OO!
WHAT ?!

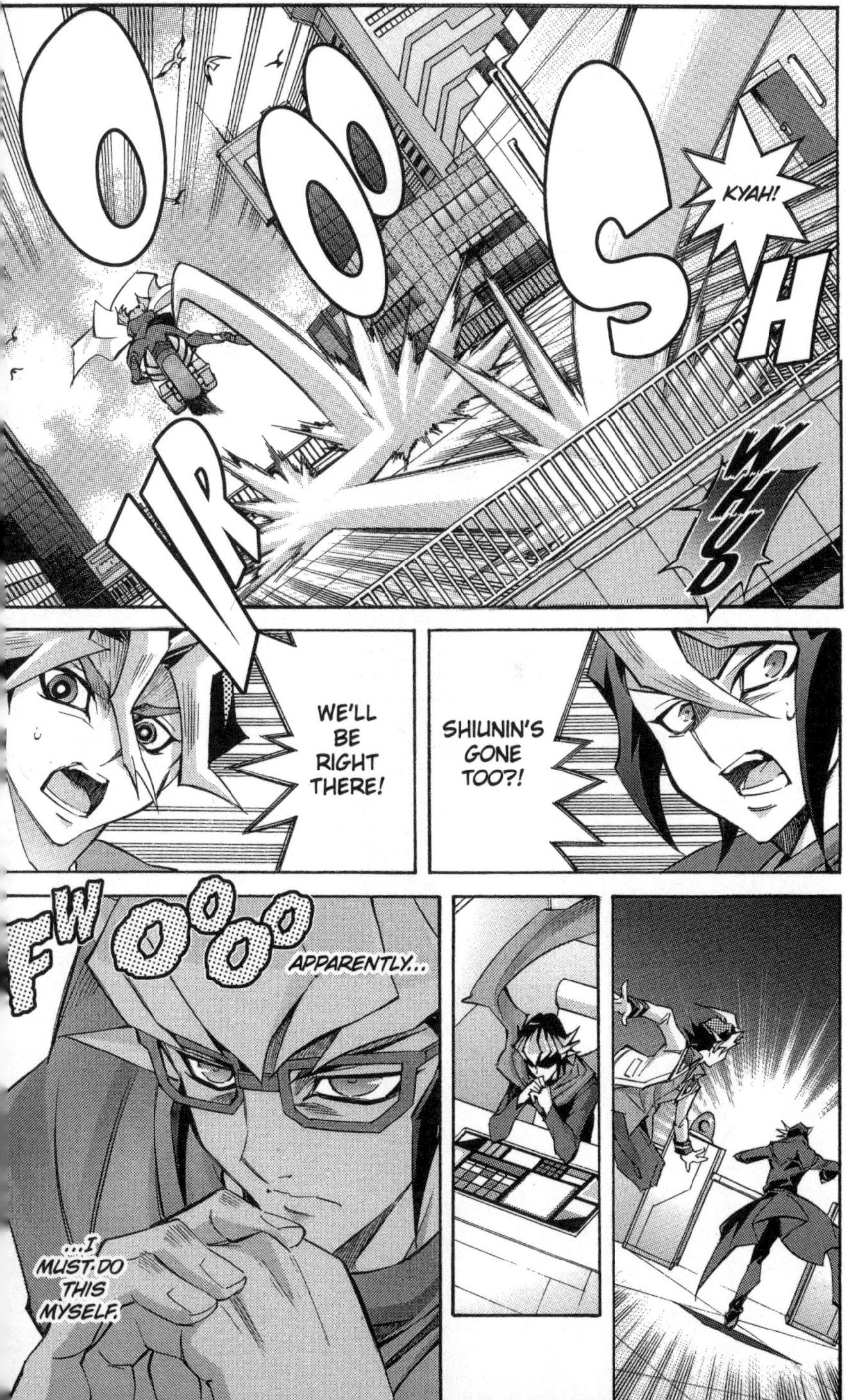
VROOOSH
KYAH!
SHIUNIN'S GONE TOO?!
WE'LL BE RIGHT THERE!
FWOOOO
APPARENTLY...
...I MUST DO THIS MYSELF.

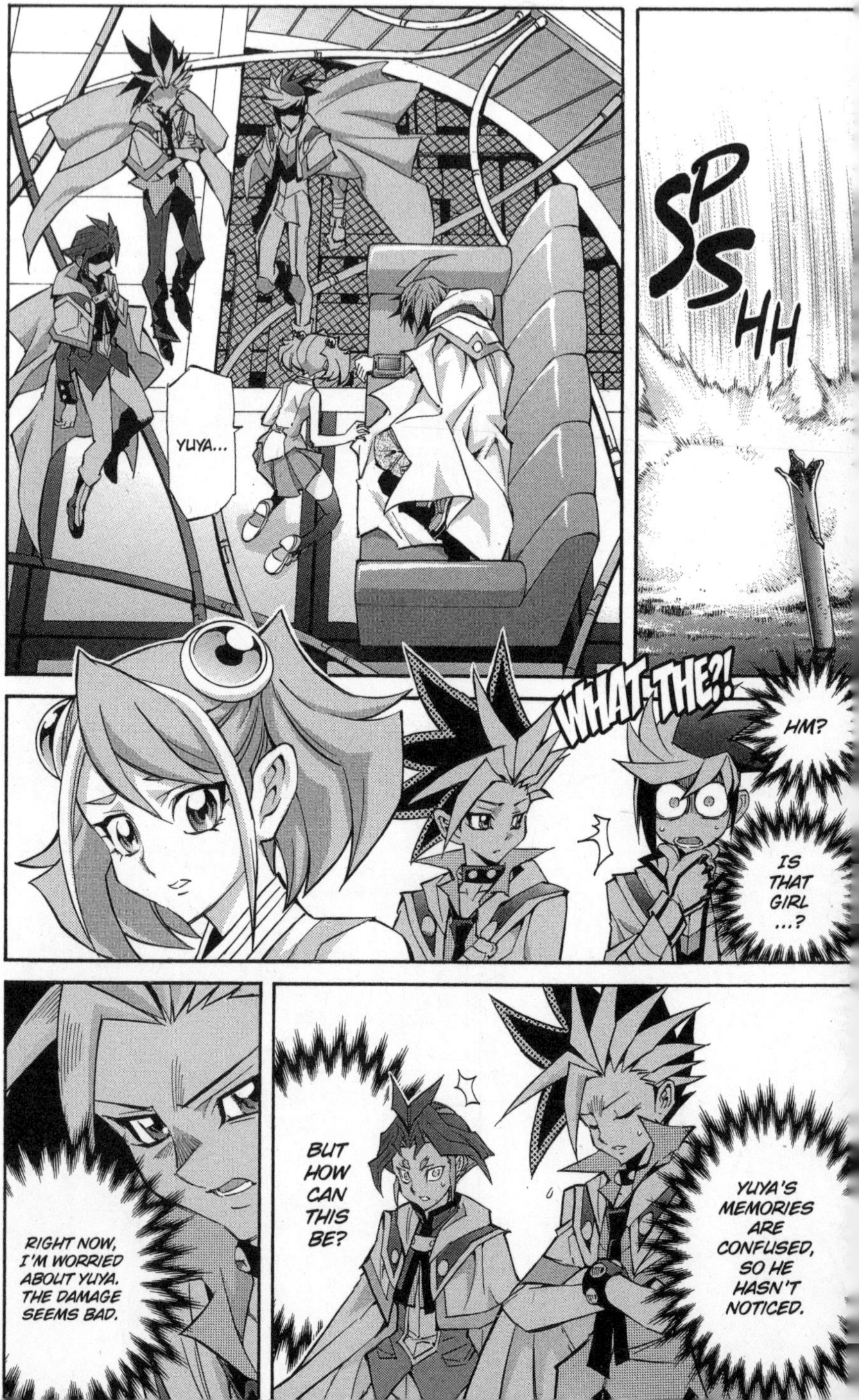
SPSHH
YUYA...
HM?
WHAT THE?!
IS THAT GIRL ...?
YUYA'S MEMORIES ARE CONFUSED, SO HE HASN'T NOTICED.
BUT HOW CAN THIS BE?
RIGHT NOW, I'M WORRIED ABOUT YUYA. THE DAMAGE SEEMS BAD.

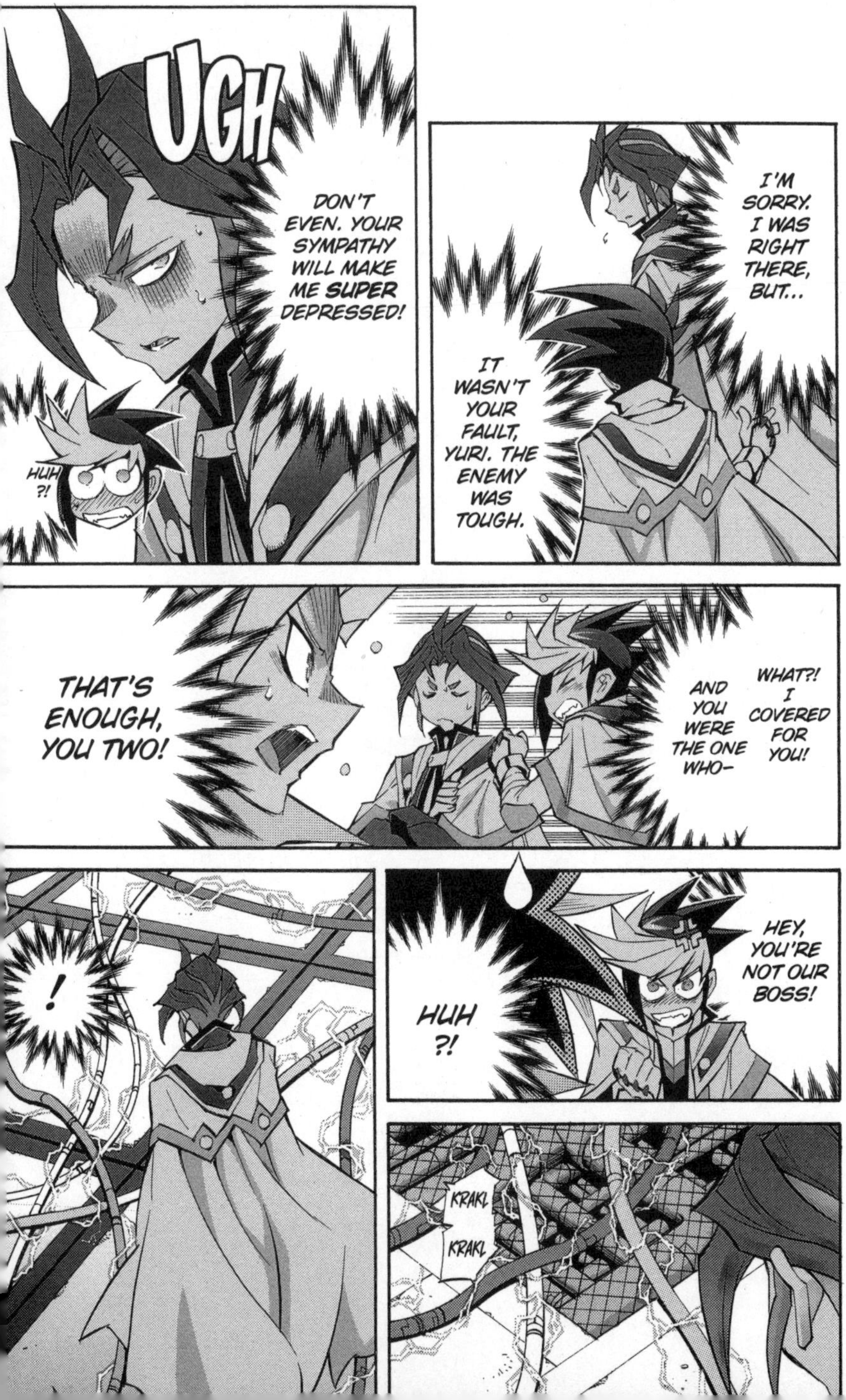
I'M SORRY. I WAS RIGHT THERE, BUT...
IT WASN'T YOUR FAULT, YURI. THE ENEMY WAS TOUGH.
UGH
DON'T EVEN. YOUR SYMPATHY WILL MAKE ME **SUPER** DEPRESSED!
HUH ?!
WHAT?! I COVERED FOR YOU!
AND YOU WERE THE ONE WHO–
THAT'S ENOUGH, YOU TWO!
HEY, YOU'RE NOT OUR BOSS!
HUH ?!
KRAKL
KRAKL
!

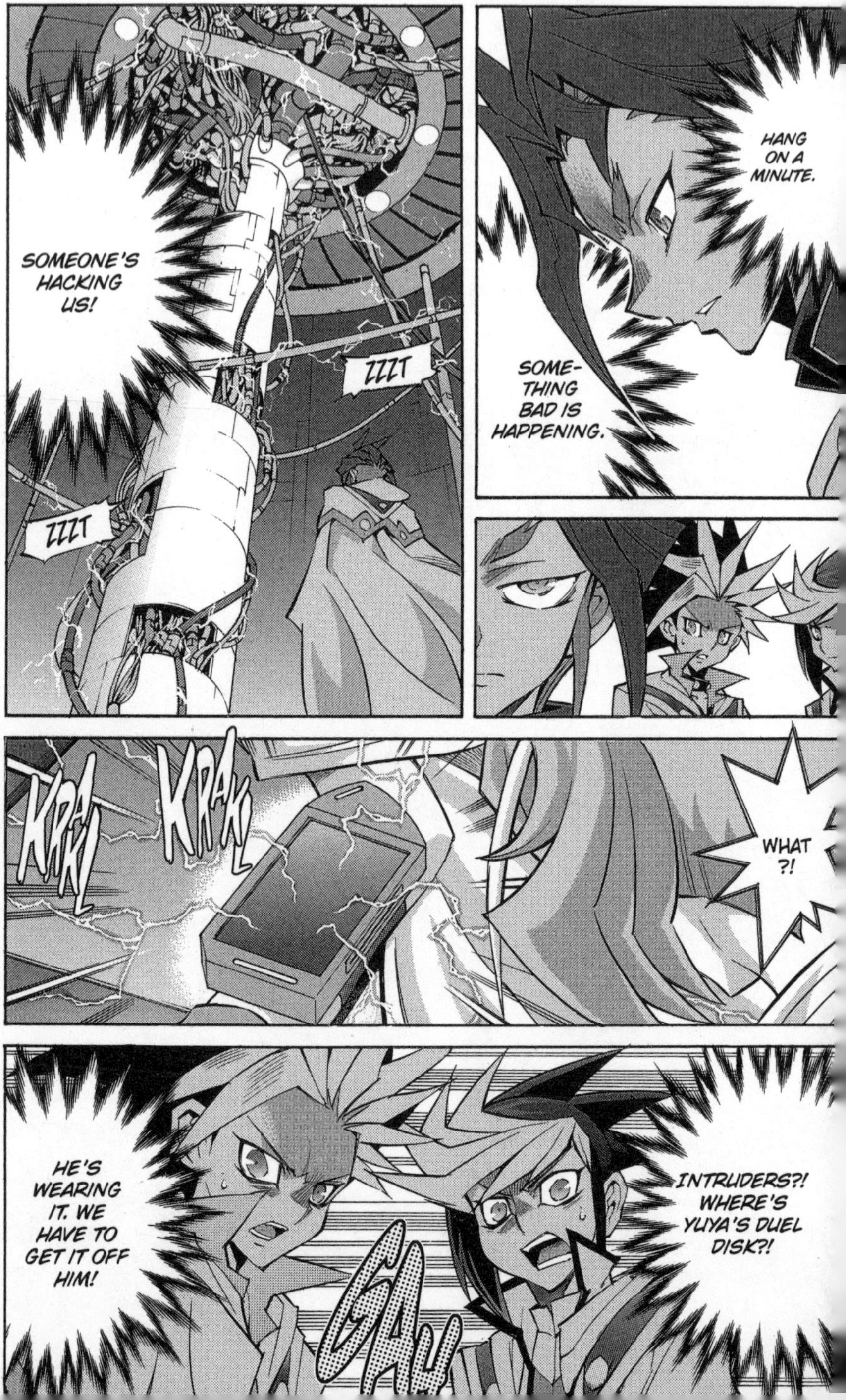
HANG ON A MINUTE.
SOME-THING BAD IS HAPPENING.
SOMEONE'S HACKING US!
ZZZT
ZZZT
WHAT ?!
KRAKL
KRAKL
INTRUDERS?! WHERE'S YUYA'S DUEL DISK?!
HE'S WEARING IT. WE HAVE TO GET IT OFF HIM!

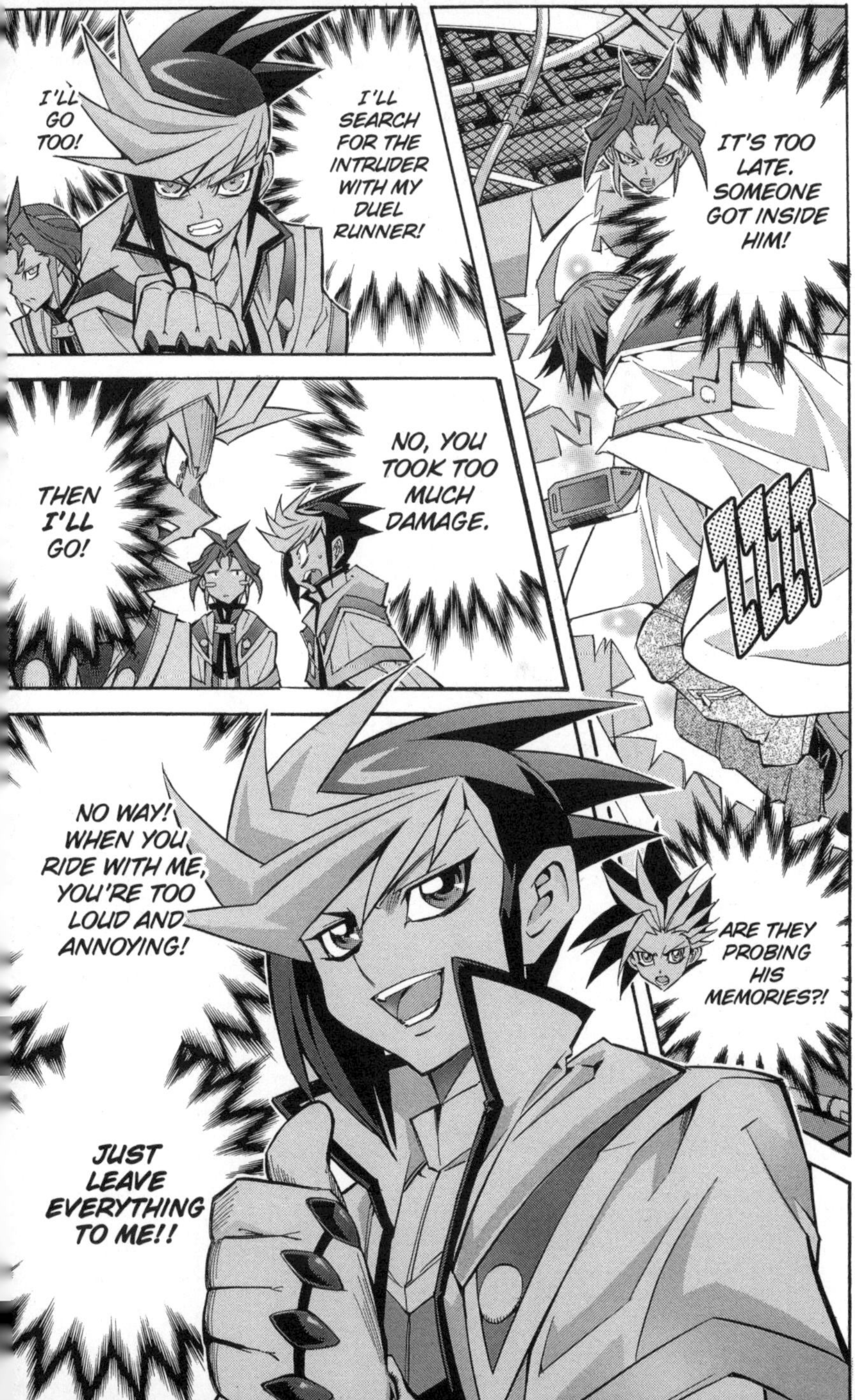
IT'S TOO LATE. SOMEONE GOT INSIDE HIM!
ZZZT
I'LL SEARCH FOR THE INTRUDER WITH MY DUEL RUNNER!
I'LL GO TOO!
NO, YOU TOOK TOO MUCH DAMAGE.
THEN I'LL GO!
ARE THEY PROBING HIS MEMORIES?!
NO WAY! WHEN YOU RIDE WITH ME, YOU'RE TOO LOUD AND ANNOYING!
JUST LEAVE EVERYTHING TO ME!!

PRESENTING MIYOSHI SENSEI'S EARLY DESIGNS!

ARC-V CHARACTER SKETCHES

YUGO

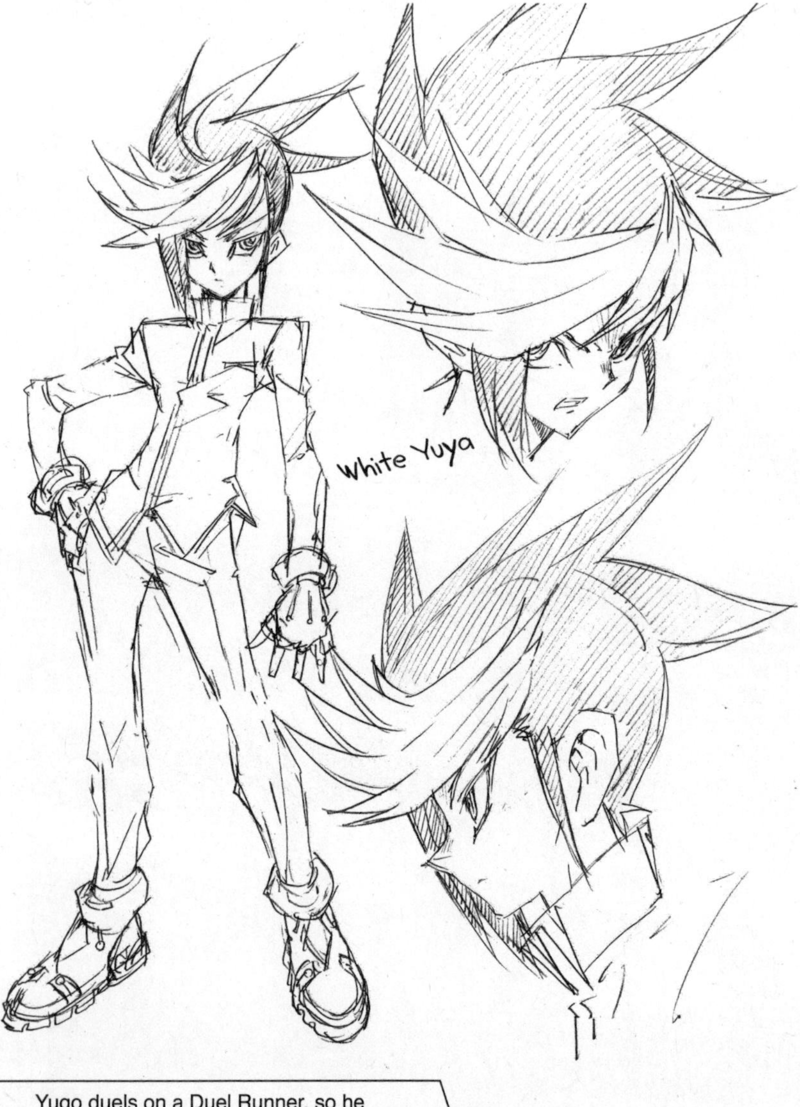
White Yuya

Yugo duels on a Duel Runner, so he wears riding gear in the main story, but he doesn't in these sketches. He also looks more laid-back.

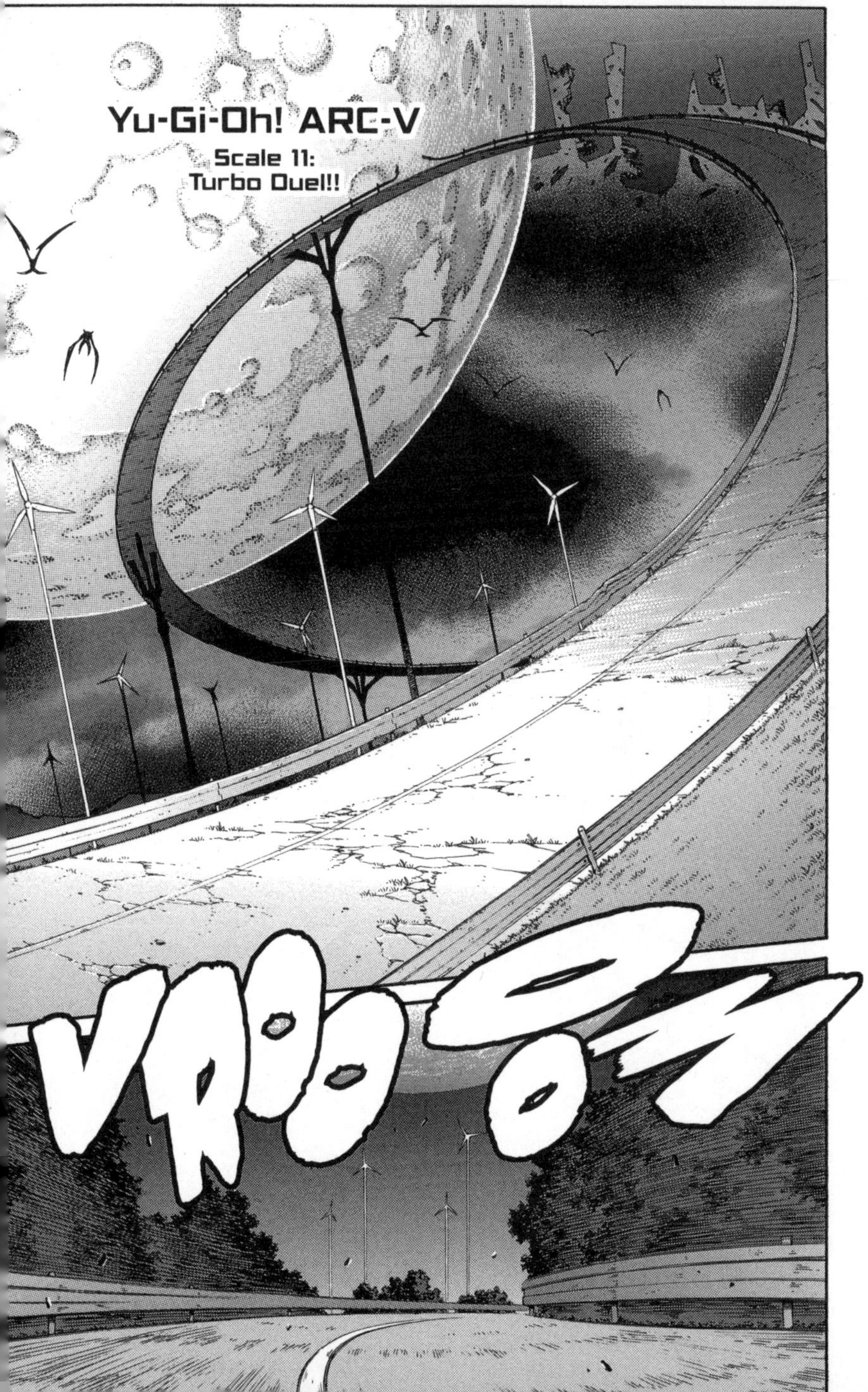
Yu-Gi-Oh! ARC-V
Scale 11:
Turbo Duel!!
VROOOOM

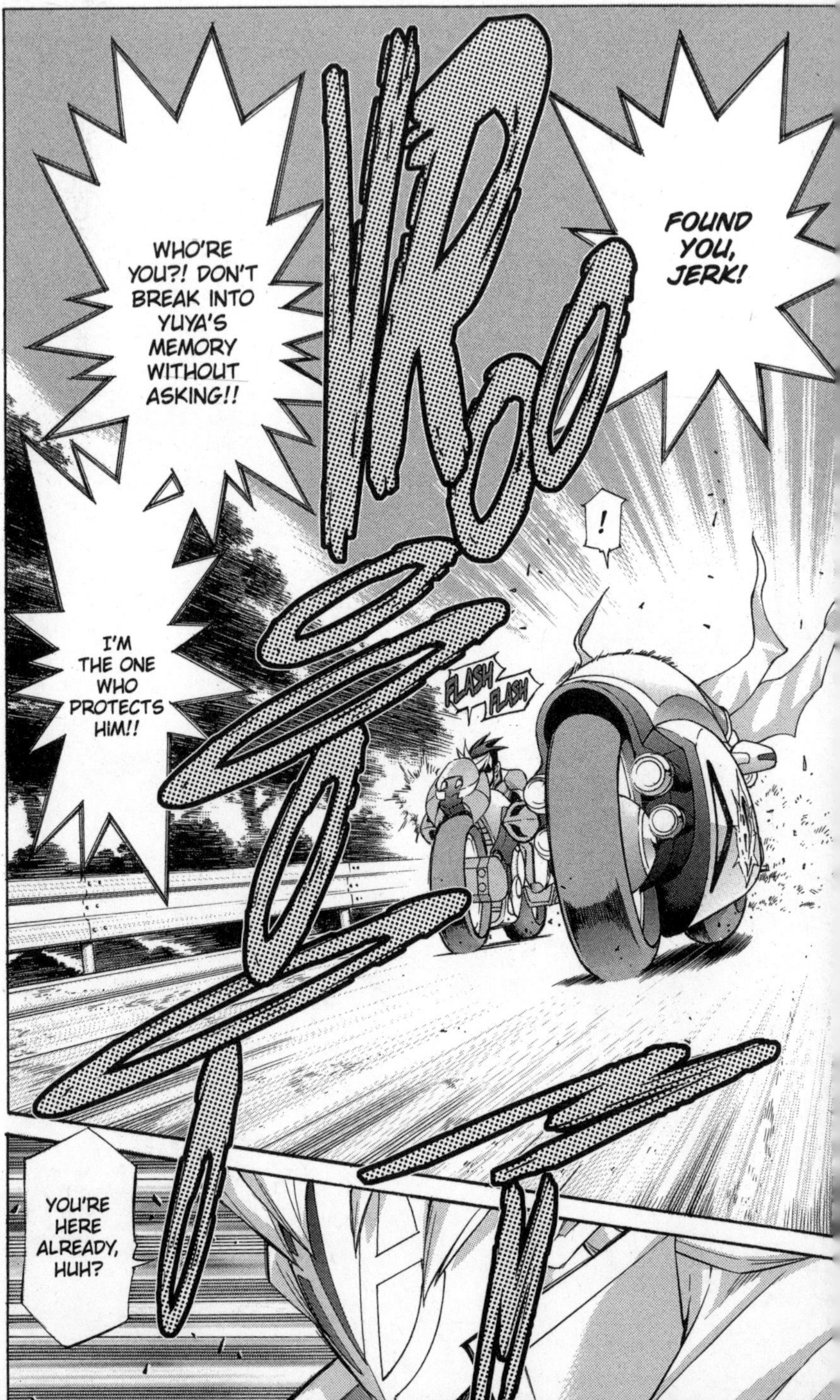
FOUND YOU, JERK!
WHO'RE YOU?! DON'T BREAK INTO YUYA'S MEMORY WITHOUT ASKING!!
I'M THE ONE WHO PROTECTS HIM!!
!
FLASH
FLASH
YOU'RE HERE ALREADY, HUH?

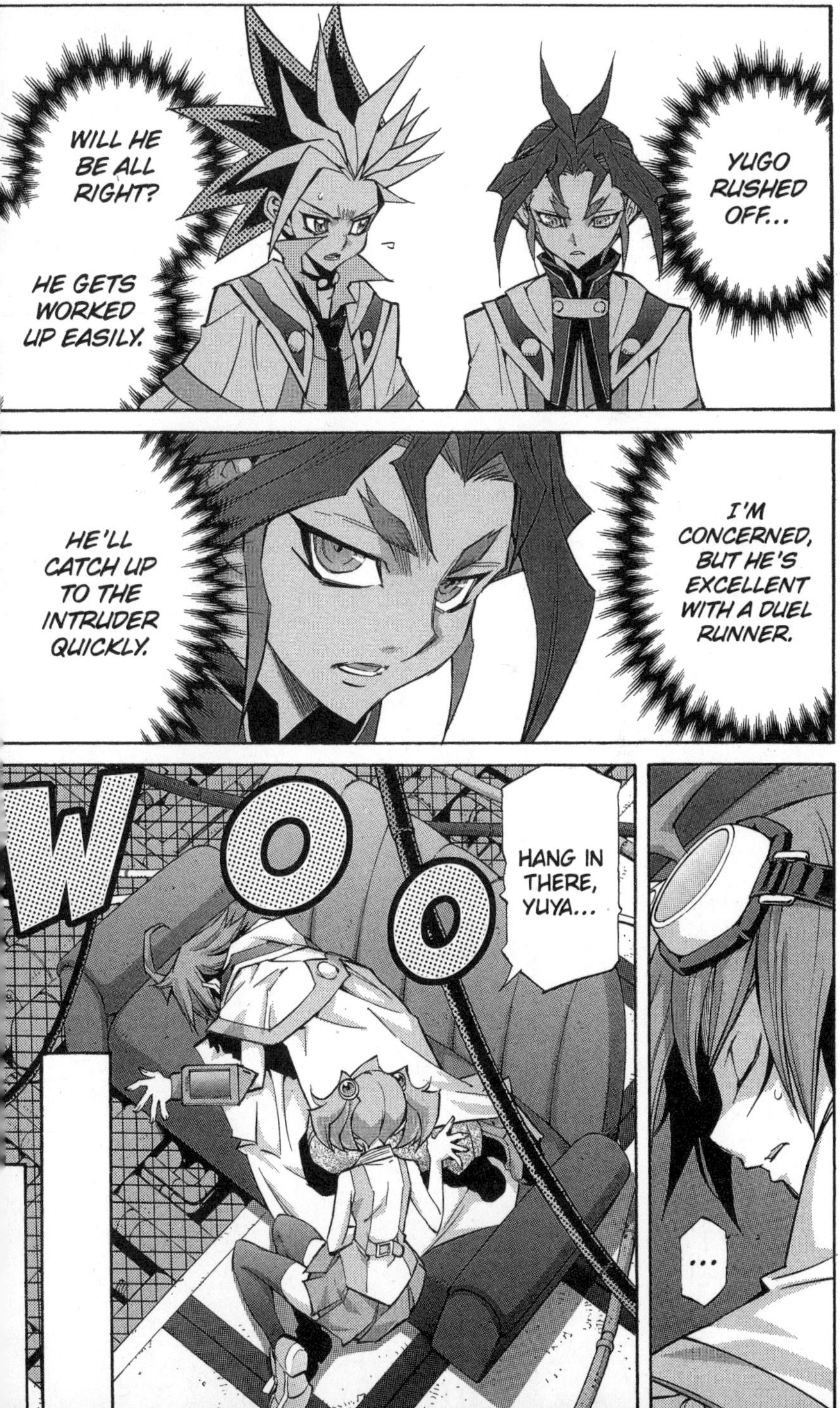
YUGO RUSHED OFF...
WILL HE BE ALL RIGHT?
HE GETS WORKED UP EASILY.
I'M CONCERNED, BUT HE'S EXCELLENT WITH A DUEL RUNNER.
HE'LL CATCH UP TO THE INTRUDER QUICKLY.
...
HANG IN THERE, YUYA...
WOOO

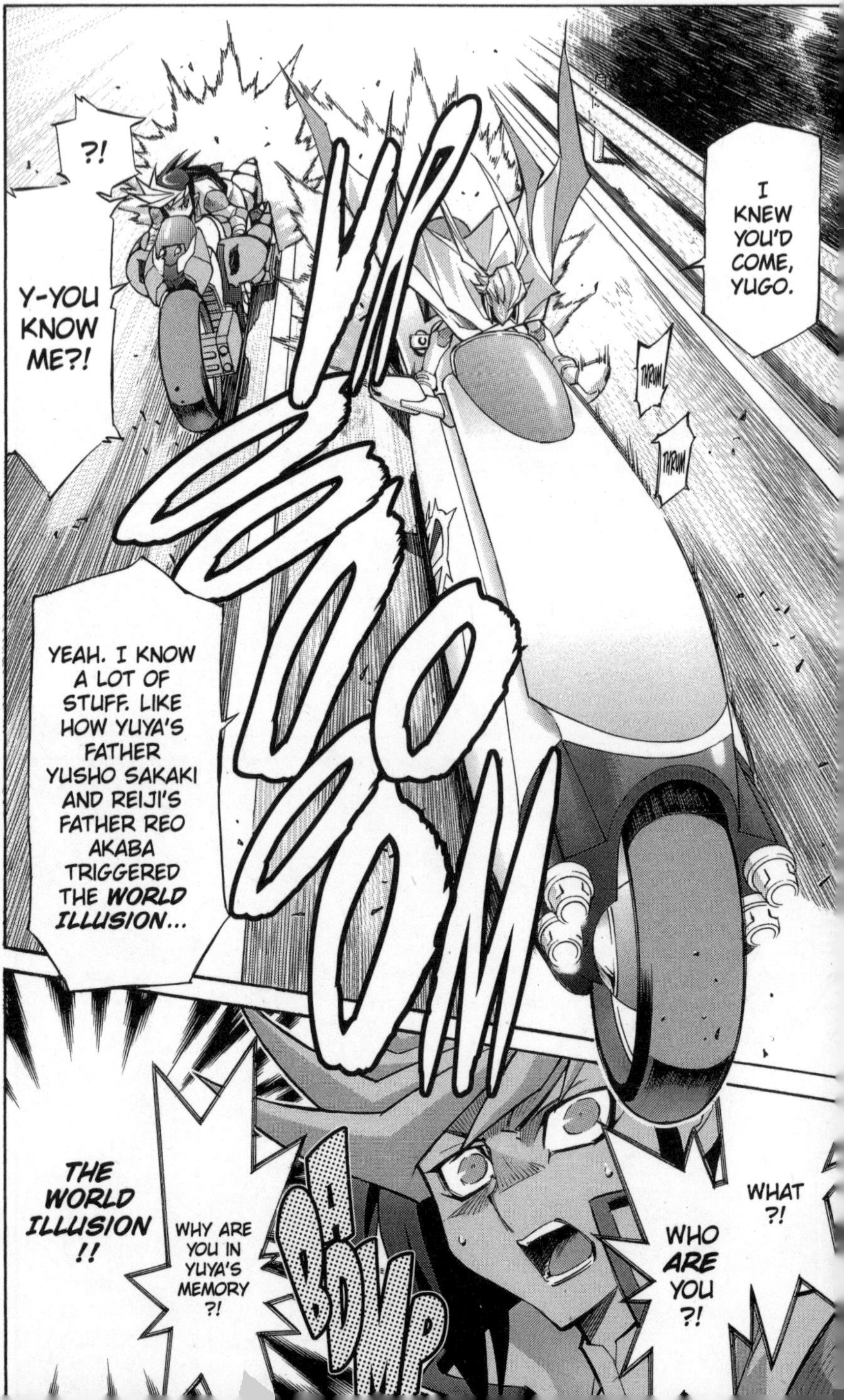
I KNEW YOU'D COME, YUGO.
THROM
THROM
?!
Y-YOU KNOW ME?!
YEAH. I KNOW A LOT OF STUFF. LIKE HOW YUYA'S FATHER YUSHO SAKAKI AND REIJI'S FATHER REO AKABA TRIGGERED THE *WORLD ILLUSION*...
WHAT ?!
WHO *ARE* YOU ?!
BA-BOMP
WHY ARE YOU IN YUYA'S MEMORY ?!
THE WORLD ILLUSION !!

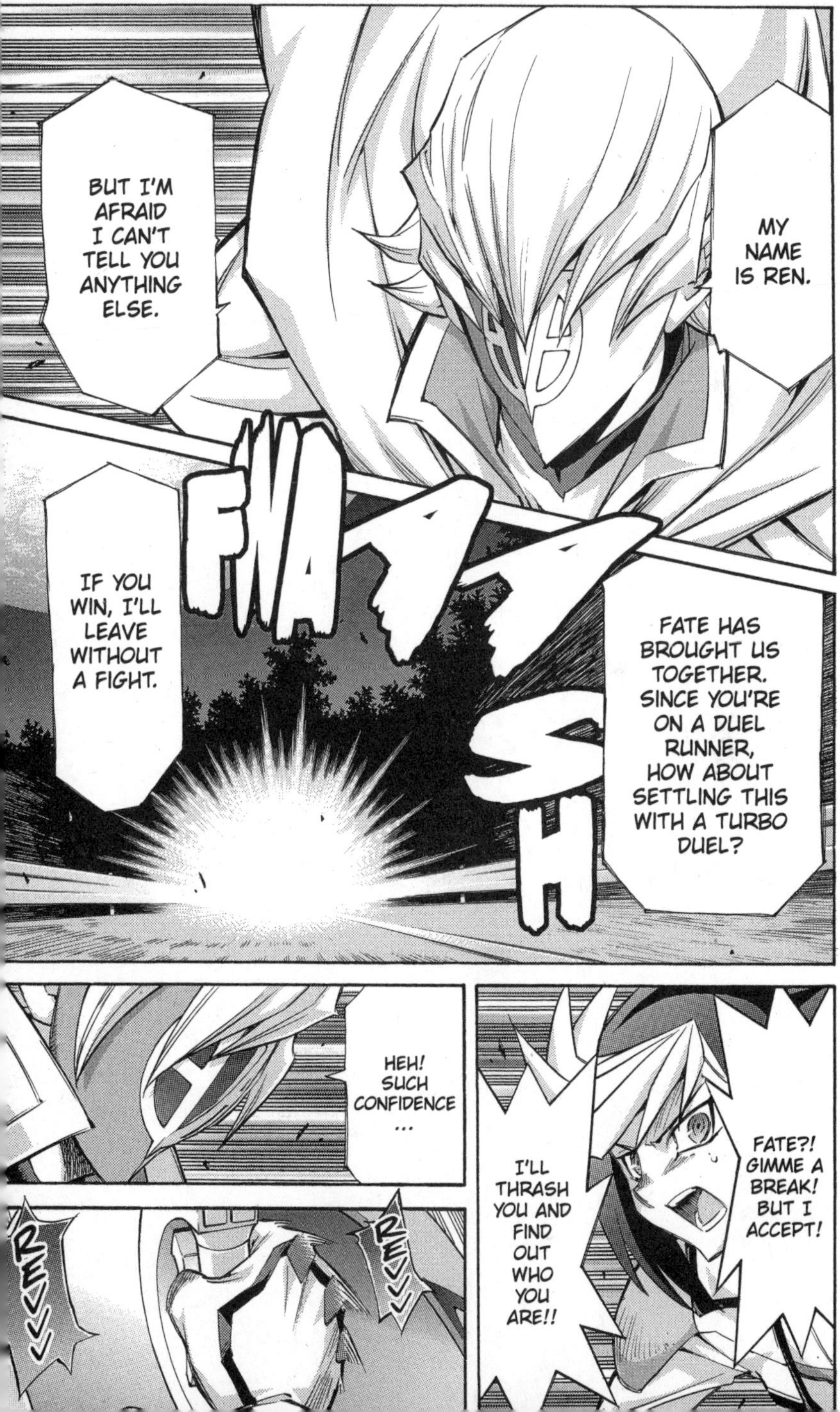
MY NAME IS REN.
BUT I'M AFRAID I CAN'T TELL YOU ANYTHING ELSE.
FATE HAS BROUGHT US TOGETHER. SINCE YOU'RE ON A DUEL RUNNER, HOW ABOUT SETTLING THIS WITH A TURBO DUEL?
IF YOU WIN, I'LL LEAVE WITHOUT A FIGHT.
FWASH
FATE?! GIMME A BREAK! BUT I ACCEPT!
I'LL THRASH YOU AND FIND OUT WHO YOU ARE!!
HEH! SUCH CONFIDENCE...
REV
REV

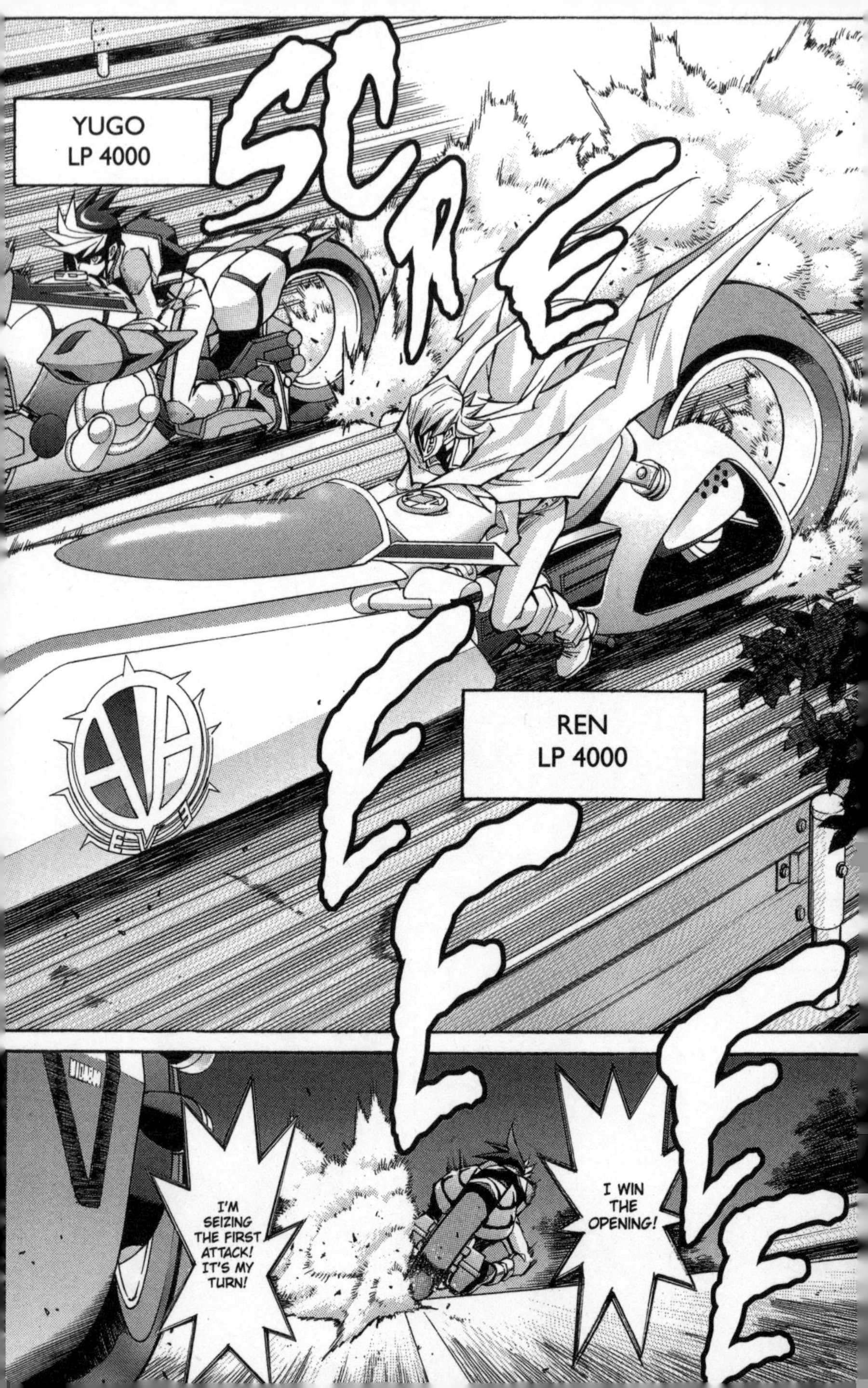
YUGO
LP 4000
SCREEEEEEE
REN
LP 4000
I WIN THE OPENING!
I'M SEIZING THE FIRST ATTACK! IT'S MY TURN!

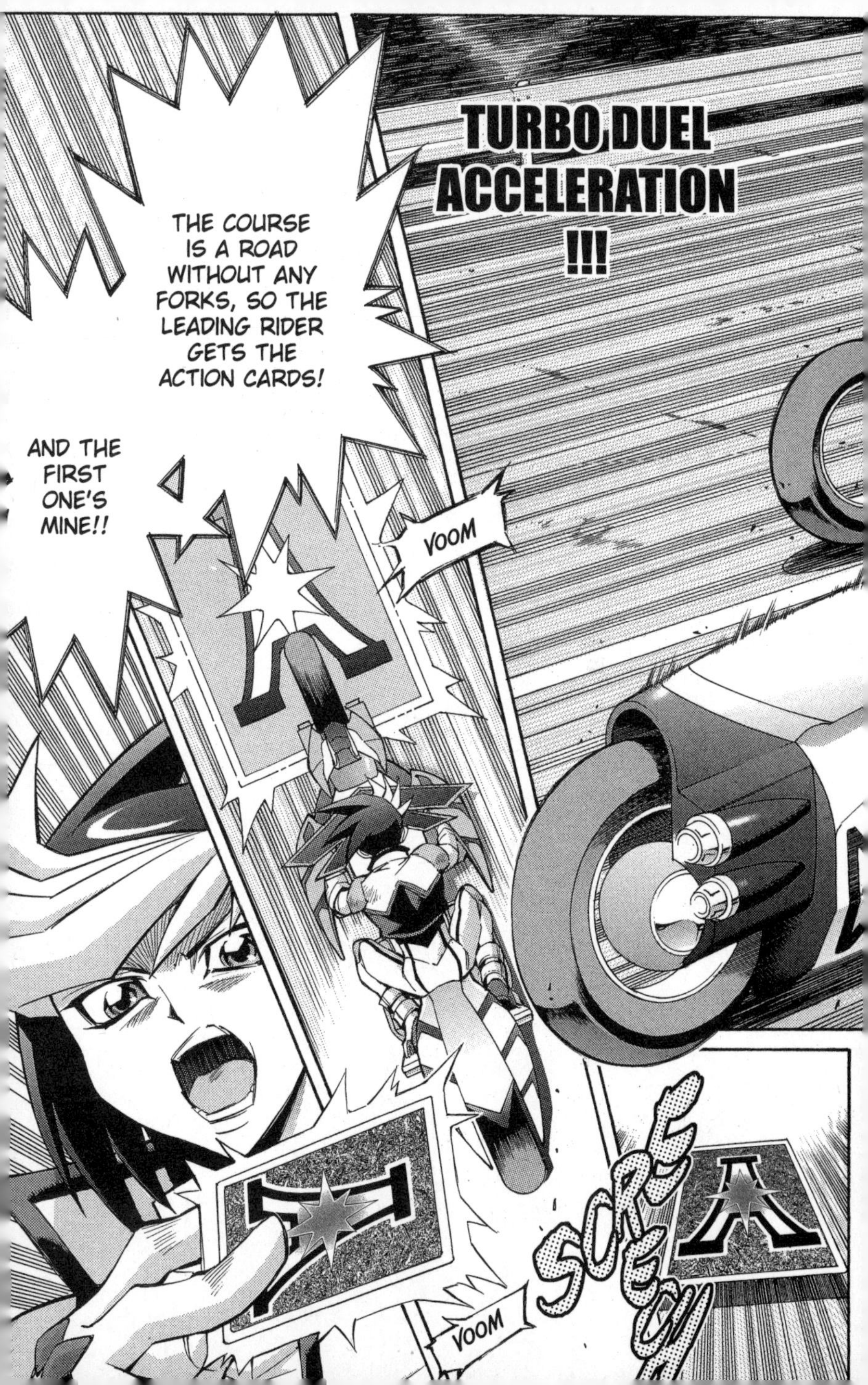
TURBO DUEL ACCELERATION !!!
VOOM
THE COURSE IS A ROAD WITHOUT ANY FORKS, SO THE LEADING RIDER GETS THE ACTION CARDS!
AND THE FIRST ONE'S MINE!!
SCREECH
VOOM

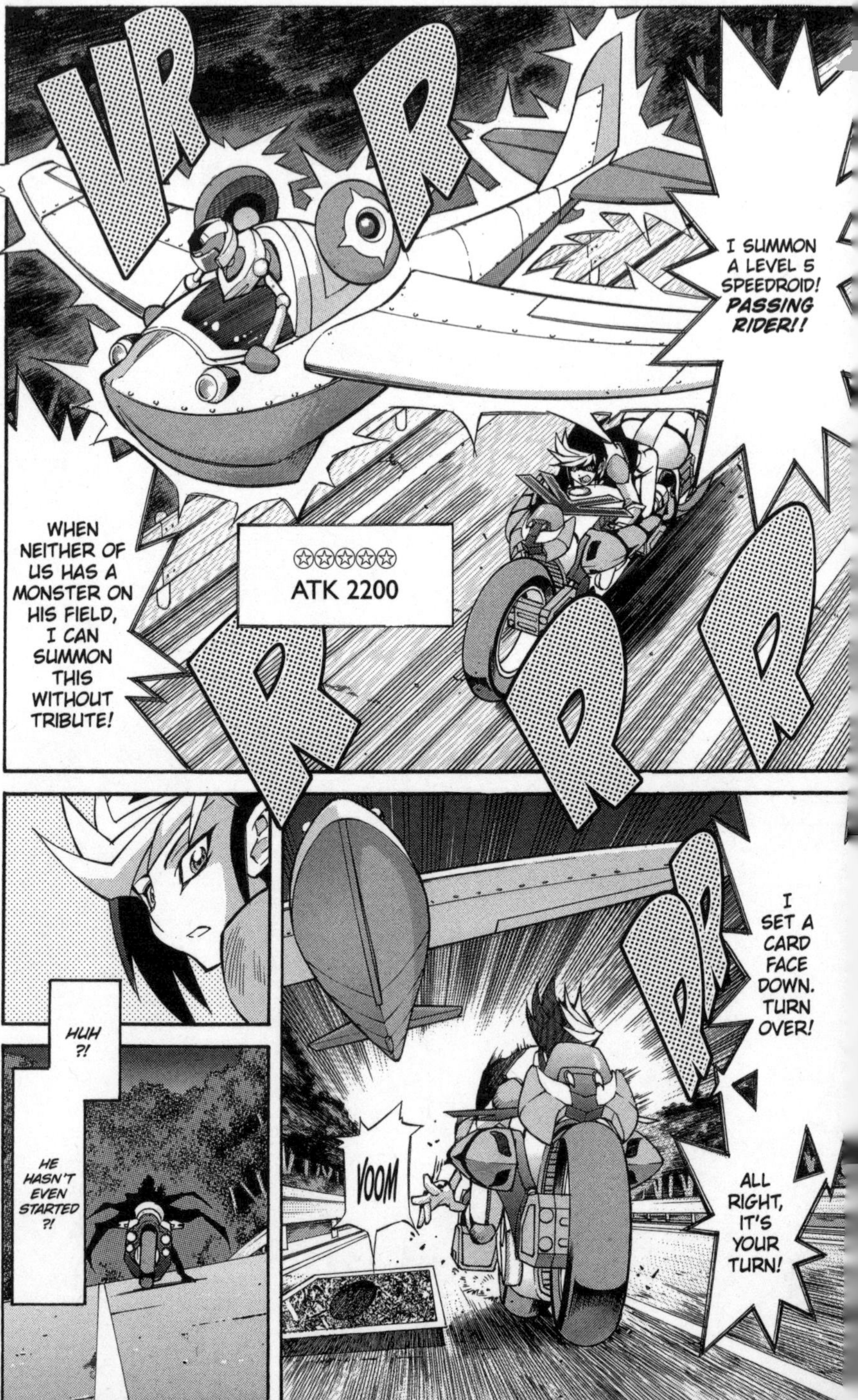
I SUMMON A LEVEL 5 SPEEDROID! PASSING RIDER!!
WHEN NEITHER OF US HAS A MONSTER ON HIS FIELD, I CAN SUMMON THIS WITHOUT TRIBUTE!
☆☆☆☆☆
ATK 2200
I SET A CARD FACE DOWN. TURN OVER!
ALL RIGHT, IT'S YOUR TURN!
VOOM
HUH?!
HE HASN'T EVEN STARTED?!

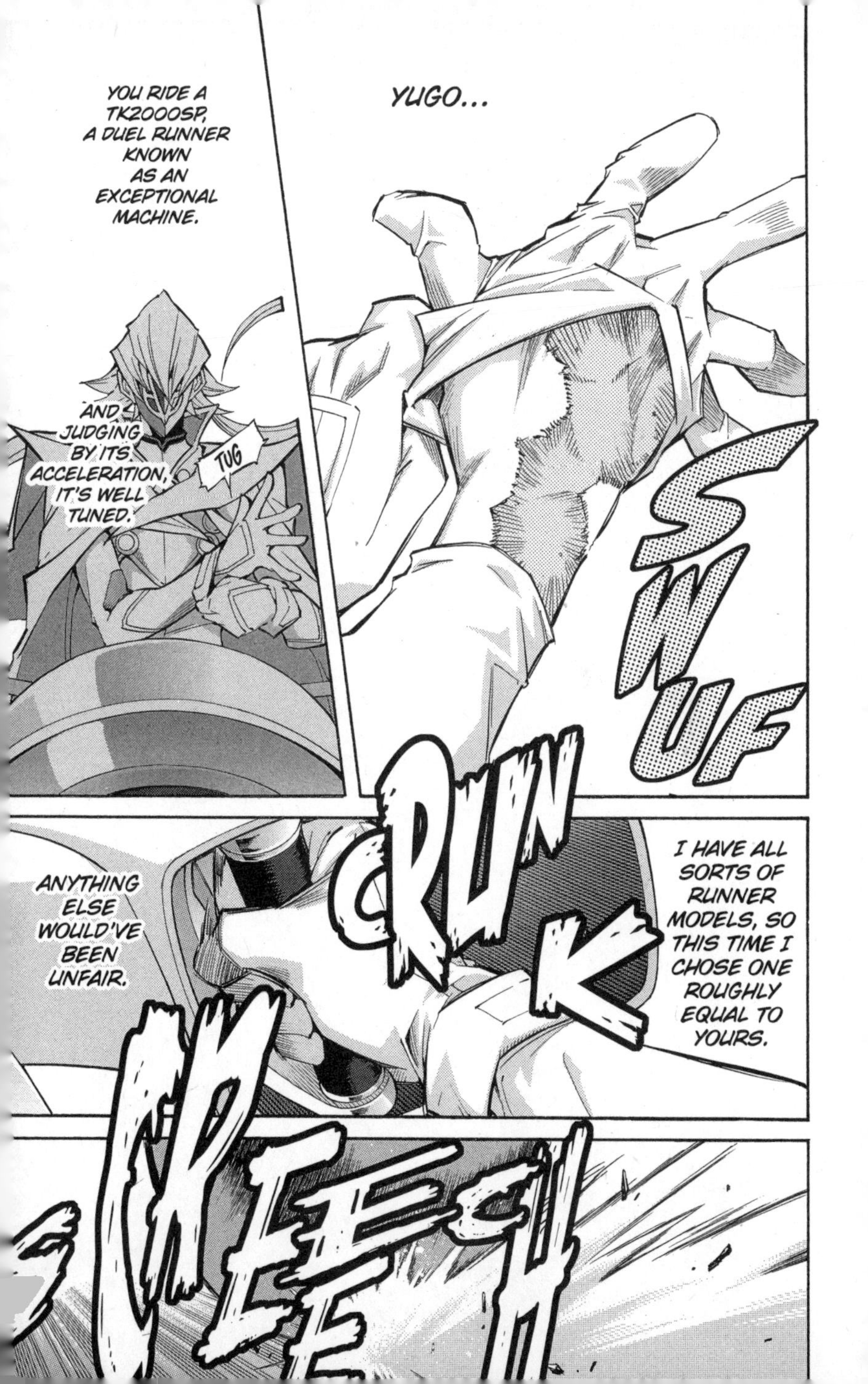
YUGO...
SWUF
YOU RIDE A TK2000SP, A DUEL RUNNER KNOWN AS AN EXCEPTIONAL MACHINE.
AND JUDGING BY ITS ACCELERATION, IT'S WELL TUNED.
TUG
I HAVE ALL SORTS OF RUNNER MODELS, SO THIS TIME I CHOSE ONE ROUGHLY EQUAL TO YOURS.
CRUNK
ANYTHING ELSE WOULD'VE BEEN UNFAIR.

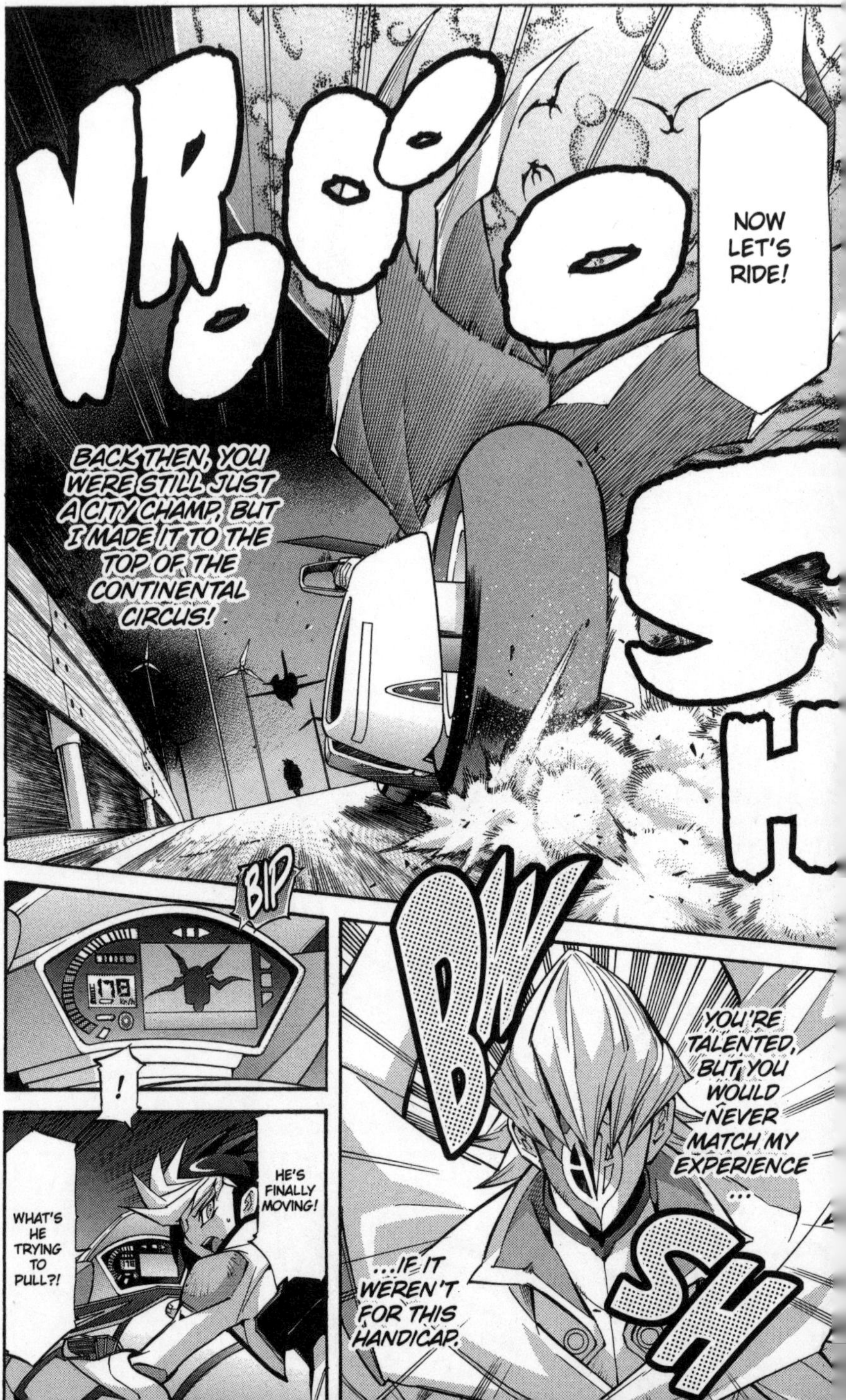
NOW LET'S RIDE!
VROOOOO
BACK THEN, YOU WERE STILL JUST A CITY CHAMP, BUT I MADE IT TO THE TOP OF THE CONTINENTAL CIRCUS!
SH
BW
YOU'RE TALENTED, BUT YOU WOULD NEVER MATCH MY EXPERIENCE...
...IF IT WEREN'T FOR THIS HANDICAP.
SH
BIP
178
!
HE'S FINALLY MOVING!
WHAT'S HE TRYING TO PULL?!

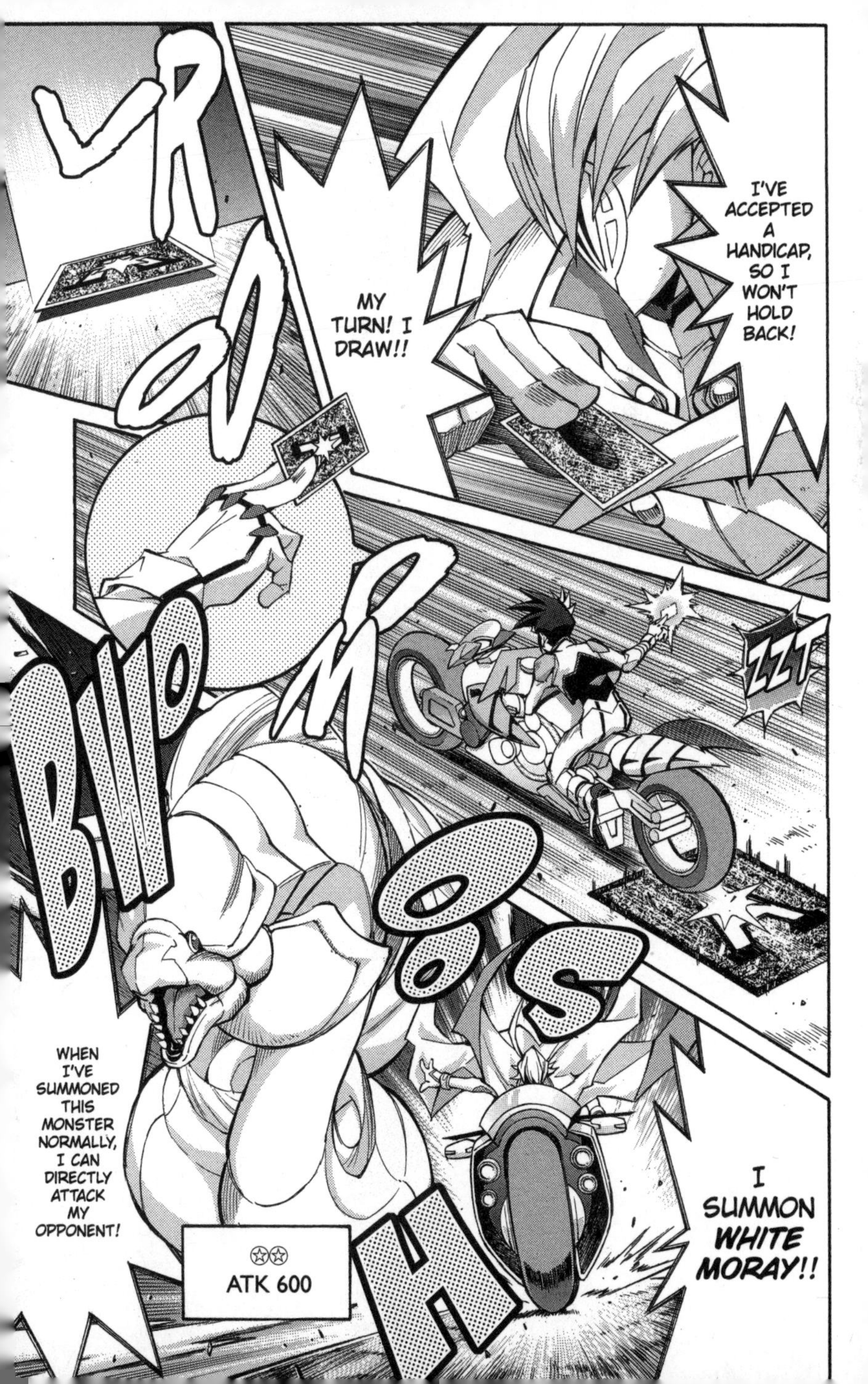
I'VE ACCEPTED A HANDICAP, SO I WON'T HOLD BACK!
MY TURN! I DRAW!!
ZZZT
I SUMMON WHITE MORAY!!
WHEN I'VE SUMMONED THIS MONSTER NORMALLY, I CAN DIRECTLY ATTACK MY OPPONENT!
☆☆
ATK 600

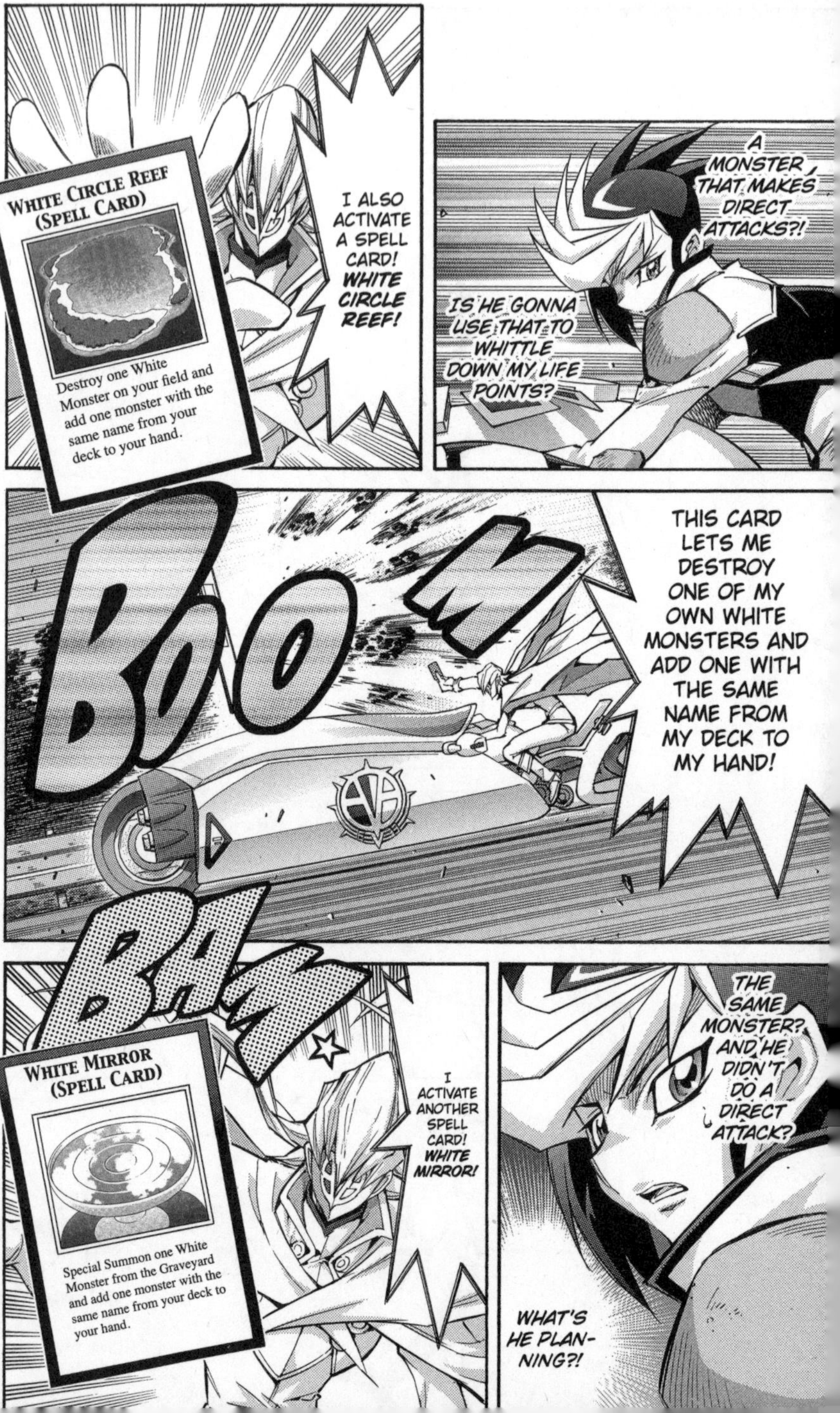
A MONSTER THAT MAKES DIRECT ATTACKS?!
IS HE GONNA USE THAT TO WHITTLE DOWN MY LIFE POINTS?
I ALSO ACTIVATE A SPELL CARD! WHITE CIRCLE REEF!
WHITE CIRCLE REEF (SPELL CARD)
Destroy one White Monster on your field and add one monster with the same name from your deck to your hand.
BOOOM
THIS CARD LETS ME DESTROY ONE OF MY OWN WHITE MONSTERS AND ADD ONE WITH THE SAME NAME FROM MY DECK TO MY HAND!
THE SAME MONSTER? AND HE DIDN'T DO A DIRECT ATTACK?
WHAT'S HE PLAN-NING?!
BAM
I ACTIVATE ANOTHER SPELL CARD! WHITE MIRROR!
WHITE MIRROR (SPELL CARD)
Special Summon one White Monster from the Graveyard and add one monster with the same name from your deck to your hand.

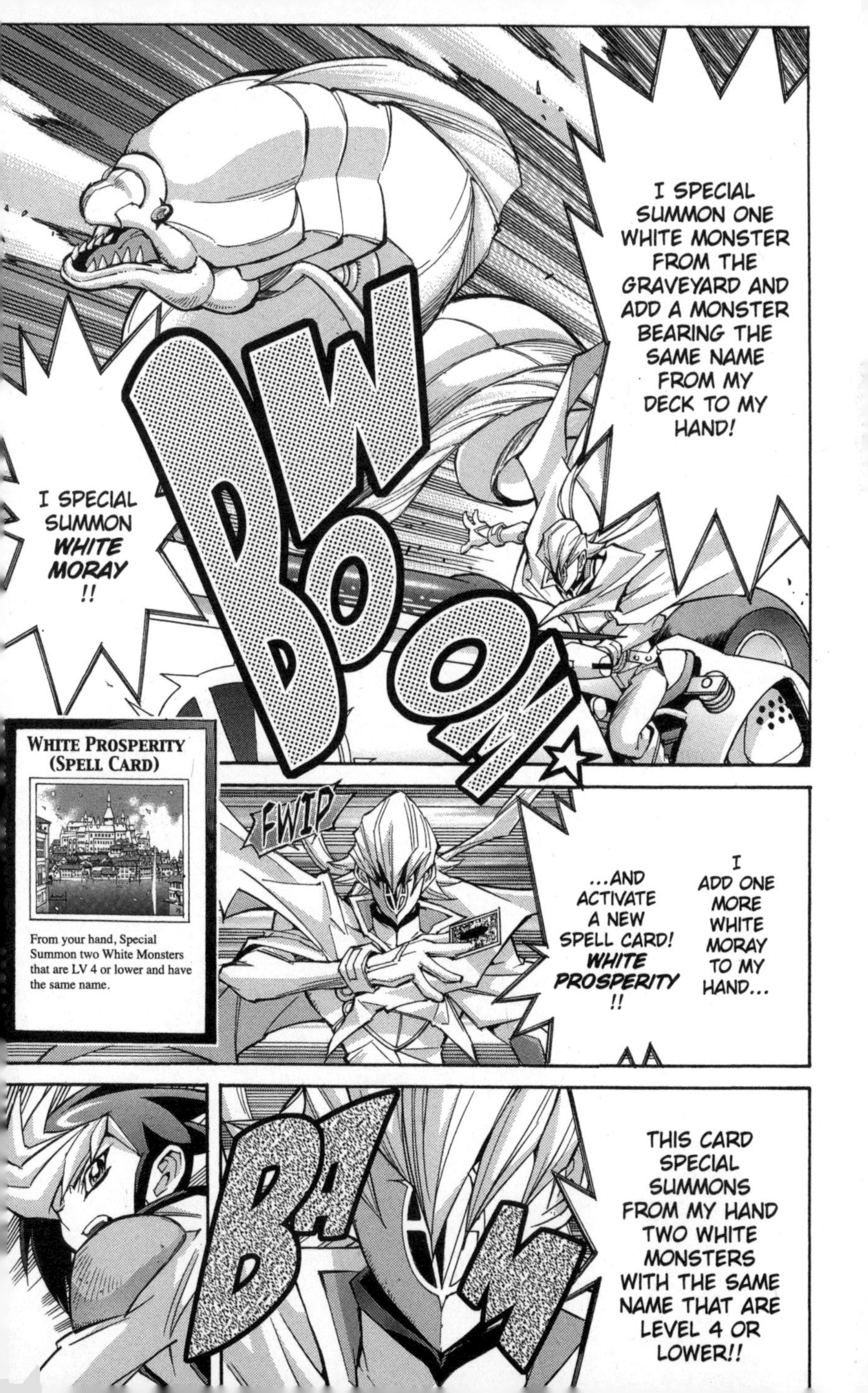
I SPECIAL SUMMON ONE WHITE MONSTER FROM THE GRAVEYARD AND ADD A MONSTER BEARING THE SAME NAME FROM MY DECK TO MY HAND!
I SPECIAL SUMMON *WHITE MORAY* !!
FWIP
I ADD ONE MORE WHITE MORAY TO MY HAND...
...AND ACTIVATE A NEW SPELL CARD! *WHITE PROSPERITY* !!
WHITE PROSPERITY (SPELL CARD)
From your hand, Special Summon two White Monsters that are LV 4 or lower and have the same name.
THIS CARD SPECIAL SUMMONS FROM MY HAND TWO WHITE MONSTERS WITH THE SAME NAME THAT ARE LEVEL 4 OR LOWER!!

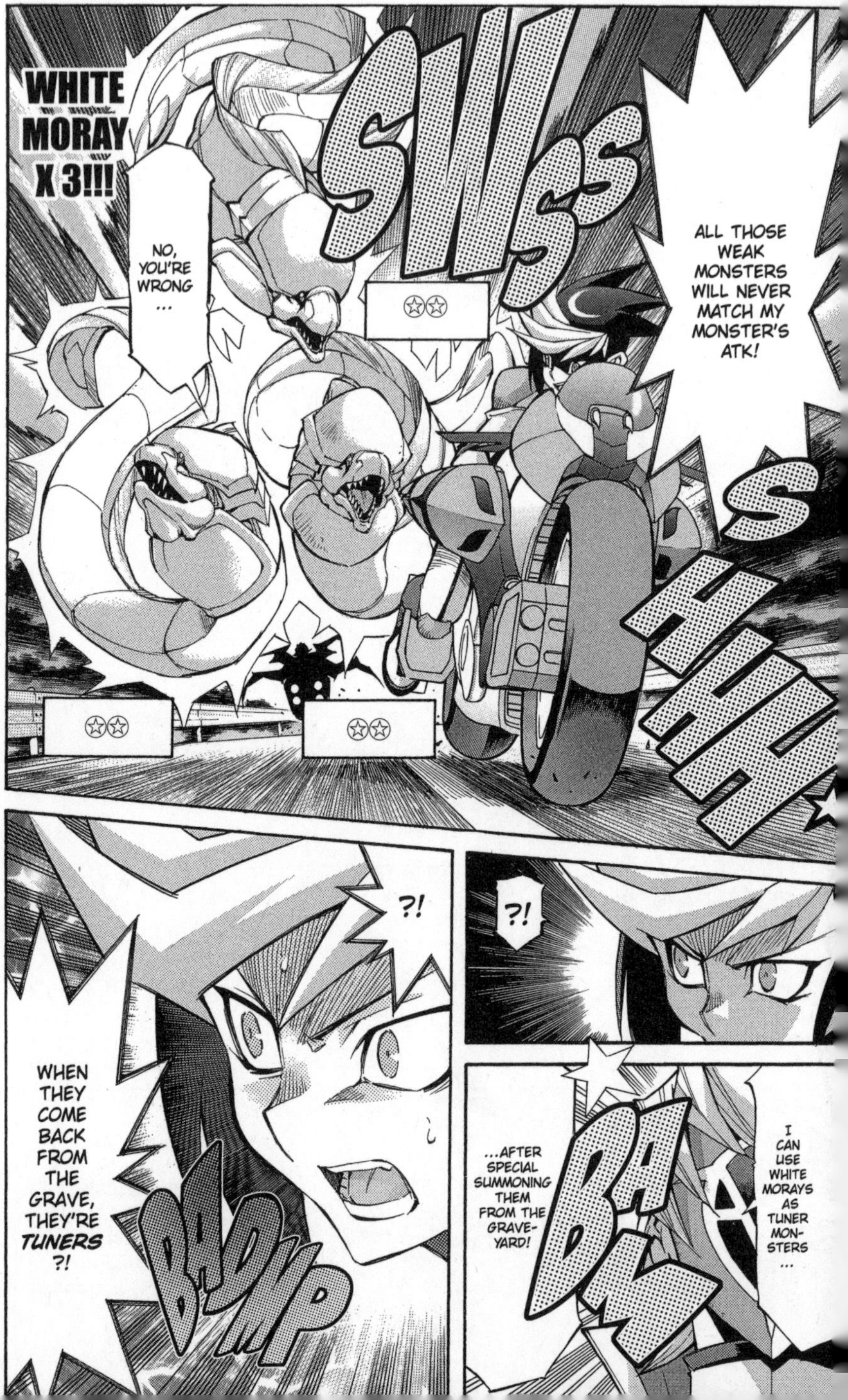
SWISS
ALL THOSE WEAK MONSTERS WILL NEVER MATCH MY MONSTER'S ATK!
SHHHH
NO, YOU'RE WRONG ...
WHITE MORAY X 3!!!
?!
I CAN USE WHITE MORAYS AS TUNER MON-STERS ...
...AFTER SPECIAL SUMMONING THEM FROM THE GRAVE-YARD!
?!
WHEN THEY COME BACK FROM THE GRAVE, THEY'RE *TUNERS* ?!

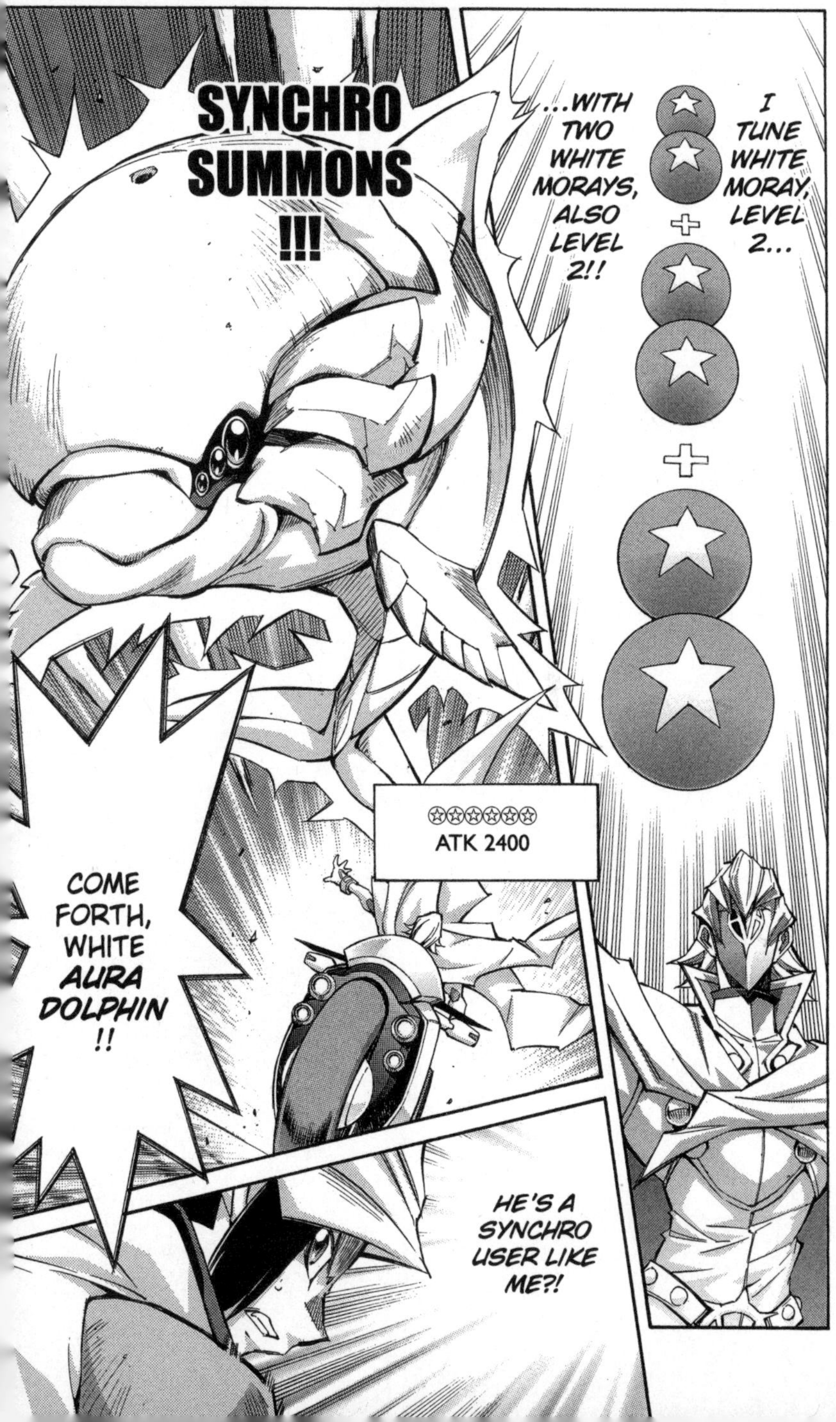
I TUNE WHITE MORAY, LEVEL 2...
...WITH TWO WHITE MORAYS, ALSO LEVEL 2!!
SYNCHRO SUMMONS !!!
ATK 2400
COME FORTH, WHITE AURA DOLPHIN !!
HE'S A SYNCHRO USER LIKE ME?!

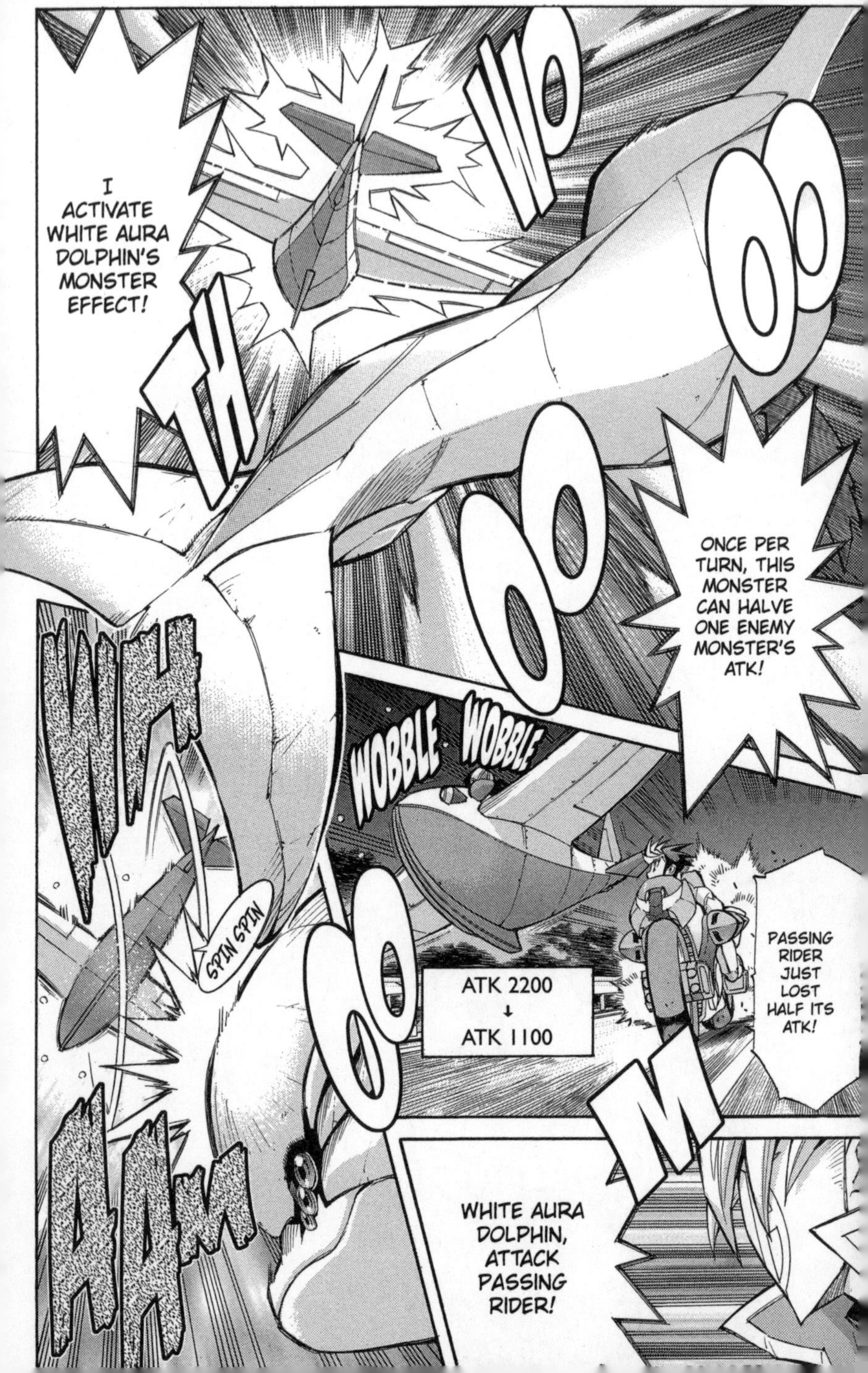
I ACTIVATE WHITE AURA DOLPHIN'S MONSTER EFFECT!
ONCE PER TURN, THIS MONSTER CAN HALVE ONE ENEMY MONSTER'S ATK!
WOBBLE WOBBLE
SPIN SPIN
PASSING RIDER JUST LOST HALF ITS ATK!
ATK 2200 ↓ ATK 1100
WHITE AURA DOLPHIN, ATTACK PASSING RIDER!

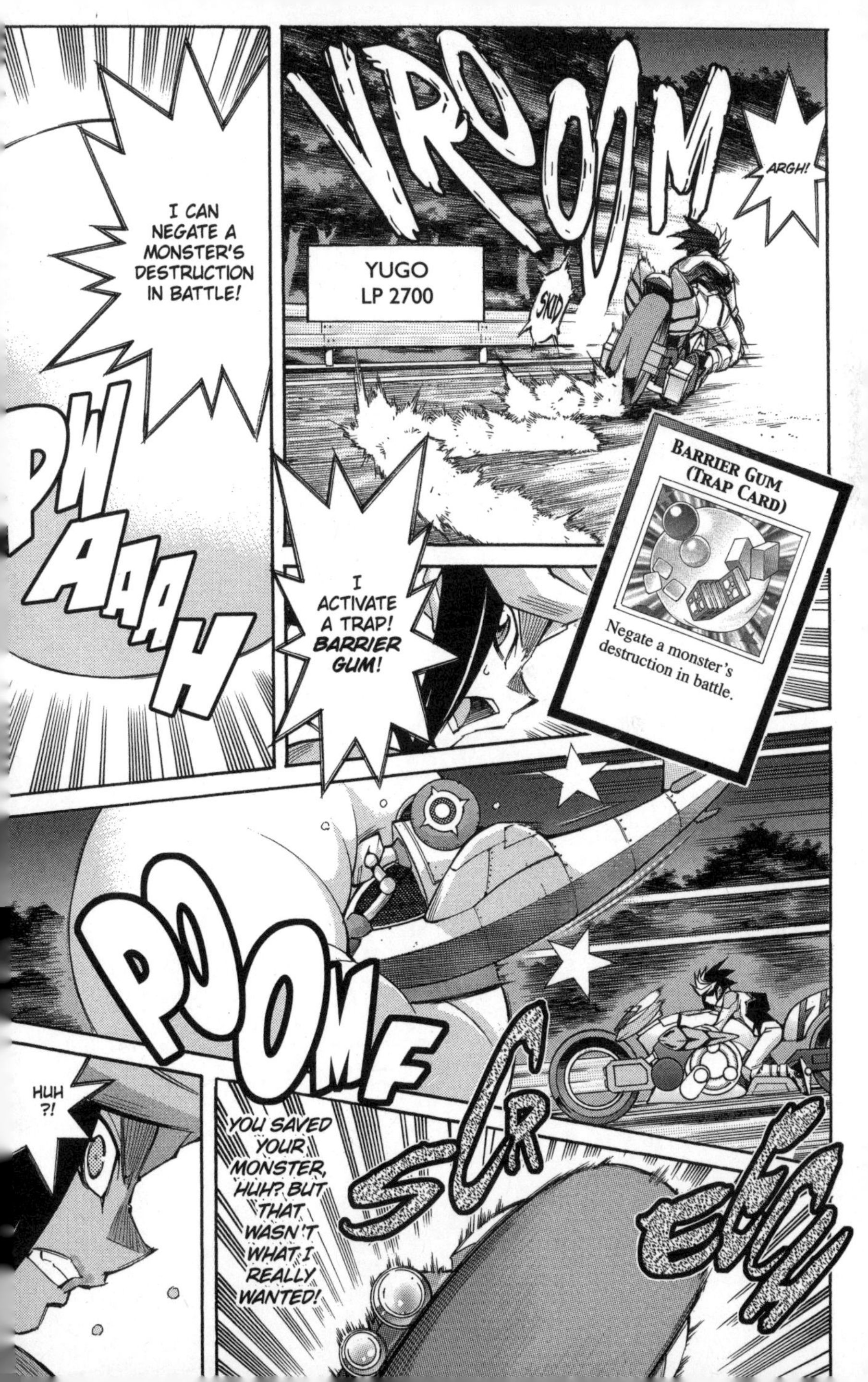
VROOOM
ARGH!
YUGO
LP 2700
SKID
I ACTIVATE A TRAP! BARRIER GUM!
BARRIER GUM (TRAP CARD)
Negate a monster's destruction in battle.
I CAN NEGATE A MONSTER'S DESTRUCTION IN BATTLE!
PWAAAAH
POOMF
YOU SAVED YOUR MONSTER, HUH? BUT THAT WASN'T WHAT I REALLY WANTED!
SCREECH
HUH?!

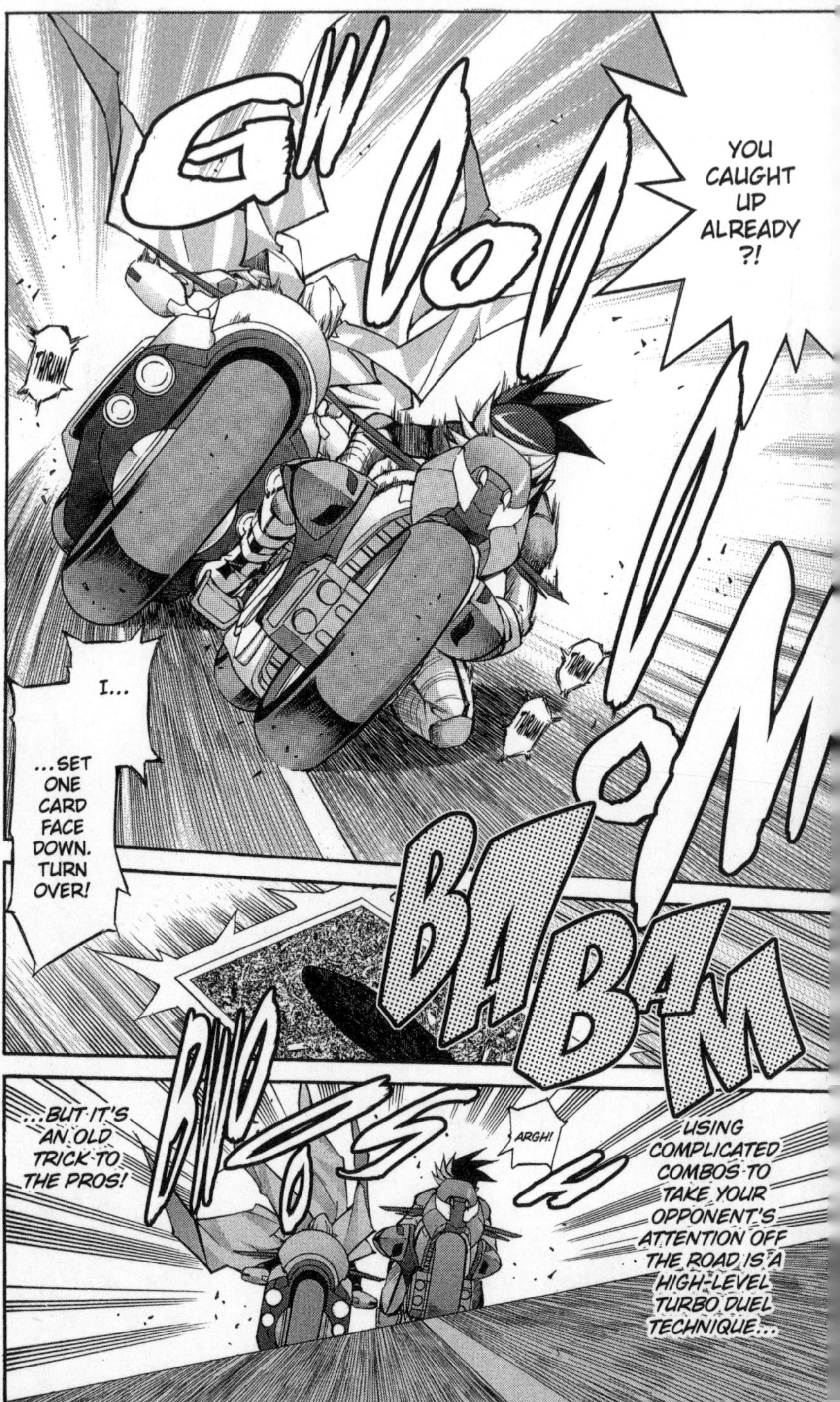
YOU CAUGHT UP ALREADY?!
THRUM
THRUM
THRUM
I...
...SET ONE CARD FACE DOWN. TURN OVER!
BABAM
USING COMPLICATED COMBOS TO TAKE YOUR OPPONENT'S ATTENTION OFF THE ROAD IS A HIGH-LEVEL TURBO DUEL TECHNIQUE...
ARGH!
...BUT IT'S AN OLD TRICK TO THE PROS!

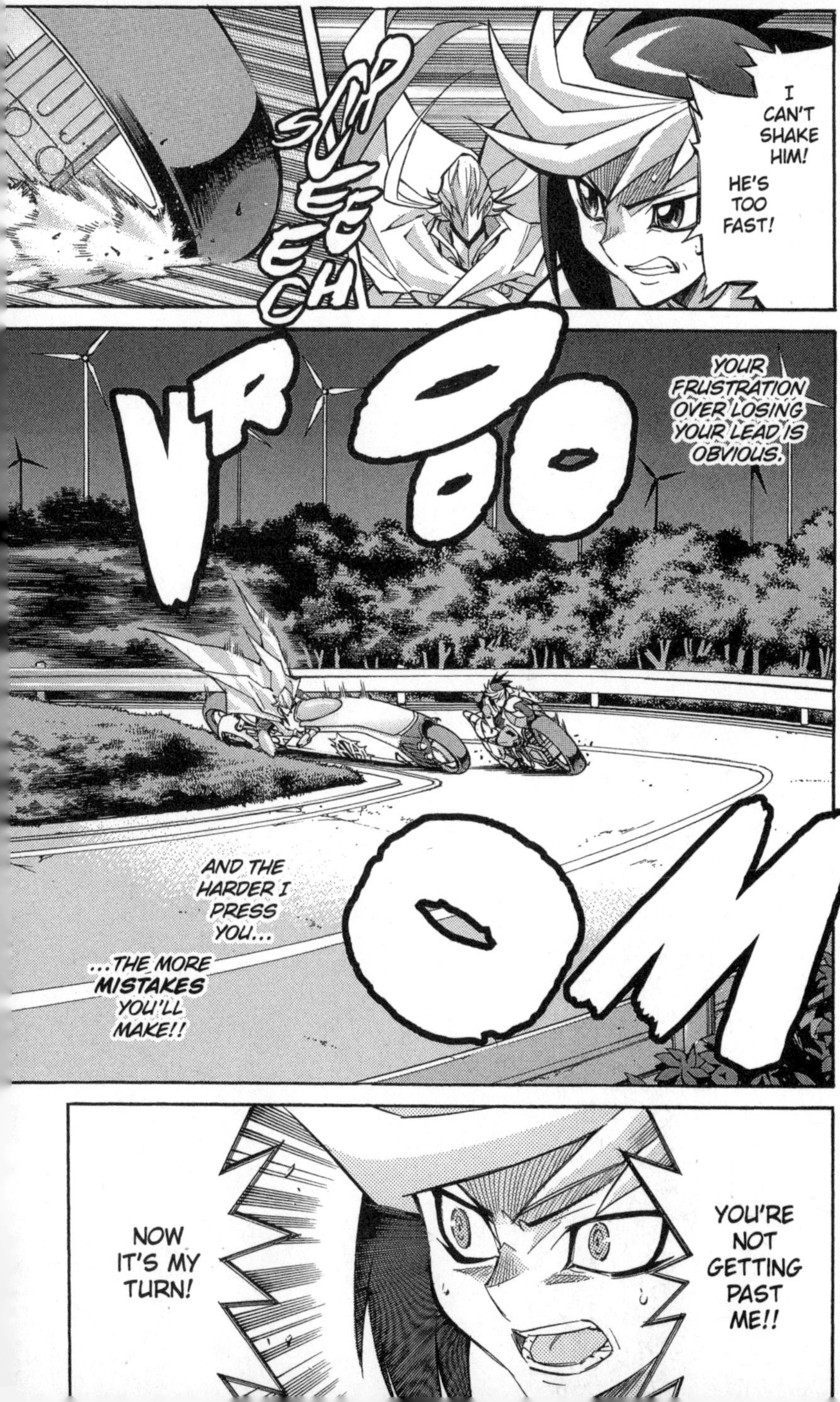
I CAN'T SHAKE HIM!
HE'S TOO FAST!
SCREEEECH
YOUR FRUSTRATION OVER LOSING YOUR LEAD IS OBVIOUS.
VROOOOM
AND THE HARDER I PRESS YOU...
...THE MORE MISTAKES YOU'LL MAKE!!
YOU'RE NOT GETTING PAST ME!!
NOW IT'S MY TURN!

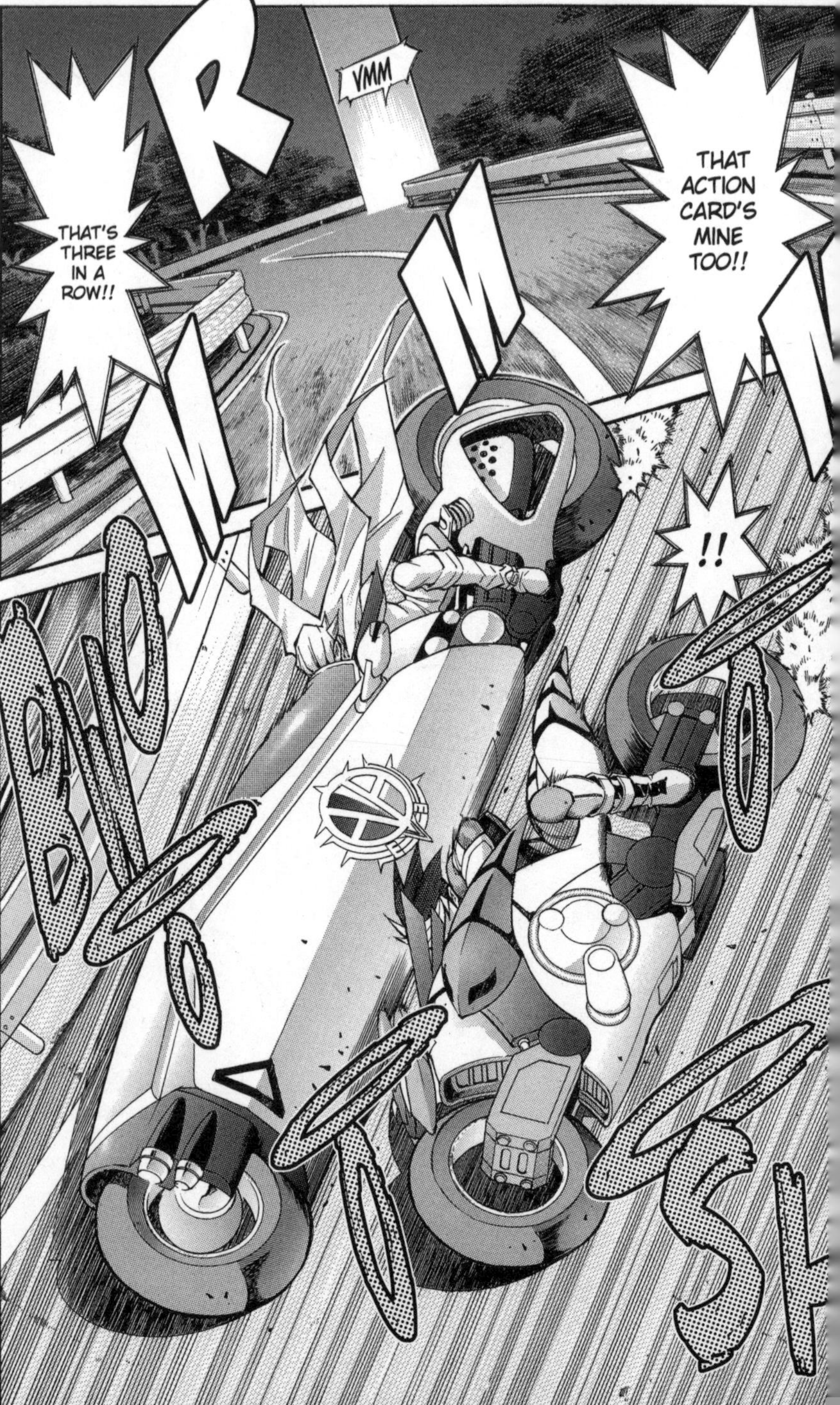
THAT ACTION CARD'S MINE TOO!!
VMM
THAT'S THREE IN A ROW!!
!!

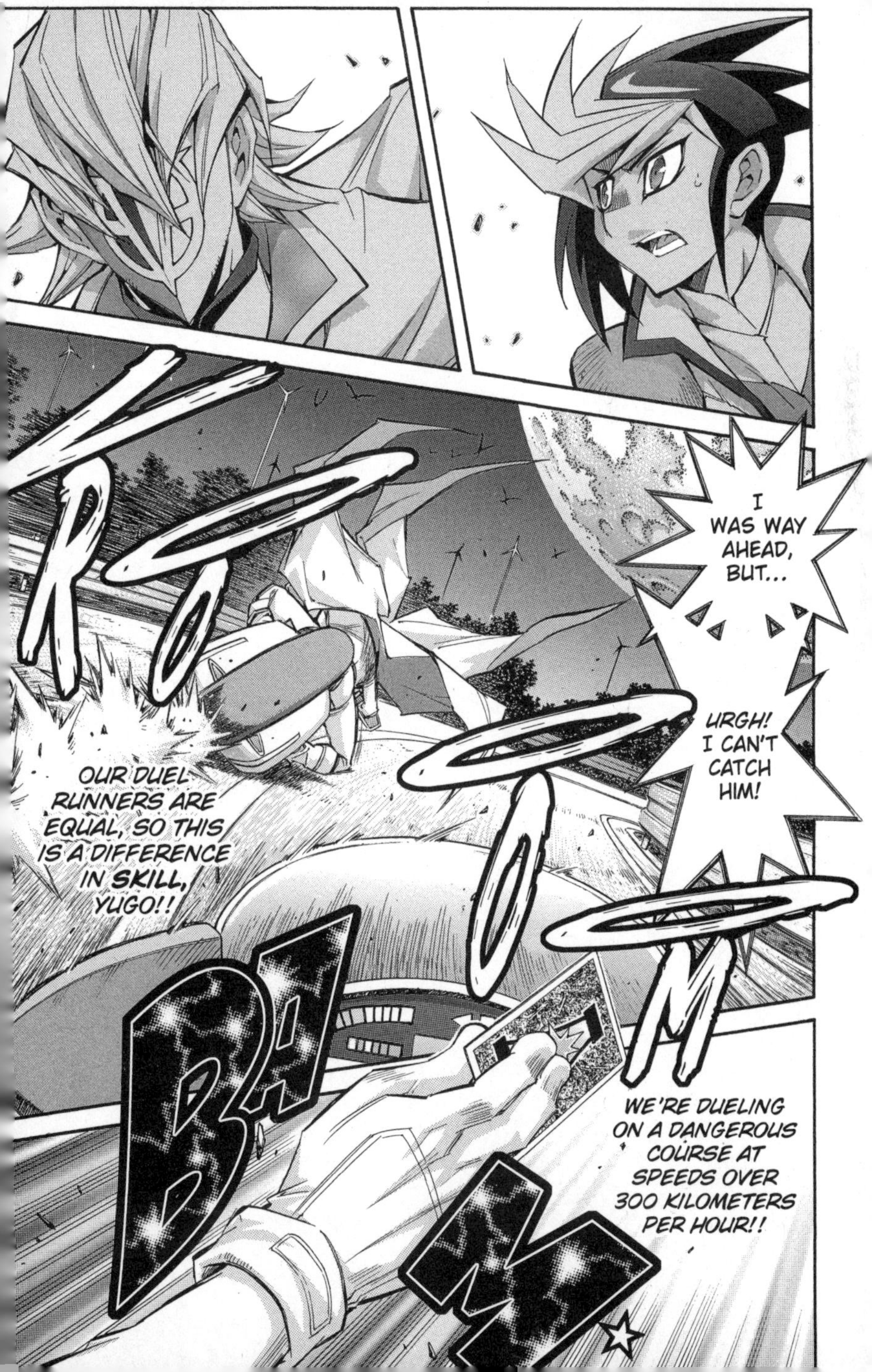
I WAS WAY AHEAD, BUT...
URGH! I CAN'T CATCH HIM!
KROOOOOM
OUR DUEL RUNNERS ARE EQUAL, SO THIS IS A DIFFERENCE IN SKILL, YUGO!!
WE'RE DUELING ON A DANGEROUS COURSE AT SPEEDS OVER 300 KILOMETERS PER HOUR!!
BAM

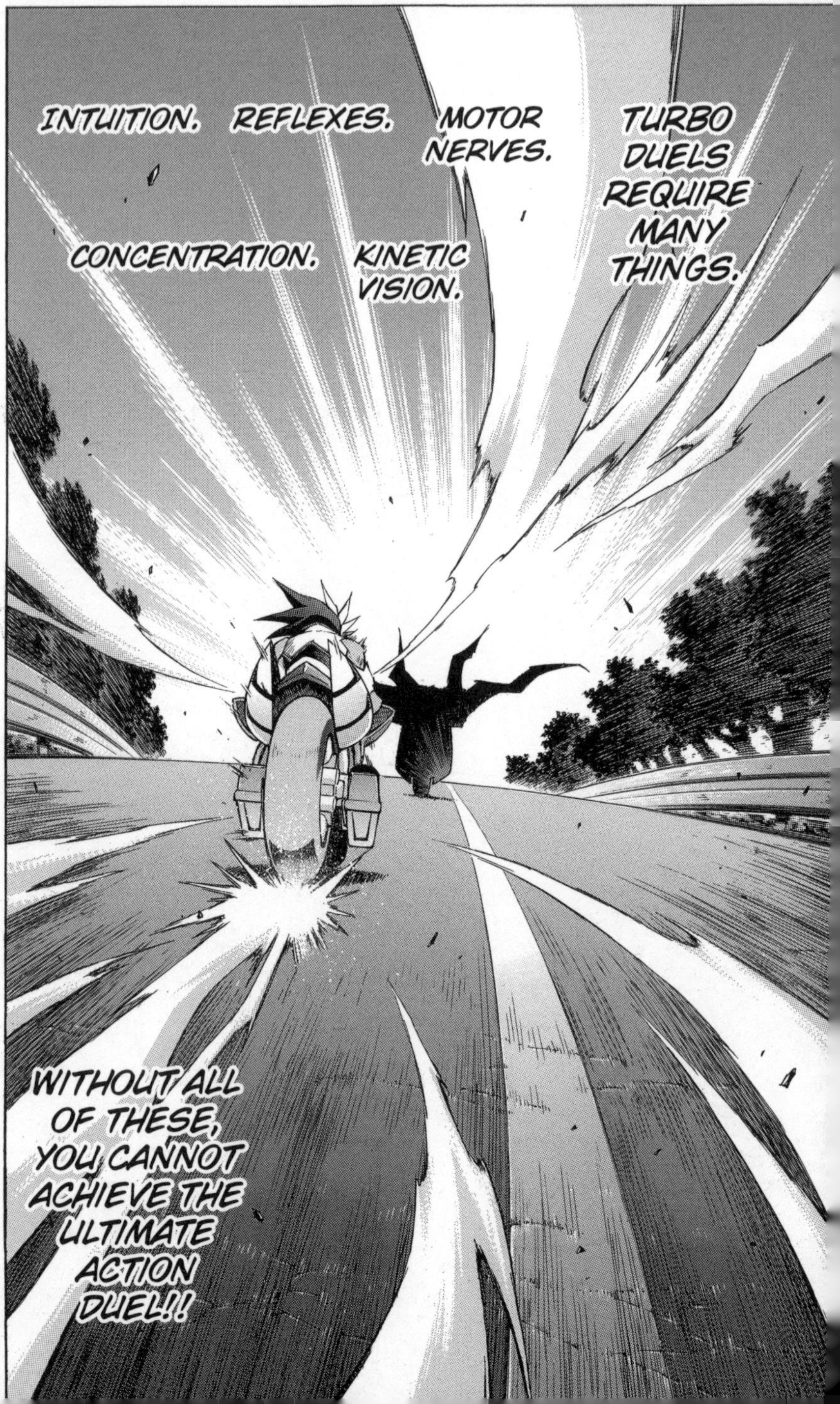

TURBO DUELS REQUIRE MANY THINGS.
MOTOR NERVES.
REFLEXES.
INTUITION.
KINETIC VISION.
CONCENTRATION.
WITHOUT ALL OF THESE, YOU CANNOT ACHIEVE THE ULTIMATE ACTION DUEL!!

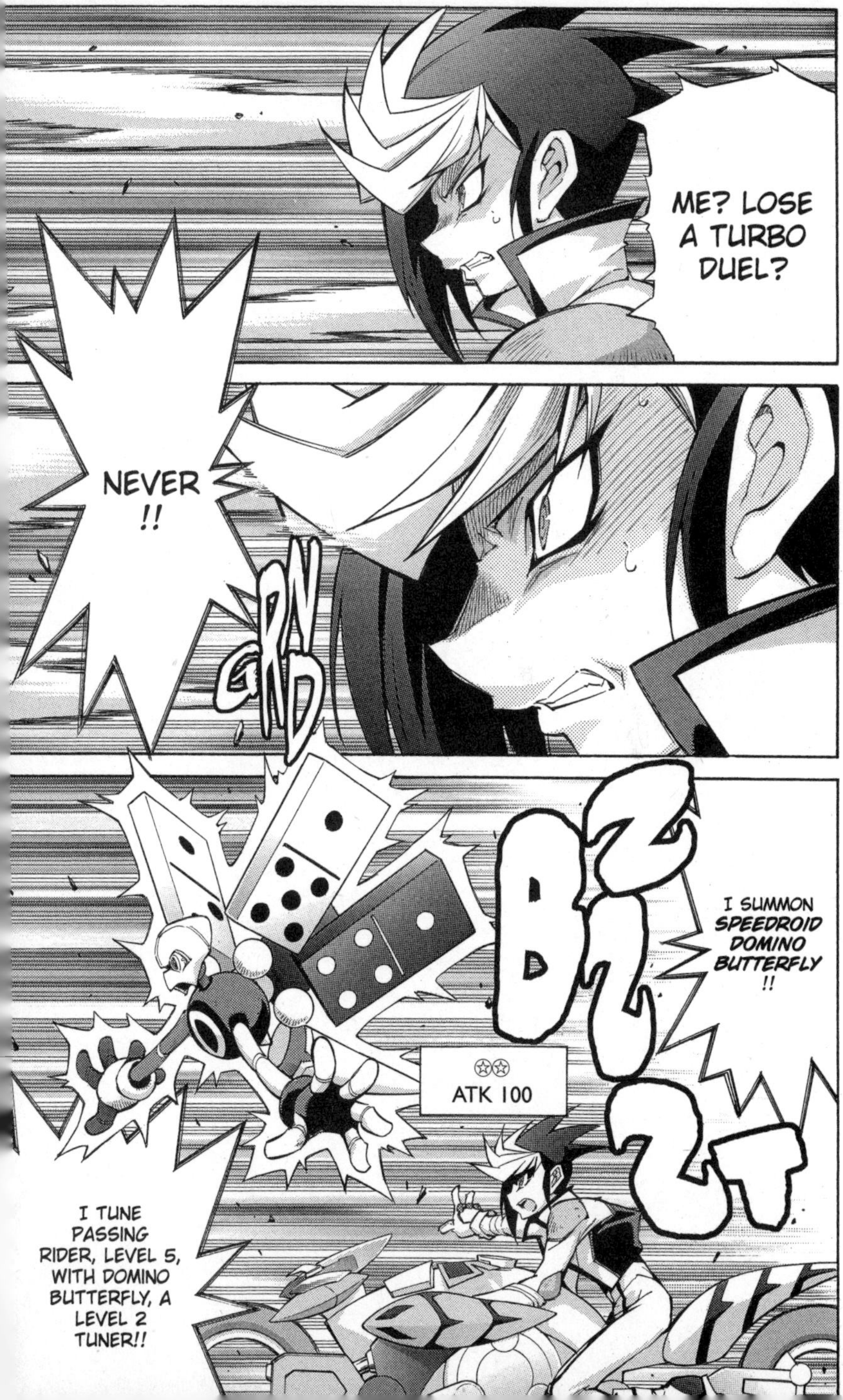
ME? LOSE A TURBO DUEL?
NEVER!!
I SUMMON SPEEDROID DOMINO BUTTERFLY!!
☆☆
ATK 100
I TUNE PASSING RIDER, LEVEL 5, WITH DOMINO BUTTERFLY, A LEVEL 2 TUNER!!

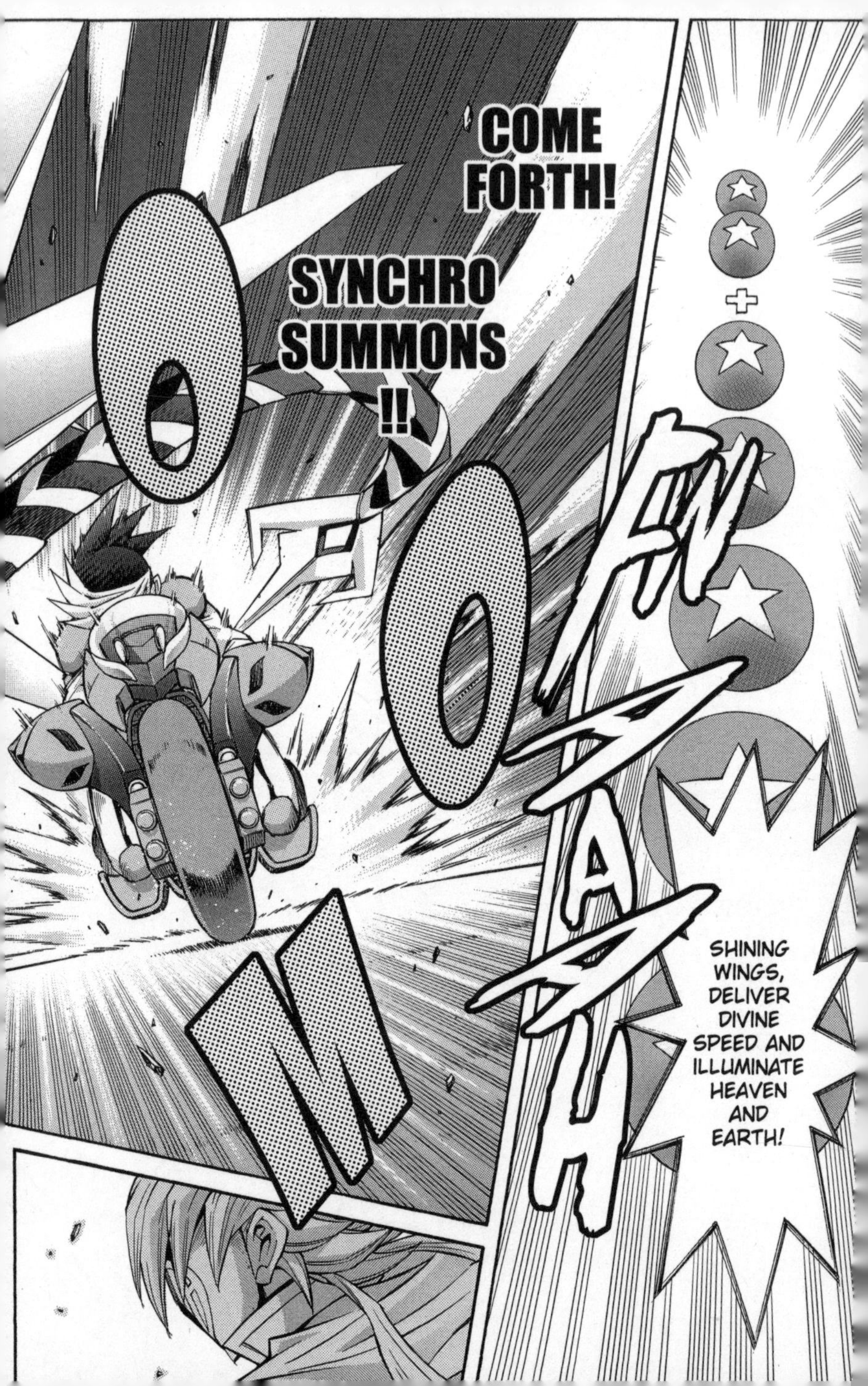
SHINING WINGS, DELIVER DIVINE SPEED AND ILLUMINATE HEAVEN AND EARTH!
COME FORTH!
SYNCHRO SUMMONS !!

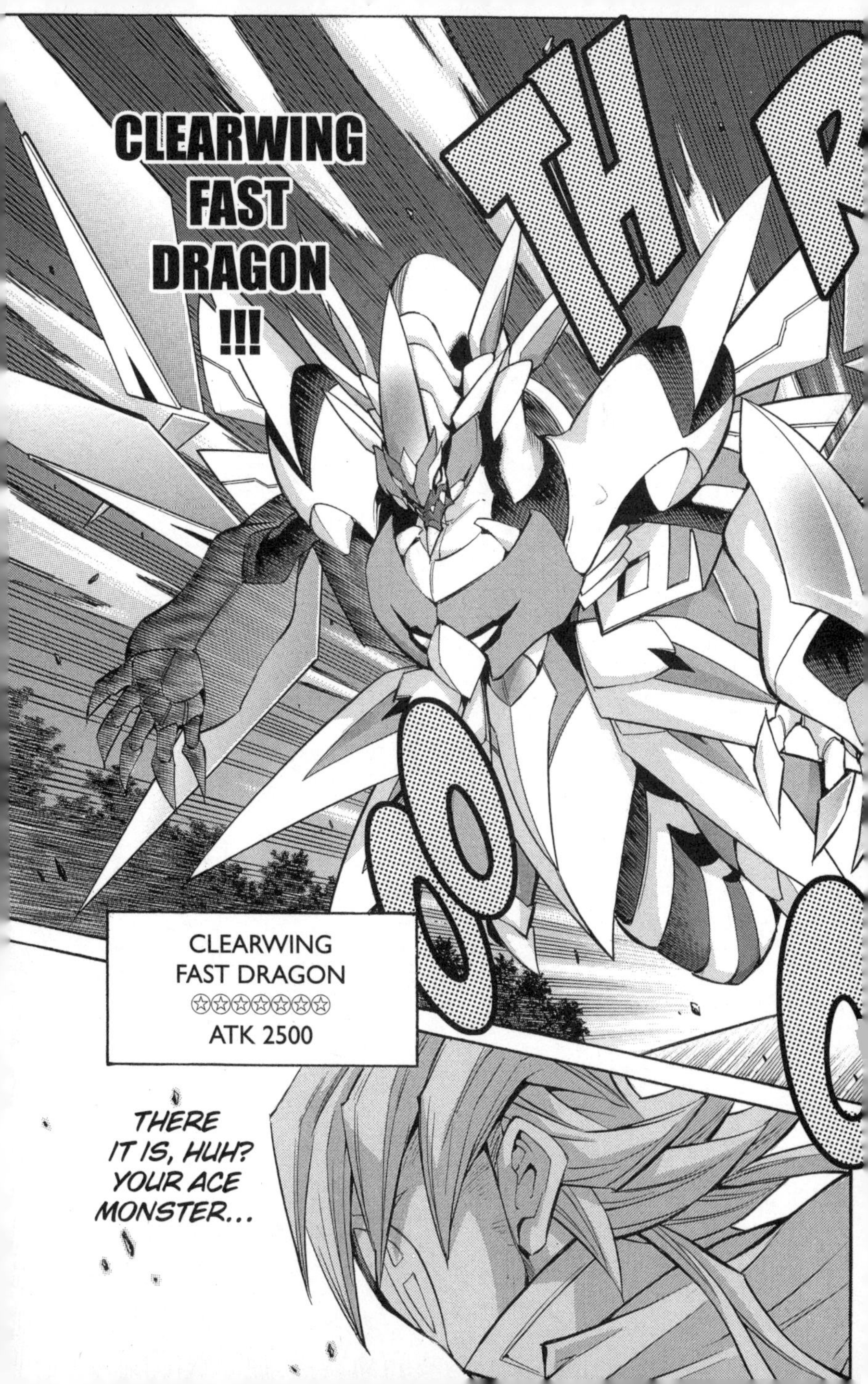
CLEARWING FAST DRAGON !!!
CLEARWING FAST DRAGON ☆☆☆☆☆☆☆ ATK 2500
THERE IT IS, HUH? YOUR ACE MONSTER...

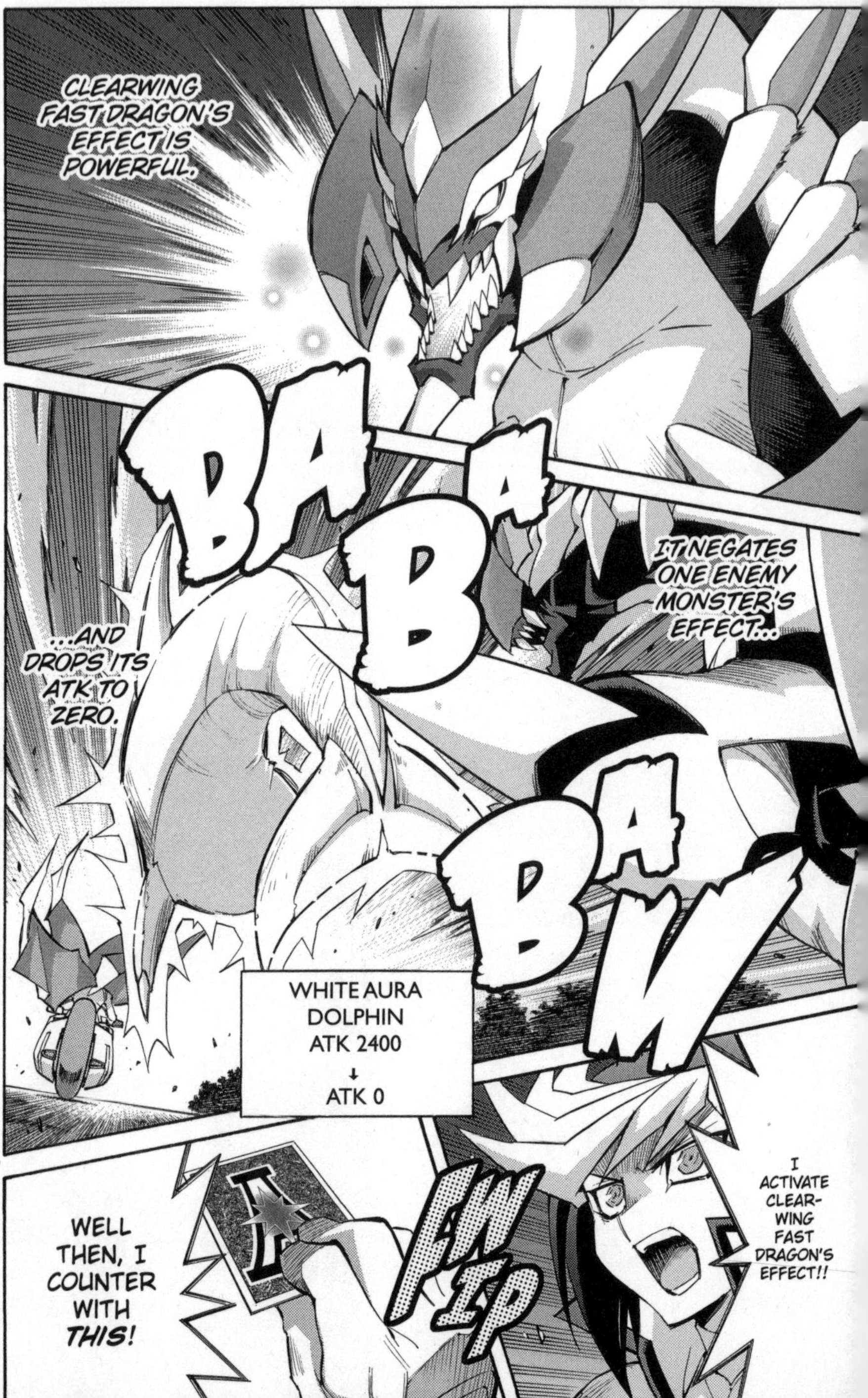
CLEARWING FAST DRAGON'S EFFECT IS POWERFUL.
IT NEGATES ONE ENEMY MONSTER'S EFFECT...
...AND DROPS ITS ATK TO ZERO.
BA BA BAM
WHITE AURA DOLPHIN ATK 2400 ↓ ATK 0
I ACTIVATE CLEARWING FAST DRAGON'S EFFECT!!
WELL THEN, I COUNTER WITH THIS!
FWIP

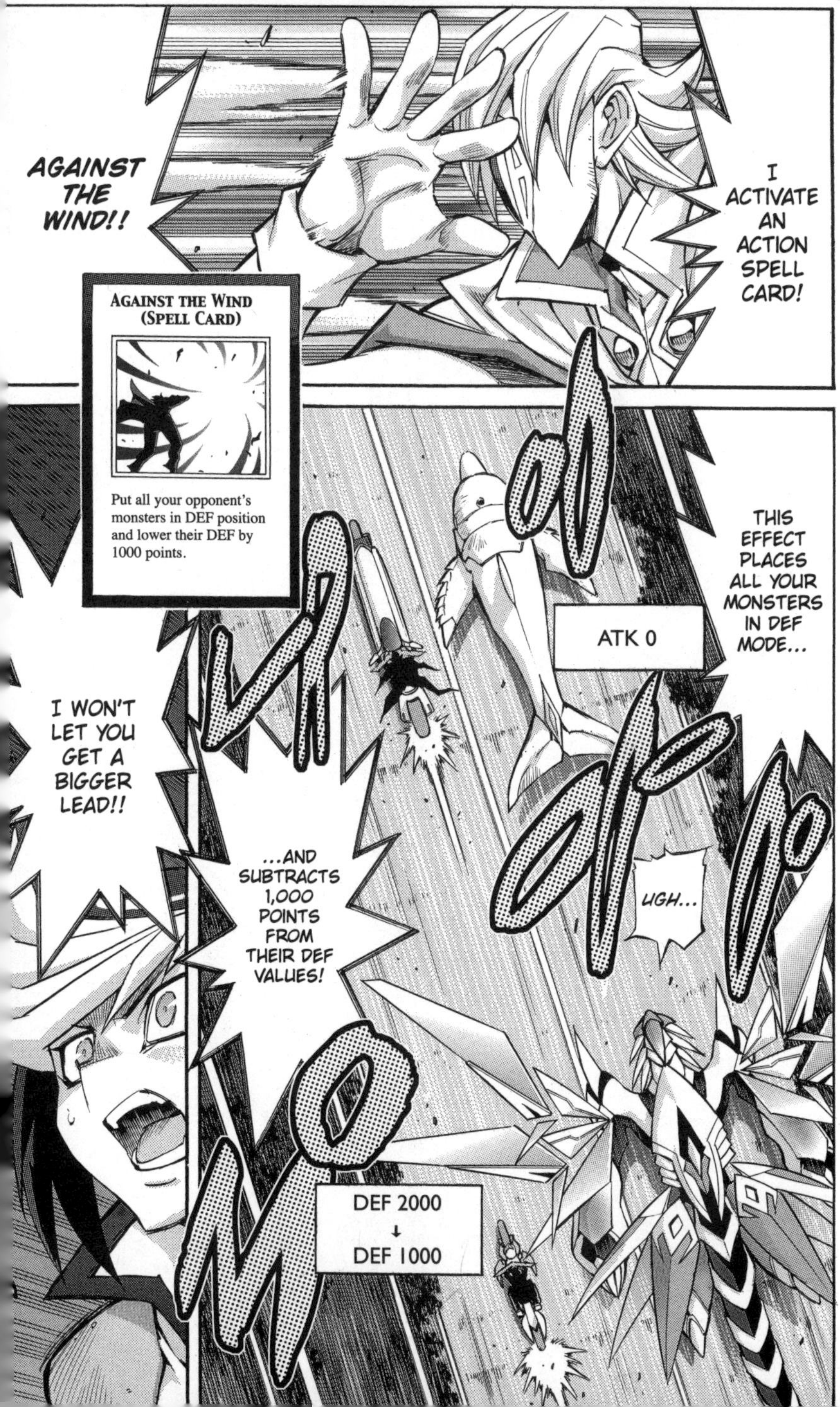
I ACTIVATE AN ACTION SPELL CARD!
AGAINST THE WIND!!
Against the Wind (Spell Card)
Put all your opponent's monsters in DEF position and lower their DEF by 1000 points.
THIS EFFECT PLACES ALL YOUR MONSTERS IN DEF MODE...
ATK 0
UGH...
...AND SUBTRACTS 1,000 POINTS FROM THEIR DEF VALUES!
I WON'T LET YOU GET A BIGGER LEAD!!
DEF 2000
↓
DEF 1000

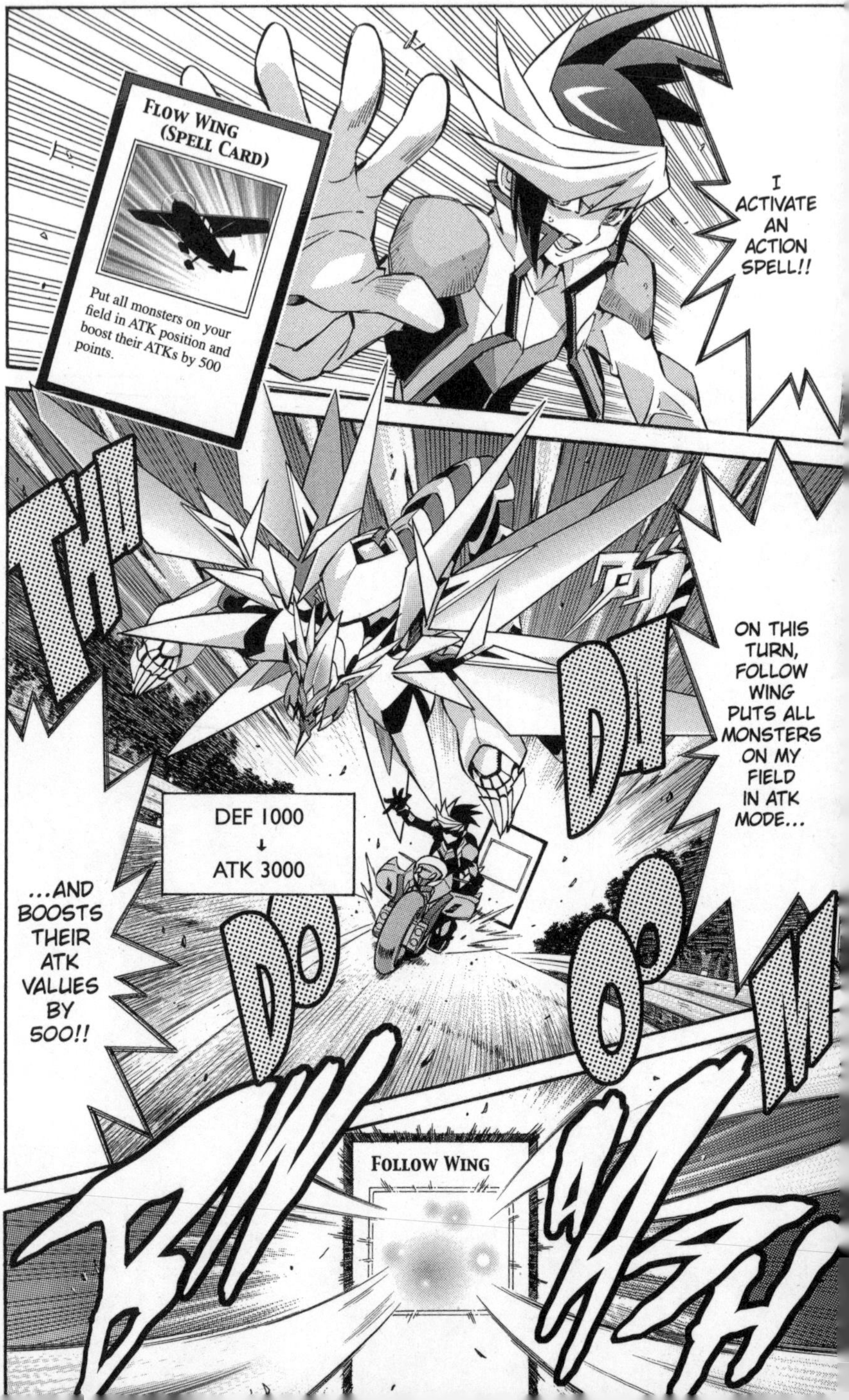
I ACTIVATE AN ACTION SPELL!!
FLOW WING (SPELL CARD)
Put all monsters on your field in ATK position and boost their ATKs by 500 points.
ON THIS TURN, FOLLOW WING PUTS ALL MONSTERS ON MY FIELD IN ATK MODE...
DEF 1000 ↓ ATK 3000
...AND BOOSTS THEIR ATK VALUES BY 500!!
FOLLOW WING

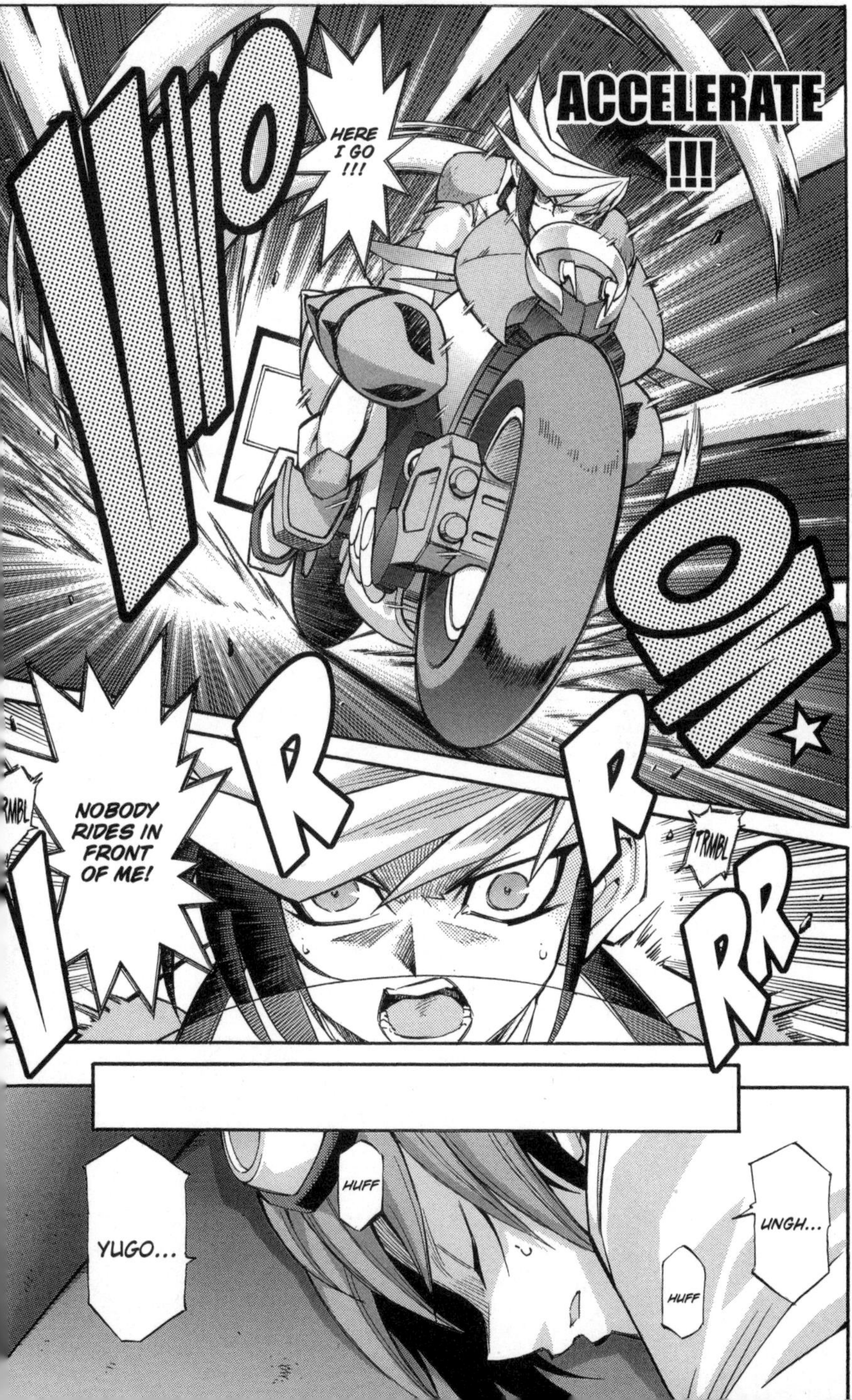
ACCELERATE !!!
HERE I GO !!!
TRMBL
NOBODY RIDES IN FRONT OF ME!
RMBL
UNGH...
HUFF
HUFF
YUGO...

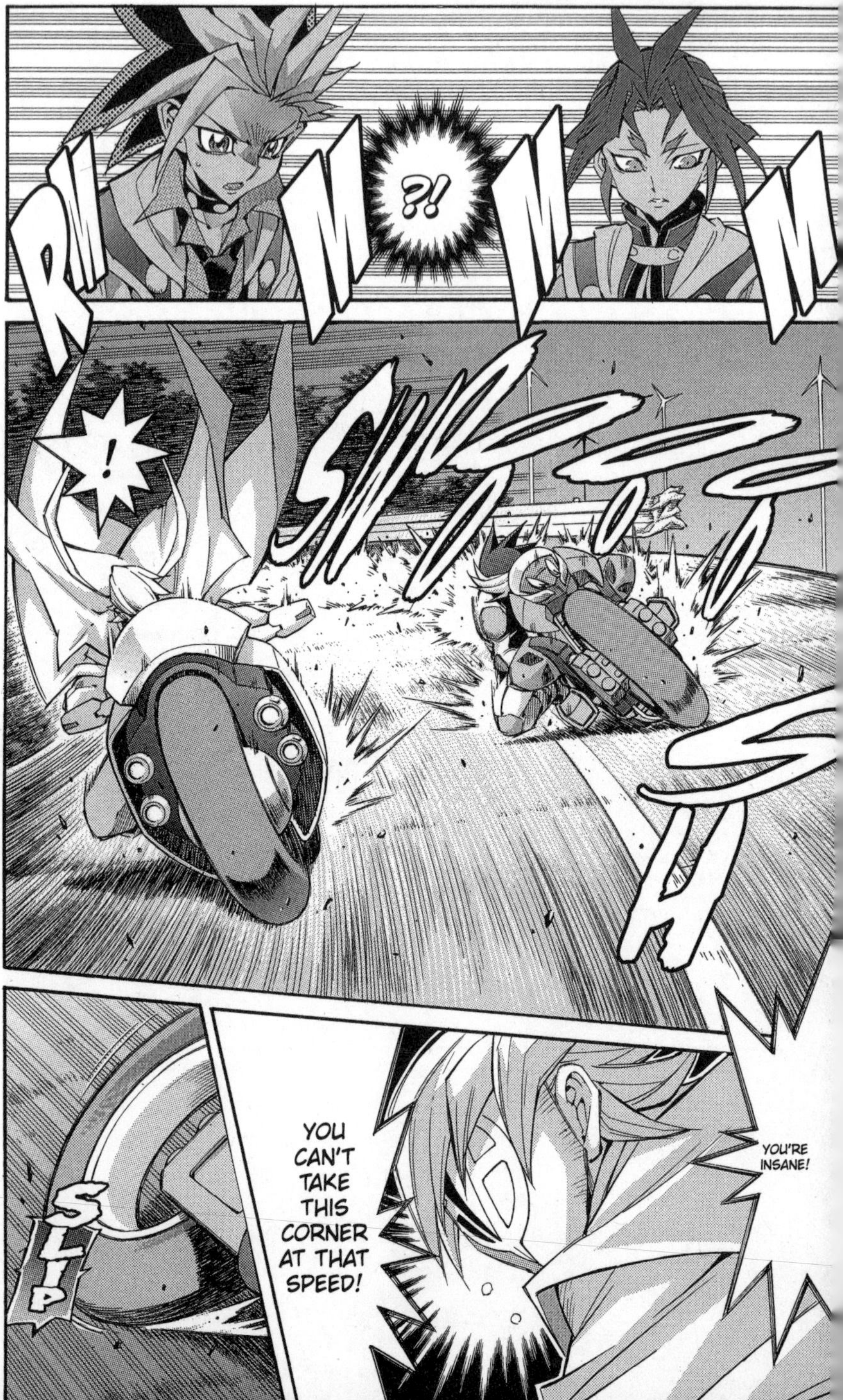

RMMMM
?!
SHOOOOOOOSH
!
YOU'RE INSANE!
YOU CAN'T TAKE THIS CORNER AT THAT SPEED!
SLIP

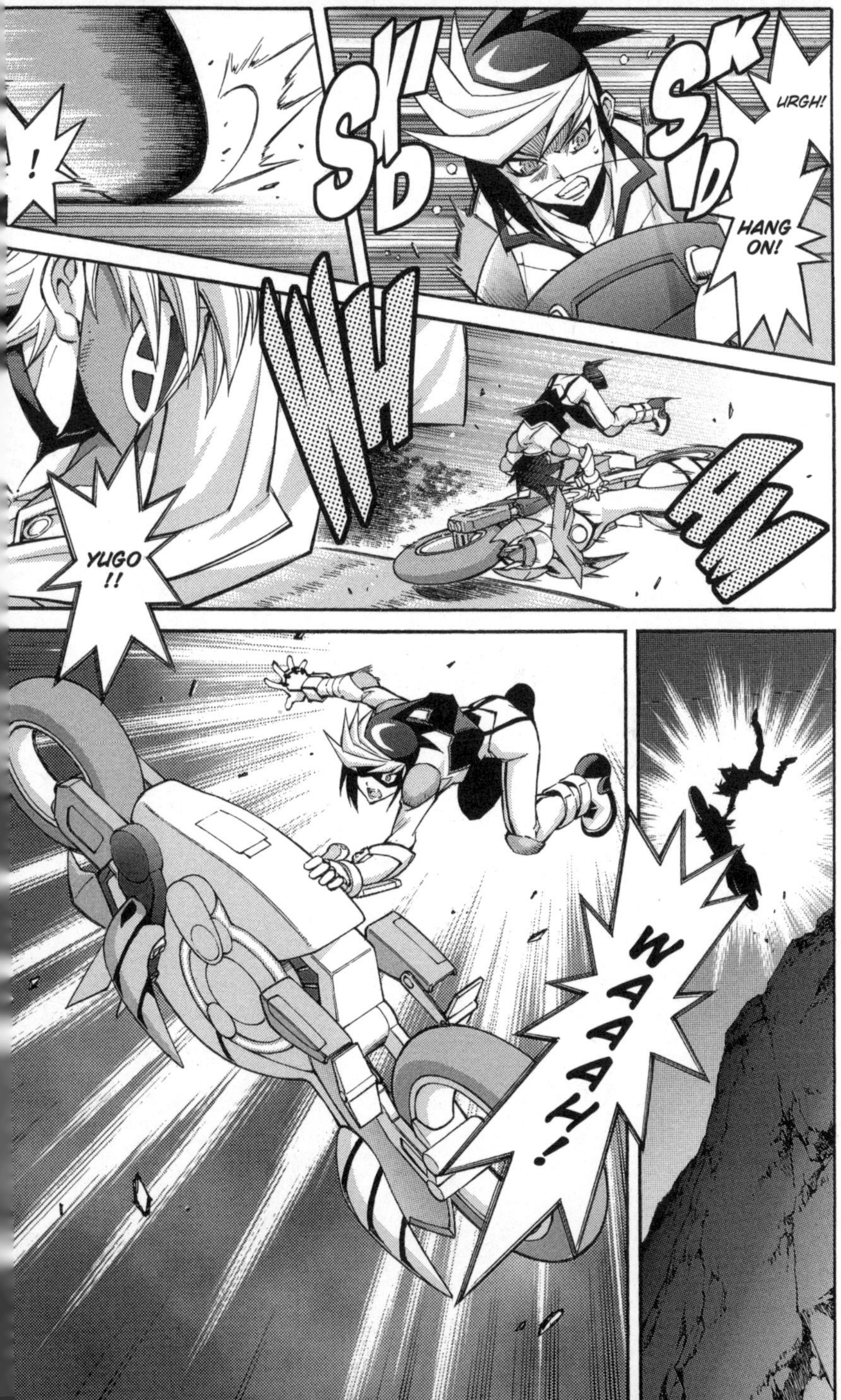
SKID
URGH!
SKID
HANG ON!
!
YUGO!!
WAAAAH!

REN

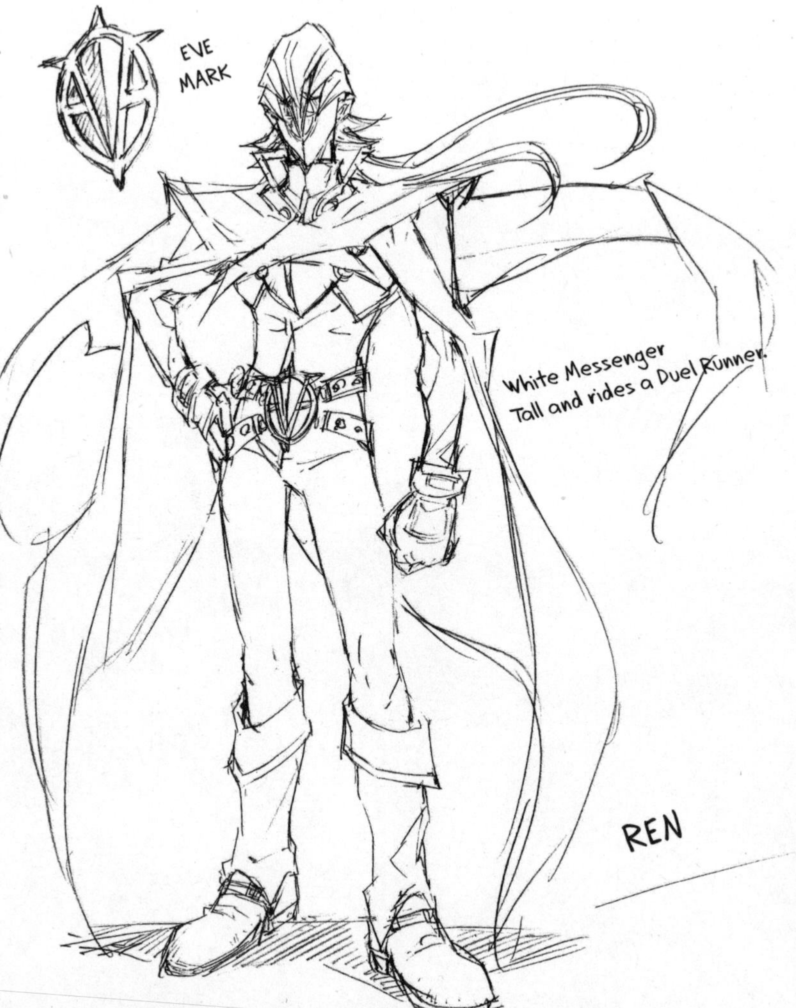
EVE
MARK
White Messenger
Tall and rides a Duel Runner.
REN

Ren is an original character created for the manga. There's probably a lot more to him than we've seen so far. Will the "Eve" character who's been appearing from time to time turn out to be a big part of the story?

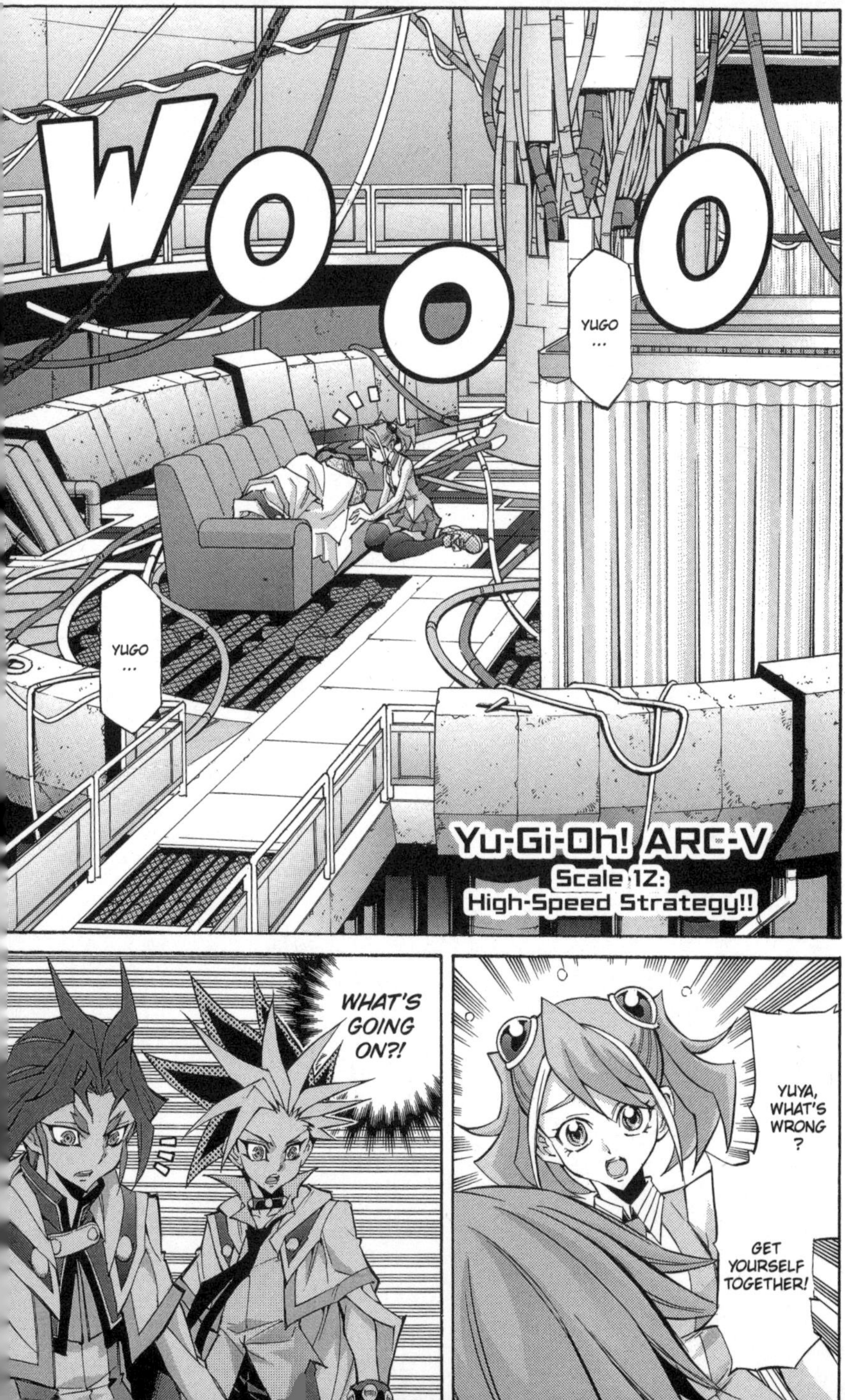
WOOOO
YUGO...
YUGO...
Yu-Gi-Oh! ARC-V
Scale 12: High-Speed Strategy!!
YUYA, WHAT'S WRONG?
GET YOURSELF TOGETHER!
WHAT'S GOING ON?!

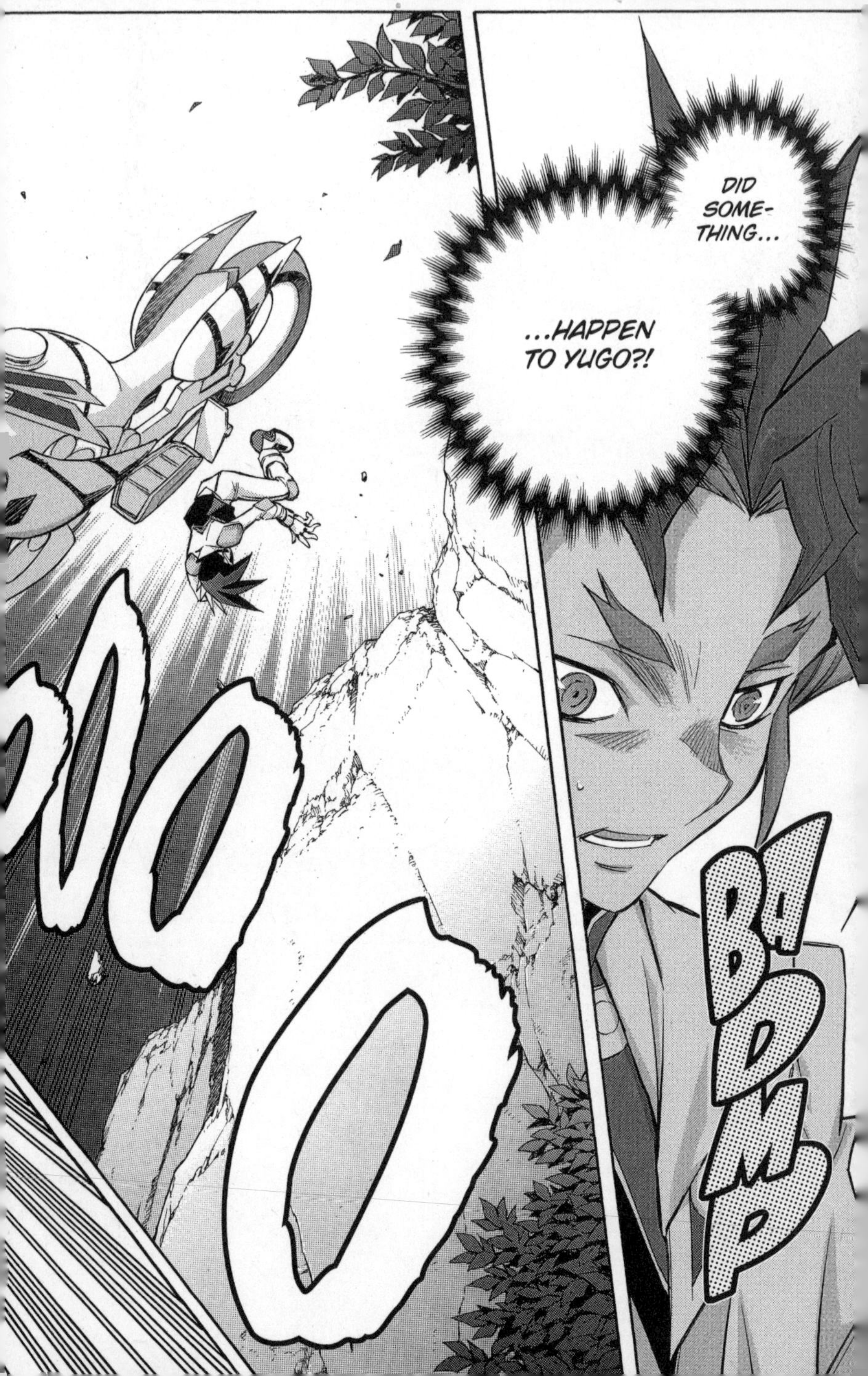
DID SOMETHING...
...HAPPEN TO YUGO?!
BA-DUMP

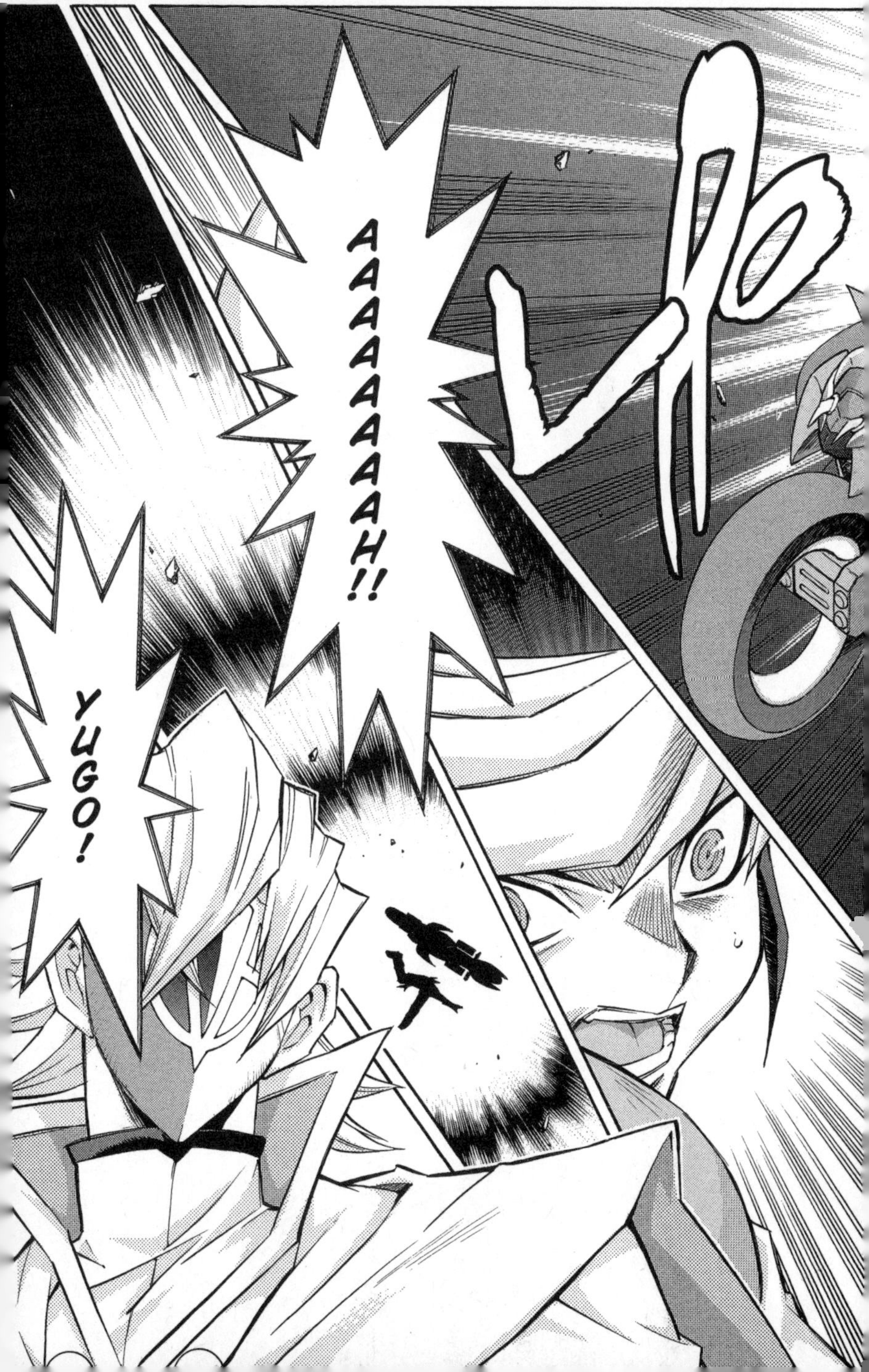
AAAAAAAAH!!
YUGO!

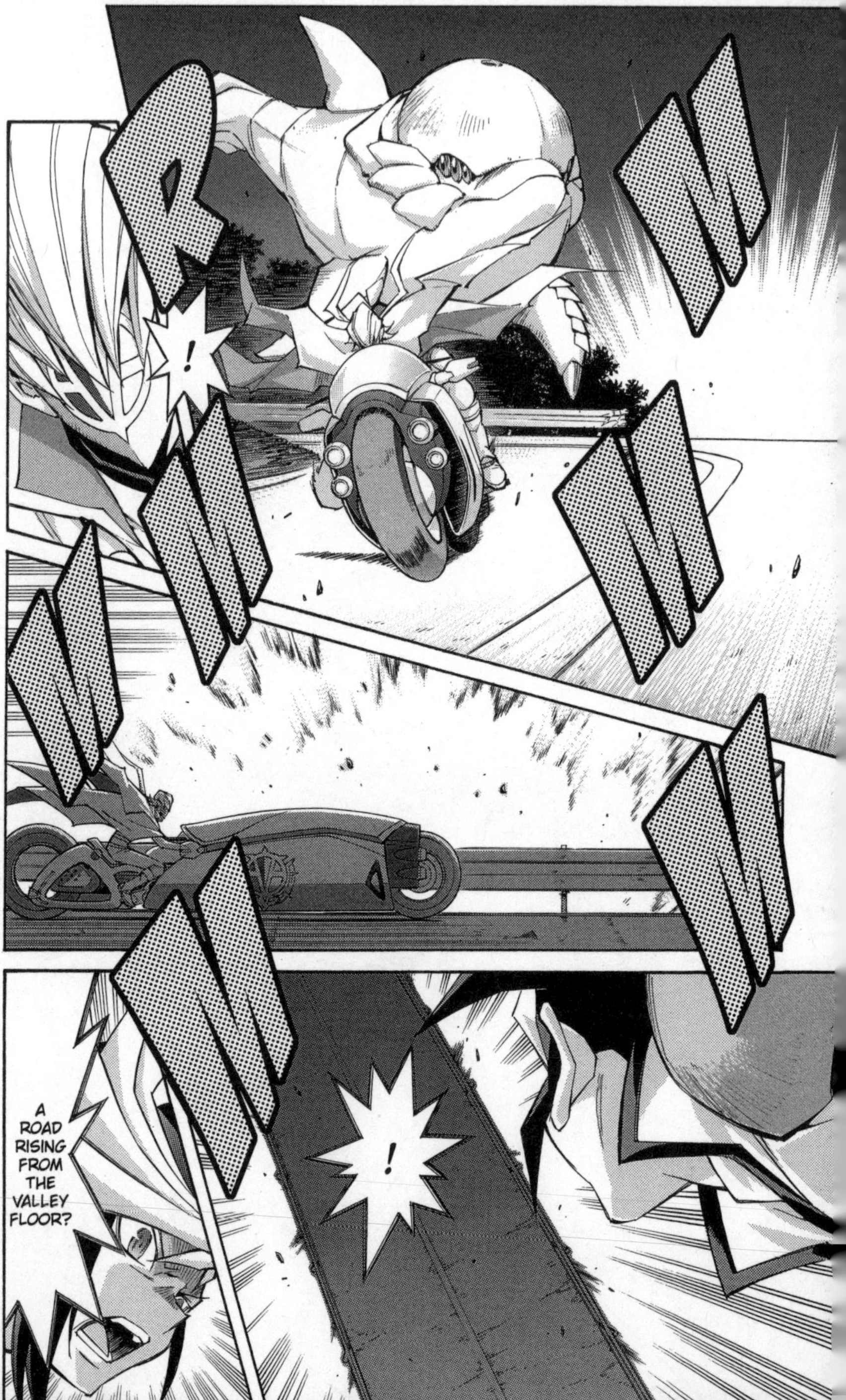
RMMMMMM
!
!
A ROAD RISING FROM THE VALLEY FLOOR?

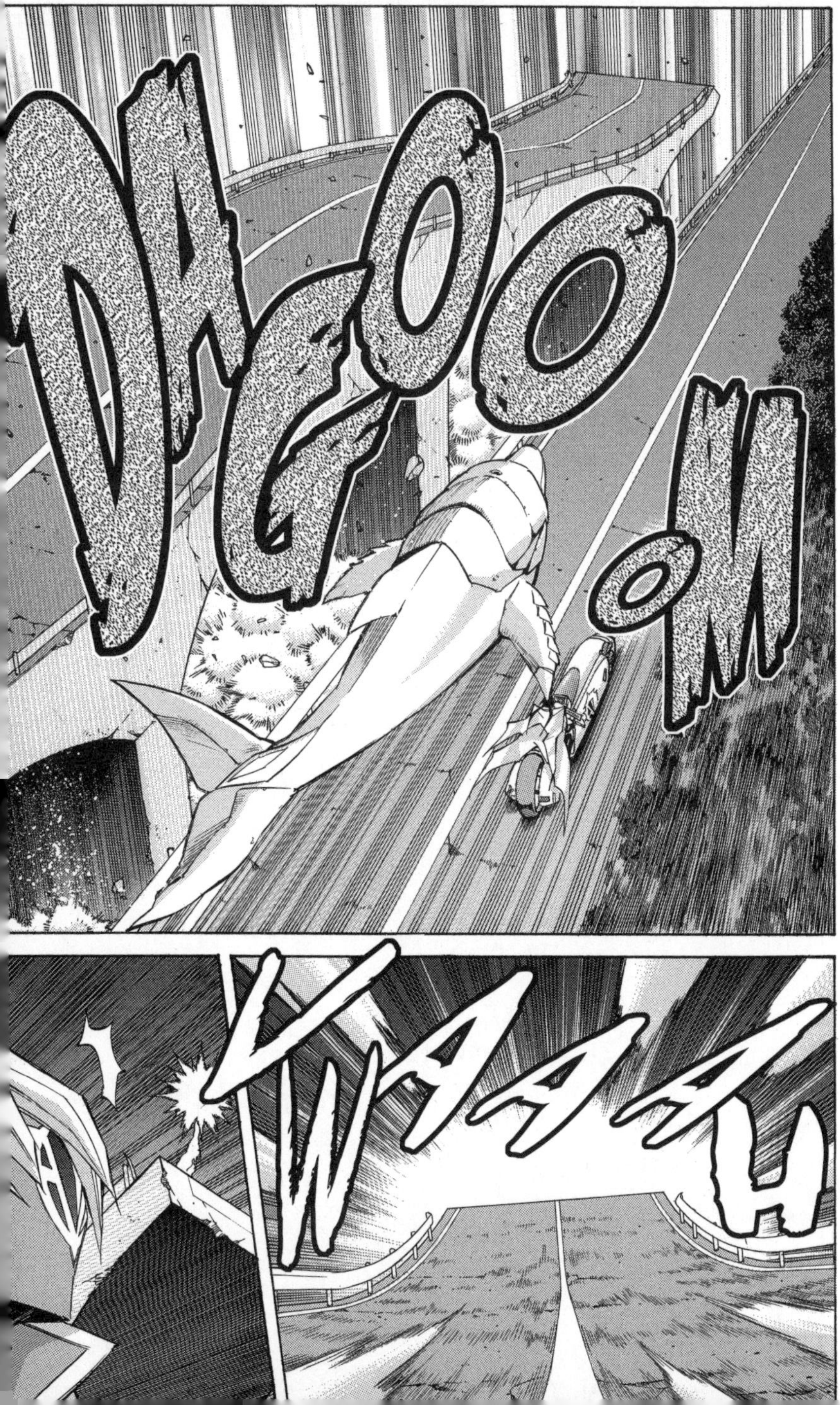
DAGOOOM
VWAAAH

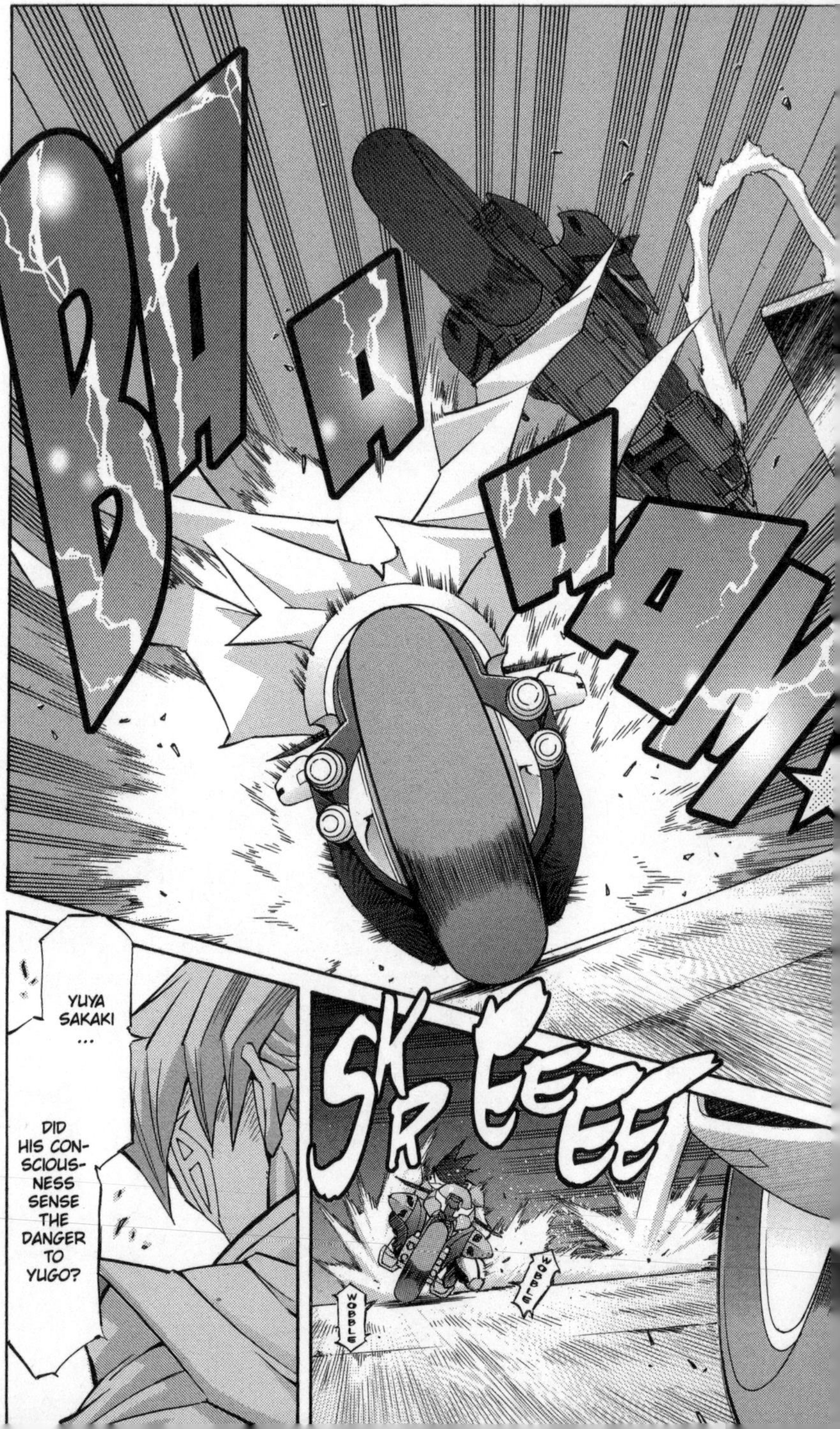
BAAAAM
SKREEEEE
WOBBLE
WOBBLE
YUYA SAKAKI ...
DID HIS CONSCIOUSNESS SENSE THE DANGER TO YUGO?

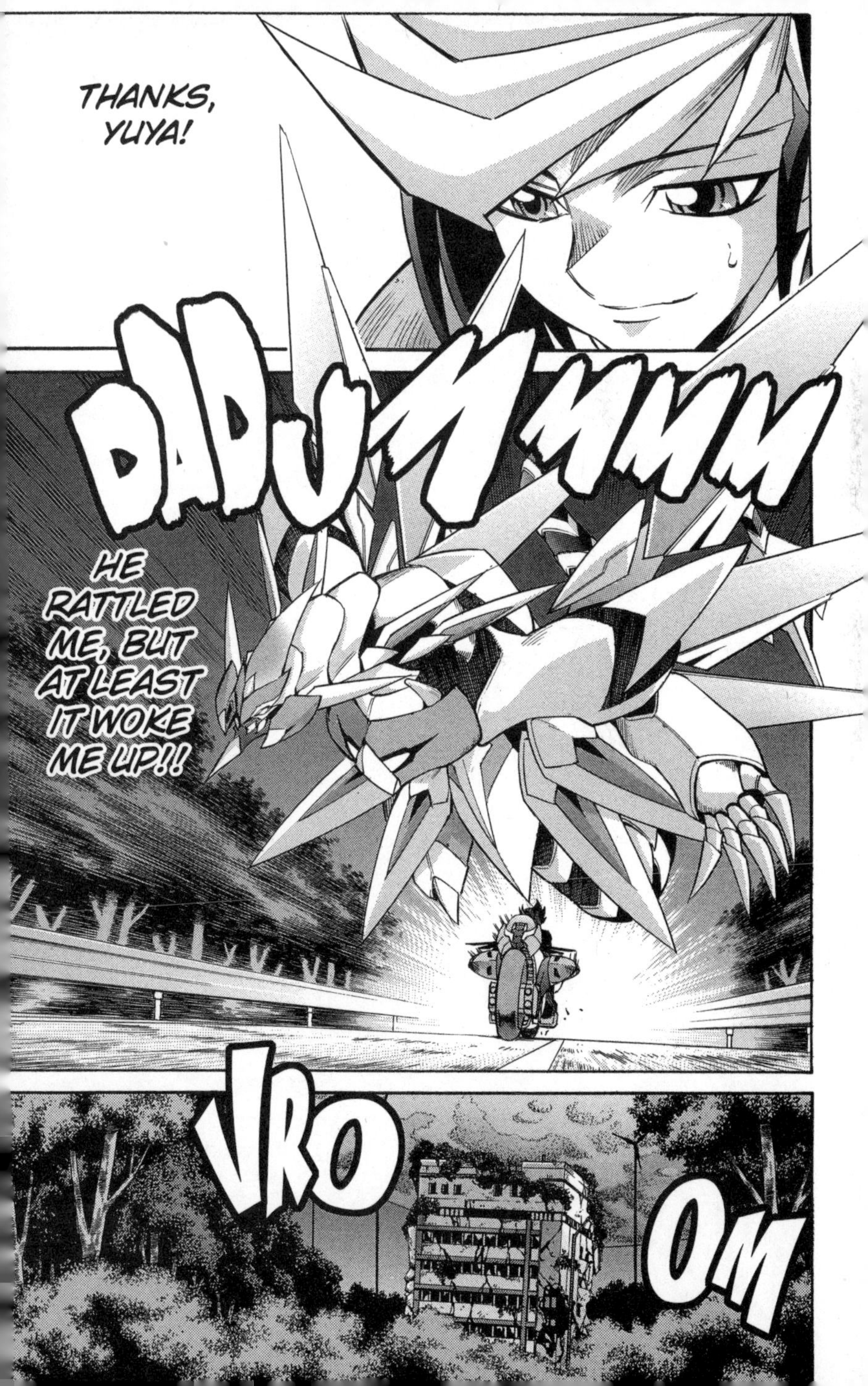
THANKS, YUYA!
DADUMMMMM
HE RATTLED ME, BUT AT LEAST IT WOKE ME UP!!
VROOM

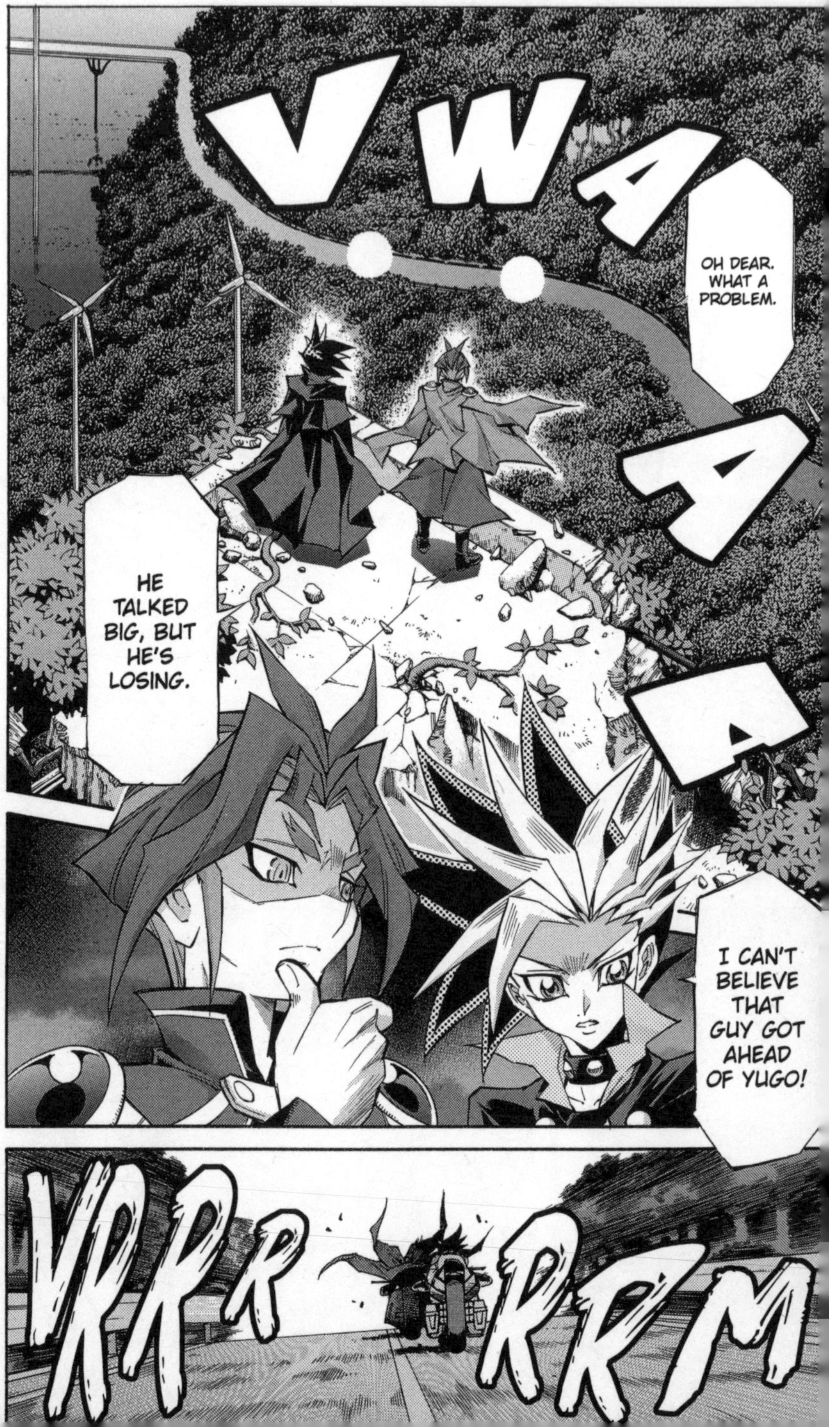
VWAAAA
OH DEAR. WHAT A PROBLEM.
HE TALKED BIG, BUT HE'S LOSING.
I CAN'T BELIEVE THAT GUY GOT AHEAD OF YUGO!
VRRR-RRRM

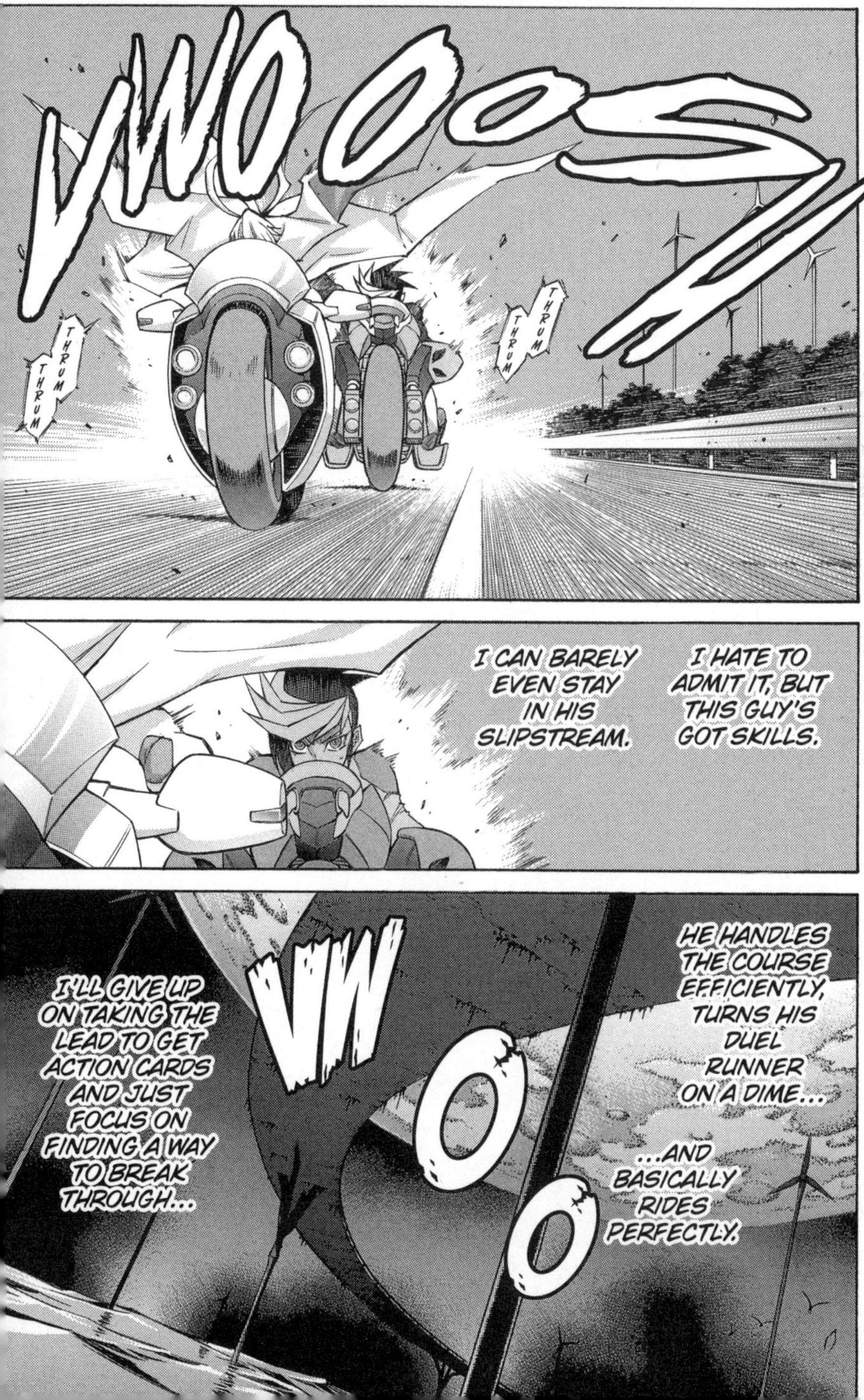
VWOOOSH
THRUM THRUM
THRUM THRUM
I HATE TO ADMIT IT, BUT THIS GUY'S GOT SKILLS.
I CAN BARELY EVEN STAY IN HIS SLIPSTREAM.
HE HANDLES THE COURSE EFFICIENTLY, TURNS HIS DUEL RUNNER ON A DIME...
...AND BASICALLY RIDES PERFECTLY.
VWOO
I'LL GIVE UP ON TAKING THE LEAD TO GET ACTION CARDS AND JUST FOCUS ON FINDING A WAY TO BREAK THROUGH...

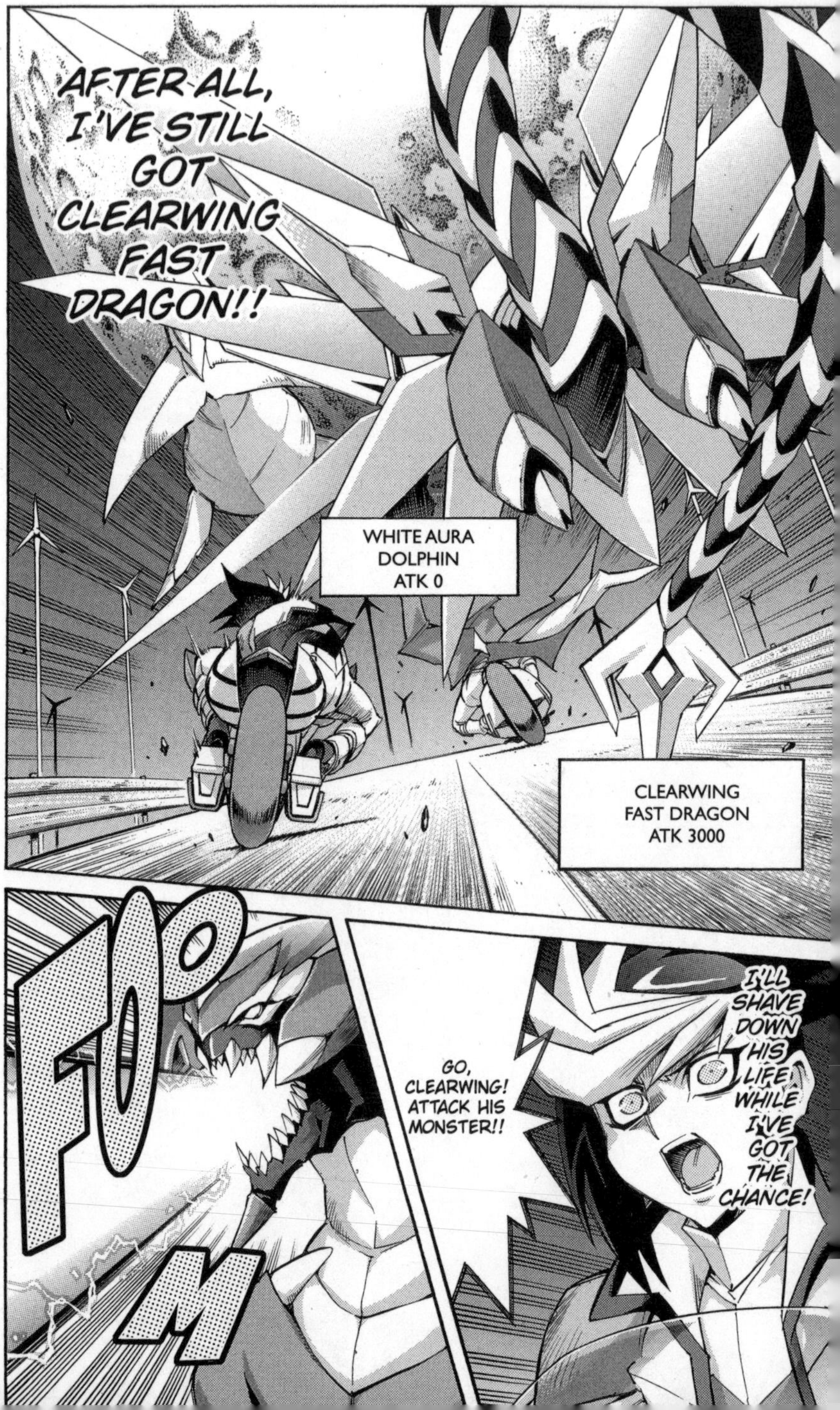
AFTER ALL, I'VE STILL GOT CLEARWING FAST DRAGON!!
WHITE AURA DOLPHIN ATK 0
CLEARWING FAST DRAGON ATK 3000
I'LL SHAVE DOWN HIS LIFE WHILE I'VE GOT THE CHANCE!
GO, CLEARWING! ATTACK HIS MONSTER!!
FOOOM

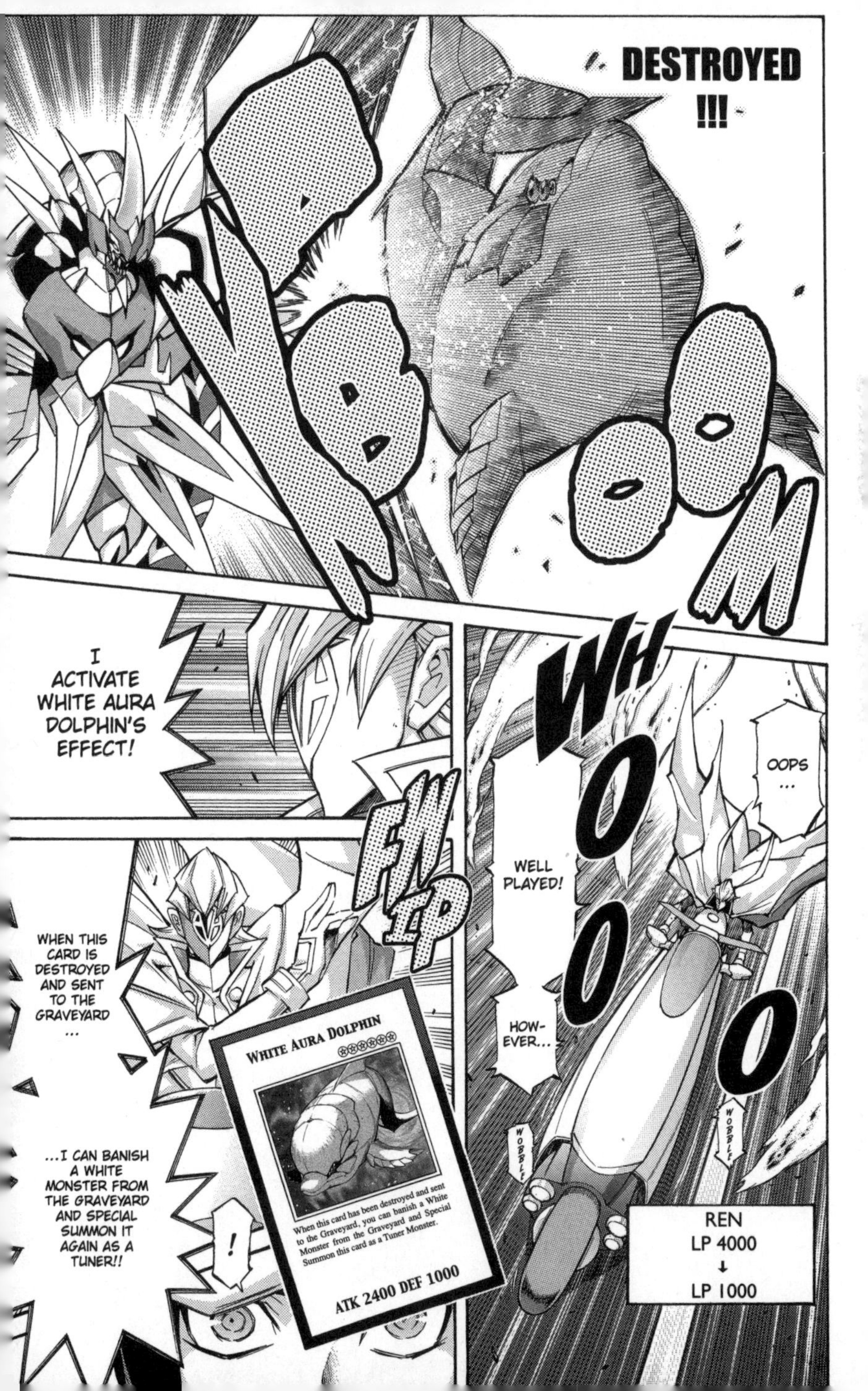
DESTROYED !!!
WHOOOOO
OOPS ...
WELL PLAYED!
HOW-EVER...
WOBBLE
WOBBLE
REN
LP 4000
↓
LP 1000
I ACTIVATE WHITE AURA DOLPHIN'S EFFECT!
FWIP
WHEN THIS CARD IS DESTROYED AND SENT TO THE GRAVEYARD ...
WHITE AURA DOLPHIN
When this card has been destroyed and sent to the Graveyard, you can banish a White Monster from the Graveyard and Special Summon this card as a Tuner Monster.
ATK 2400 DEF 1000
...I CAN BANISH A WHITE MONSTER FROM THE GRAVEYARD AND SPECIAL SUMMON IT AGAIN AS A TUNER!!
!

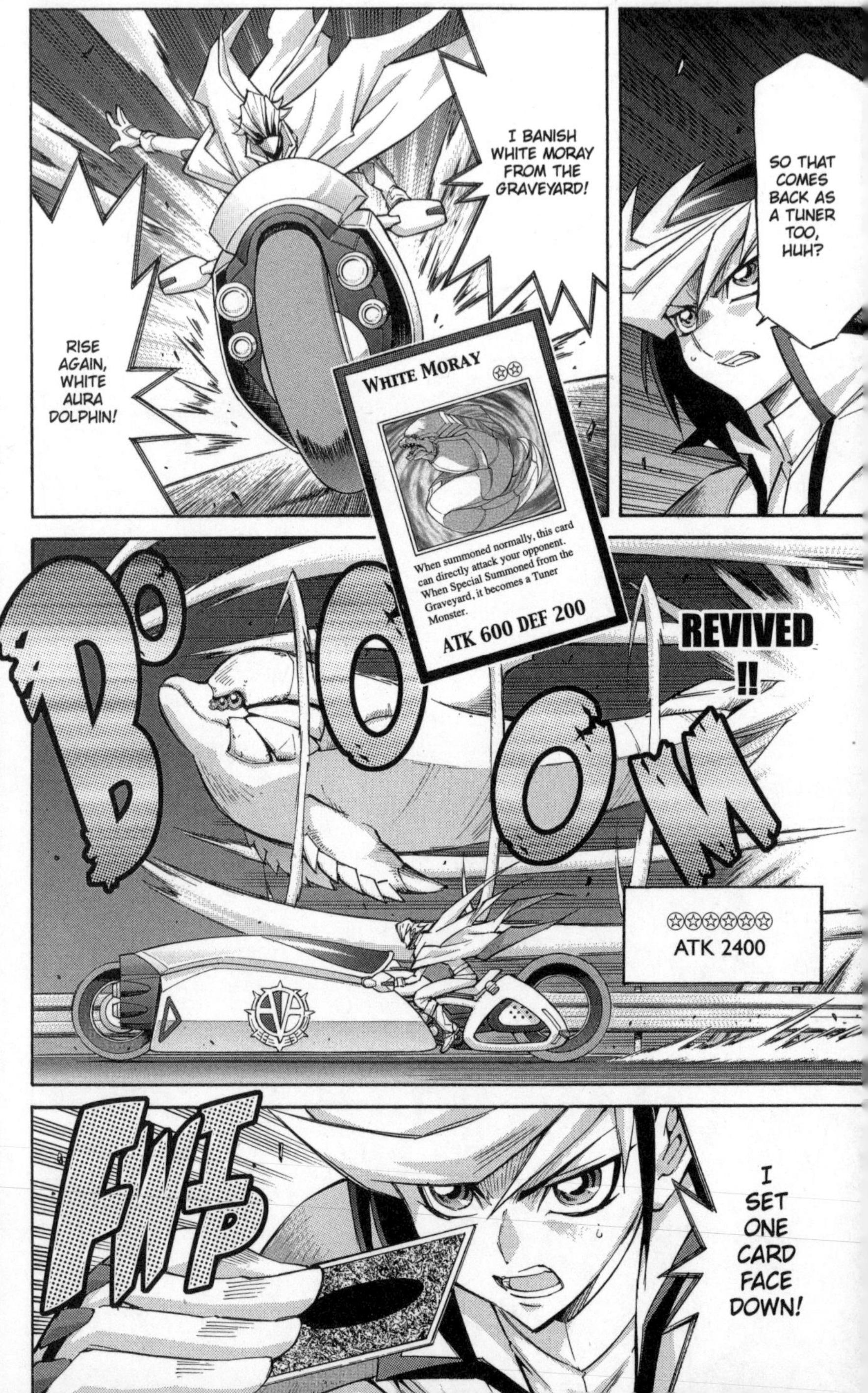
SO THAT COMES BACK AS A TUNER TOO, HUH?
I BANISH WHITE MORAY FROM THE GRAVEYARD!
RISE AGAIN, WHITE AURA DOLPHIN!
WHITE MORAY
When summoned normally, this card can directly attack your opponent. When Special Summoned from the Graveyard, it becomes a Tuner Monster.
ATK 600 DEF 200
BOOOM
REVIVED!!
ATK 2400
FWIP
I SET ONE CARD FACE DOWN!

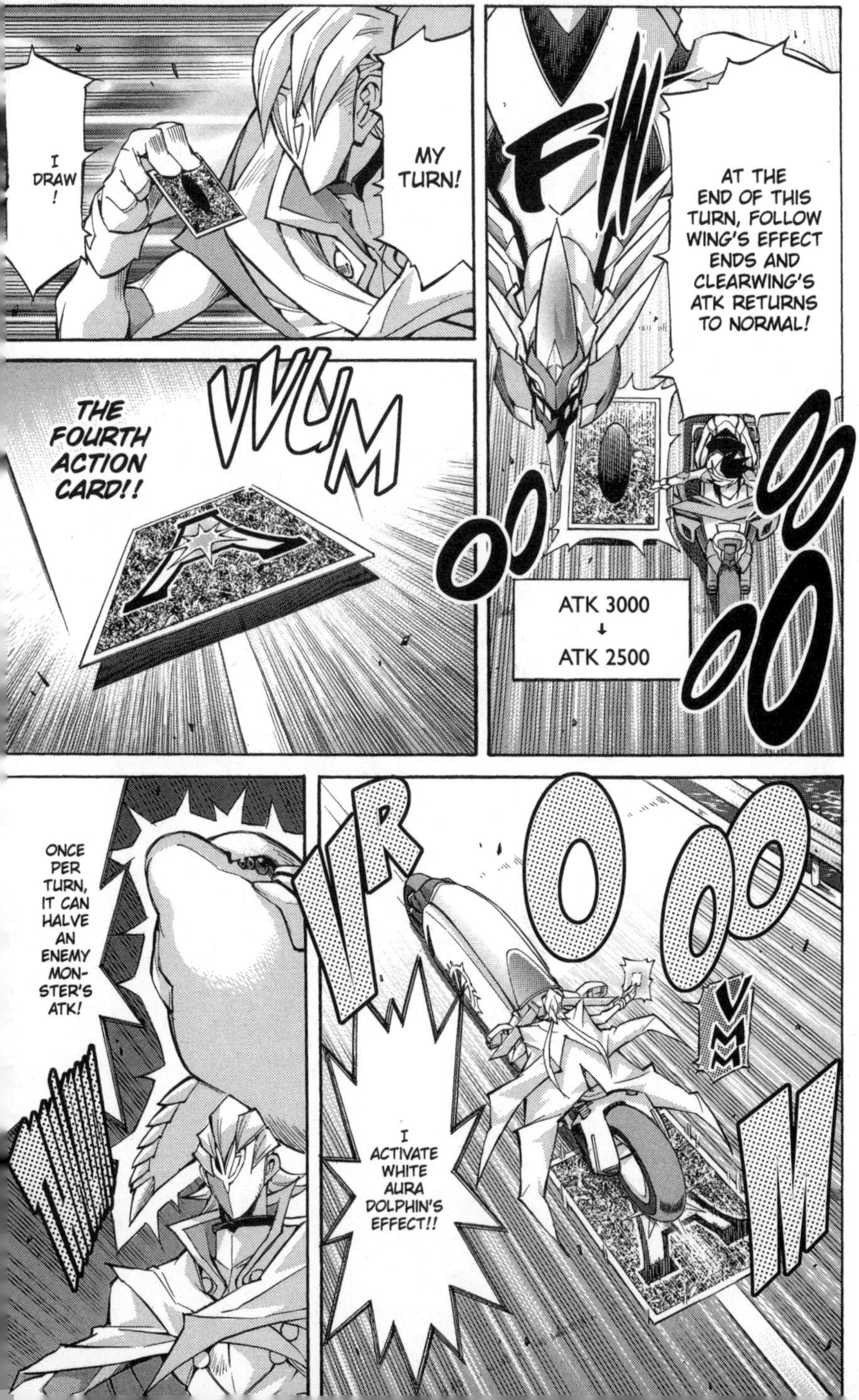
FW
AT THE END OF THIS TURN, FOLLOW WING'S EFFECT ENDS AND CLEARWING'S ATK RETURNS TO NORMAL!
VOOOOOO
ATK 3000 ↓ ATK 2500
MY TURN!
I DRAW!
VVUM
THE FOURTH ACTION CARD!!
VROOOOOM
VVMM
I ACTIVATE WHITE AURA DOLPHIN'S EFFECT!!
ONCE PER TURN, IT CAN HALVE AN ENEMY MONSTER'S ATK!

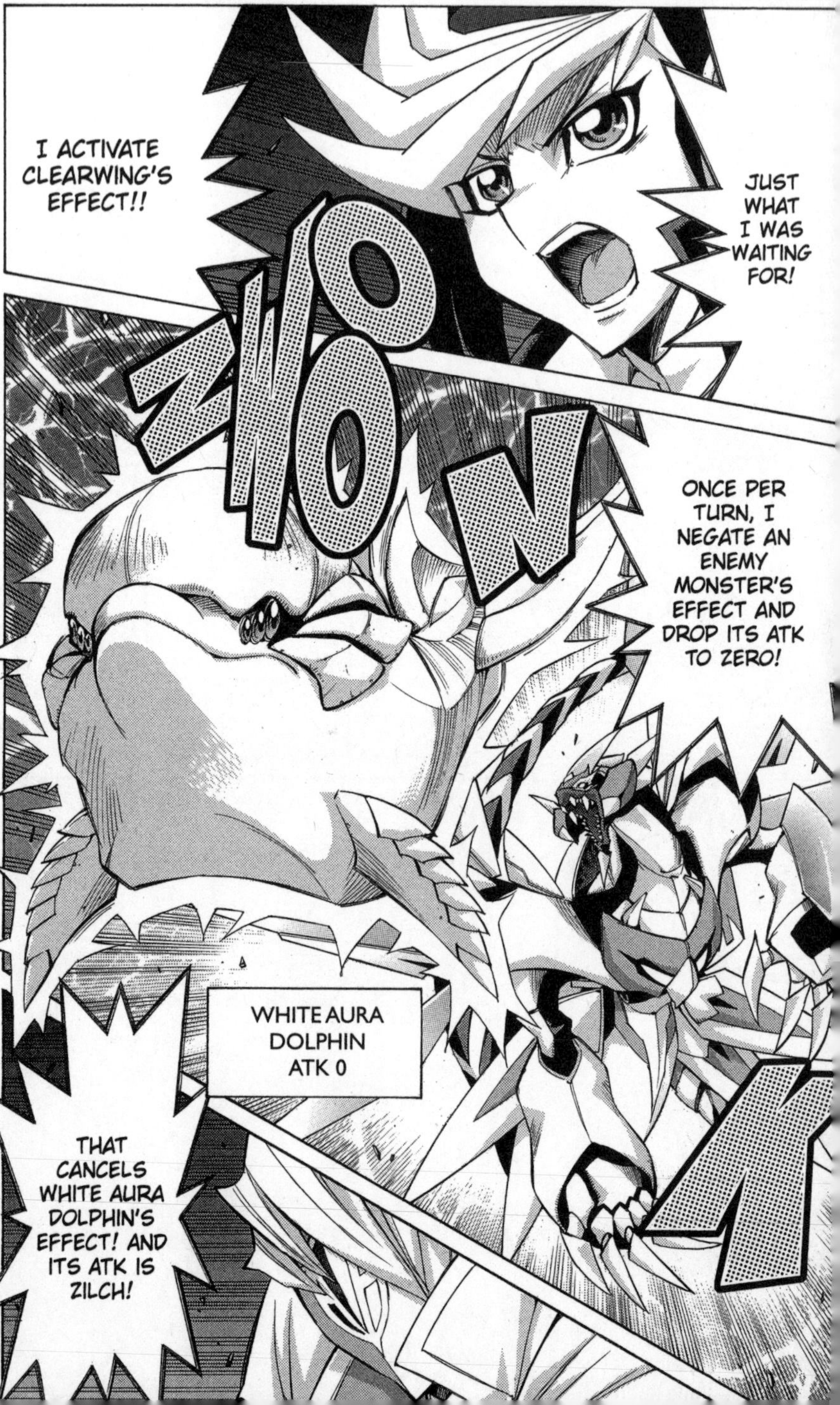
JUST WHAT I WAS WAITING FOR!
I ACTIVATE CLEARWING'S EFFECT!!
ONCE PER TURN, I NEGATE AN ENEMY MONSTER'S EFFECT AND DROP ITS ATK TO ZERO!
WHITE AURA DOLPHIN ATK 0
THAT CANCELS WHITE AURA DOLPHIN'S EFFECT! AND ITS ATK IS ZILCH!

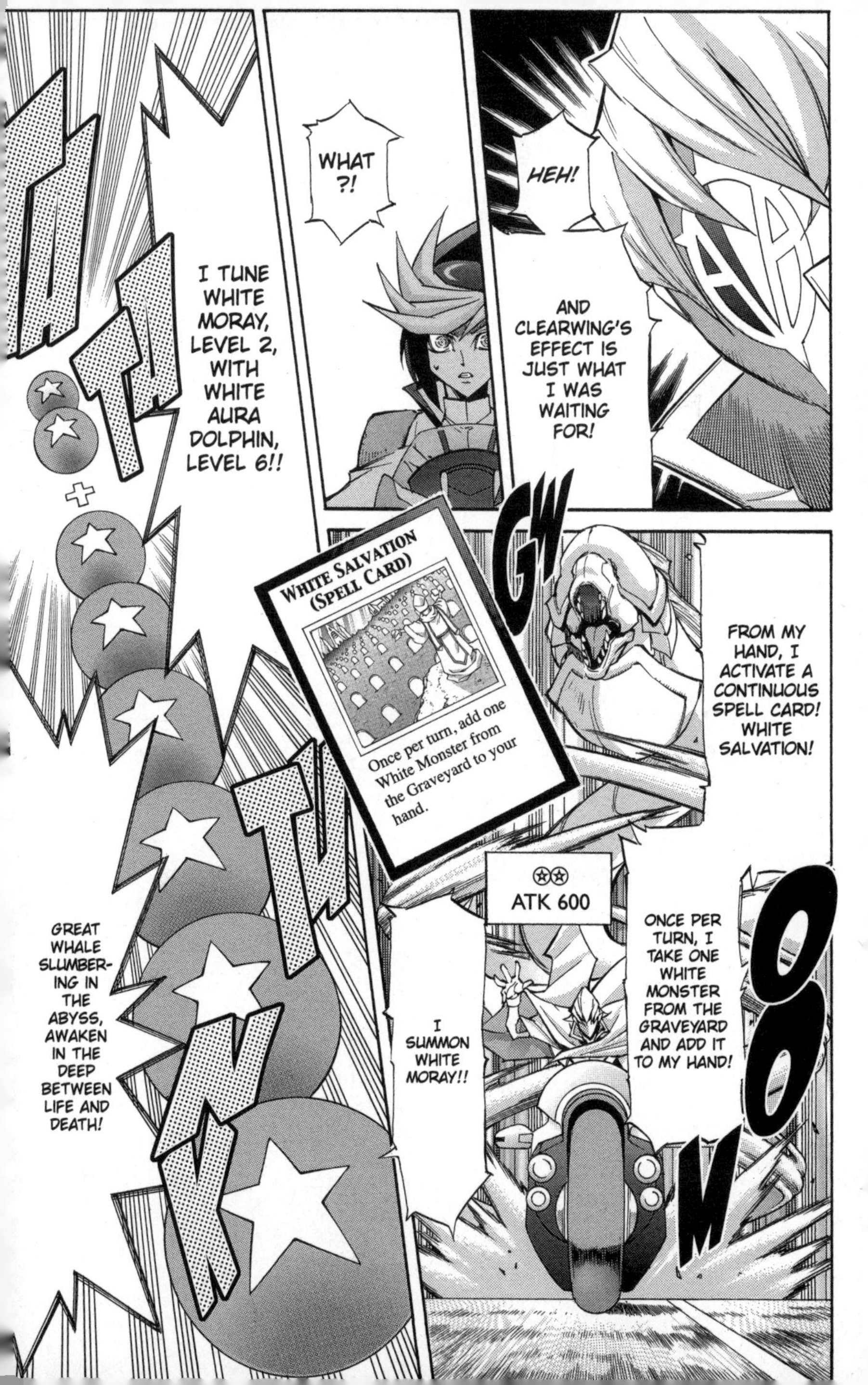
HEH!
AND CLEARWING'S EFFECT IS JUST WHAT I WAS WAITING FOR!
WHAT ?!
FROM MY HAND, I ACTIVATE A CONTINUOUS SPELL CARD! WHITE SALVATION!
WHITE SALVATION (SPELL CARD)
Once per turn, add one White Monster from the Graveyard to your hand.
ONCE PER TURN, I TAKE ONE WHITE MONSTER FROM THE GRAVEYARD AND ADD IT TO MY HAND!
ATK 600
I SUMMON WHITE MORAY!!
I TUNE WHITE MORAY, LEVEL 2, WITH WHITE AURA DOLPHIN, LEVEL 6!!
GREAT WHALE SLUMBER-ING IN THE ABYSS, AWAKEN IN THE DEEP BETWEEN LIFE AND DEATH!

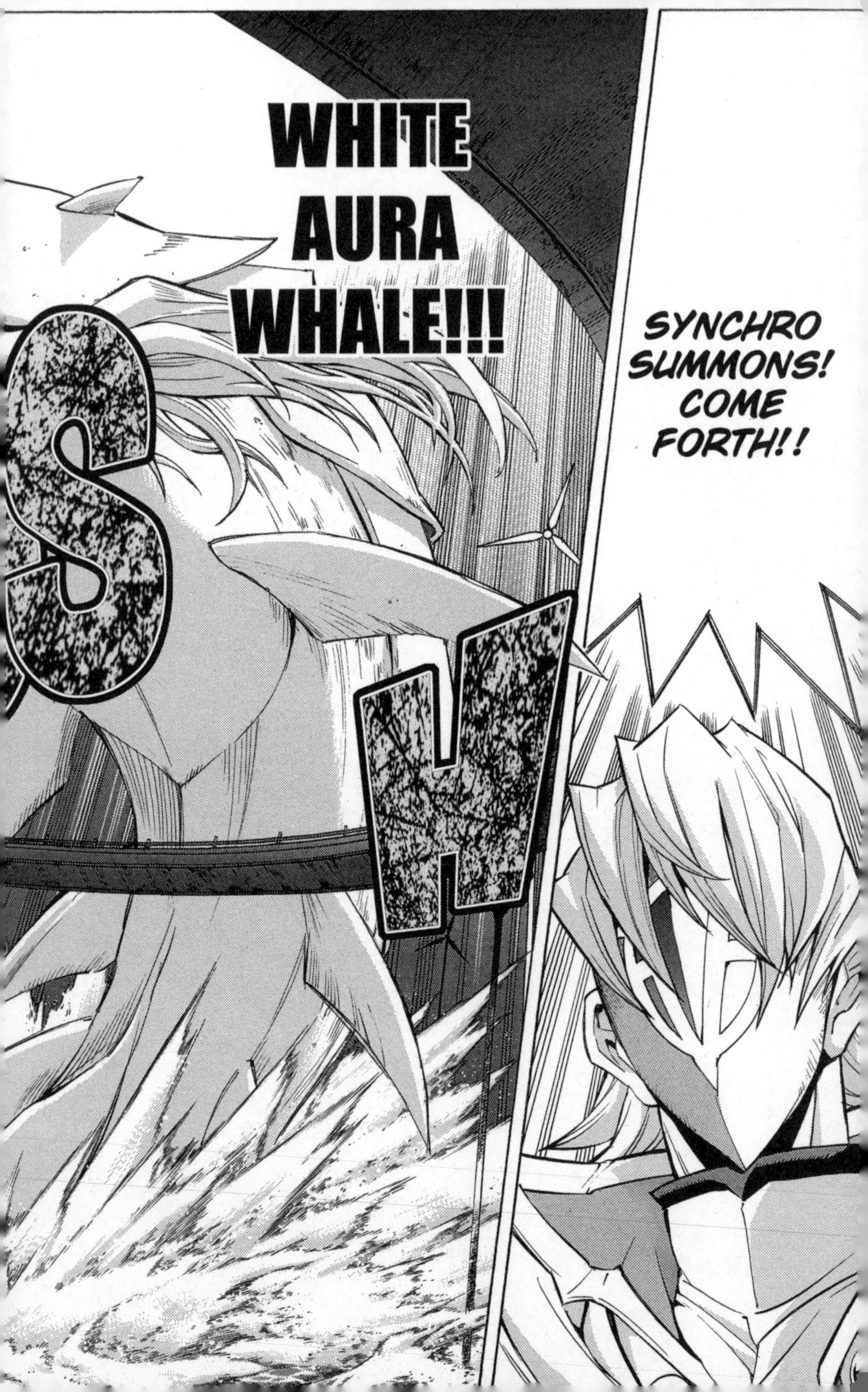
SYNCHRO SUMMONS! COME FORTH!!
WHITE AURA WHALE!!!

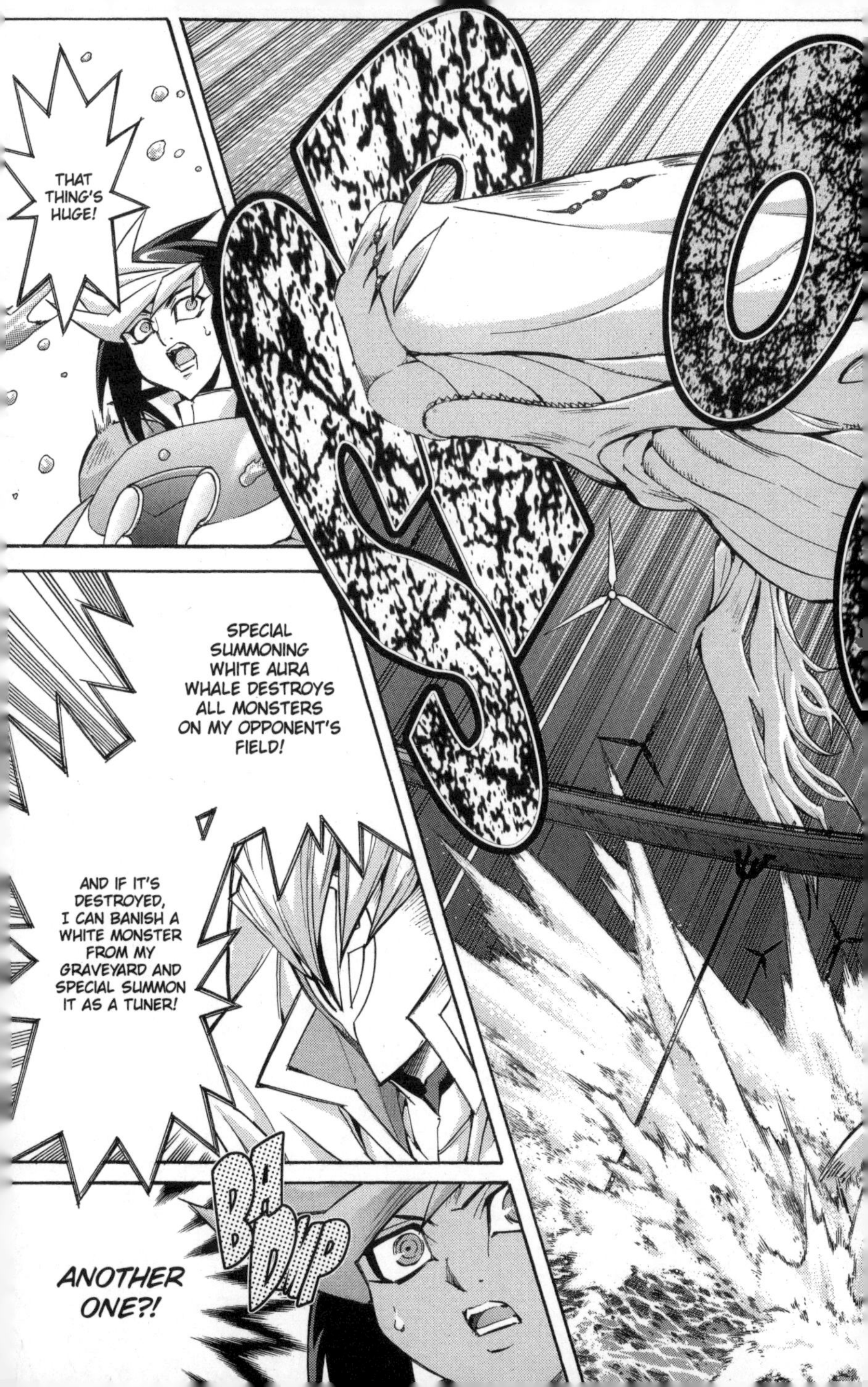
THAT THING'S HUGE!
SPECIAL SUMMONING WHITE AURA WHALE DESTROYS ALL MONSTERS ON MY OPPONENT'S FIELD!
AND IF IT'S DESTROYED, I CAN BANISH A WHITE MONSTER FROM MY GRAVEYARD AND SPECIAL SUMMON IT AS A TUNER!
ANOTHER ONE?!

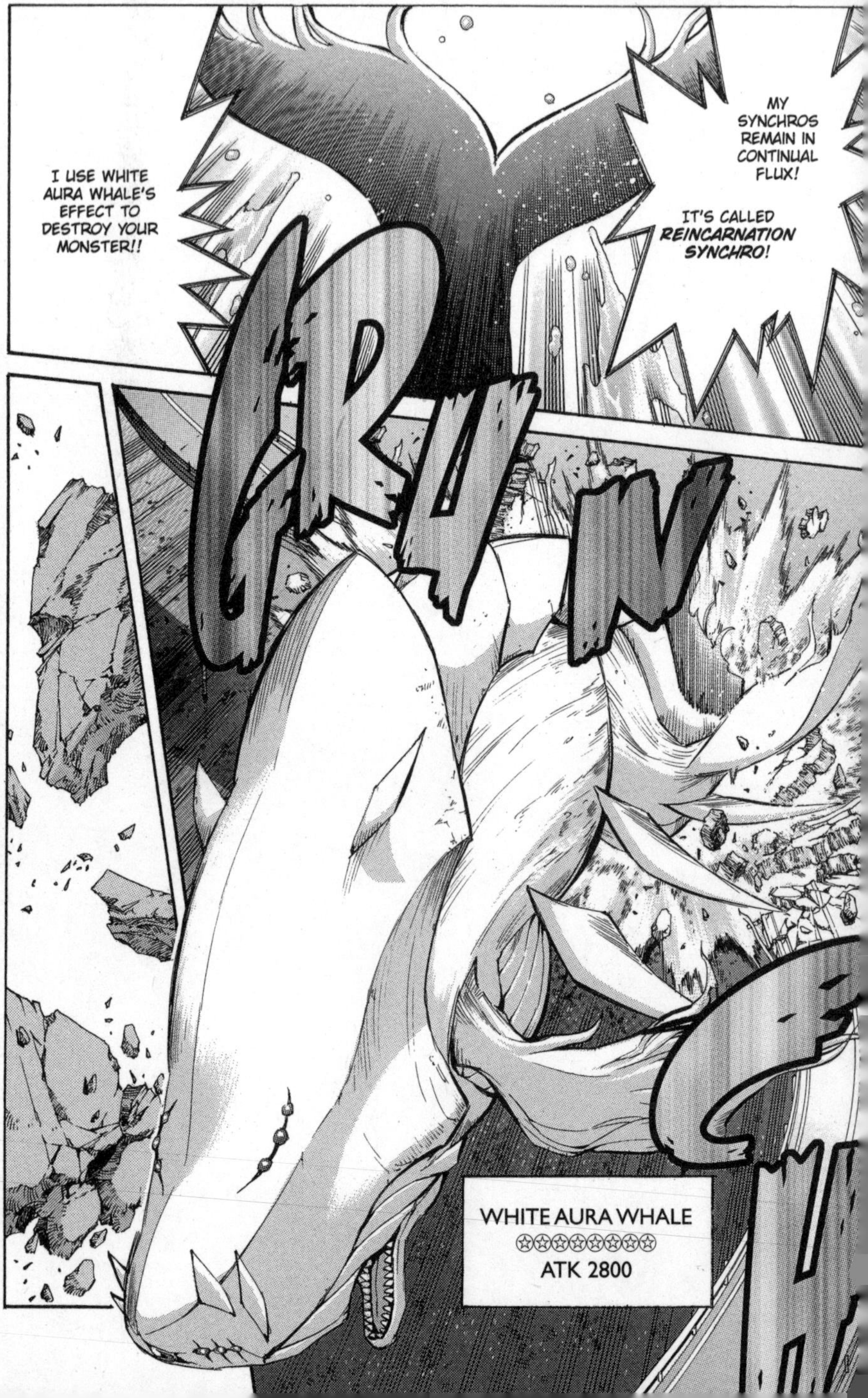
MY SYNCHROS REMAIN IN CONTINUAL FLUX!
IT'S CALLED *REINCARNATION SYNCHRO!*
I USE WHITE AURA WHALE'S EFFECT TO DESTROY YOUR MONSTER!!
WHITE AURA WHALE
ATK 2800

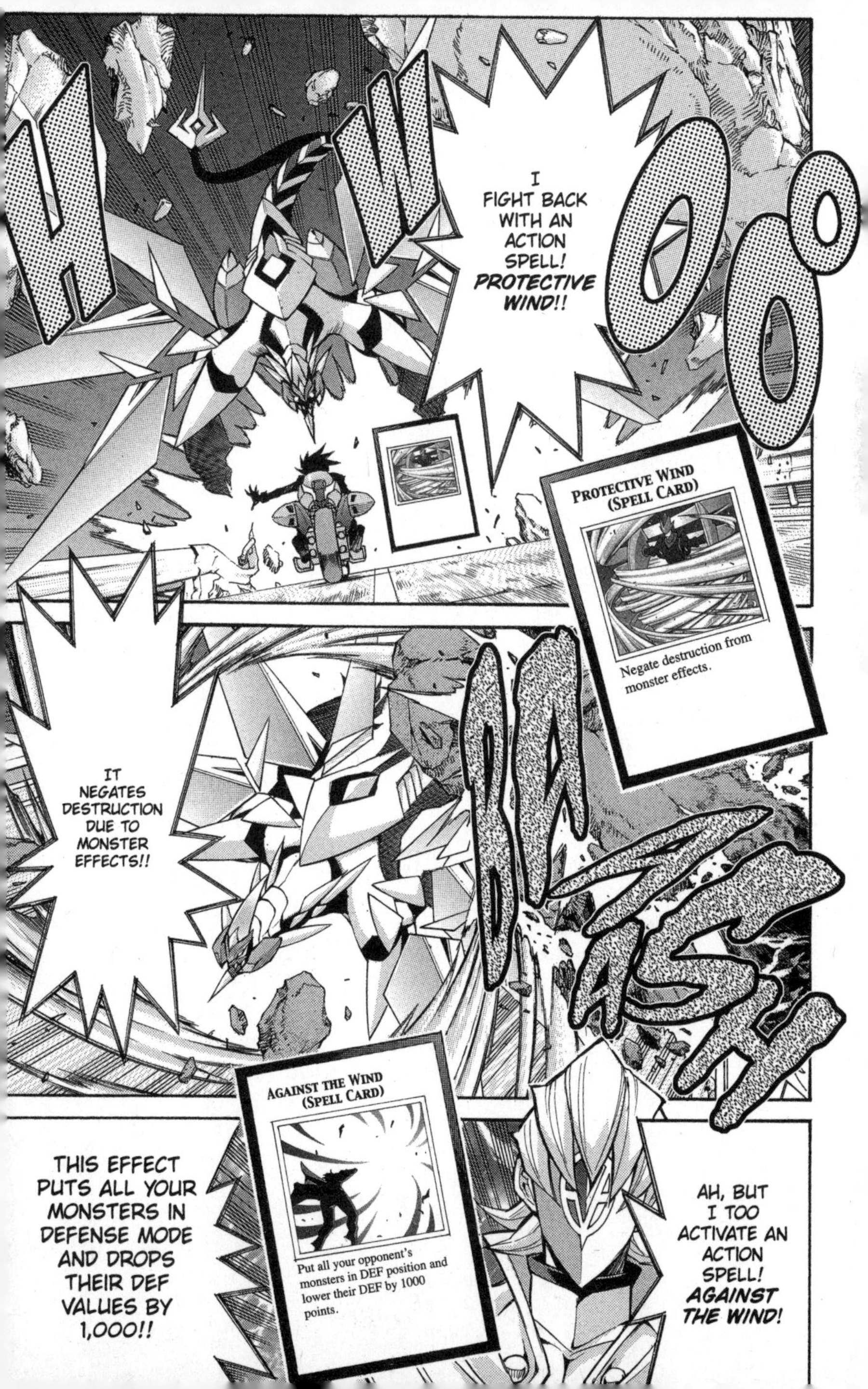

I FIGHT BACK WITH AN ACTION SPELL! PROTECTIVE WIND!!
PROTECTIVE WIND (SPELL CARD)
Negate destruction from monster effects.
IT NEGATES DESTRUCTION DUE TO MONSTER EFFECTS!!
AH, BUT I TOO ACTIVATE AN ACTION SPELL! AGAINST THE WIND!
AGAINST THE WIND (SPELL CARD)
Put all your opponent's monsters in DEF position and lower their DEF by 1000 points.
THIS EFFECT PUTS ALL YOUR MONSTERS IN DEFENSE MODE AND DROPS THEIR DEF VALUES BY 1,000!!

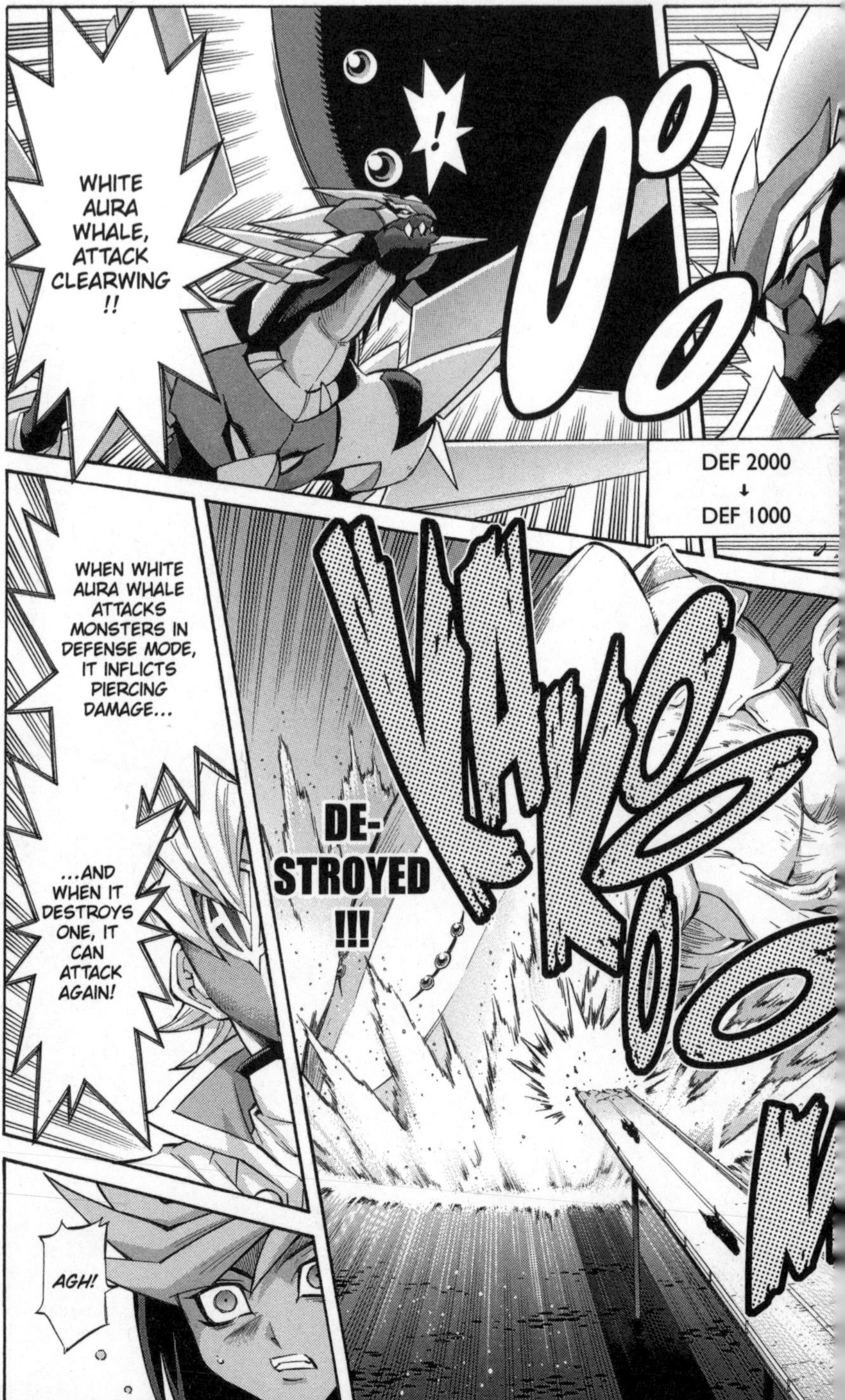
!
WHITE AURA WHALE, ATTACK CLEARWING !!
DEF 2000 ↓ DEF 1000
DE-STROYED !!!
WHEN WHITE AURA WHALE ATTACKS MONSTERS IN DEFENSE MODE, IT INFLICTS PIERCING DAMAGE...
...AND WHEN IT DESTROYS ONE, IT CAN ATTACK AGAIN!
AGH!

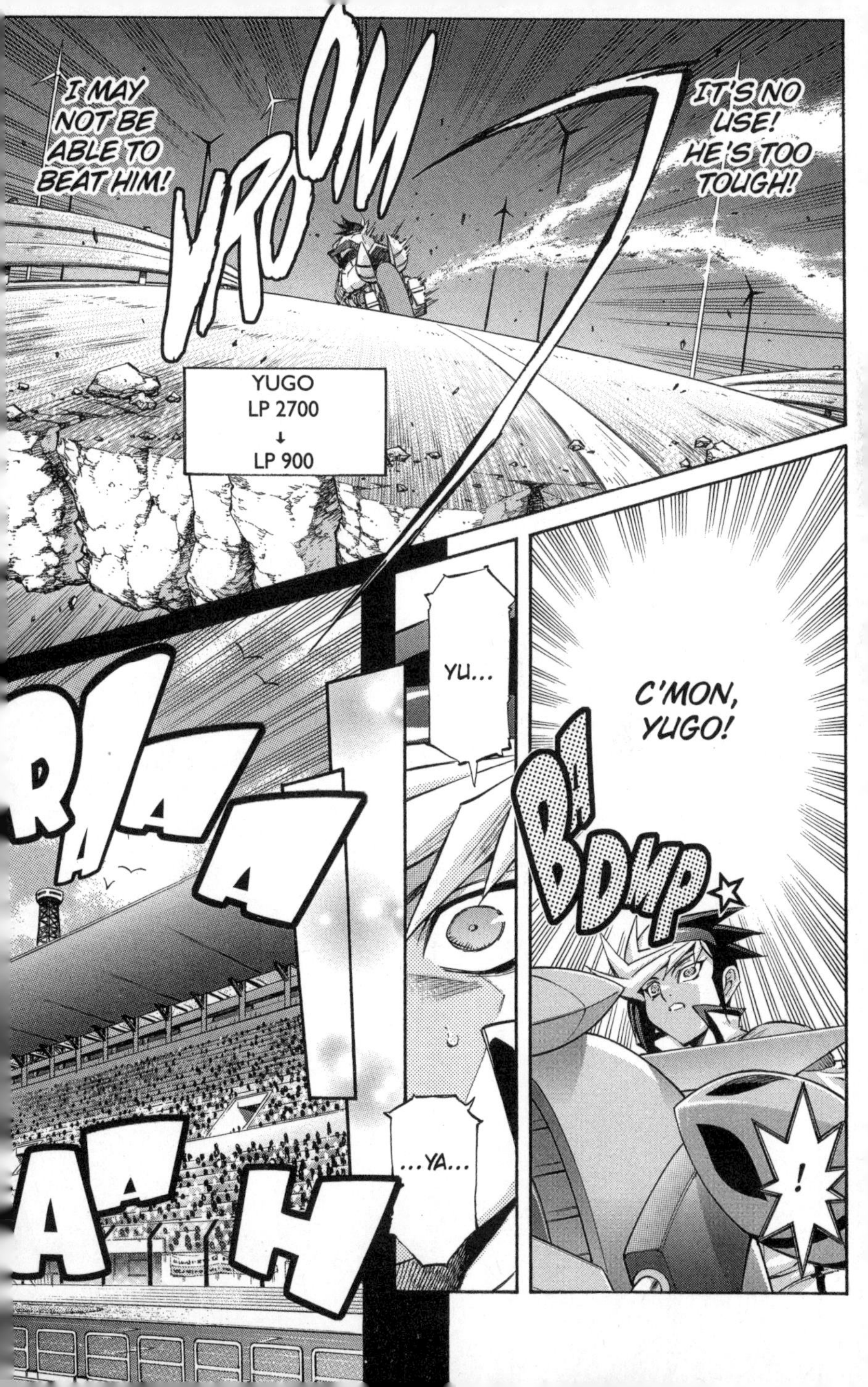
IT'S NO USE! HE'S TOO TOUGH!
I MAY NOT BE ABLE TO BEAT HIM!
VROOM
YUGO
LP 2700
↓
LP 900
C'MON, YUGO!
BADUMP
!
YU...
...YA...
RAAAAAH

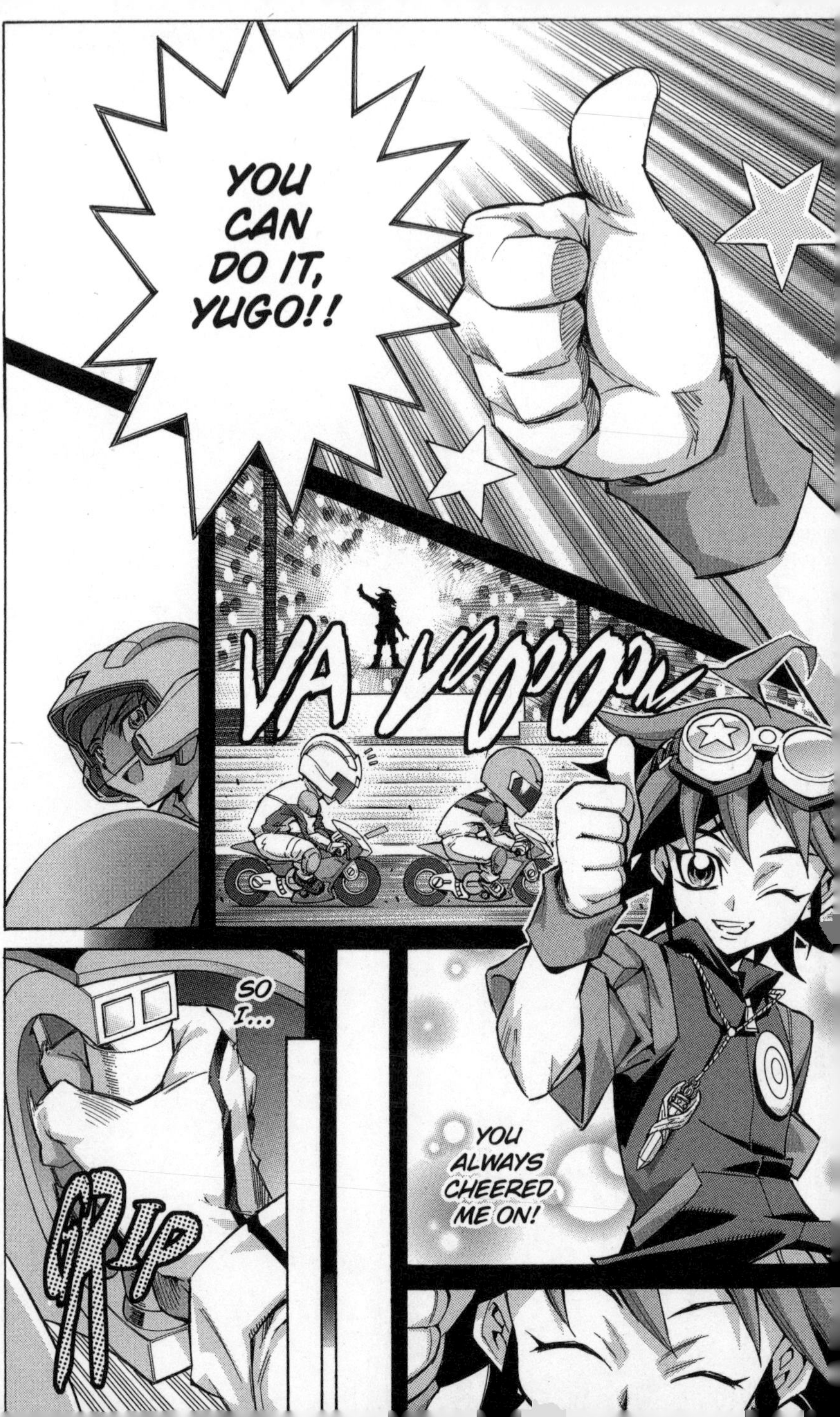
YOU CAN DO IT, YUGO!!
VA VOOOOM
YOU ALWAYS CHEERED ME ON!
SO I...
GRIP

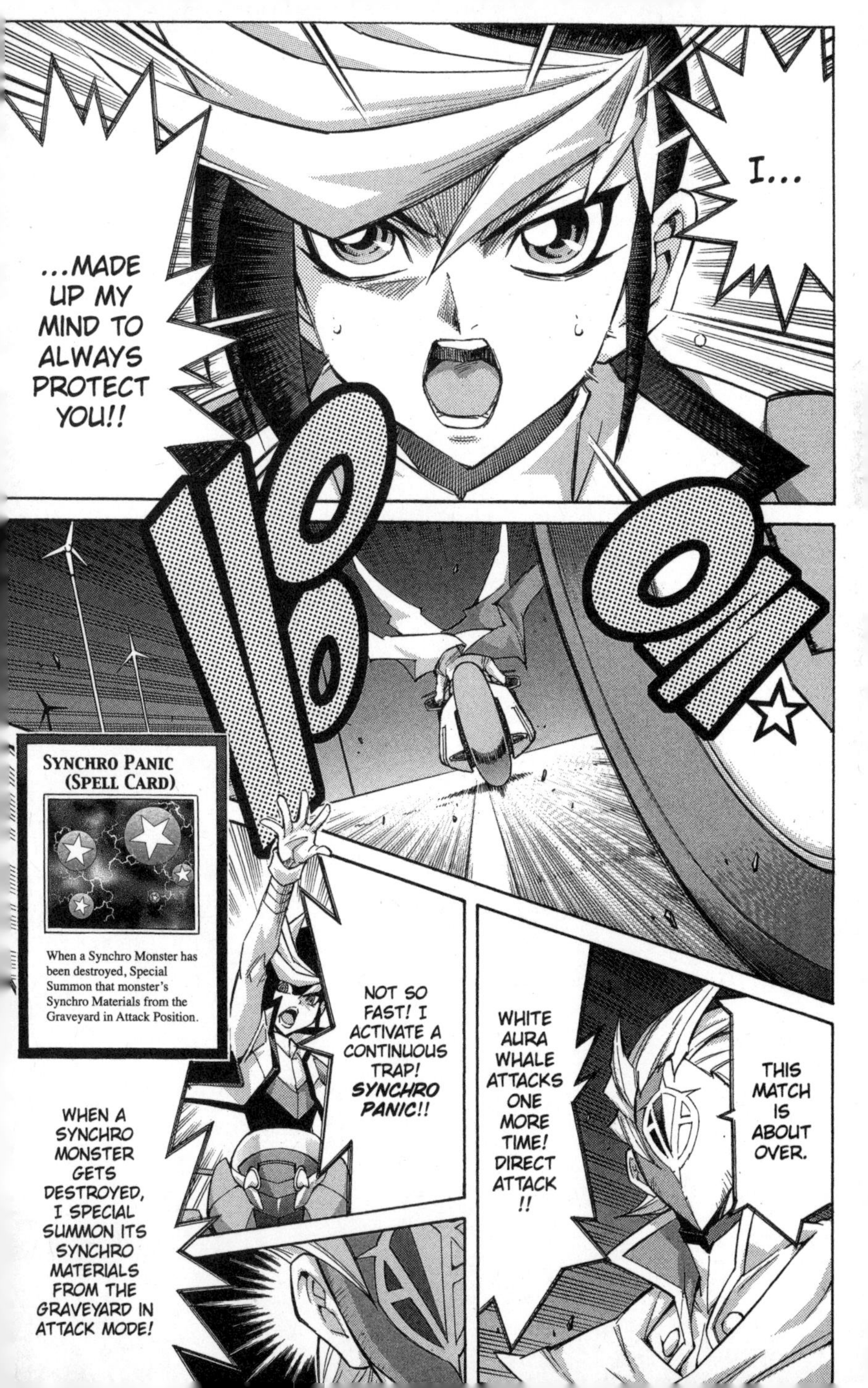
I...
...MADE UP MY MIND TO ALWAYS PROTECT YOU!!
Synchro Panic (Spell Card)
When a Synchro Monster has been destroyed, Special Summon that monster's Synchro Materials from the Graveyard in Attack Position.
THIS MATCH IS ABOUT OVER.
WHITE AURA WHALE ATTACKS ONE MORE TIME! DIRECT ATTACK!!
NOT SO FAST! I ACTIVATE A CONTINUOUS TRAP! SYNCHRO PANIC!!
WHEN A SYNCHRO MONSTER GETS DESTROYED, I SPECIAL SUMMON ITS SYNCHRO MATERIALS FROM THE GRAVEYARD IN ATTACK MODE!

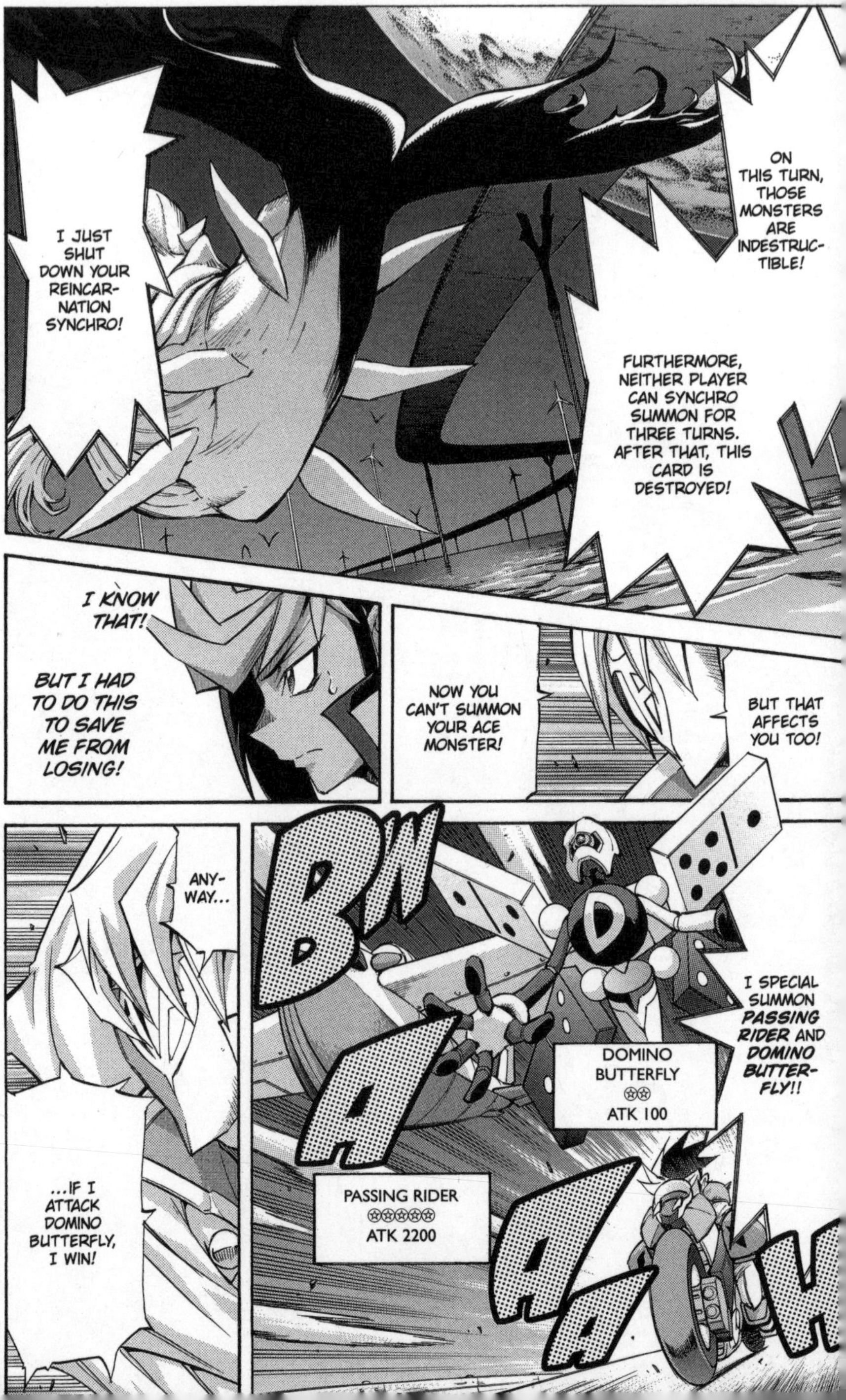
ON THIS TURN, THOSE MONSTERS ARE INDESTRUCTIBLE!
I JUST SHUT DOWN YOUR REINCARNATION SYNCHRO!
FURTHERMORE, NEITHER PLAYER CAN SYNCHRO SUMMON FOR THREE TURNS. AFTER THAT, THIS CARD IS DESTROYED!
BUT THAT AFFECTS YOU TOO!
NOW YOU CAN'T SUMMON YOUR ACE MONSTER!
I KNOW THAT!
BUT I HAD TO DO THIS TO SAVE ME FROM LOSING!
BWAAAAH
I SPECIAL SUMMON PASSING RIDER AND DOMINO BUTTERFLY!!
DOMINO BUTTERFLY ☆☆ ATK 100
PASSING RIDER ☆☆☆☆☆ ATK 2200
ANYWAY...
...IF I ATTACK DOMINO BUTTERFLY, I WIN!

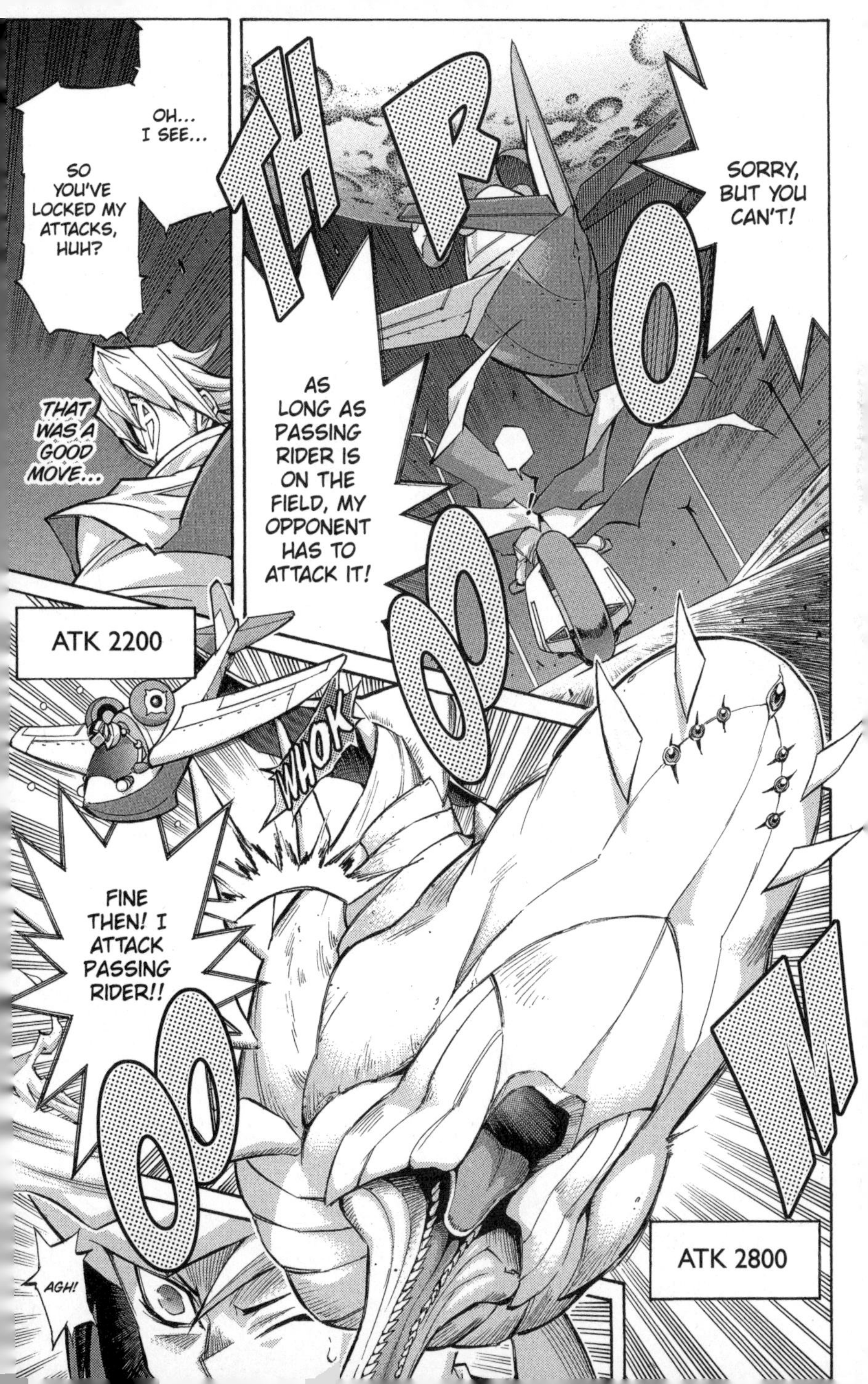

SORRY, BUT YOU CAN'T!
AS LONG AS PASSING RIDER IS ON THE FIELD, MY OPPONENT HAS TO ATTACK IT!
THROOOOOOOOOM
OH... I SEE...
SO YOU'VE LOCKED MY ATTACKS, HUH?
THAT WAS A GOOD MOVE...
ATK 2200
WHOK
FINE THEN! I ATTACK PASSING RIDER!!
ATK 2800
AGH!

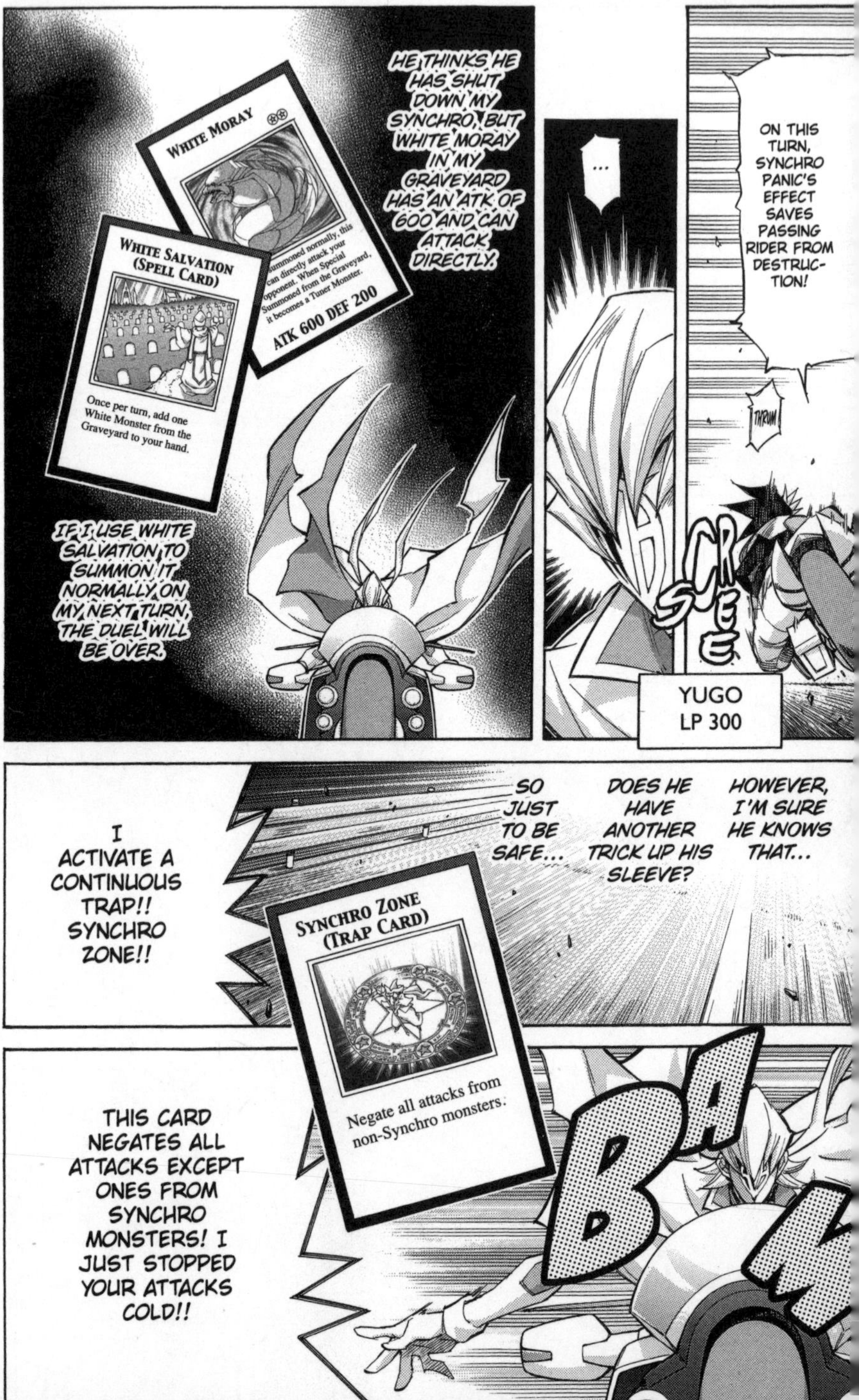

ON THIS TURN, SYNCHRO PANIC'S EFFECT SAVES PASSING RIDER FROM DESTRUCTION!
THRUM
SCREEE
YUGO
LP 300
...
HE THINKS HE HAS SHUT DOWN MY SYNCHRO, BUT WHITE MORAY IN MY GRAVEYARD HAS AN ATK OF 600 AND CAN ATTACK DIRECTLY.
WHITE MORAY
summoned normally, this can directly attack your opponent. When Special Summoned from the Graveyard, it becomes a Tuner Monster.
ATK 600 DEF 200
WHITE SALVATION (SPELL CARD)
Once per turn, add one White Monster from the Graveyard to your hand.
IF I USE WHITE SALVATION TO SUMMON IT NORMALLY ON MY NEXT TURN, THE DUEL WILL BE OVER.
HOWEVER, I'M SURE HE KNOWS THAT...
DOES HE HAVE ANOTHER TRICK UP HIS SLEEVE?
SO JUST TO BE SAFE...
I ACTIVATE A CONTINUOUS TRAP!! SYNCHRO ZONE!!
SYNCHRO ZONE (TRAP CARD)
Negate all attacks from non-Synchro monsters.
BAM
THIS CARD NEGATES ALL ATTACKS EXCEPT ONES FROM SYNCHRO MONSTERS! I JUST STOPPED YOUR ATTACKS COLD!!

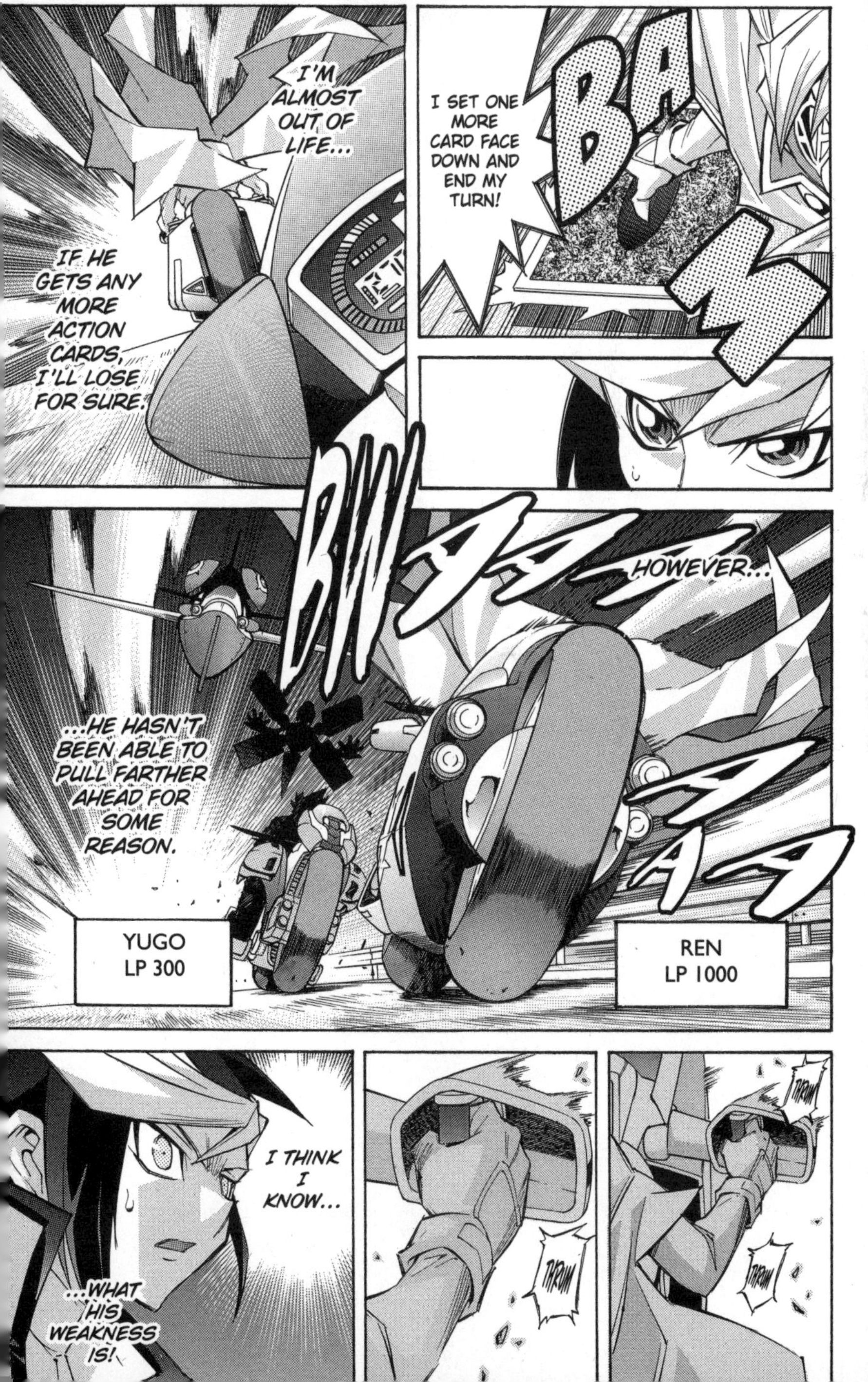
I SET ONE MORE CARD FACE DOWN AND END MY TURN!
BAM
I'M ALMOST OUT OF LIFE...
IF HE GETS ANY MORE ACTION CARDS, I'LL LOSE FOR SURE.
BWAAAA
HOWEVER...
...HE HASN'T BEEN ABLE TO PULL FARTHER AHEAD FOR SOME REASON.
REN
LP 1000
YUGO
LP 300
THROM
THROM
THROM
I THINK I KNOW...
...WHAT HIS WEAKNESS IS!

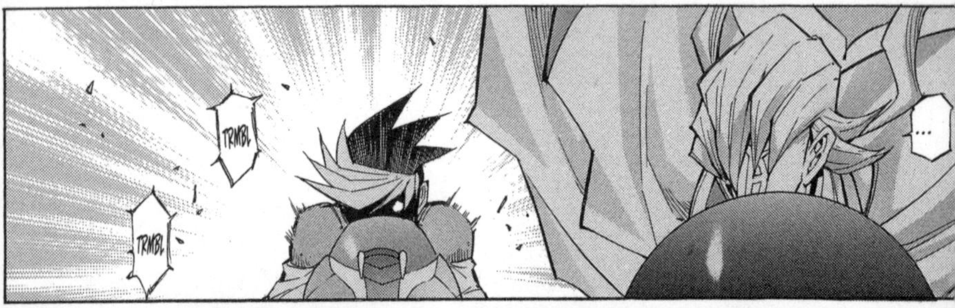
...
TRMBL
TRMBL

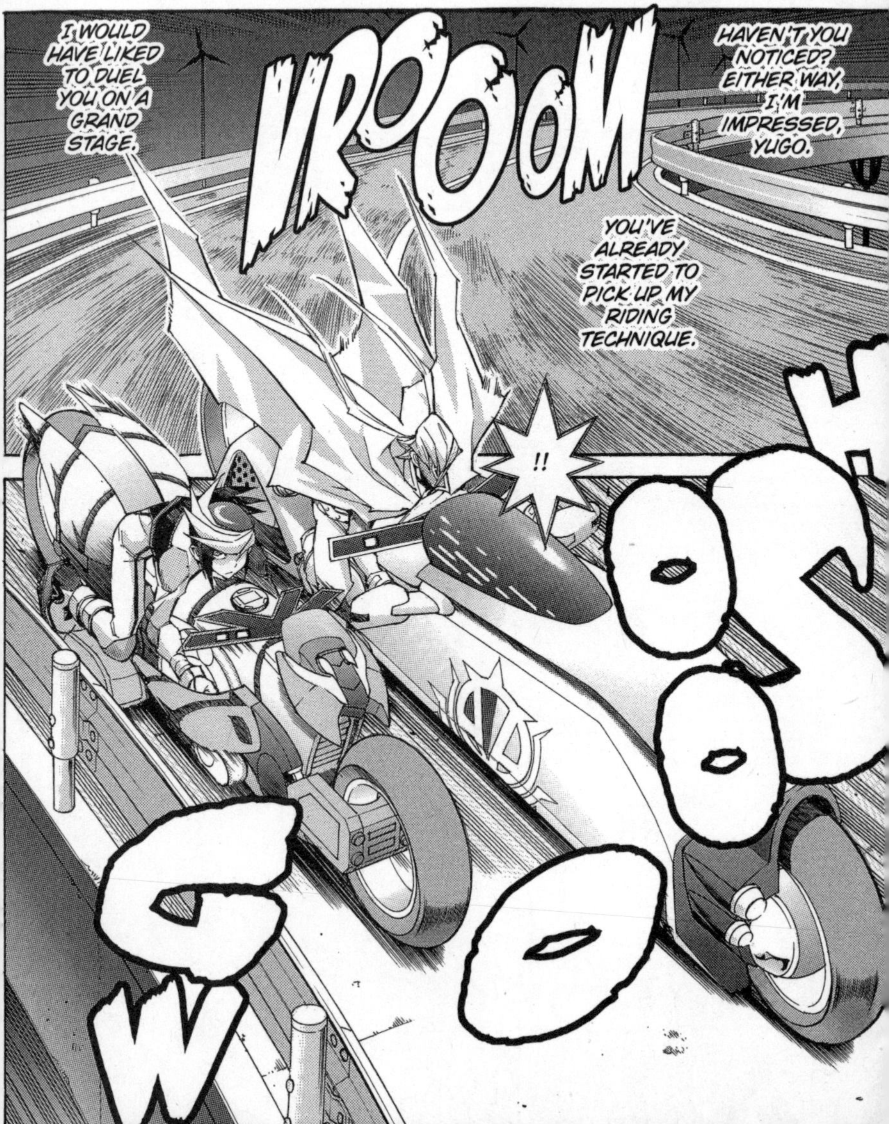
HAVEN'T YOU NOTICED? EITHER WAY, I'M IMPRESSED, YUGO.
YOU'VE ALREADY STARTED TO PICK UP MY RIDING TECHNIQUE.
VROOOM
I WOULD HAVE LIKED TO DUEL YOU ON A GRAND STAGE.
!!

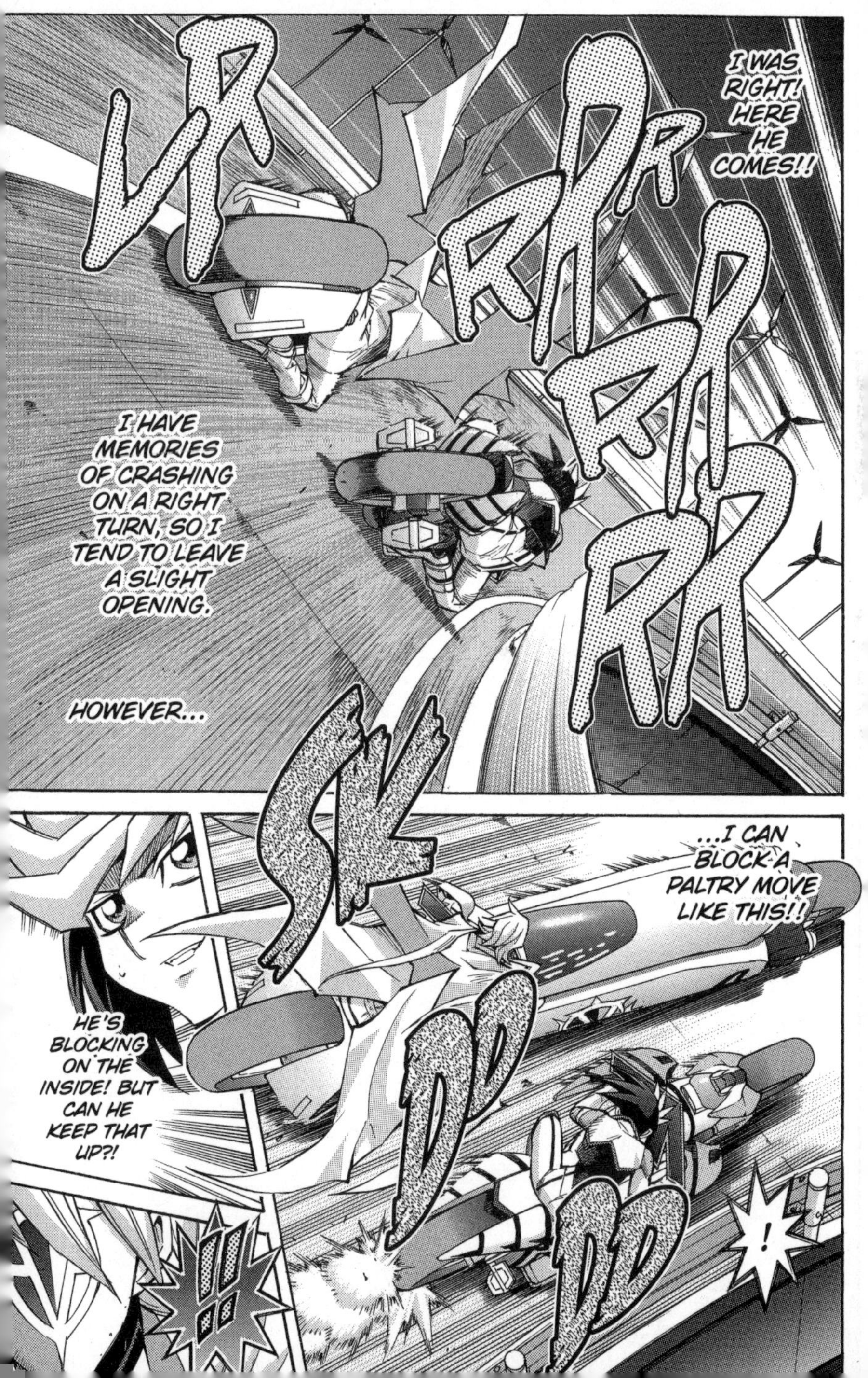
I WAS RIGHT! HERE HE COMES!!
VR
I HAVE MEMORIES OF CRASHING ON A RIGHT TURN, SO I TEND TO LEAVE A SLIGHT OPENING.
HOWEVER...
...I CAN BLOCK A PALTRY MOVE LIKE THIS!!
SK
HE'S BLOCKING ON THE INSIDE! BUT CAN HE KEEP THAT UP?!
!
!!

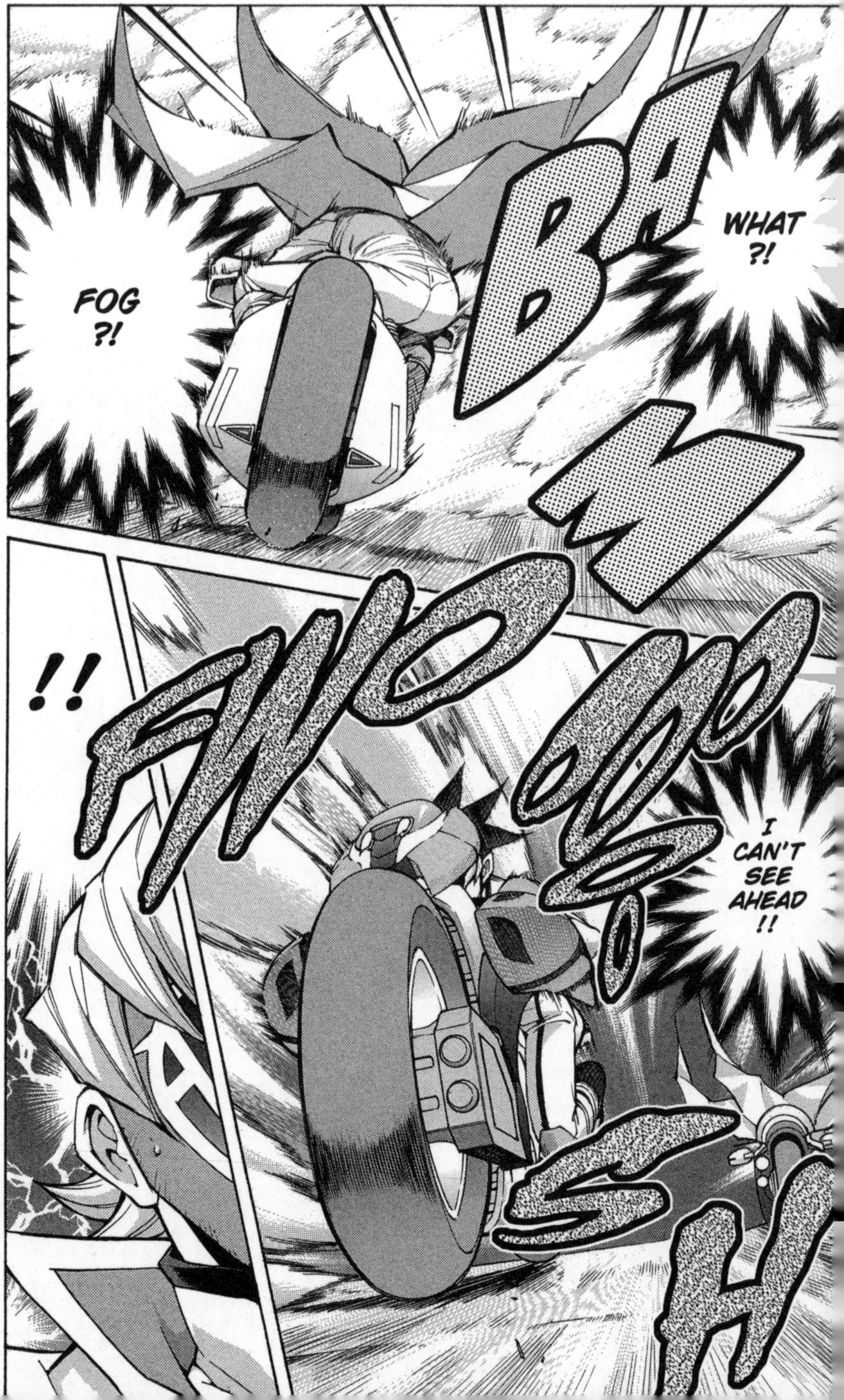
WHAT ?!
BAM
FOG ?!
I CAN'T SEE AHEAD !!
FWOOOSH
!!

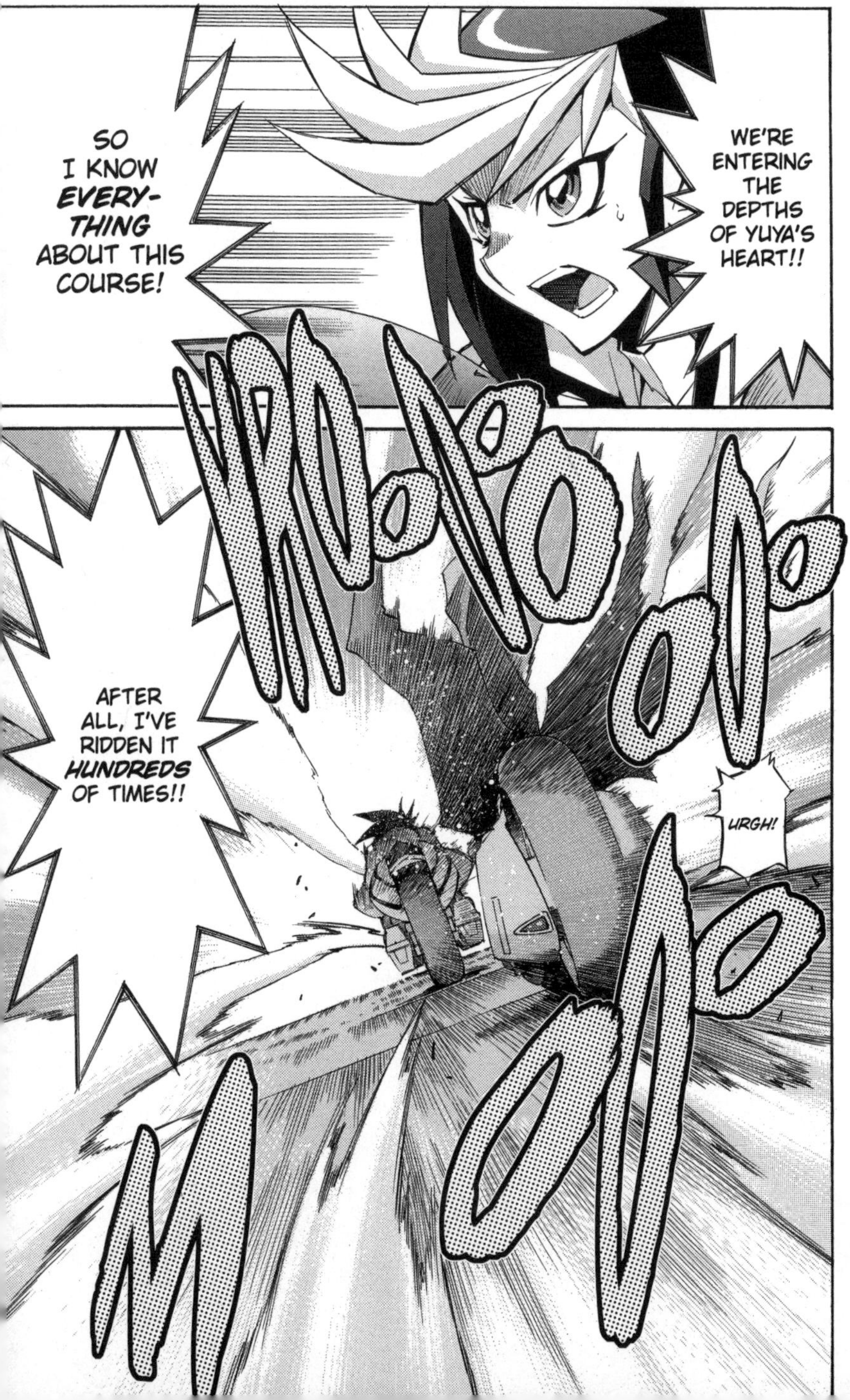
WE'RE ENTERING THE DEPTHS OF YUYA'S HEART!!
SO I KNOW ***EVERYTHING*** ABOUT THIS COURSE!
AFTER ALL, I'VE RIDDEN IT ***HUNDREDS*** OF TIMES!!
URGH!

Yu-Gi-Oh! ARC-V

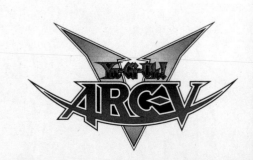

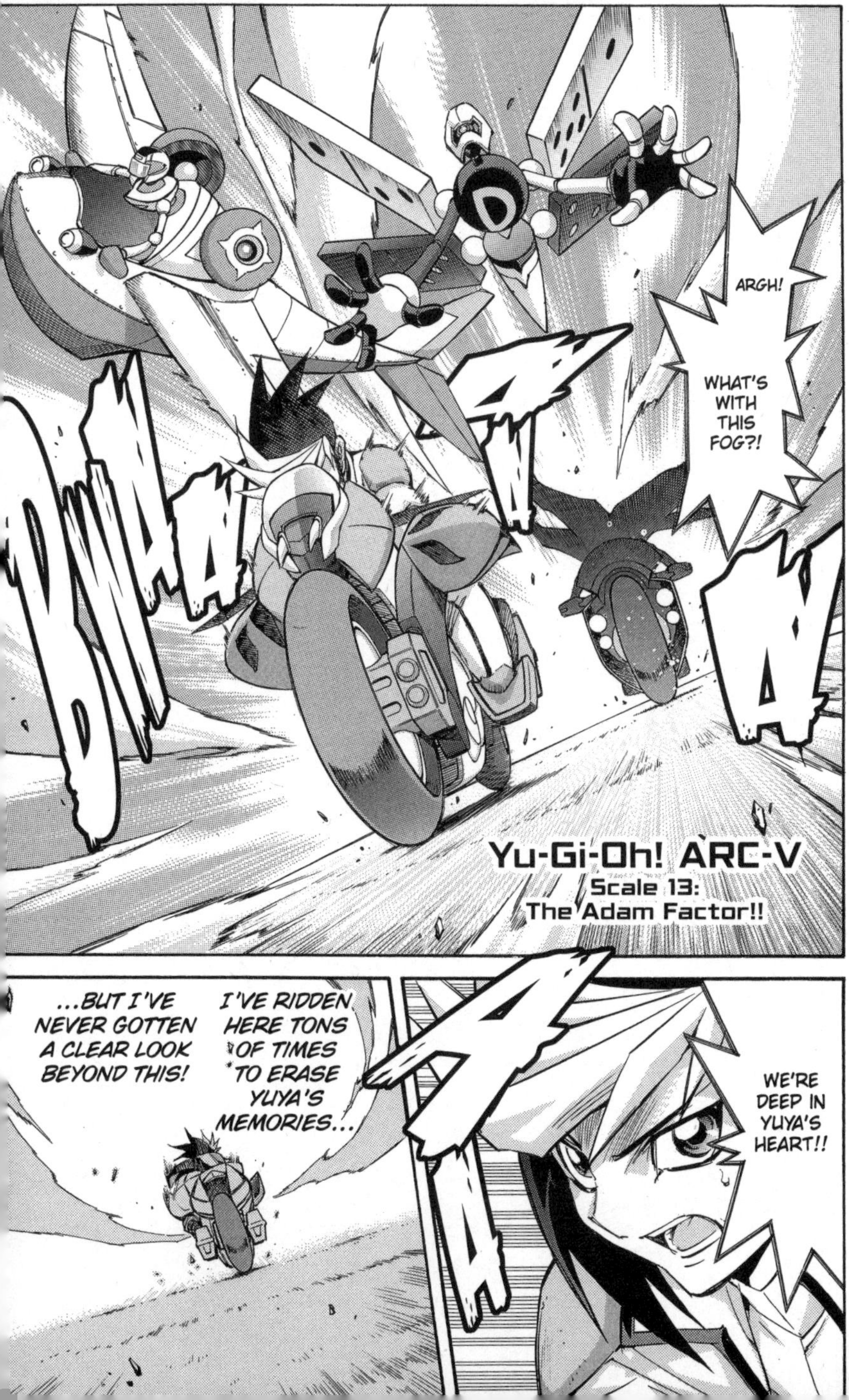
ARGH!
WHAT'S WITH THIS FOG?!
Yu-Gi-Oh! ARC-V
Scale 13: The Adam Factor!!
WE'RE DEEP IN YUYA'S HEART!!
I'VE RIDDEN HERE TONS OF TIMES TO ERASE YUYA'S MEMORIES...
...BUT I'VE NEVER GOTTEN A CLEAR LOOK BEYOND THIS!

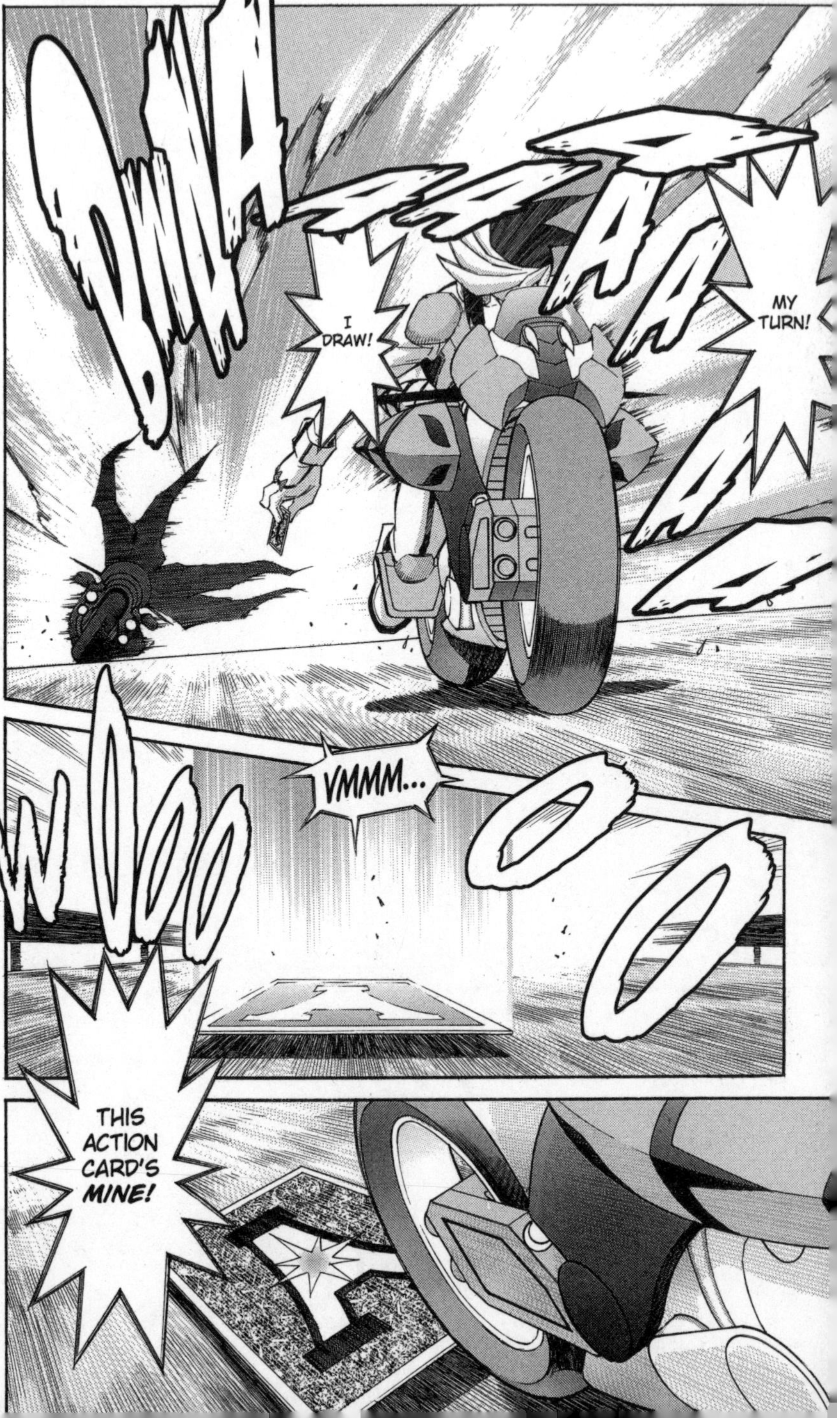
MY TURN!
I DRAW!
VMMM...
THIS ACTION CARD'S MINE!

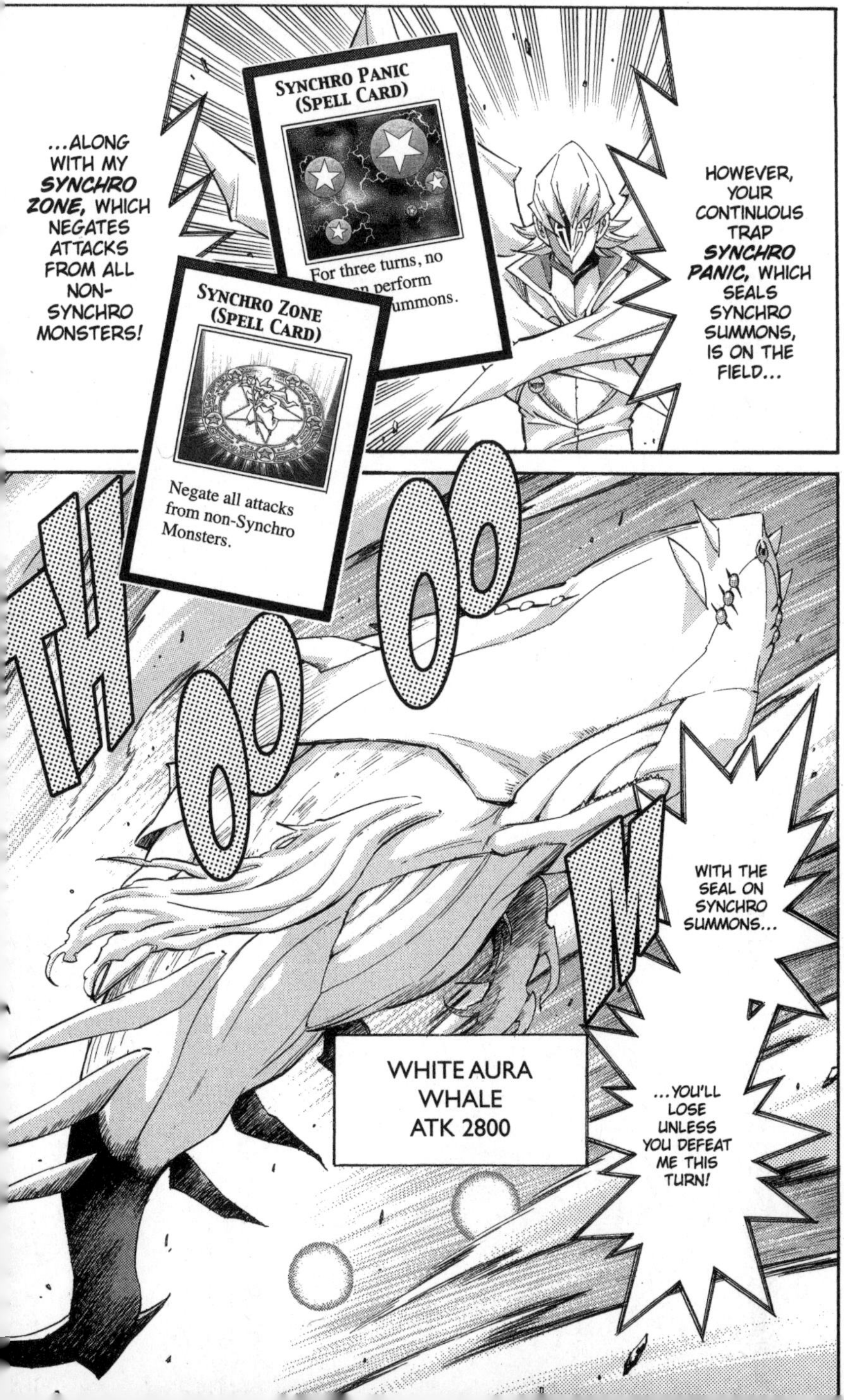
HOWEVER, YOUR CONTINUOUS TRAP SYNCHRO PANIC, WHICH SEALS SYNCHRO SUMMONS, IS ON THE FIELD...
...ALONG WITH MY SYNCHRO ZONE, WHICH NEGATES ATTACKS FROM ALL NON-SYNCHRO MONSTERS!
SYNCHRO PANIC (SPELL CARD)
For three turns, no
perform
SYNCHRO ZONE (SPELL CARD)
Negate all attacks from non-Synchro Monsters.
THOOOOM
WITH THE SEAL ON SYNCHRO SUMMONS...
WHITE AURA WHALE ATK 2800
...YOU'LL LOSE UNLESS YOU DEFEAT ME THIS TURN!

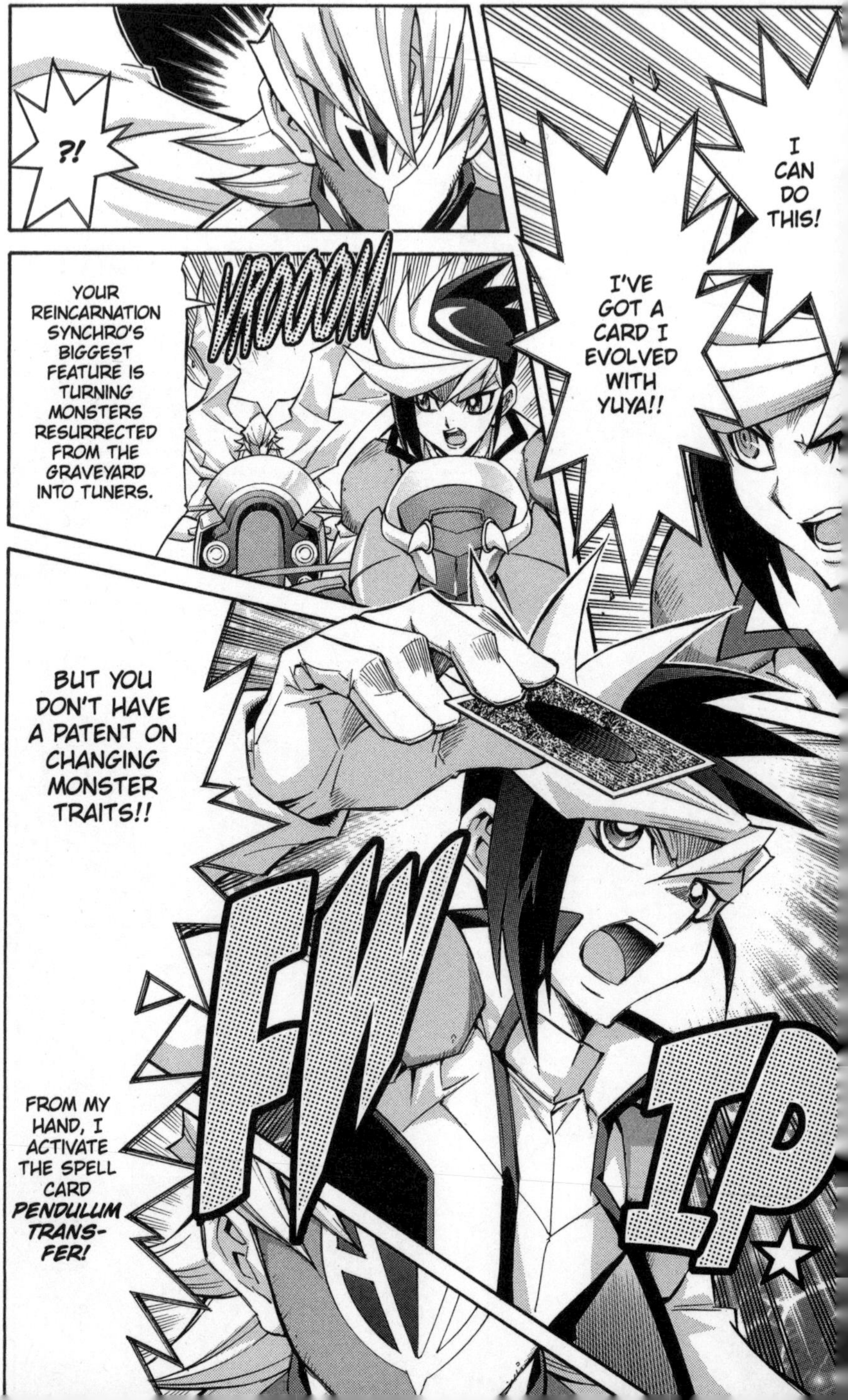
I CAN DO THIS!
I'VE GOT A CARD I EVOLVED WITH YUYA!!
?!
VROOOM
YOUR REINCARNATION SYNCHRO'S BIGGEST FEATURE IS TURNING MONSTERS RESURRECTED FROM THE GRAVEYARD INTO TUNERS.
BUT YOU DON'T HAVE A PATENT ON CHANGING MONSTER TRAITS!!
FWIP
FROM MY HAND, I ACTIVATE THE SPELL CARD *PENDULUM TRANSFER*!

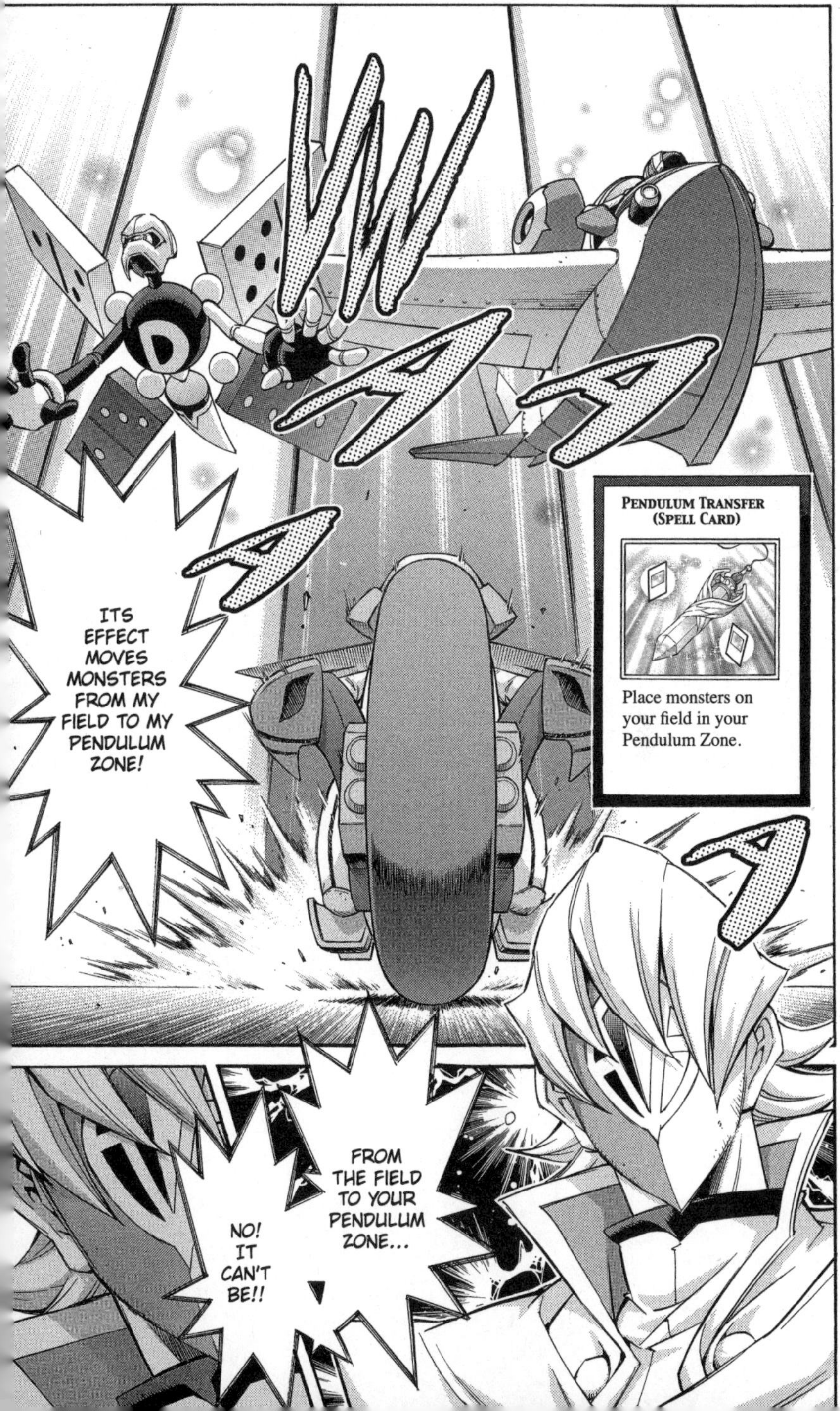
VWAAAA
PENDULUM TRANSFER
(SPELL CARD)
Place monsters on your field in your Pendulum Zone.
ITS EFFECT MOVES MONSTERS FROM MY FIELD TO MY PENDULUM ZONE!
FROM THE FIELD TO YOUR PENDULUM ZONE...
NO! IT CAN'T BE!!

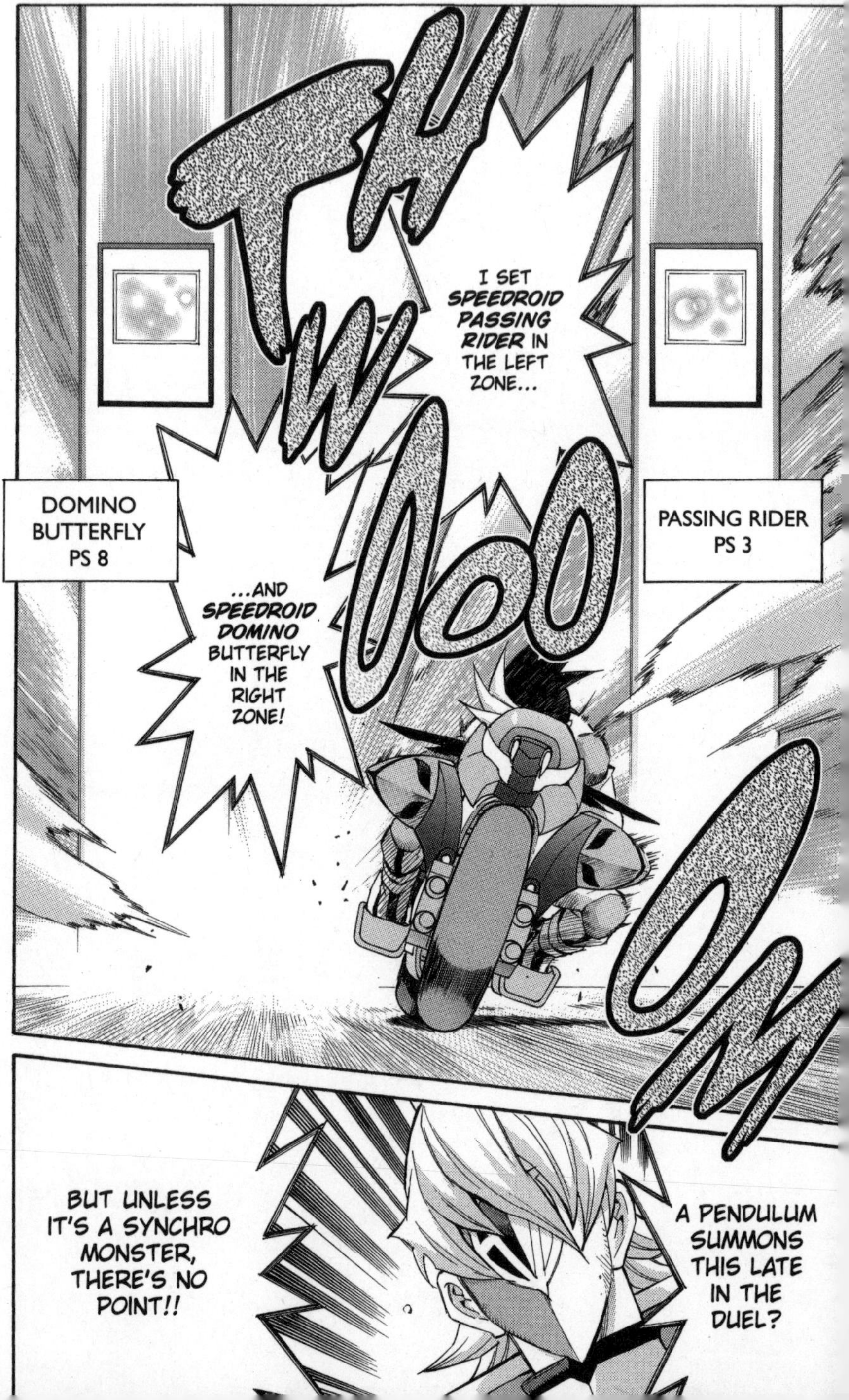
THWOOOOM
PASSING RIDER PS 3
I SET SPEEDROID PASSING RIDER IN THE LEFT ZONE...
DOMINO BUTTERFLY PS 8
...AND SPEEDROID DOMINO BUTTERFLY IN THE RIGHT ZONE!
A PENDULUM SUMMONS THIS LATE IN THE DUEL?
BUT UNLESS IT'S A SYNCHRO MONSTER, THERE'S NO POINT!!

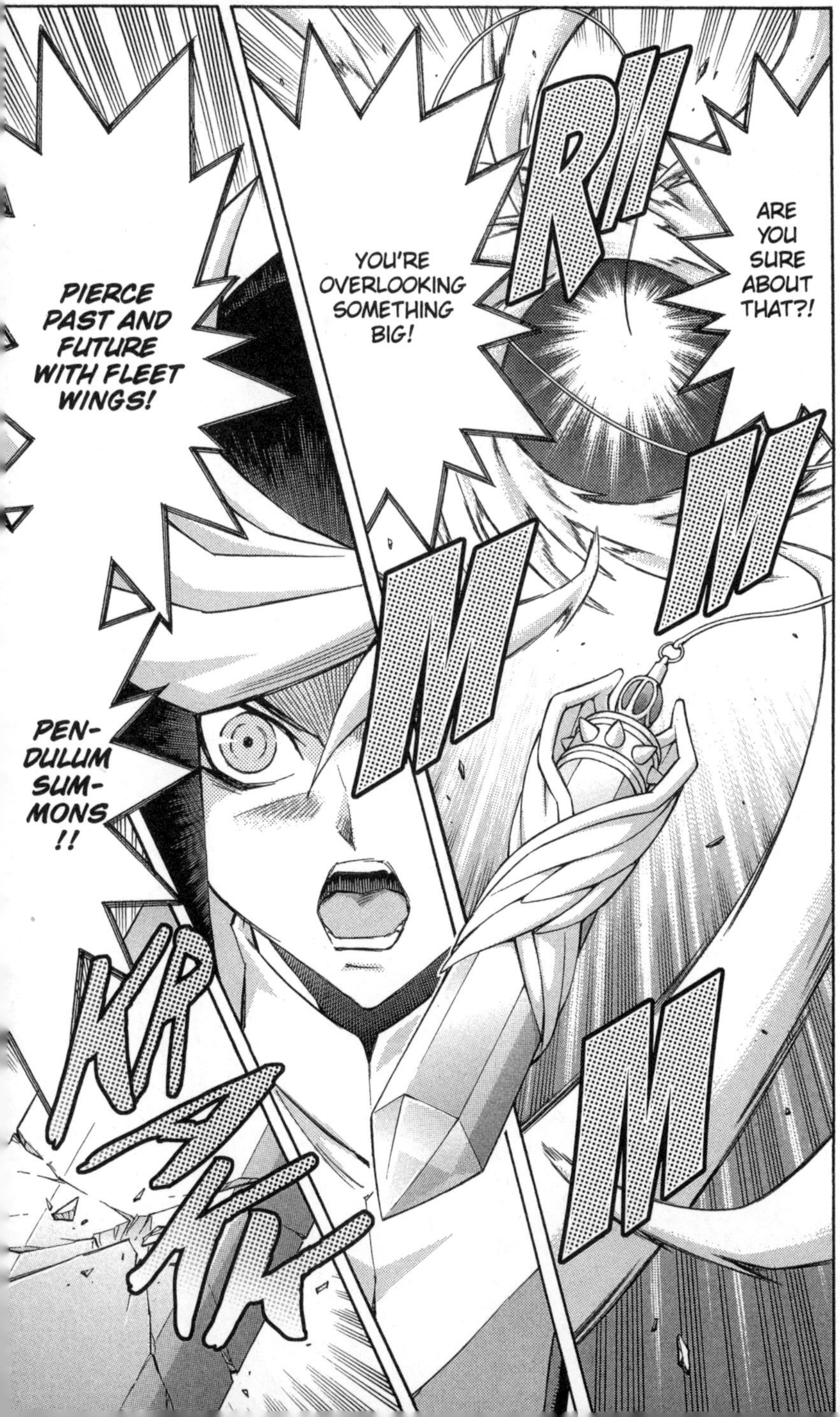
ARE YOU SURE ABOUT THAT?!
RII
YOU'RE OVERLOOKING SOMETHING BIG!
MMMM
PIERCE PAST AND FUTURE WITH FLEET WINGS!
PENDULUM SUMMONS!!
KRAAK

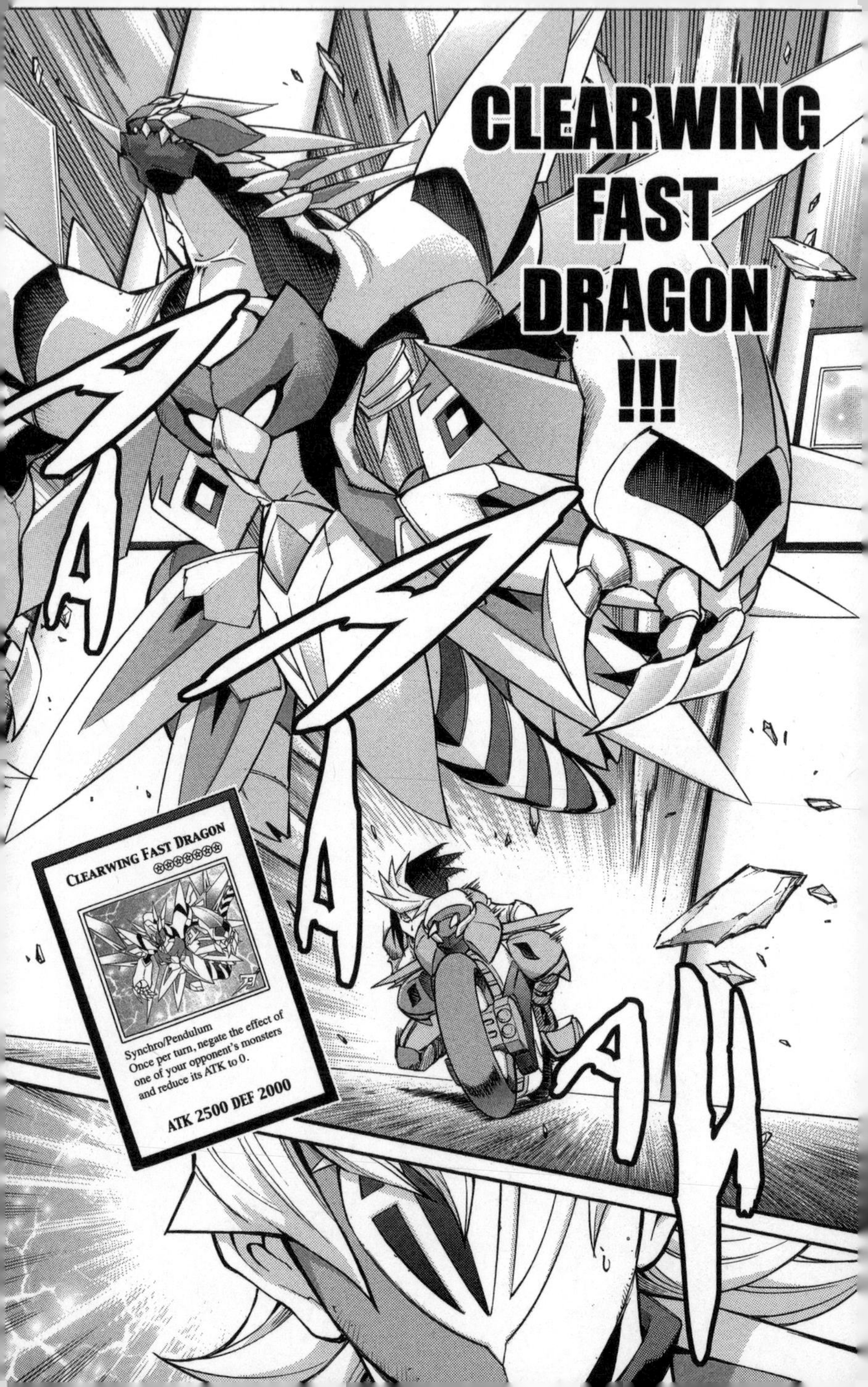
CLEARWING FAST DRAGON !!!
AAAAAAAAH
CLEARWING FAST DRAGON
Synchro/Pendulum
Once per turn, negate the effect of one of your opponent's monsters and reduce its ATK to 0.
ATK 2500 DEF 2000

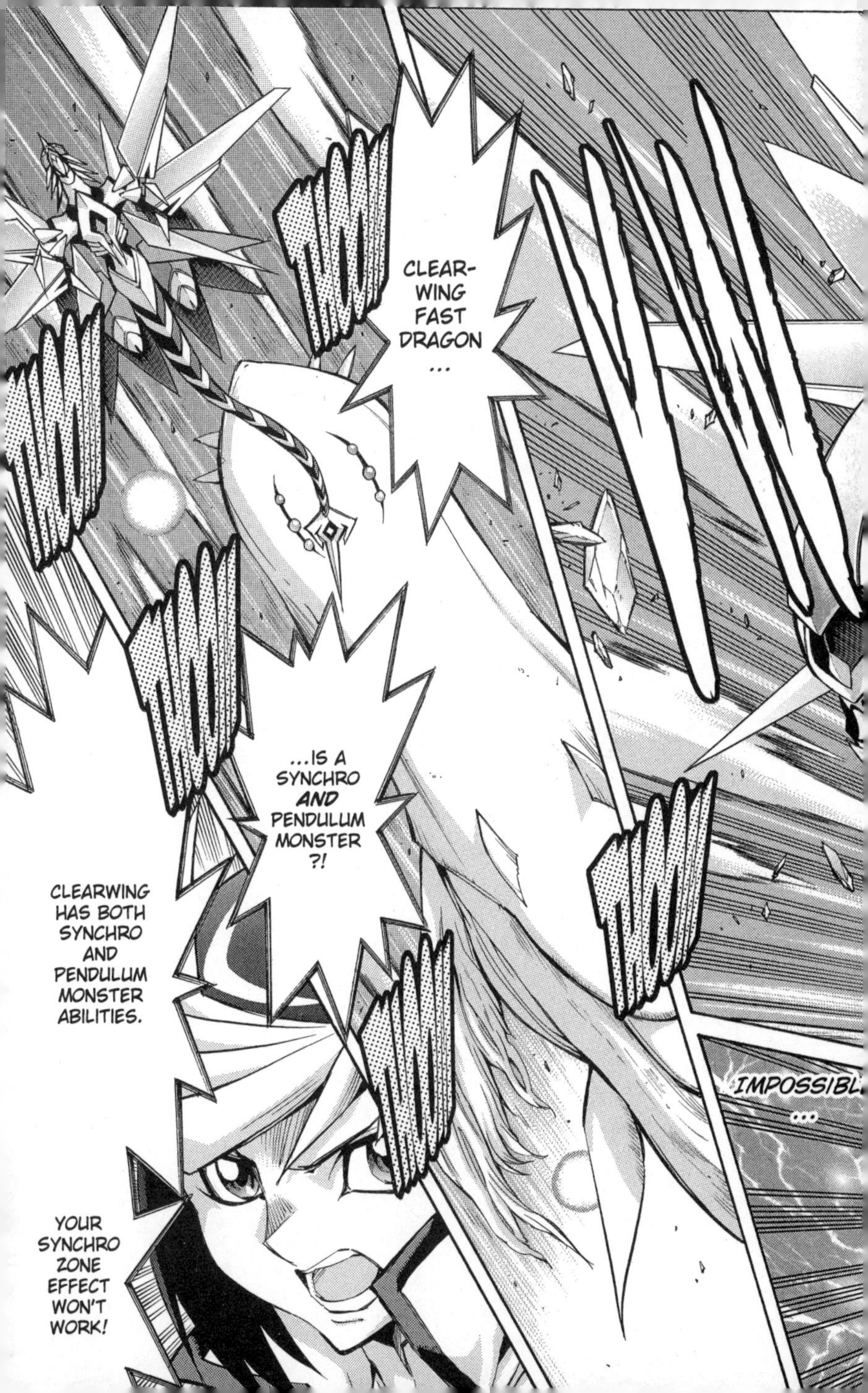
CLEAR-WING FAST DRAGON...
...IS A SYNCHRO AND PENDULUM MONSTER?!
IMPOSSIBL...
CLEARWING HAS BOTH SYNCHRO AND PENDULUM MONSTER ABILITIES.
YOUR SYNCHRO ZONE EFFECT WON'T WORK!

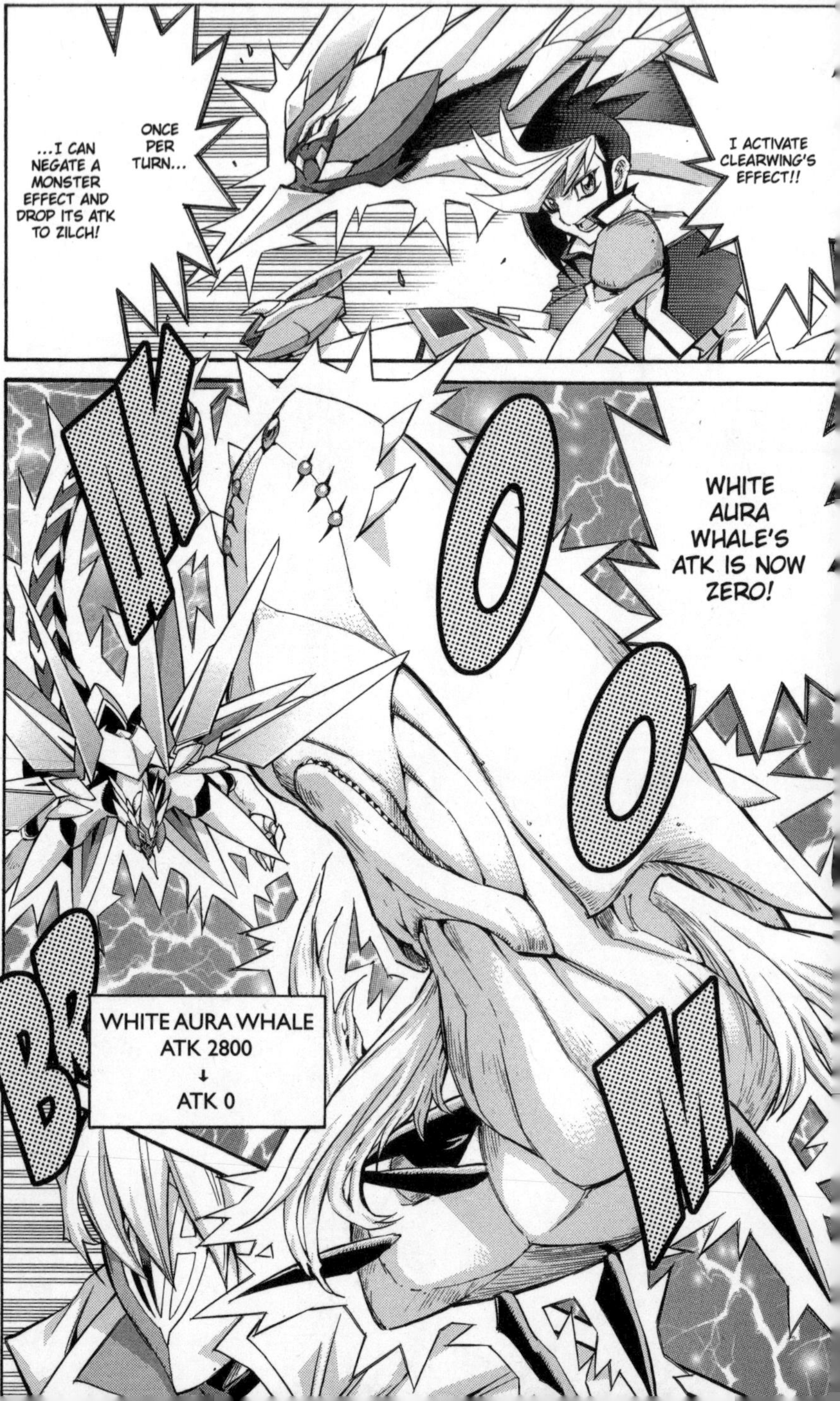
I ACTIVATE CLEARWING'S EFFECT!!
ONCE PER TURN...
...I CAN NEGATE A MONSTER EFFECT AND DROP ITS ATK TO ZILCH!
WHITE AURA WHALE'S ATK IS NOW ZERO!
WHITE AURA WHALE
ATK 2800
↓
ATK 0

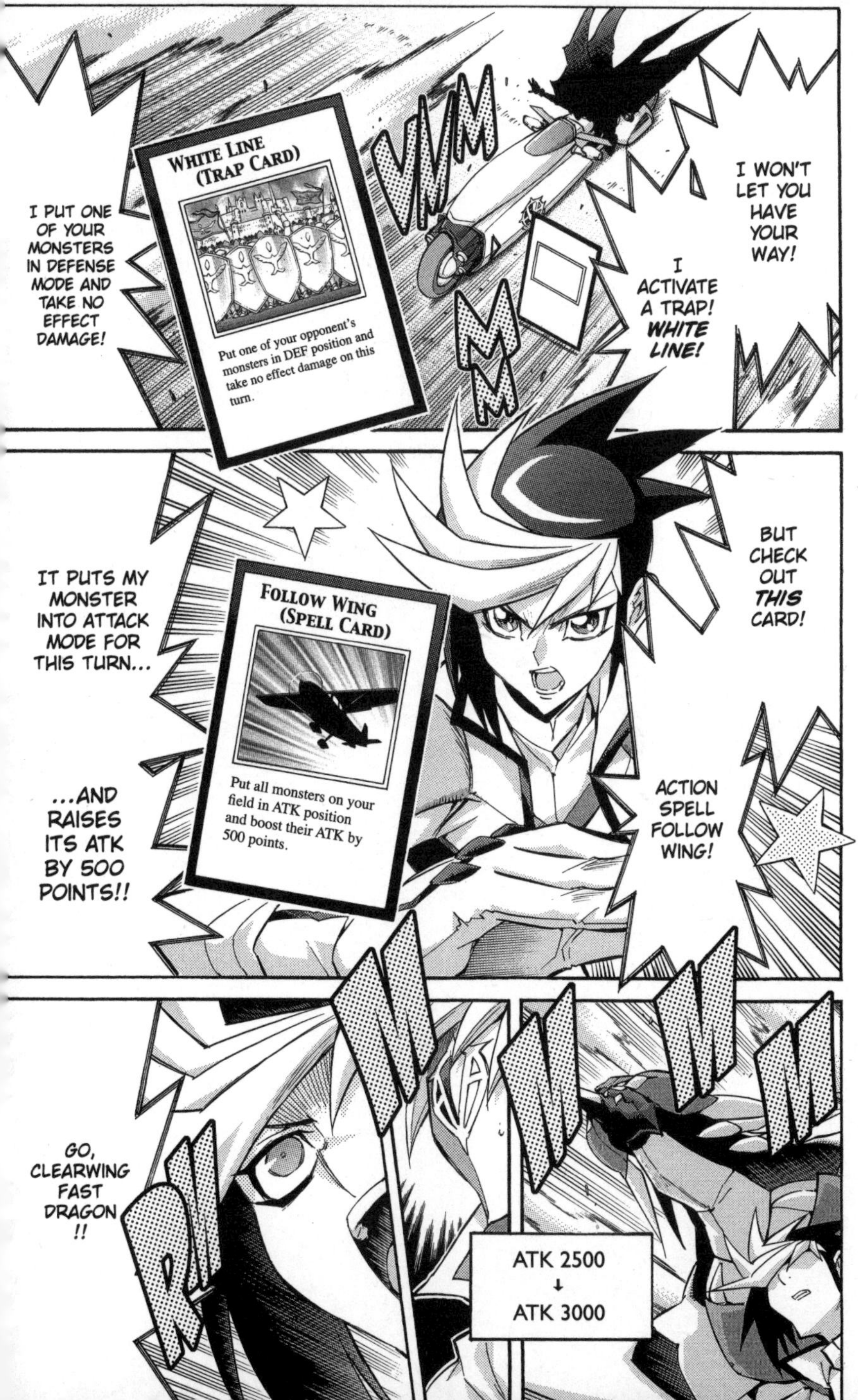
I WON'T LET YOU HAVE YOUR WAY!
I ACTIVATE A TRAP! *WHITE LINE!*
WHITE LINE (TRAP CARD)
Put one of your opponent's monsters in DEF position and take no effect damage on this turn.
I PUT ONE OF YOUR MONSTERS IN DEFENSE MODE AND TAKE NO EFFECT DAMAGE!
BUT CHECK OUT *THIS* CARD!
ACTION SPELL FOLLOW WING!
FOLLOW WING (SPELL CARD)
Put all monsters on your field in ATK position and boost their ATK by 500 points.
IT PUTS MY MONSTER INTO ATTACK MODE FOR THIS TURN...
...AND RAISES ITS ATK BY 500 POINTS!!
ATK 2500
↓
ATK 3000
GO, CLEARWING FAST DRAGON!!

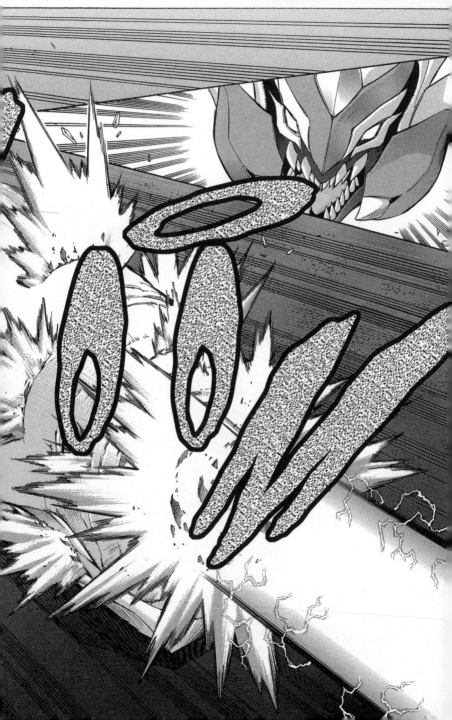

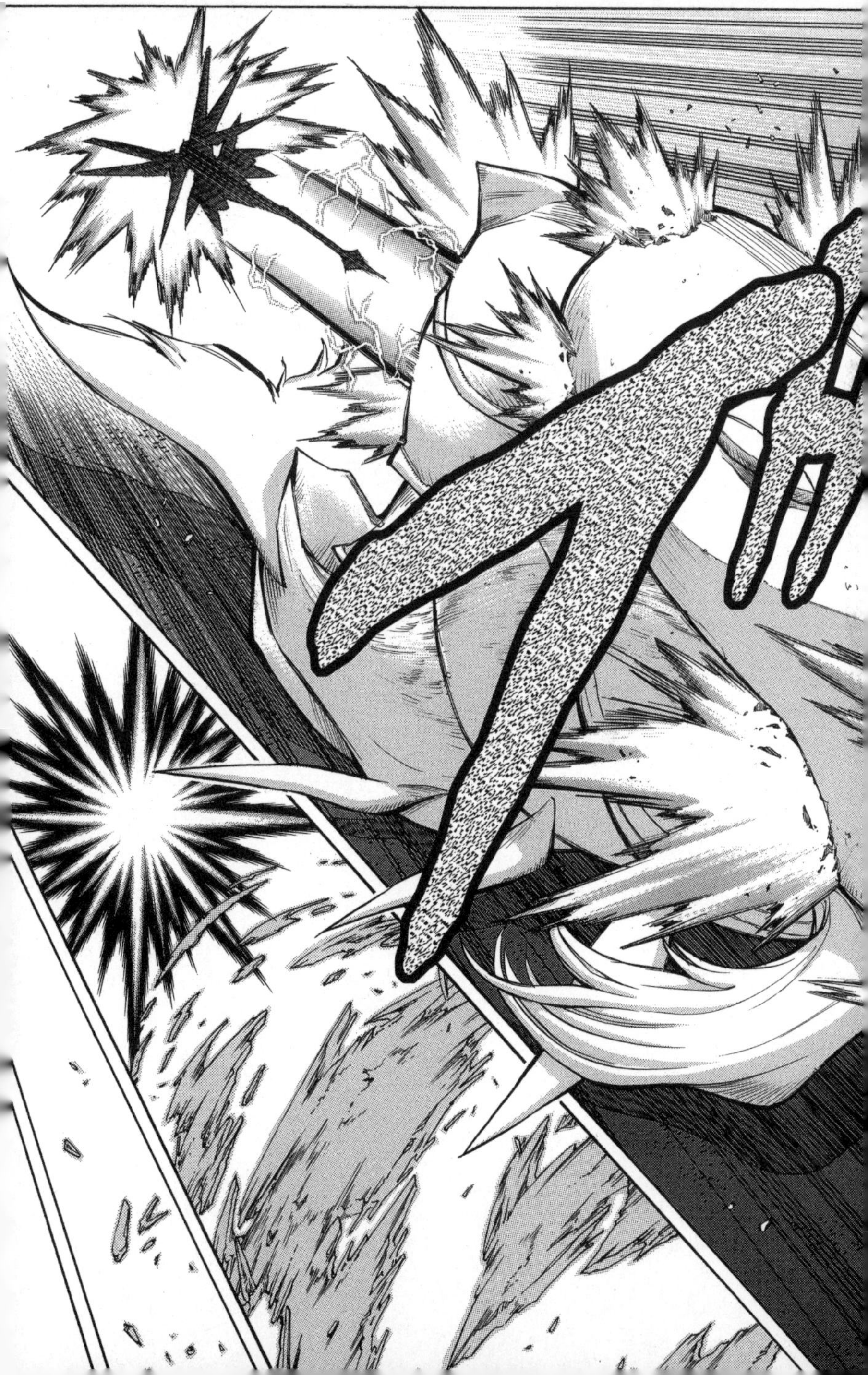

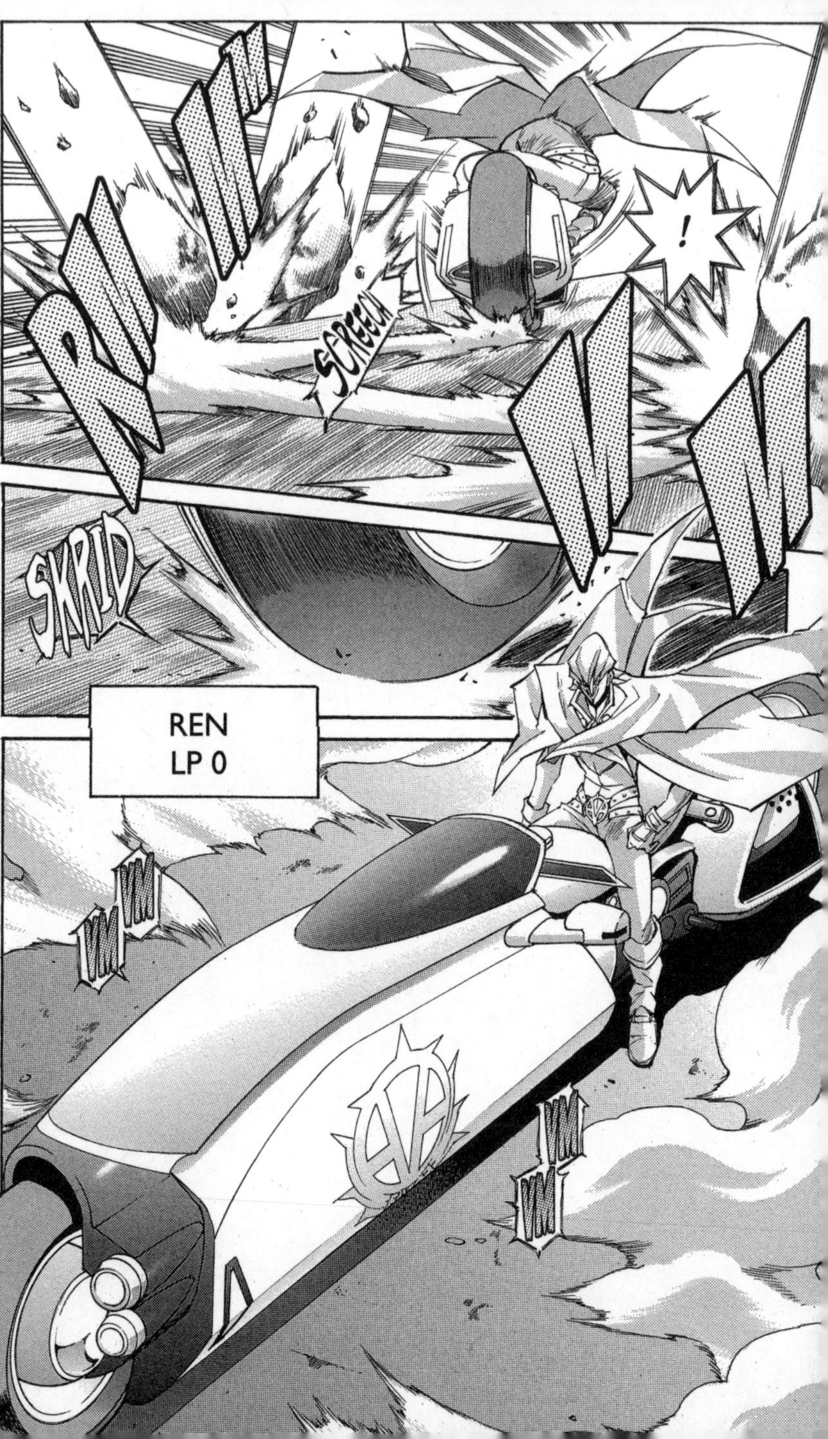
!
SCREECH
RMMM
SKRID
REN
LP 0
VMM VMM
VMM VMM

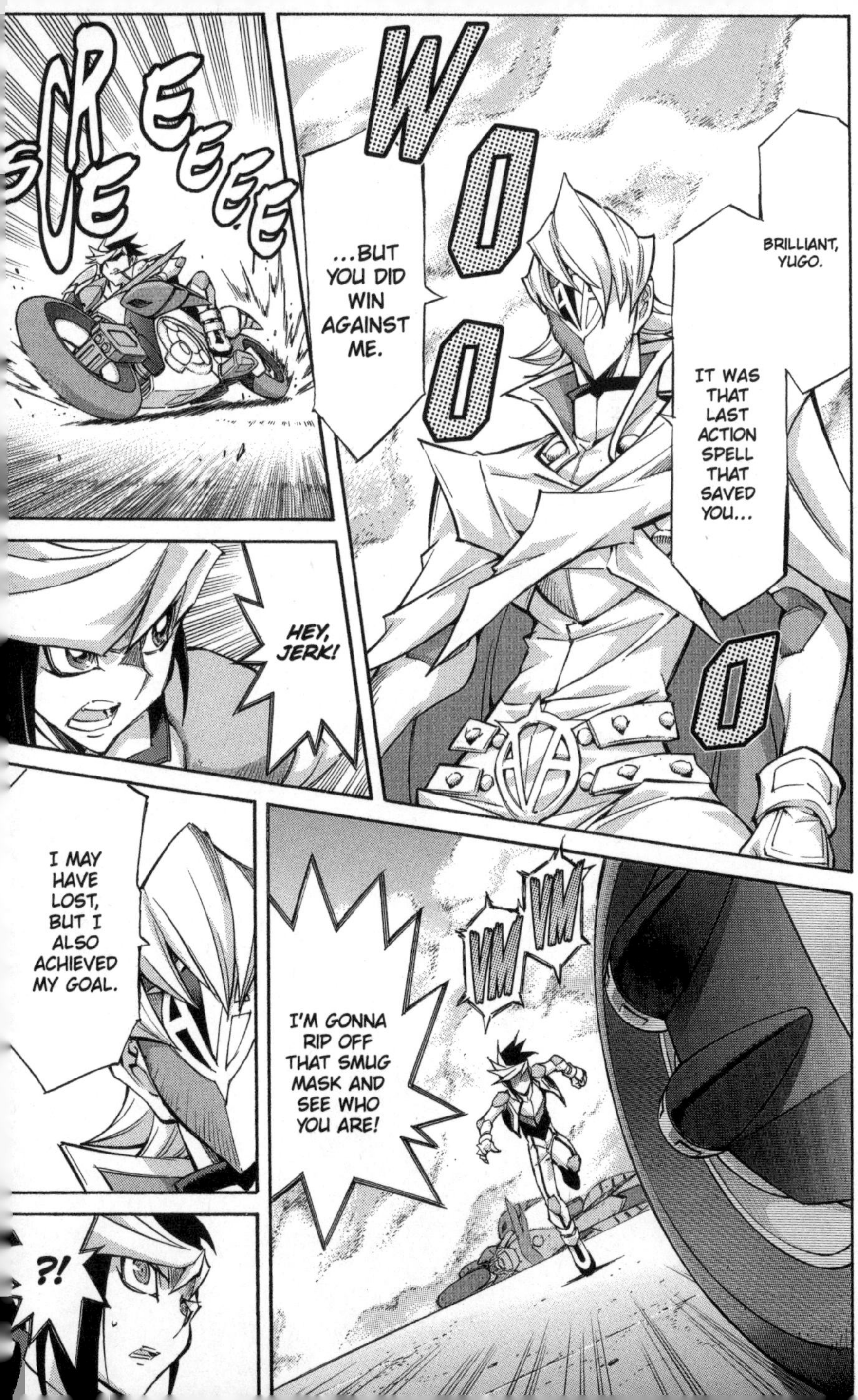

WOOO
BRILLIANT, YUGO.
IT WAS THAT LAST ACTION SPELL THAT SAVED YOU...
...BUT YOU DID WIN AGAINST ME.
SCREEEEEE
HEY, JERK!
VM VM
I'M GONNA RIP OFF THAT SMUG MASK AND SEE WHO YOU ARE!
I MAY HAVE LOST, BUT I ALSO ACHIEVED MY GOAL.
?!

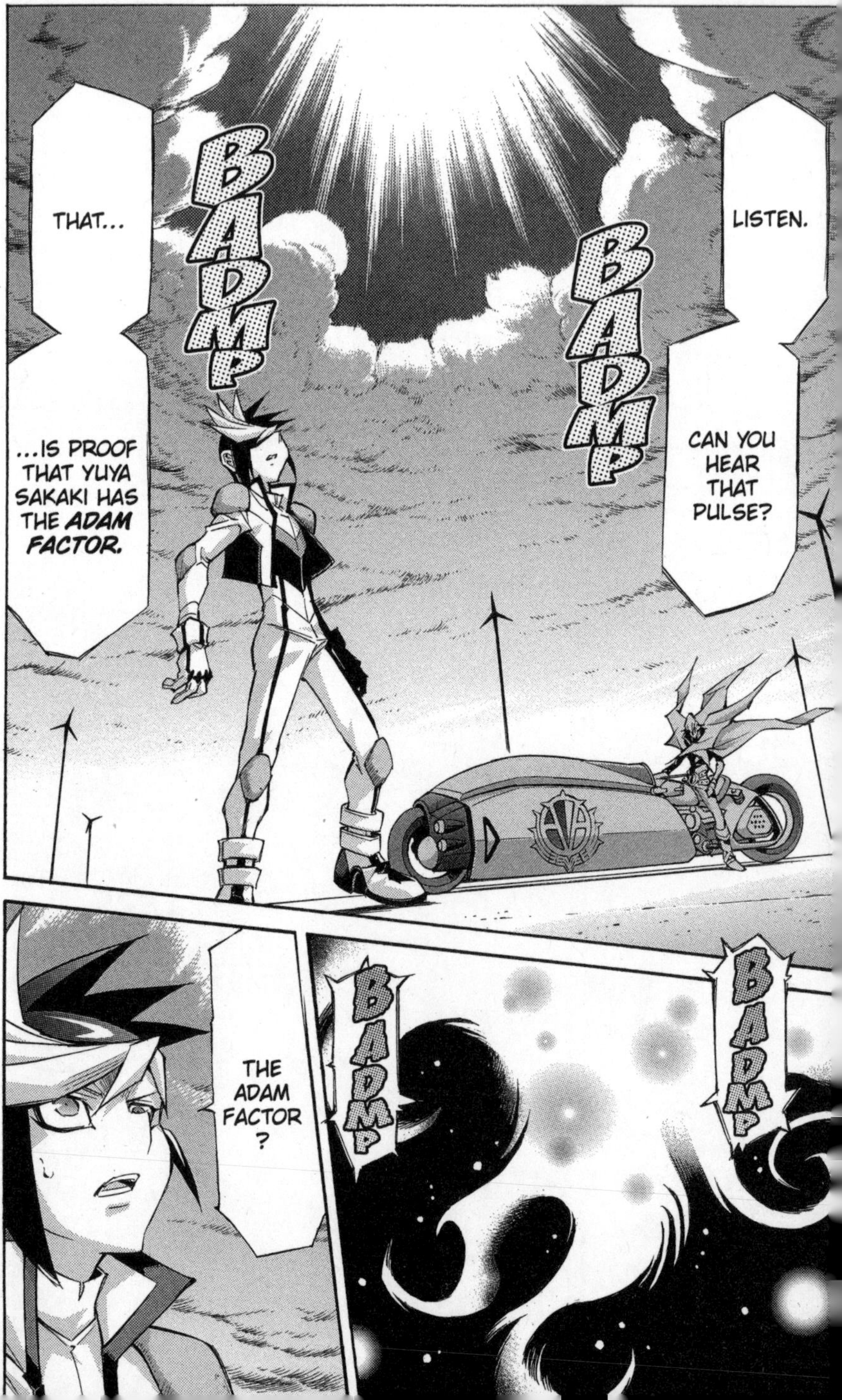
LISTEN.
BADMP
CAN YOU HEAR THAT PULSE?
BADMP
THAT...
...IS PROOF THAT YUYA SAKAKI HAS THE *ADAM FACTOR.*
BADMP
BADMP
THE ADAM FACTOR?

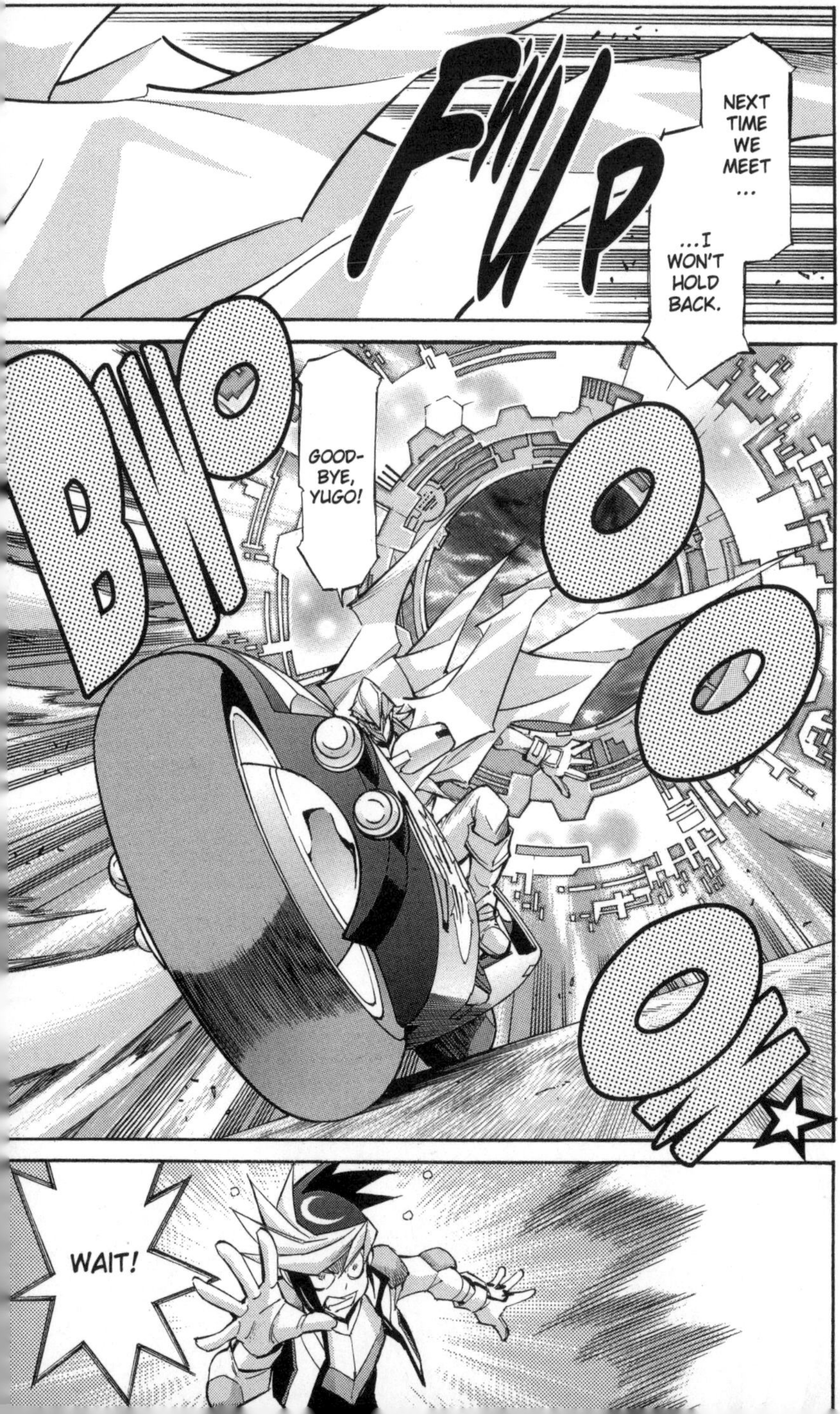
NEXT TIME WE MEET ...
...I WON'T HOLD BACK.
FWUP
GOOD-BYE, YUGO!
BWOOOOOM
WAIT!

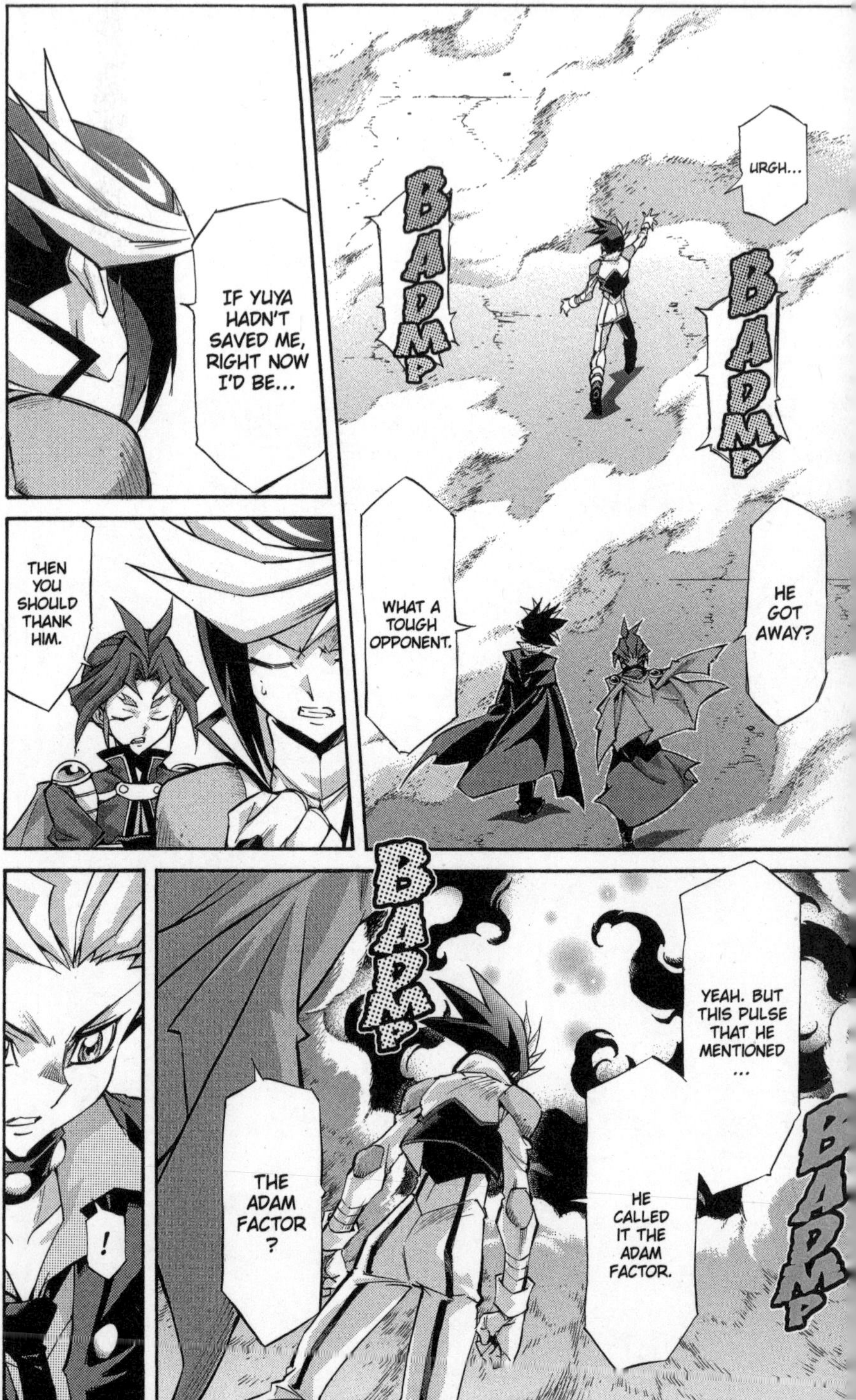
URGH...
BADMP
BADMP
HE GOT AWAY?
WHAT A TOUGH OPPONENT.
IF YUYA HADN'T SAVED ME, RIGHT NOW I'D BE...
THEN YOU SHOULD THANK HIM.
BADMP
YEAH. BUT THIS PULSE THAT HE MENTIONED...
HE CALLED IT THE ADAM FACTOR.
THE ADAM FACTOR?
BADMP
!

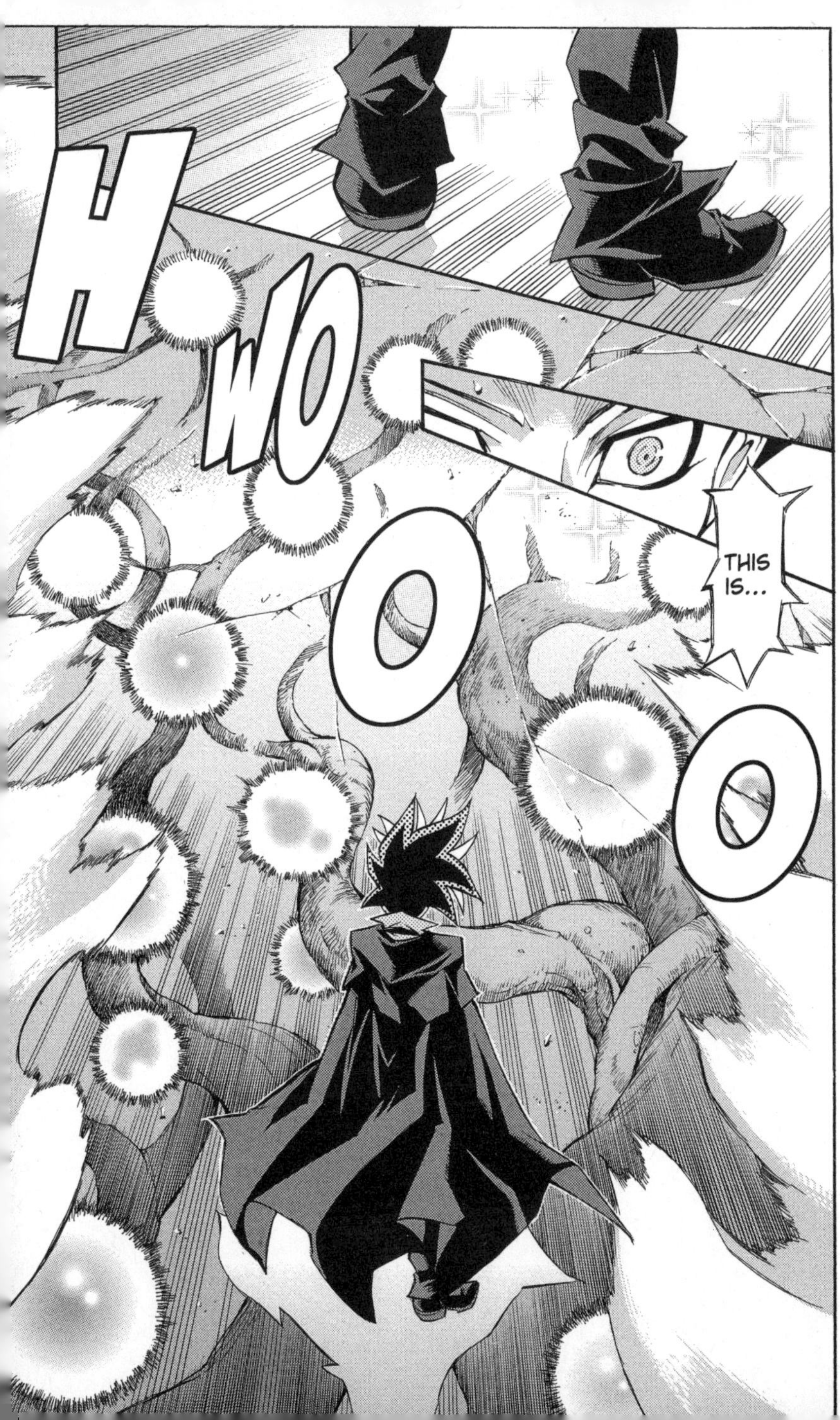
HWOOOO
THIS IS...

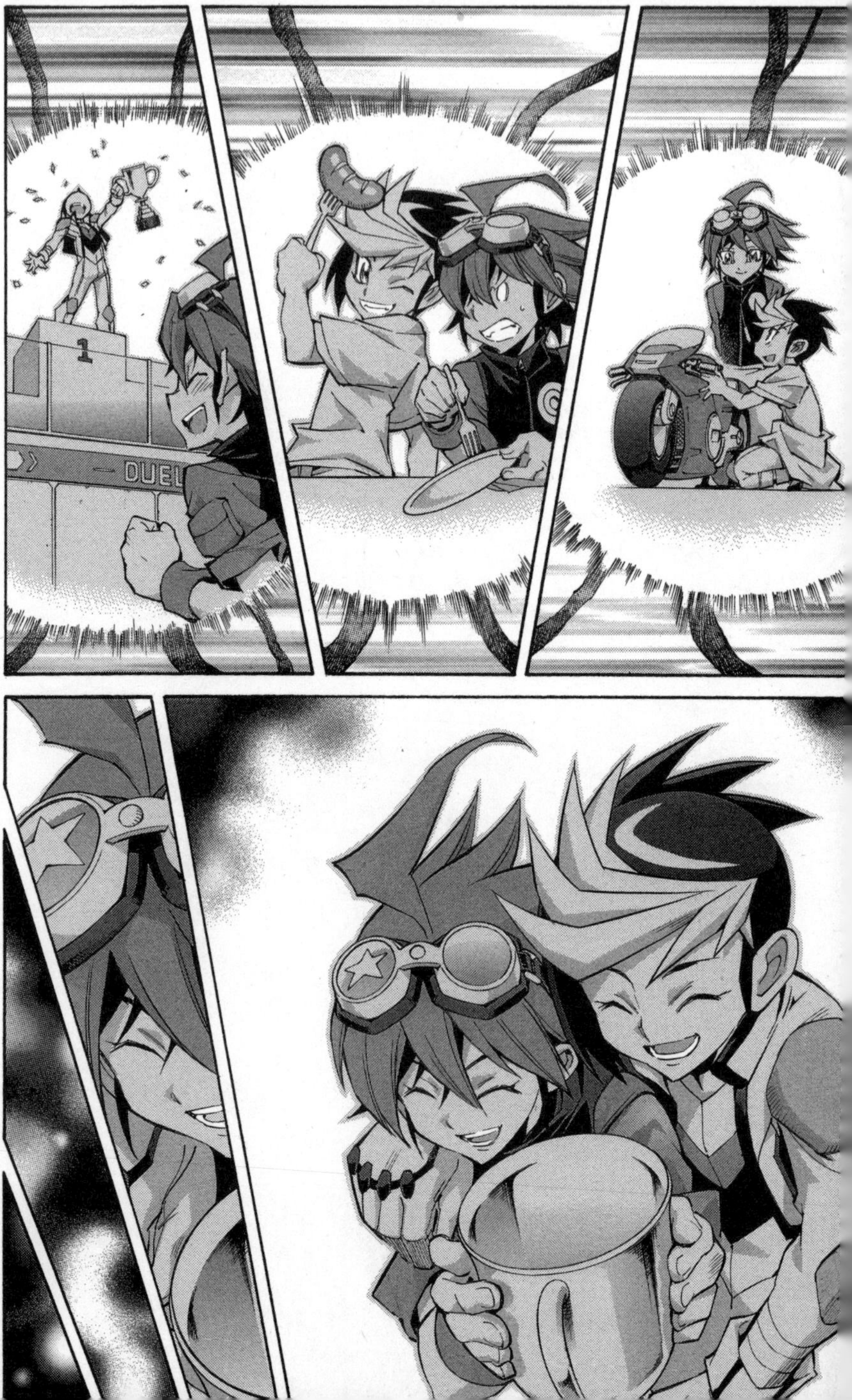
1
DUEL

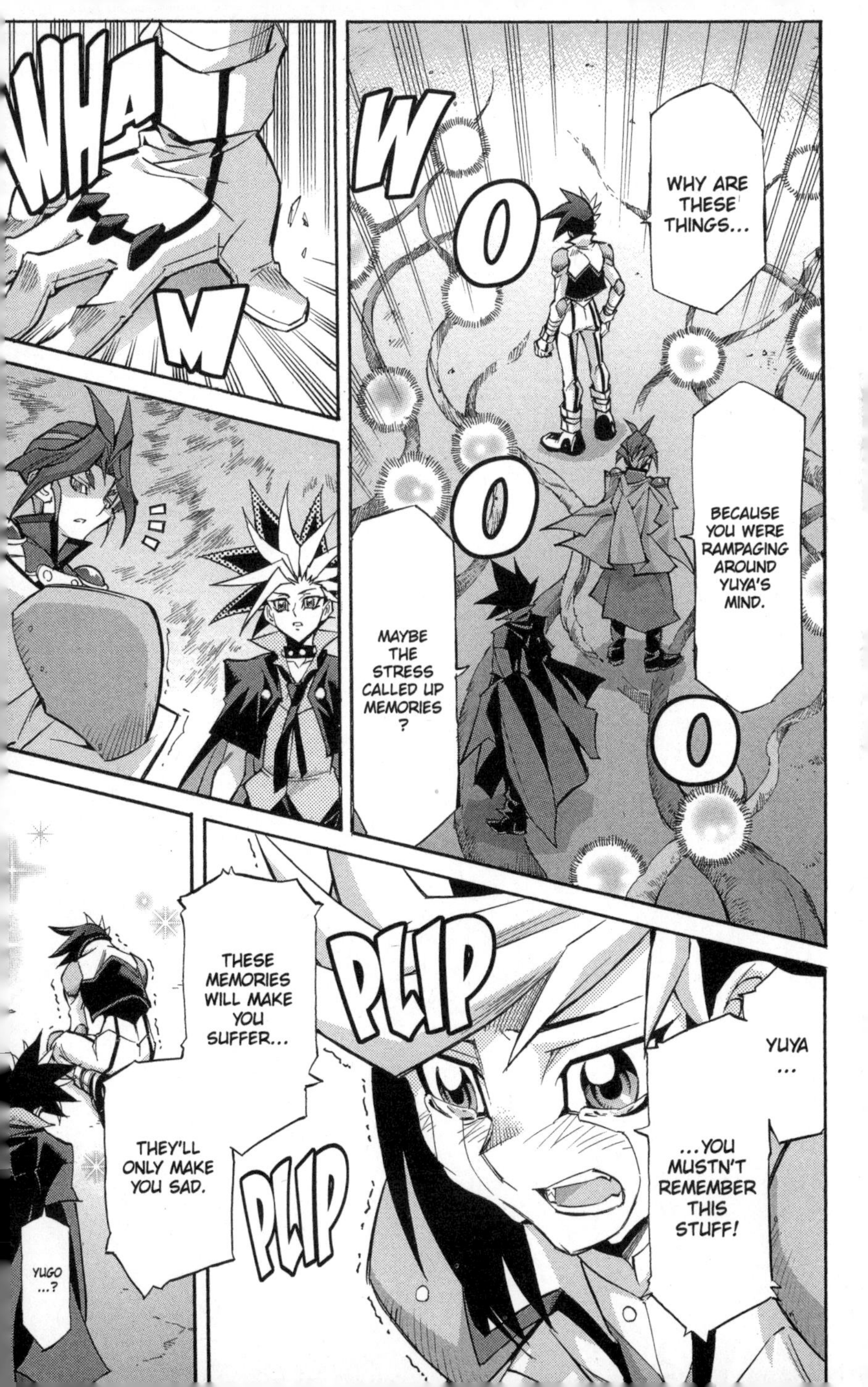
WOOO
WHY ARE THESE THINGS...
BECAUSE YOU WERE RAMPAGING AROUND YUYA'S MIND.
MAYBE THE STRESS CALLED UP MEMORIES?
WHAM
...
PLIP
YUYA...
...YOU MUSTN'T REMEMBER THIS STUFF!
THESE MEMORIES WILL MAKE YOU SUFFER...
THEY'LL ONLY MAKE YOU SAD.
PLIP
YUGO...?

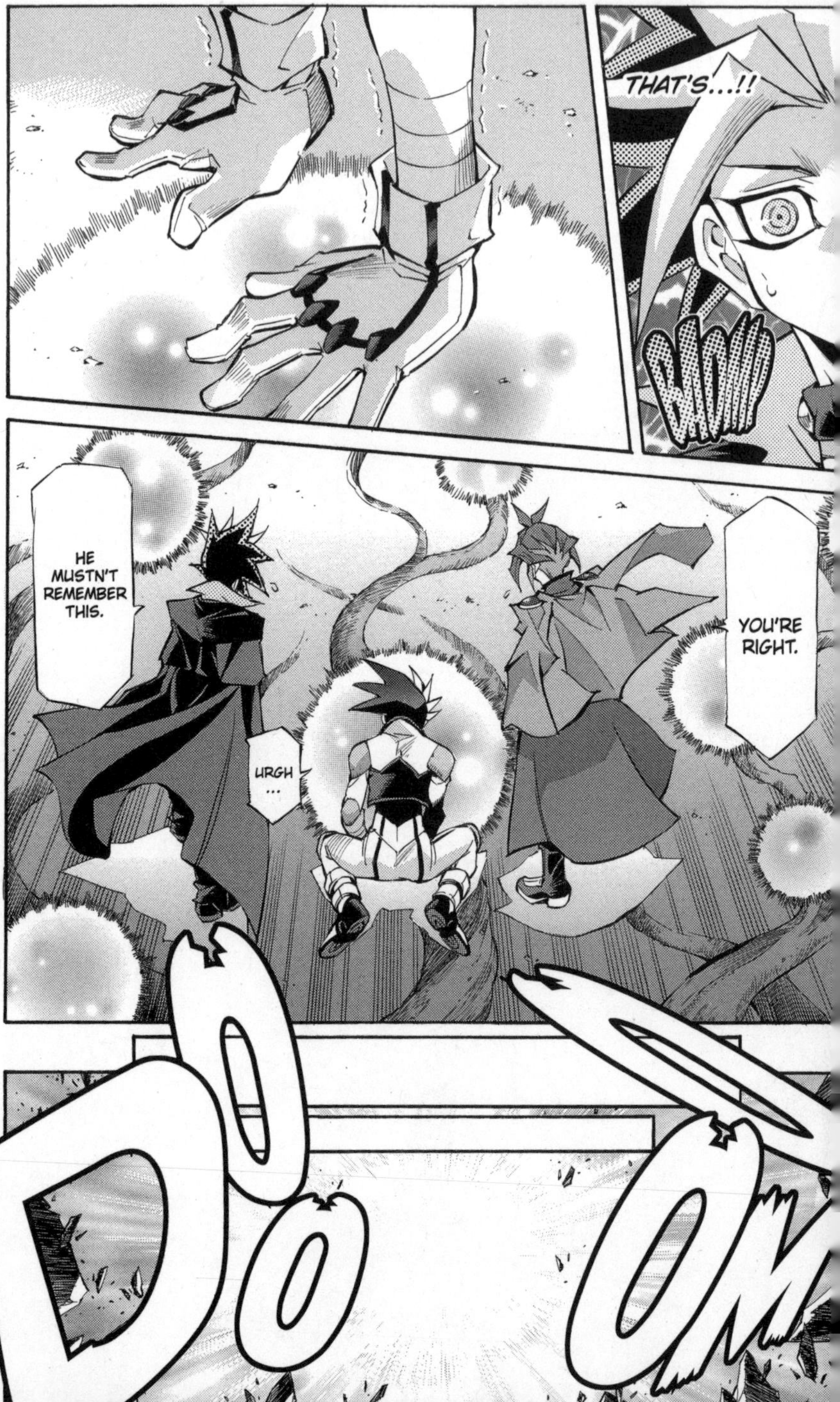
THAT'S...!!
HE MUSTN'T REMEMBER THIS.
YOU'RE RIGHT.
URGH ...
DOOOOM

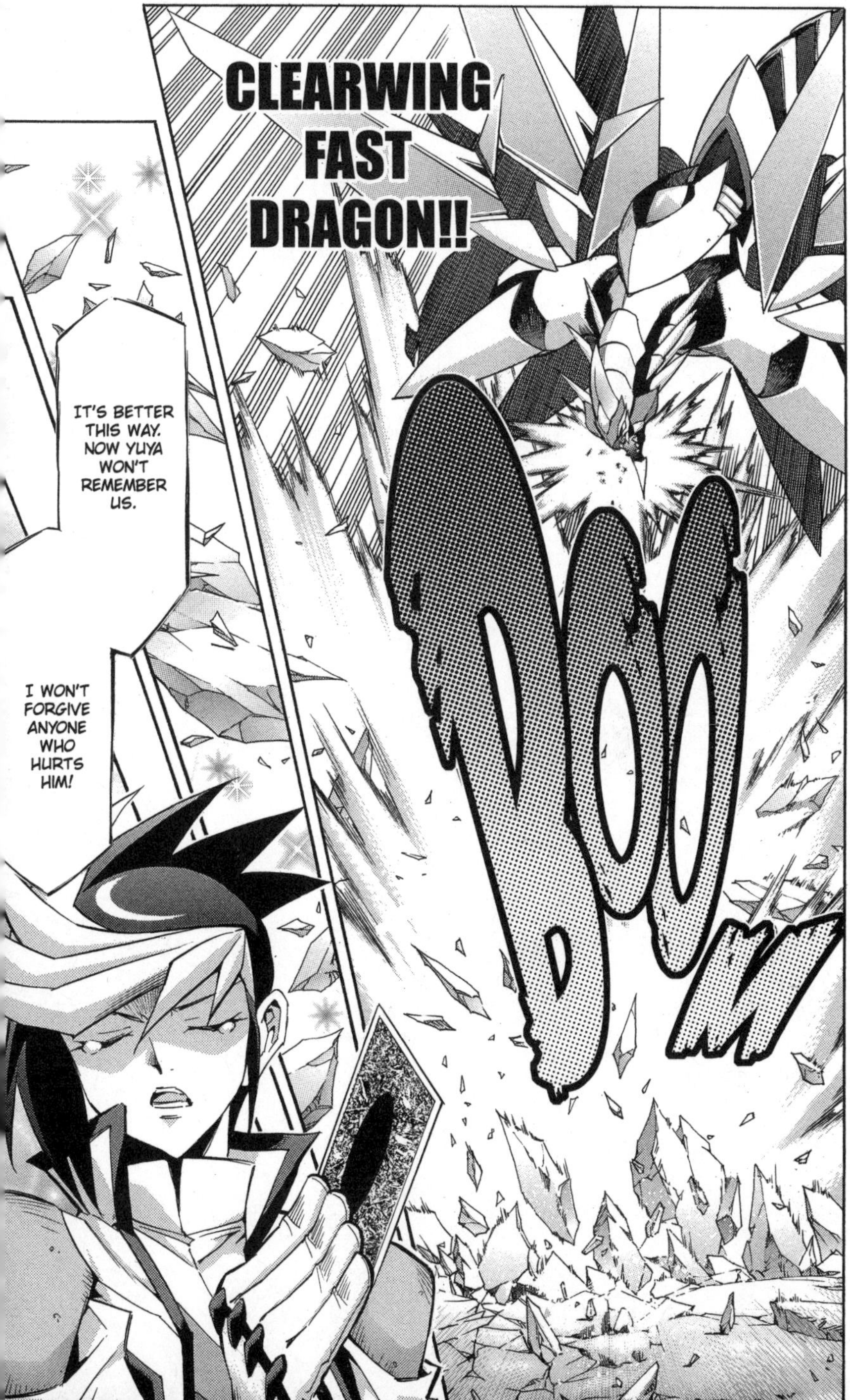
CLEARWING FAST DRAGON!!
BOOM
IT'S BETTER THIS WAY. NOW YUYA WON'T REMEMBER US.
I WON'T FORGIVE ANYONE WHO HURTS HIM!

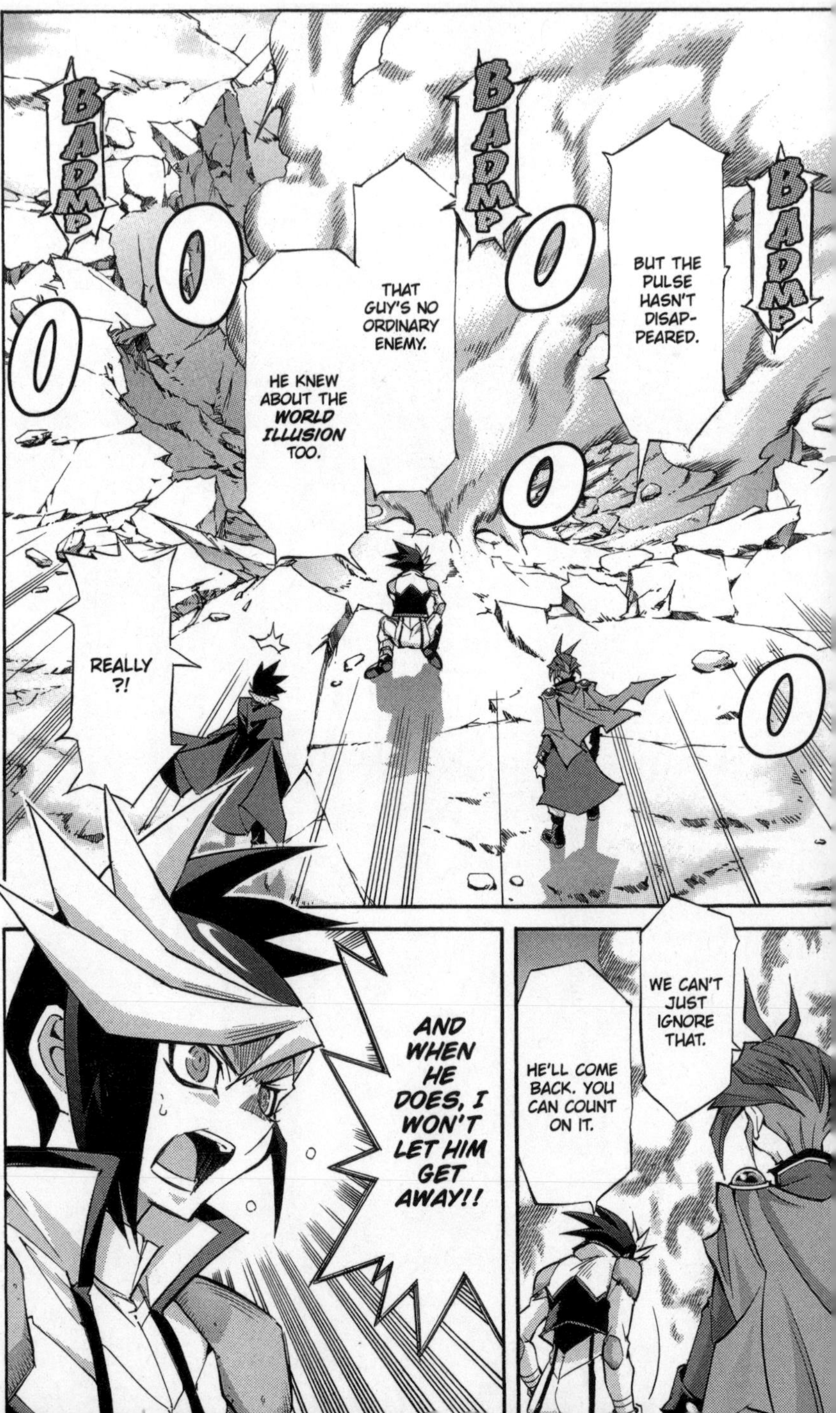
BADMP
BUT THE PULSE HASN'T DISAP-PEARED.
BADMP
THAT GUY'S NO ORDINARY ENEMY.
HE KNEW ABOUT THE *WORLD ILLUSION* TOO.
BADMP
REALLY?!
WE CAN'T JUST IGNORE THAT.
HE'LL COME BACK. YOU CAN COUNT ON IT.
AND WHEN HE DOES, I WON'T LET HIM GET AWAY!!

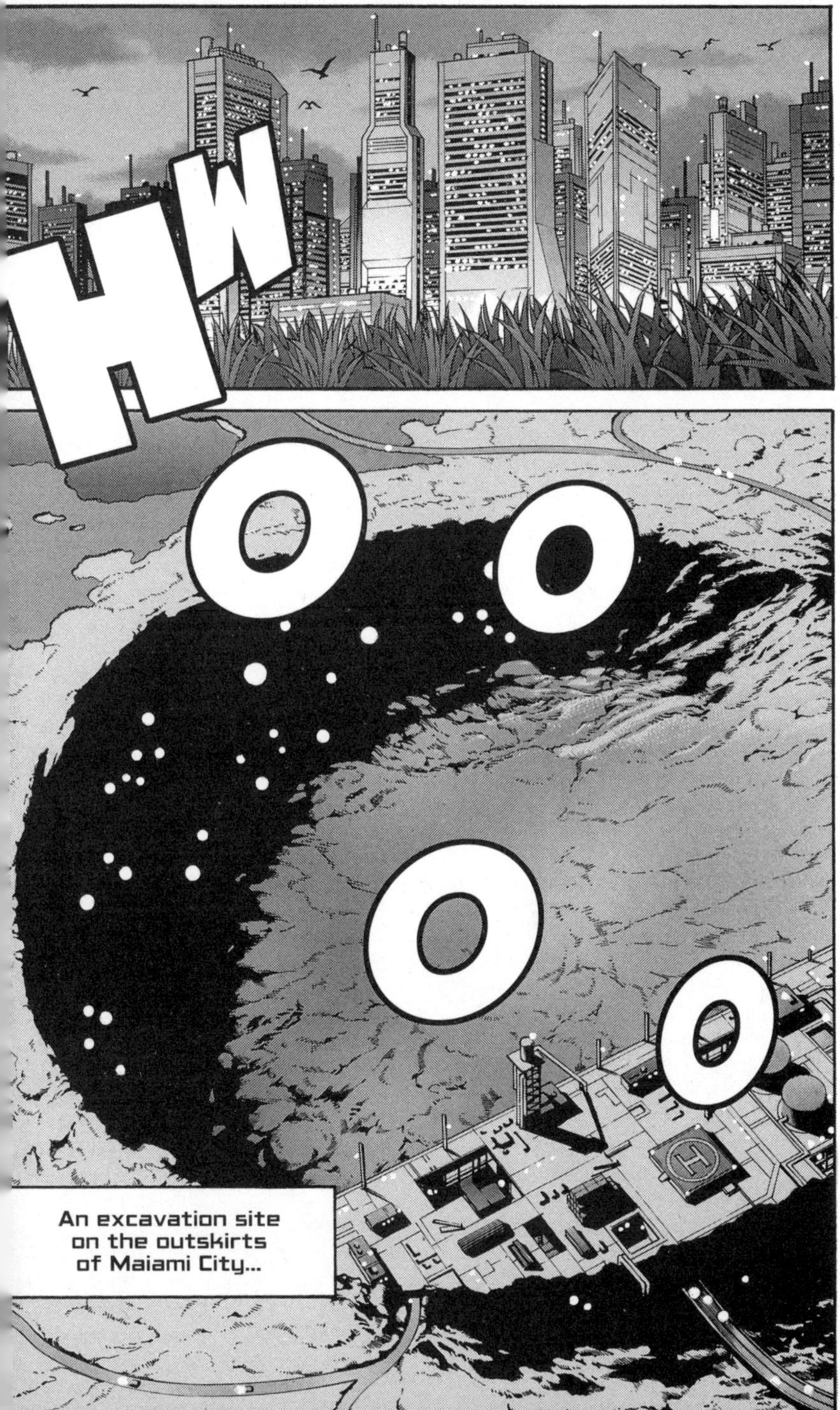
HWOOOO
An excavation site on the outskirts of Maiami City...

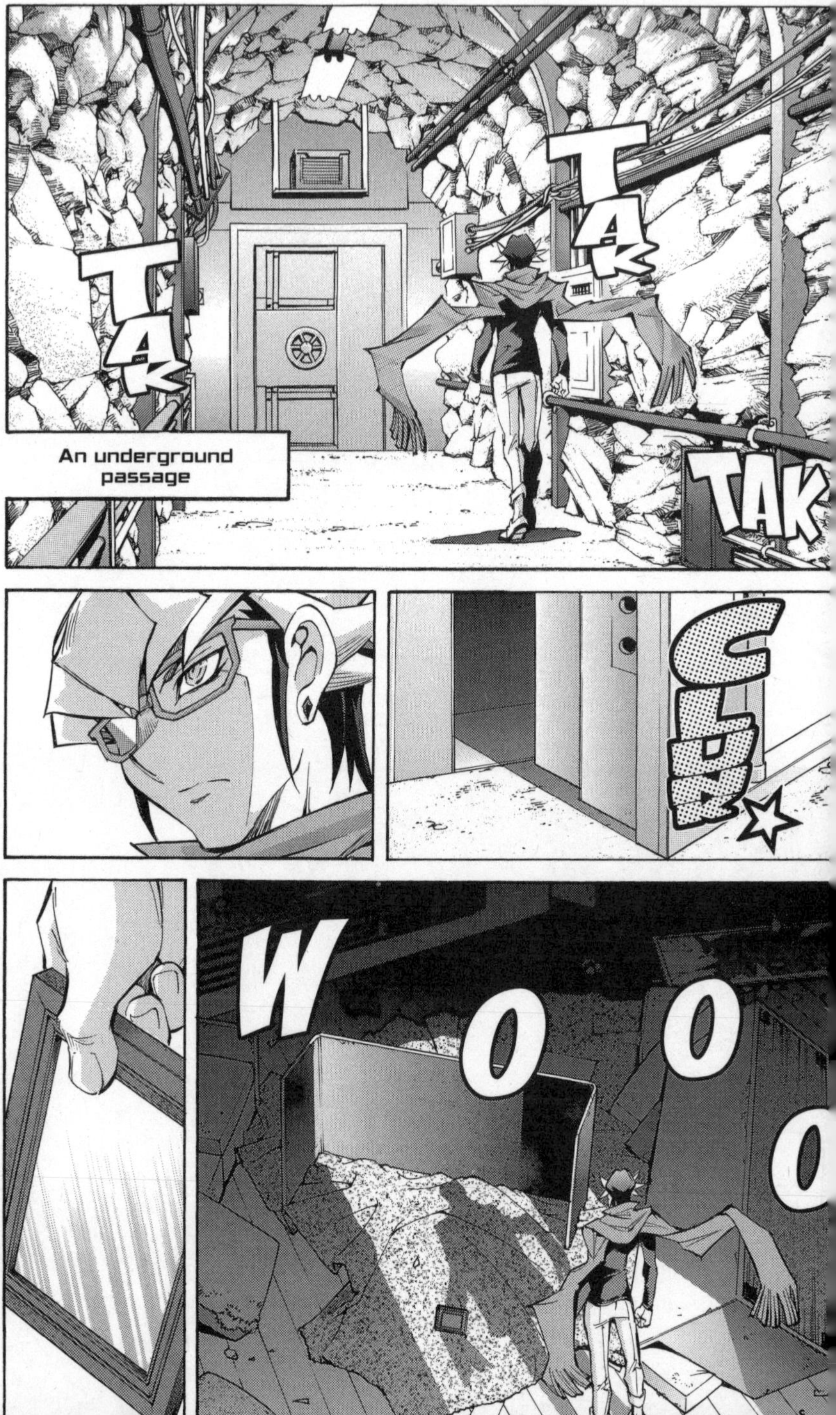
TAK
TAK
TAK
An underground passage
WOOO

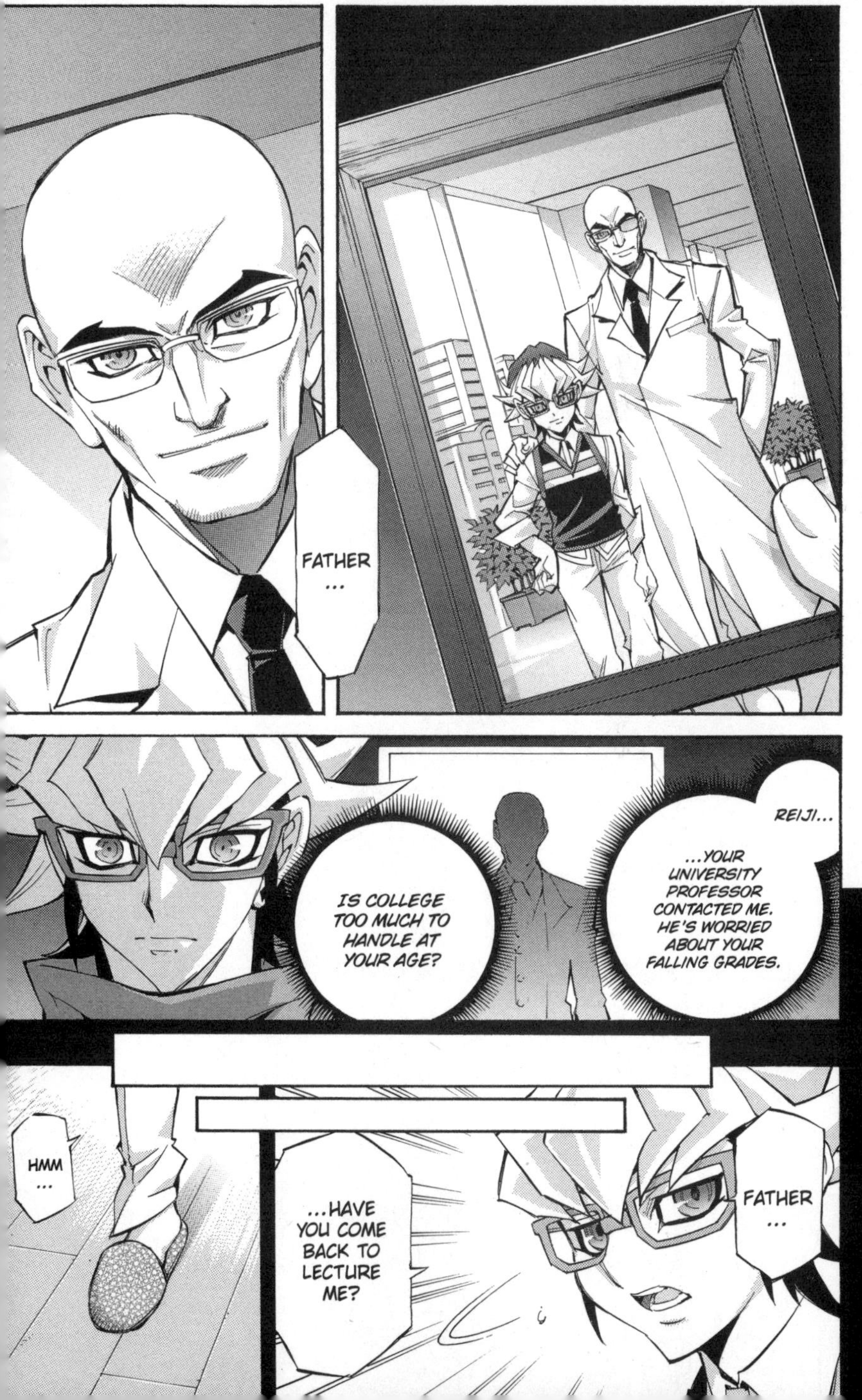
FATHER ...
REIJI...
...YOUR UNIVERSITY PROFESSOR CONTACTED ME. HE'S WORRIED ABOUT YOUR FALLING GRADES.
IS COLLEGE TOO MUCH TO HANDLE AT YOUR AGE?
FATHER ...
...HAVE YOU COME BACK TO LECTURE ME?
HMM ...

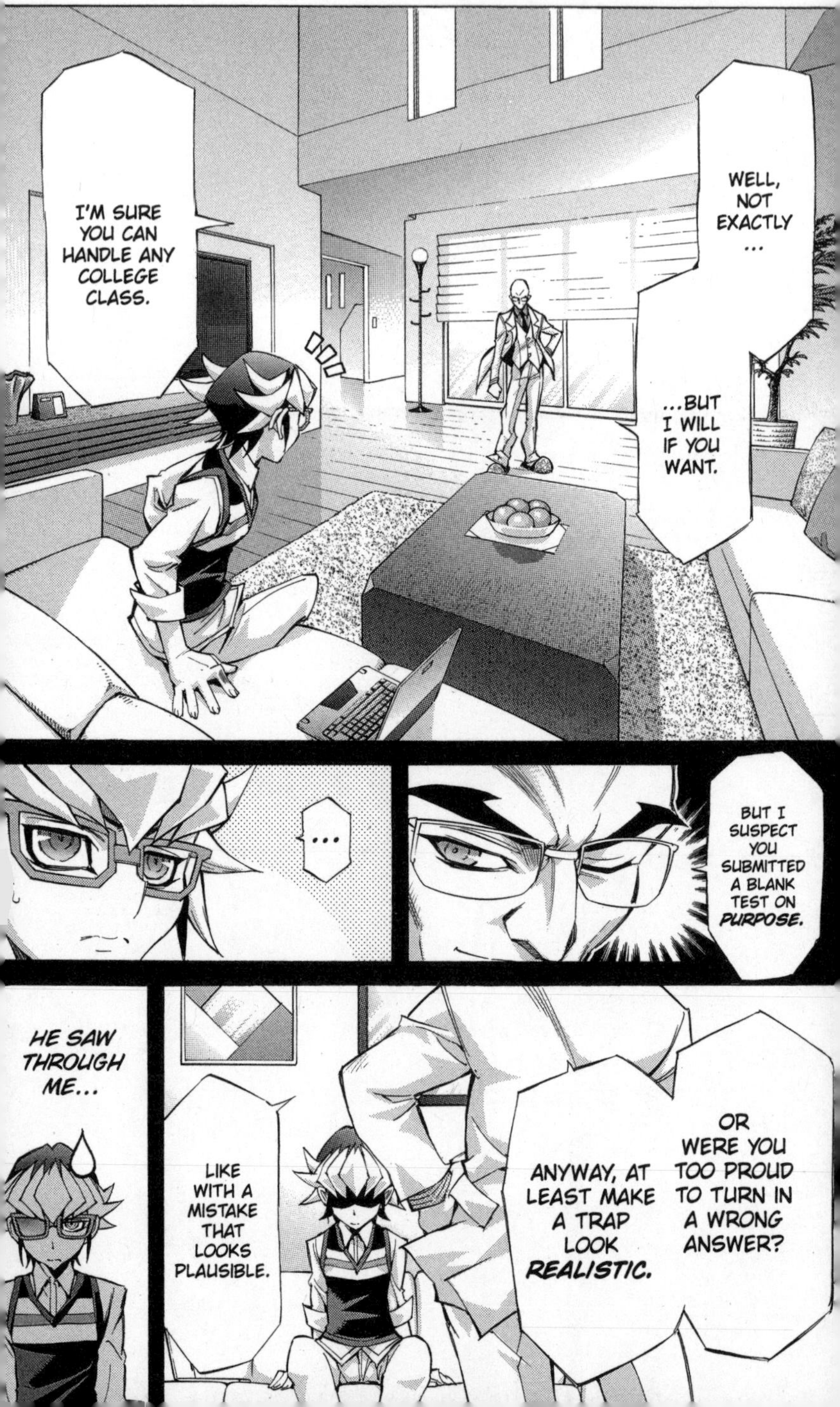
WELL, NOT EXACTLY ...
...BUT I WILL IF YOU WANT.
I'M SURE YOU CAN HANDLE ANY COLLEGE CLASS.
BUT I SUSPECT YOU SUBMITTED A BLANK TEST ON *PURPOSE.*
...
OR WERE YOU TOO PROUD TO TURN IN A WRONG ANSWER?
ANYWAY, AT LEAST MAKE A TRAP LOOK *REALISTIC.*
LIKE WITH A MISTAKE THAT LOOKS PLAUSIBLE.
HE SAW THROUGH ME...

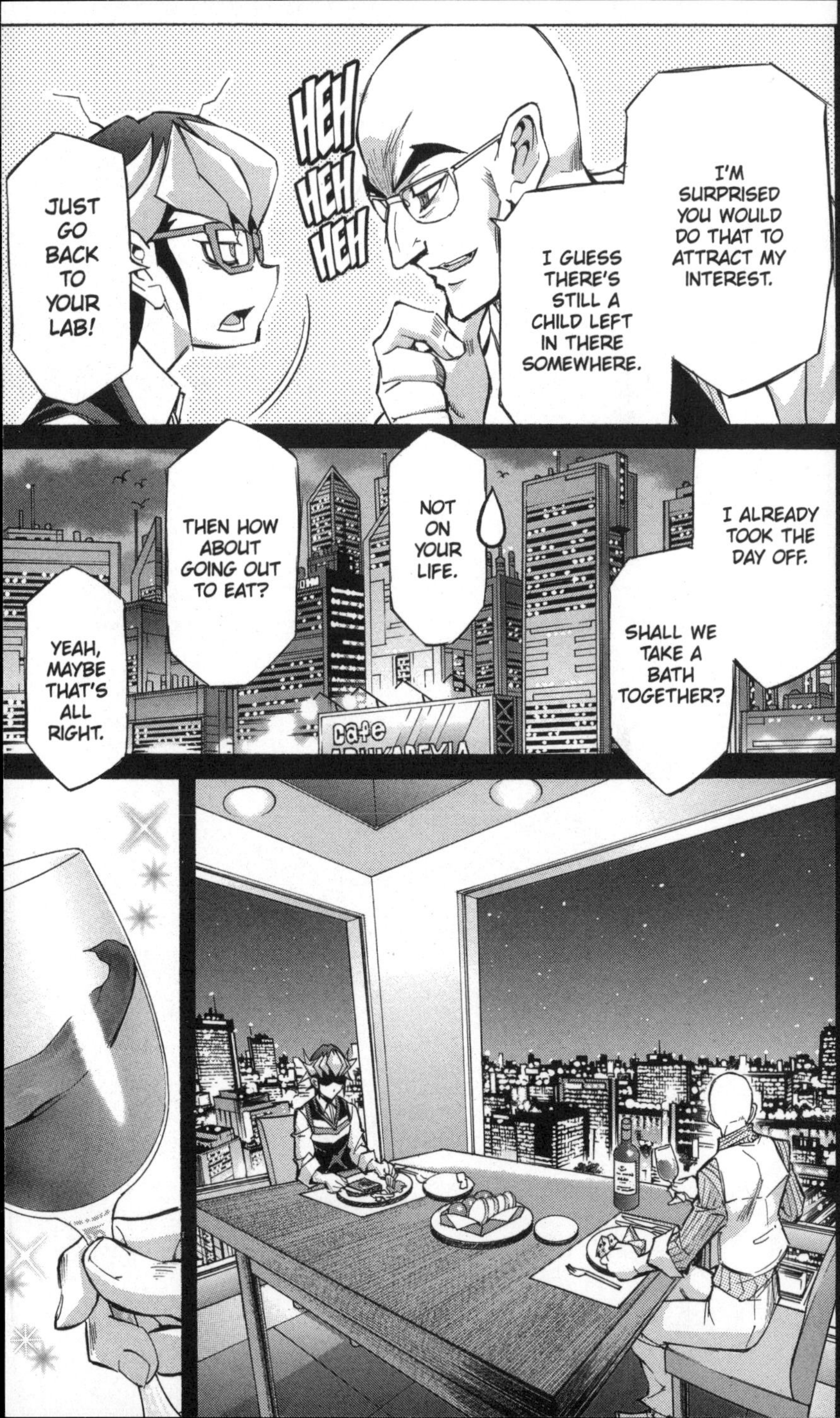
I'M SURPRISED YOU WOULD DO THAT TO ATTRACT MY INTEREST.
I GUESS THERE'S STILL A CHILD LEFT IN THERE SOMEWHERE.
HEH HEH HEH
JUST GO BACK TO YOUR LAB!
I ALREADY TOOK THE DAY OFF.
SHALL WE TAKE A BATH TOGETHER?
NOT ON YOUR LIFE.
THEN HOW ABOUT GOING OUT TO EAT?
YEAH, MAYBE THAT'S ALL RIGHT.
cafe

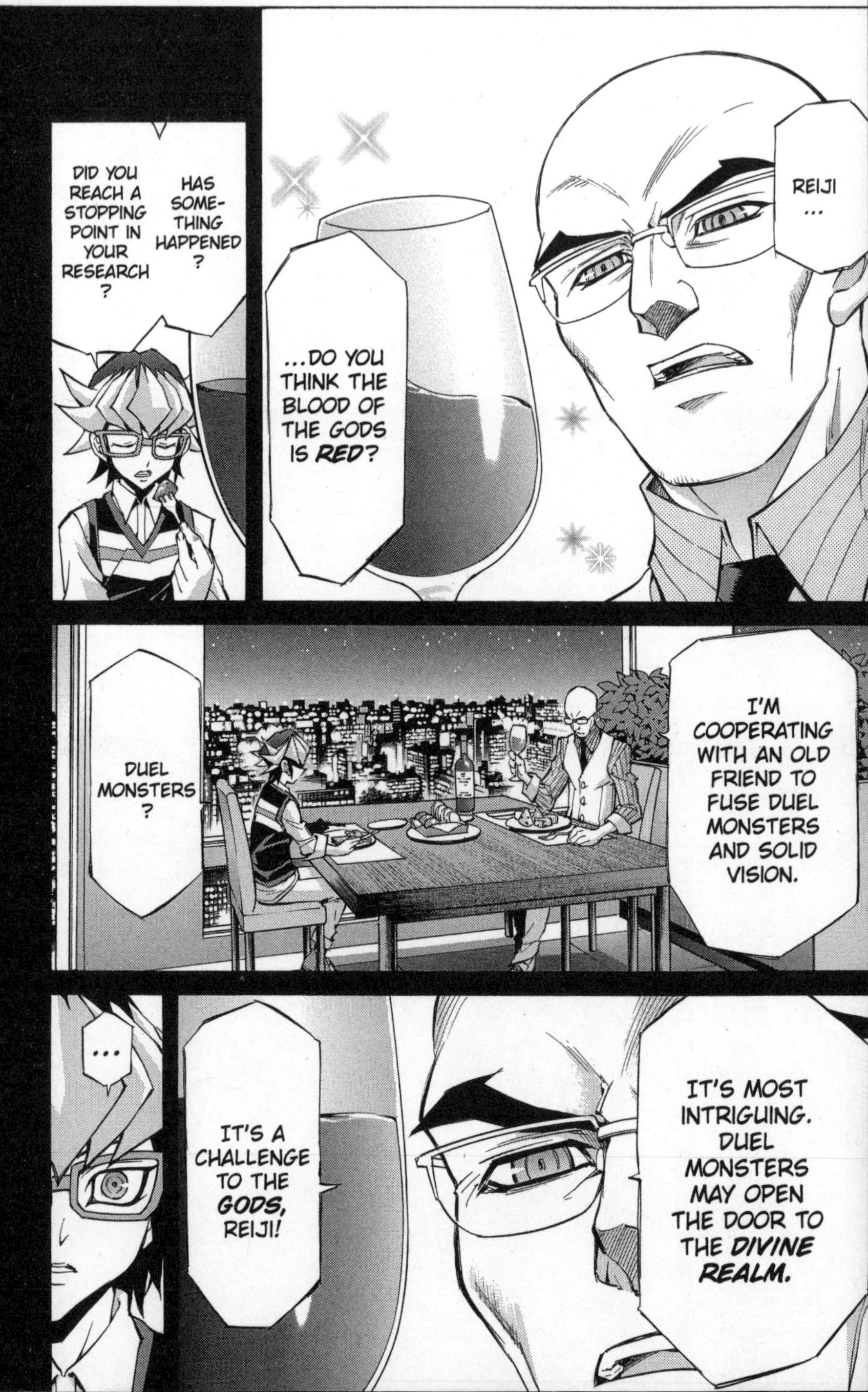
REIJI ...
...DO YOU THINK THE BLOOD OF THE GODS IS *RED*?
HAS SOMETHING HAPPENED?
DID YOU REACH A STOPPING POINT IN YOUR RESEARCH?
I'M COOPERATING WITH AN OLD FRIEND TO FUSE DUEL MONSTERS AND SOLID VISION.
DUEL MONSTERS?
IT'S MOST INTRIGUING. DUEL MONSTERS MAY OPEN THE DOOR TO THE *DIVINE REALM.*
IT'S A CHALLENGE TO THE *GODS,* REIJI!
...

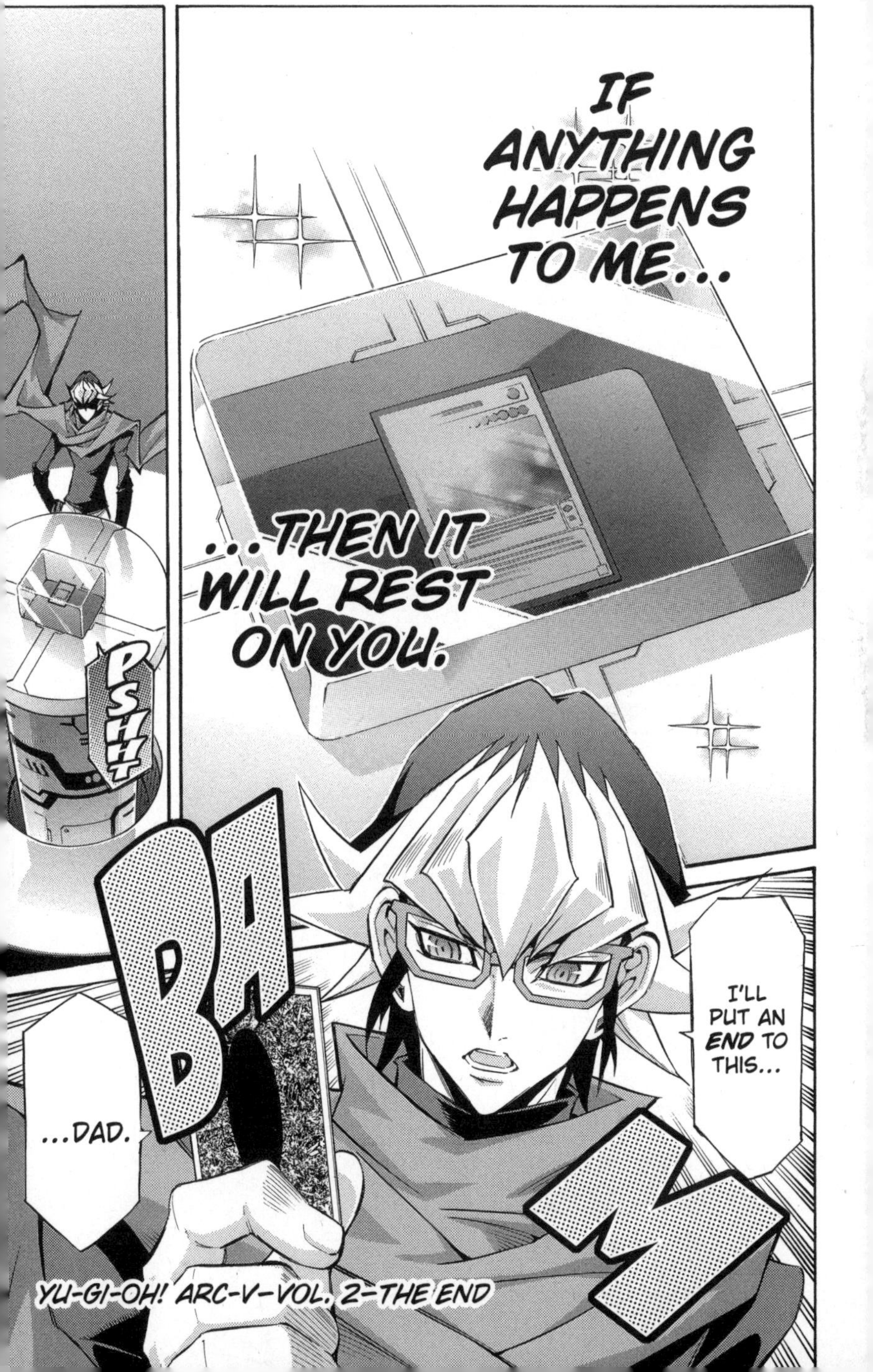
IF ANYTHING HAPPENS TO ME...
...THEN IT WILL REST ON YOU.
PSHHT
I'LL PUT AN *END* TO THIS...
BAM
...DAD.
YU-GI-OH! ARC-V—VOL. 2—THE END

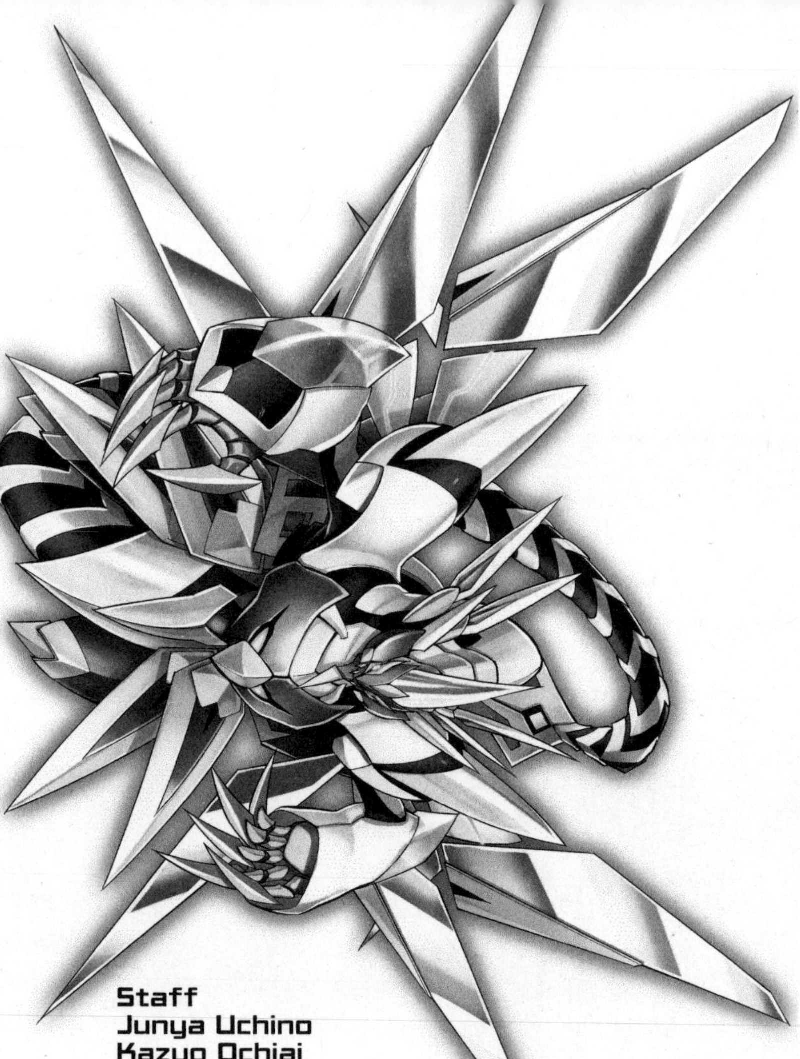

Staff
Junya Uchino
Kazuo Ochiai
Toshiaki Kato

Editing
Takahiko Aikawa

Coloring
Toru Shimizu

Support
Gallop
Wedge Holdings

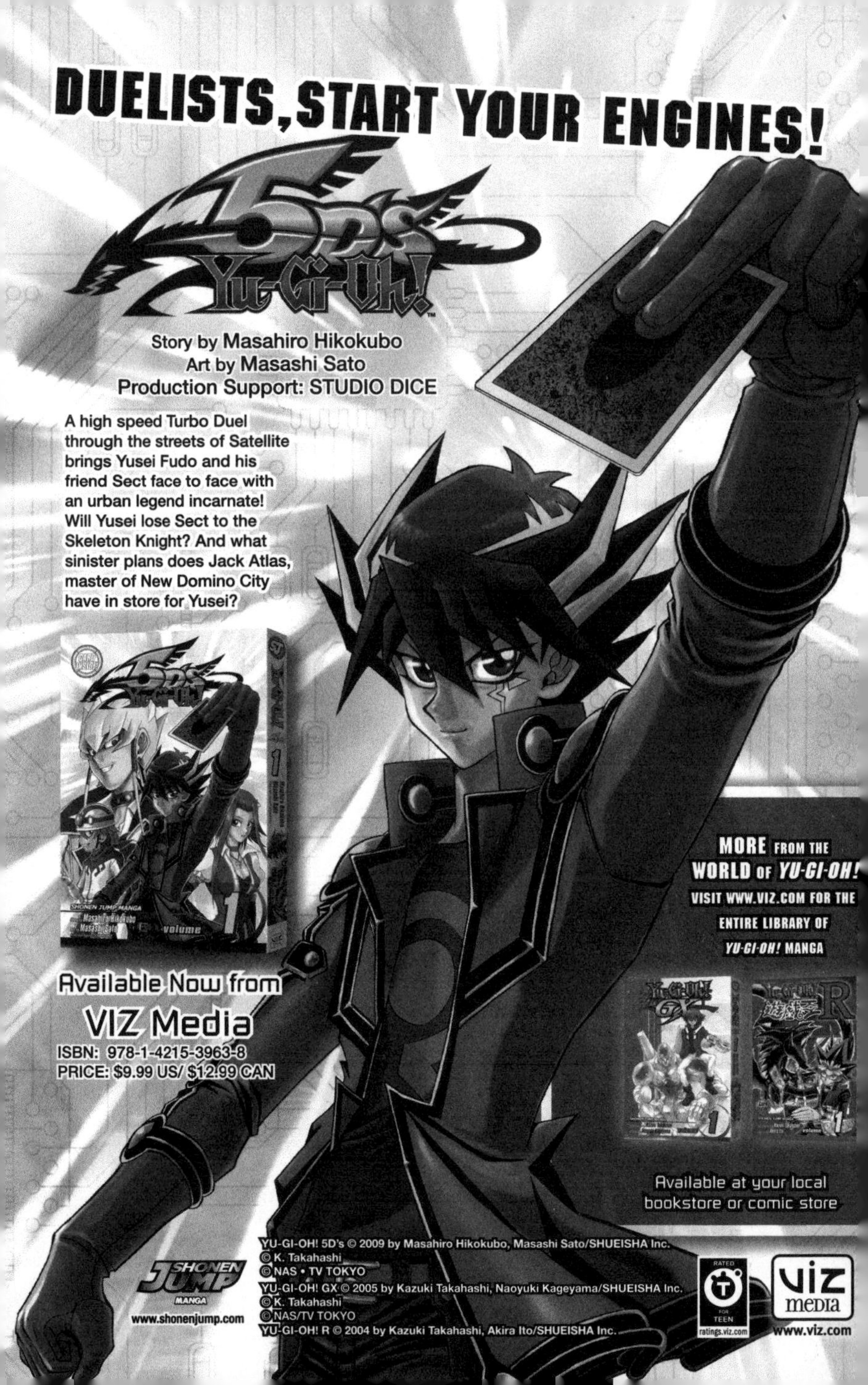
DUELISTS, START YOUR ENGINES!
5D's YU-GI-OH!
Story by Masahiro Hikokubo
Art by Masashi Sato
Production Support: STUDIO DICE
A high speed Turbo Duel through the streets of Satellite brings Yusei Fudo and his friend Sect face to face with an urban legend incarnate! Will Yusei lose Sect to the Skeleton Knight? And what sinister plans does Jack Atlas, master of New Domino City have in store for Yusei?
Available Now from
VIZ Media
ISBN: 978-1-4215-3963-8
PRICE: $9.99 US/ $12.99 CAN
MORE FROM THE WORLD OF YU-GI-OH!
VISIT WWW.VIZ.COM FOR THE ENTIRE LIBRARY OF YU-GI-OH! MANGA
Available at your local bookstore or comic store
SHONEN JUMP MANGA
www.shonenjump.com
YU-GI-OH! 5D's © 2009 by Masahiro Hikokubo, Masashi Sato/SHUEISHA Inc.
© K. Takahashi
© NAS • TV TOKYO
YU-GI-OH! GX © 2005 by Kazuki Takahashi, Naoyuki Kageyama/SHUEISHA Inc.
© K. Takahashi
© NAS/TV TOKYO
YU-GI-OH! R © 2004 by Kazuki Takahashi, Akira Ito/SHUEISHA Inc.
RATED T FOR TEEN
ratings.viz.com
VIZ media
www.viz.com

STOP!

YOU'RE READING THE WRONG WAY!

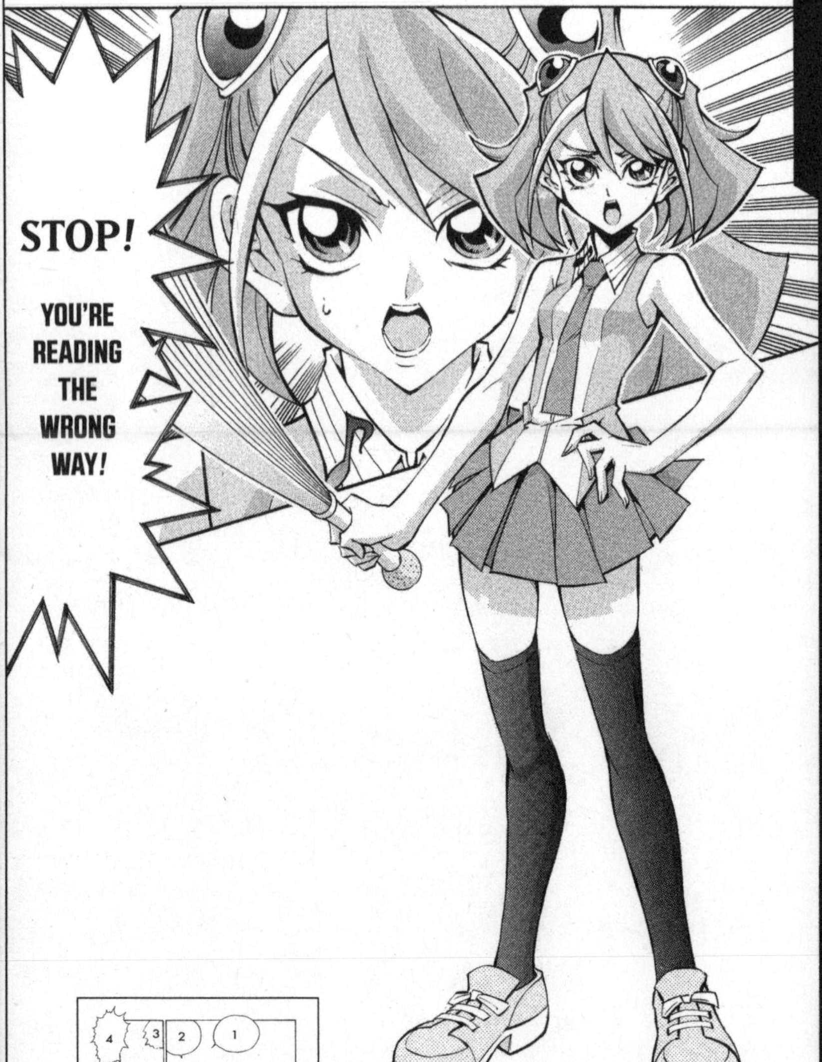

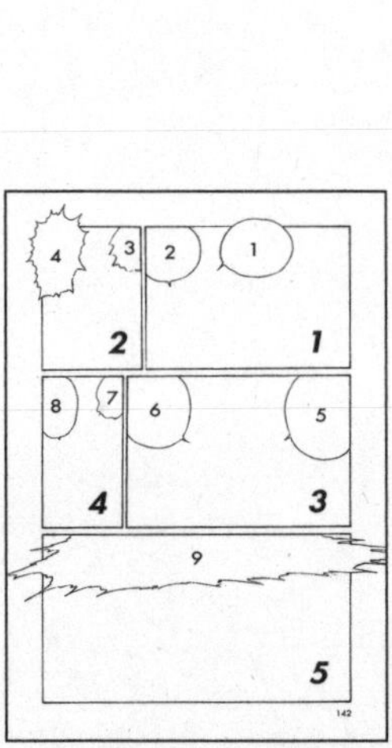
1
2
3
4
1
2
5
6
7
8
3
4
9
5
142

Yu-Gi-Oh! ARC-V

reads from right to left, starting in the upper-right corner. Japanese is read from right to left, meaning that action, sound effects and word-balloon order are completely reversed from English order.